THE

Praxis
— *Series*™ —

Official Guide

THE
Praxis
Series™
Official Guide

New York | Chicago | San Francisco | Lisbon
London | Madrid | Mexico City | Milan | New Delhi
San Juan | Seoul | Singapore | Sydney | Toronto

The McGraw·Hill Companies

Library of Congress Cataloging-in-Publication Data

The praxis series official guide.—2nd ed.

   p.   cm.
   ISBN-13: 978-0-07-162656-9
   ISBN-10: 0-07-162656-5
   ISBN-13: 978-0-07-162660-6
   ISBN-10: 0-07-162660-3
   1. Pre-Professional Skills Tests—Study guides.   2. Principles of Learning and Teaching Test—Study guides.   3. Teachers—Certification—United States.   I. Educational Testing Service.
   LB2367.75.P735   2010
   370.76—dc22

                                                                          2009030258

1 2 3 4 5 6 7 8 9 0 QPD/QPD 0 1 2 1 0 9

Book alone:
ISBN 978-0-07-162656-9
MHID 0-07-162656-5

Book/CD set:
ISBN: P/N 978-0-07-162658-3 of set
            978-07-162660-6
MHID: P/N 0-07-162658-1 of set
            0-07-162660-3

Printed and bound by Quebecor/Dubuque.

McGraw-Hill books are available at special quantity discounts to use as premiums and sales promotions, or for use in corporate training programs. To contact a representative please e-mail us at bulksales@mcgraw-hill.com.

This publication is designed to provide accurate and authoritative information in regard to the subject matter covered. It is sold with the understanding that neither the author nor the publisher is engaged in rendering legal, accounting, or other professional service. If legal advice or other expert assistance is required, the services of a competent professional person should be sought.

ETS, the ETS logo, *PRAXIS I*, *PRAXIS II*, and *PRAXIS III* are registered trademarks of Educational Testing Service (ETS) in the United States of America and other countries throughout the world. *PRAXIS* and *THE PRAXIS SERIES* are trademarks of Educational Testing Service (ETS).

CONTENTS

PART VI. *PRAXIS*™ II SUBJECT ASSESSMENTS

APPENDICES

How to Use This Book

The *Praxis*™ tests are designed for three different testing populations. The test for which you prepare will depend on the population to which you belong.

If you are an undergraduate who is just starting out on the path toward becoming a prospective teacher, you will probably want to prepare for the PPST®, which tests your basic academic skills.

If you are in a teacher preparation program and are moving toward certification, you will most likely want to prepare for one or more of the *Praxis II* tests—the PLT®, the Elementary Education tests, and/or the Subject Assessments.

If you are in the classroom, you will want to prepare for *Praxis III*, which assesses your teaching skills.

This book will help you

- Familiarize yourself with the test formats.
- Review some key concepts that appear on the *Praxis* tests.
- Practice your test-taking skills, using real* *Praxis* test questions.

Here is a step-by-step plan for using this book.

Step 1: Determine Your Requirements

Appendix A on page 467 includes a state-by-state list of testing requirements for certification. The tests you must take vary depending on where you plan to teach. Use the list to determine which tests you must take. That will tell you which parts of this book to use as you prepare.

Step 2: Read Part I

This overview gives you practical information about the different *Praxis* tests, including how to register and how to get your scores. Part I is for everyone who plans to take a *Praxis* test.

Step 3: Focus on the Upcoming Test

Are you preparing for the PPST?
Read Part II and take the sample tests in Part III.

---

* When we refer to "real tests," we mean that literally. Since this book is prepared by ETS®, the same company that prepares the *Praxis* tests, all the questions you see in this book are taken directly from actual tests from years past. You will have a chance to answer the exact kinds of questions you will find on the *Praxis* test you are about to take.

Are you preparing for the PLT?

Read Part IV and work through the sample test questions in Chapter 16.

Are you preparing for the Elementary Education tests?

Read Part V and work through the sample test questions in Chapters 17–19.

Are you preparing for one or more of the Subject Assessments?

Read Part VI and work through the sample test questions in Chapters 20–23.

Working teachers who are preparing for evaluation and review via the *Praxis III* tests should visit www.ets.org/praxis to learn more about those in-class assessments.

Step 4: Review and Improve

Each set of the real test questions is followed by explanatory answers. Use the information you gain from these answers to figure out areas where you need to study and improve your skills.

PART I

Getting Started

Your Goals for This Part:

- Identify the purposes and components of *Praxis I*®, *Praxis II*®, and *Praxis III*® tests.
- Review basic information on test registration and scoring for *Praxis I* and *Praxis II* tests.
- Learn general test-preparation strategies to apply to *Praxis*™ tests.

CHAPTER 1

Introducing the *Praxis*™ Tests

The Praxis Series™ Assessments provide tests and other services that states use as part of their teaching licensing certification process. The *Praxis I®* tests measure basic academic skills. The *Praxis II®* tests measure general and subject-specific knowledge and teaching skills. The *Praxis III®* tests assess classroom performance.

PRAXIS I PRE-PROFESSIONAL SKILLS TESTS (PPST®)

The PPST Reading, Writing, and Mathematics tests are designed to be taken early in a student's college career. They measure whether the student has the academic skills needed to prepare for a career in education. The tests are available in a paper-based or computer-based format.

About the PPST

The PPST reflect the most current research and the professional judgment and experience of educators across the country. This group of tests includes the following:

Test Subject	Test Name and Code	Length of Test	Major Content Areas Covered and Approximate Number and Percentage of Questions in Each Area
Reading	*Computerized Pre-Professional Skills Test: Reading (5710)*	75 minutes	• Literal Comprehension (21 questions, 45%) • Critical and Inferential Comprehension (25 questions, 55%)
	Pre-Professional Skills Test: Reading (0710)	60 minutes	• Literal Comprehension (18 questions, 45%) • Critical and Inferential Comprehension (22 questions, 55%)

(Continued)

Test Subject	Test Name and Code	Length of Test	Major Content Areas Covered and Approximate Number and Percentage of Questions in Each Area
Writing	*Computerized Pre-Professional Skills Test: Writing (5720)*	68 minutes (38 minutes multiple-choice, 30 minutes essay)	• Grammatical Relationships (15 questions, 17%) • Structural Relationships (16 questions, 18.5%) • Word Choice and Mechanics (13 questions, 14.5%) • Essay (1 question, 50%)
	Pre-Professional Skills Test: Writing (0720)	60 minutes (30 minutes multiple-choice, 30 minutes essay)	• Grammatical Relationships (13 questions, 17%) • Structural Relationships (14 questions, 18.5%) • Word Choice and Mechanics (11 questions, 14.5%) • Essay (1 question, 50%) **Note:** A pencil or pen can be used to write the essay for the paper-based test.
Mathematics	*Computerized Pre-Professional Skills Test: Mathematics (5730)*	75 minutes	• Number and Operations (15 questions, 32.5%) • Algebra (9 questions, 20%) • Geometry and Measurement (10 questions, 22.5%) • Data Analysis and Probability (12 questions, 25%) **Note:** Calculators are prohibited.

Test Subject	Test Name and Code	Length of Test	Major Content Areas Covered and Approximate Number and Percentage of Questions in Each Area
Mathematics	*Pre-Professional Skills Test: Mathematics (0730)*	60 minutes	• Number and Operations (13 questions, 32.5%) • Algebra (8 questions, 20%) • Geometry and Measurement (9 questions, 22.5%) • Data Analysis and Probability (10 questions, 25%) **Note:** Calculators are prohibited.

PRAXIS II PRINCIPLES OF LEARNING AND TEACHING (PLT), ELEMENTARY EDUCATION, AND SUBJECT ASSESSMENTS

Praxis II is for individuals entering the teaching profession, who take these tests as part of the teacher licensing and certification process required by many states. These tests are different from the *Praxis I* tests as they assess both subject matter knowledge and teaching skills.

Principles of Learning and Teaching

The Principles of Learning and Teaching (PLT) tests are designed to assess a prospective teacher's knowledge of a broad range of job-related topics. Students typically attain such knowledge in undergraduate courses in educational psychology, human growth and development, classroom management, instructional design and delivery techniques, evaluation and assessment, and other areas of professional preparation. Educational Testing Service (ETS) has aligned the content of this test with principles developed by INTASC (Interstate New Teacher Assessment and Support Consortium) and published in the *INTASC Model Standards*. To develop test questions for the PLT tests, ETS works in collaboration with teacher educators and higher education content specialists to keep the test updated and representative of current standards.

There are four Principles of Learning and Teaching tests:

Principles of Learning and Teaching: Early Childhood
Principles of Learning and Teaching: Grades K–6
Principles of Learning and Teaching: Grades 5–9
Principles of Learning and Teaching: Grades 7–12

Elementary Education

The Elementary Education tests are a series of three tests, two in multiple-choice format and one that requires written answers. The first test assesses prospective elementary teachers' understanding of curriculum, instruction, and assessment in the major K–6 subject areas. The second test measures knowledge of content in Language Arts and Reading, Mathematics, Social Studies, and Science. The third test assesses content knowledge in a more open-ended, constructed-response format.

Subject Assessments

Praxis II Subject Assessment tests measure knowledge of specific subjects that K–12 educators teach, as well as general and subject-specific teaching skills and knowledge.

Individuals entering the teaching profession take these tests as part of the teacher licensing and certification process required by many states. A number of professional associations and organizations require these tests as one criterion for professional licensing decisions.

Teaching Foundations tests, which are part of *Praxis II*: Subject Assessments, measure pedagogy in five areas: multisubject (elementary), English Language Arts, Mathematics, Science, and Social Science.

PRAXIS III ASSESSMENTS

Praxis III Classroom Performance Assessments comprise a system for assessing the skills of beginning teachers in classroom settings. ETS developed *Praxis III* assessments for states or local agencies to use in teacher licensing decisions. Under the guidelines that govern its use, *Praxis III* may not be used to make employment decisions about teachers who are currently licensed.

This direct classroom assessment recognizes the importance of the teaching context as well as the many diverse forms that excellent teaching can take. The *Praxis III* system uses a three-pronged method to assess the beginning teacher's competence and success in the classroom. This includes direct observation of classroom practice, review of documentation prepared by the teacher, and semi-structured interviews.

The *Praxis III* assessment is not just a test. It is comprised of three separate, yet strongly interconnected components. Individually, each component augments the value of the assessment. Collectively, the system offers a thorough understanding of the teaching skills of a beginning teacher. The *Praxis III* assessment also provides insights into pedagogical areas in which a teacher may benefit from additional development.

- Component 1: Framework of knowledge and skills for a beginning teacher that assess the teaching performance across all grade levels and content areas.
- Component 2: Instruments used by trained assessors to collect data, analyze, and score the teacher's performance.
- Component 3: Training of assessors to facilitate consistent, accurate, and fair assessments of a beginning teacher.

Beginning teachers residing and planning to teach in states that require *Praxis III*: Classroom Performance Assessments as part of the criteria for teacher licensing decisions have their teaching skills assessed in classroom settings by trained assessors.

CHAPTER 2

Praxis™ Assessments Practical Matters

HOW TO REGISTER FOR THE *PRAXIS* ASSESSMENTS

The *Praxis I* PPST Tests are offered as computer-based or paper-based tests. *Praxis II* tests are available only as paper-based tests. *Praxis III* is an in-class assessment authorized by state or local agencies.

> To find out which tests are required in your state, see Appendix A.

Registering for *Praxis* Computer-Based Testing

Computer-based testing (CBT) registration is made by appointment at more than 300 Prometric **test sites** throughout the United States.

To schedule an appointment, call Prometric Candidate Services Monday through Friday, 8 a.m.–8 p.m. Eastern Time (New York) (excluding holidays), at 1-800-853-6773, 1-443-751-4859, or call the test center directly. A list of computer-based test centers can be found at http://etsis4.ets.org/tcenter/tcenter.jsp. If you are deaf or hard of hearing and use a TTY, call 1-800-529-3590 to schedule an appointment.

- You must use an American Express®, Discover® Network, JCB®, Visa®, or MasterCard® credit card, or an authorization voucher.
- To obtain an authorization voucher, send payment to the Educational Testing Service (ETS) with a completed CBT Authorization Voucher Request Form, which is available at http://www.ets.org/Media/Tests/PRAXIS/pdf/01361cbtav.pdf.
- An authorization voucher will be sent to you. It is valid for 90 days from the date of issue. After receiving the voucher, make your test appointment.
- Be sure to take the voucher when you report for testing. It will be collected at the test center.

If you are a test taker with disabilities, refer to the Test Takers with Disabilities page or visit the ETS Test Center List page, at http://etsis4.ets.org/tcenter/tcenter.jsp.

You may test as a walk-in if space allows. Walk-in registrants may pay all test fees by check,* money order, credit card, or authorization voucher. If your check,

---

* *When you pay by check, you authorize ETS to convert the check into an electronic fund transfer. Please be aware that your account may be debited the same day we receive your payment. Please also note that you will no longer receive a canceled check.*

money order, or credit card is declined, charged back, or returned for insufficient funds or stopped payment, you will be billed for the amount due plus an additional $20 processing fee.

You may take the Computerized PPST only once per calendar month, and no more than six times within a 12-month period. This applies even if you canceled your scores on a test taken previously. If you violate this restriction, the scores from your retest will not be reported, and your test fees will not be refunded.

Registering for *Praxis* Paper-Based Testing

Register Online   Register online for a paper-based test using a credit card, Monday–Friday, 7 a.m.–10 p.m. (ET) and 7 a.m. Saturday through 8 p.m. Sunday (ET). The online registration page is available at https://www.ets.org/portal/site/iserpraxis/menuitem.97b5ae768b3cbd815cb7dd107beb1509.

Online registration is **not available** for the following:

- *Praxis I* computer-based testing
- Test-takers with disabilities
- Sabbath/Monday testing
- Examinees whose primary language is not English
- Fee waivers

Defense Activity for Nontraditional Education Support (DANTES) test takers: If you register for a national test date, you may not register to take a test at a DANTES center immediately prior to or following that date. If you register for and take a test, only the first answer sheet received by ETS will be scored and your fees will not be refunded.

Register by Mail   Download and complete the *Praxis Series* 2008-09 Paper-Based Test Registration Form and Background Information Questionnaire (PDF). Then follow the instructions in the 2008-09 version of *The Praxis Series Information Bulletin* (PDF), at http://www.ets.org/Media/Tests/PRAXIS/pdf/01361.pdf.

GETTING YOUR SCORES

If you take a paper-based test, your official score report will arrive in the mail approximately four weeks after your test date. Your score report will contain your overall score and six area scores.

If you take the computer-based version of the PPST, you do not have to pre-register with ETS. To take the computer-based version, contact the appropriate person in your school or prospective district to find out how you can arrange a day and time for taking the test. Once you are seated at the computer and the school or district administrator has entered the correct codes to start the test, you will be asked to fill in your name, address, and other information on the registration screen. At the end of the testing session, you will receive an unofficial report of your score. Two weeks later, you will receive an official score report in the mail that will contain your overall score and six area scores.

CHAPTER 3

General Strategies for Test-Takers

GENERAL TEST PREPARATION STRATEGIES

Praxis tests contain a mixture of types of questions. Some of these are simple identification questions, such as "What is the name of the shape shown above?" Other questions require you to analyze situations, synthesize material, and apply knowledge to specific examples. In short, they require you to think and solve problems. This type of question is usually longer than a simple identification question and takes more time to answer. You may be presented with something to read (a description of a classroom situation, a sample of student work, a chart or graph) and then asked to answer questions based on your reading. Good reading skills are required, and you must read carefully.

Strengthen Your Reading Skills

Both on these tests and as a teacher, you will need to process and use what you read efficiently. If you know that your reading skills are not strong, you may want to take a reading course. Community colleges and night schools often have reading labs that can help you strengthen your reading skills.

Find Out the Test Specifications in Advance

Praxis multiple-choice test content specifications for a multiple-choice test can be found in the Tests at a Glance available on the *Praxis* Web site, at www.ets. org/praxis/testprep. You may have heard there are several different test "forms" (or versions of the same test). It's true. You might take one version of the test in January, and your friend might take a different version of the test in April. The two of you will have different questions covering the same subject area. But the tests are "parallel"—they measure the same content domain, because both are built to the same specifications. ETS continually monitors the performance of test-takers to ensure that all test forms measure content knowledge in the same ways.

The specifications are like a recipe for the test; every version of the test covers the same specifications and contains the same proportion of questions on each topic. This coverage makes the test parallel from form to form. The actual questions may be different (a question on the Civil War may ask you about the surrender at Appomattox on one test form, and about Sherman's March to the Sea on another test form), but the content coverage will still be that required by the specifications (in this case, a question on a significant event of the Civil War).

The specifications lists within the Tests at a Glance, called "Topics Covered," contain the percent of the whole test that each topic will represent. The greater the percent, the more questions there will be on that topic, and the greater your knowledge of that area will need to be. Knowing the test specifications in advance can help you guide your study.

Learn to Pace Yourself as You Answer Questions

To help pace yourself through a test, try answering the practice questions in this study guide several times. You may want to use the practice questions to identify areas in which you need more studying, but you should also answer the practice questions several times without worrying about "content" issues. Instead, your goal should be simply to get used to taking the test. Time yourself, and notice the amount of concentration you need to stay focused on the test for the duration of the testing period. Discover the level of pacing that works best for you, and take the test until the pacing starts to feel natural.

STRATEGIES FOR TAKING *PRAXIS* TESTS

Useful Facts About the Tests

1. **You can answer the questions in any order.** You can go through the questions from beginning to end, as many test-takers do, or you can create your own path. Perhaps you will want to answer questions in your strongest subject first and then move from your strengths to your weaker areas. There is no right or wrong way. Use the approach that works for you.
2. **Don't worry about answer patterns.** One test-taking myth claims that answers on multiple-choice tests follow patterns. Another myth insists that there will never be more than two questions with the same lettered answer following each other. There is no truth to either of these myths. Select the answer you think is correct based on your knowledge of the subject.
3. **There is no penalty for guessing.** Your test score is based on the number of correct answers you have, and incorrect answers do not count against you. When you don't know the answer to a question on a multiple-choice test, try to eliminate any obviously wrong answers and then guess at the correct one.
4. **It's OK to write in your test booklet.** If you are taking the paper-based version of a test, you can work problems right on the pages of the booklet, make notes to yourself, or mark questions you want to review later. Your test booklet will be destroyed after you have finished with it, so use it in any way that is helpful to you. If you are taking the PPST test on a computer, you can work problems on scratch paper, and you can click the "Mark" button to note questions for later review.

Smart Tips for Taking the Tests

1. **Put your answers in the right "bubbles."** It seems obvious, but if you are taking the paper-based version of a multiple-choice test, you should make sure you are "bubbling in" the answer to the right question on your answer sheet. Check the question number each time you fill in an answer. Use a Number 2 lead pencil, and be sure that each mark is heavy and dark, and completely fills the answer space. If you change an answer, be sure the previous mark is erased completely. For the PPST computer-based version, be sure the circle next to your chosen answer is dark after you have clicked on it.

2. **Be prepared for questions that use the words _LEAST, EXCEPT,_ or _NOT._** Some questions may ask you to select the choice that doesn't fit or that contains information that is not true. Questions in this format use the words LEAST, EXCEPT, or NOT. The words are capitalized when they appear in test questions. This alerts you to the fact that you are looking for the single answer choice that is different in some specified way from the other answer choices. Here is an example of a question in this format that might be on the math part of the PPST:

> *Some values of x are less than 100.*

Which of the following is NOT consistent with the sentence above?

(A) 5 is not a value of x.
(B) 95 is a value of x.
(C) Some values of x are greater than 100.
(D) All values of x are less than 100.
(E) No numbers less than 100 are values of x.

> *Note that the PPST offers you five answer choices. On most* Praxis II *tests, you will see four choices though some tests have five.*

In the question above, four of the five sentences are consistent with the boxed sentence, and one is NOT. The sentence that is NOT consistent is the correct answer choice—in this case, (E). If no numbers less than 100 are values of x, as stated in (E), there will not be at least one value of x less than 100, as stated in the boxed sentence.

When you encounter a NOT, LEAST, or EXCEPT question, it is a good idea to reread the question after you select your answer to make sure that you have answered the question correctly.

3. **Skip the questions you find to be extremely difficult.** There are bound to be some questions that you think are hard. Rather than trying to answer these on your first pass through the test, leave them blank and mark

them in your test booklet so that you can come back to them. (If you are taking the PPST on a computer, you can click the "Mark" button to mark a question and then use the "Review" listing to see which questions you have marked and/or left unanswered.) Pay attention to the time as you answer the rest of the questions on the test. Try to finish with 10 or 15 minutes remaining so that you can go back over the questions that you left blank. Even if you don't know the answers the second time around, see whether you can narrow down the possible answers, and then guess.

4. **Keep track of the time.** For paper-based tests, wear a watch, just in case the clock in the test room is difficult for you to see. (For the computer-based version of the PPST tests, there is a clock on the screen.) Remember that on an average you have a little more than 1½ minutes to answer each of the questions. One and one-half (1½) minutes may not seem like much time, but you will be able to answer many questions in only a few seconds each. You will probably have plenty of time to answer all the questions, but if you find yourself becoming bogged down in one section, move on and come back to that section later.

5. **Read all the possible answers before selecting one.** Then reread the question to be sure the answer you have selected really answers the question being asked.

6. **Check your answers.** If you have extra time left over at the end of the test, look over each question. Make sure you have filled in the "bubble" on the answer sheet (or on the computer screen) as you intended. Many test-takers make careless mistakes that could have been corrected if they had checked their answers.

7. **Don't worry about your score as you take the test.** No one expects you to get all the questions correct. This is not like the SAT® or other similar tests, where a higher score means a better chance for success. On this test your score does not matter as long as you pass. If you meet the minimum passing scores for your state or district, you will have fulfilled the requirement.

Do Tests Make You Nervous? Try These Strategies

It's natural to be nervous before a test such as the *Praxis* tests. You can use your nervous energy to strengthen your performance if you approach the test with these facts in mind:

- There are no trick questions on the test. (Some questions may be difficult for you, but they were not written in order to trick you or other test-takers.)
- You should have plenty of time to complete the test. The times allotted for the tests are designed to be adequate. You should not feel rushed.

- Test developers have worded the test questions very carefully and reviewed them many times to make sure they are clear. If a question seems confusing at first, take some time to reread it more slowly.
- You have choices during the test. You can skip a question and come back to it later. You can change your answer to any question at any time during the testing session. You can mark questions you want to return to later.

The Day of the Test. You should complete your review process a day or two before the actual test date. Remember, many clichés you may have heard about the day of the test are true. You should:

- Be well rested
- Take photo identification with you
- Take a supply of No. 2 pencils (at least three) if you are taking a paper-based test
- Eat before you take the test
- Be prepared to stand in line to check in or to wait while other test-takers are being checked in

You can't control the testing situation, but you can control yourself. Stay calm. The supervisors are well trained and make every effort to provide uniform testing conditions, but don't let it bother you if the test doesn't start exactly on time. You will have the necessary amount of time once it does start.

Think of preparing for the test as you would train for an athletic event. Once you've trained and prepared and rested, give it everything you've got. Good luck.

PART II

Preparing for the PPST™ Tests

Your Goals for This Part:

- Learn the purpose and format of the PPST.
- Review some strategies for approaching the PPST.
- Practice answering all types of PPST questions.

CHAPTER 4

All About the PPST Tests

This chapter will give you an overview of the PPST, information about taking the test on computer, and general test-taking suggestions. The following three chapters present review courses in Reading, Math, and Writing so you can refresh your understanding of the important principles you'll need to know for the test. These chapters also contain sample questions to help you become familiar with the question formats that appear on the test. The guided practice you'll get with these questions will help you understand the kinds of knowledge and reasoning you will need to choose correct answers.

PLANNING YOUR TEST PREPARATION PROGRAM

You will probably want to begin with the following steps:

Become familiar with the test content.

Consider how well you know the content in each subject area. You may already know that you need to improve your skills in a particular area—Reading, Math, or Writing. If you're not sure, skim those sections to see what topics they cover. If you encounter materials that feel unfamiliar or difficult, tag them with sticky notes to remind yourself to spend extra time in these sections.

In addition, all users of this section of the book will probably want to end with these two steps:

Familiarize yourself with test taking. You can simulate the experience of the test by taking the practice questions within the specified time limits. Choose a time and place where you will not be interrupted or distracted. Then, score your responses. Look over the explanations of the questions you missed, and see whether you understand them and could answer similar questions correctly. Next, plan any additional studying according to your understanding of the topics.

Register for the test and consider last-minute tips. See the section in Part I on how to register for the test, and review the PPST checklist on page 21 of this chapter to make sure you are ready for the test.

What you do between these first steps and the last steps depends on whether you intend to use this book to prepare on your own or as part of a class or study group.

Preparing on Your Own

If you are working by yourself to prepare for the PPST, you may find it helpful to use the following approach:

Fill out the PPST Study Plan Sheet. The worksheet on page 22 will help you to focus on what topics you need to study most, identify materials that will help you study, and set a schedule for doing the studying. The last item is particularly important if you tend to procrastinate.

Use other materials to reinforce your skills. The following chapters contain review courses in Reading, Math, and Writing, but you may want to get additional help for the topics that give you the most trouble. For example, if you know you have a problem with spelling, you can find lists of frequently misspelled words in books and on the Internet. Math textbooks can provide instruction and give you additional practice with math problems. Computer-based instruction with a system such as the PLATO® SimTest for the PPST® tests may also help you improve your skills in Reading, Math, and Writing.

Preparing as Part of a Study Group

It is sometimes helpful to form a study group with others who are preparing for the same test. Study groups give members opportunities to ask questions and get detailed answers. In a group, some members may be good at some topics, while others may be better at other topics. As members take turns explaining concepts to one another, everyone builds self-confidence. If the group encounters a question that none of the members can answer well, the members can go as a group to a teacher or other expert and get answers efficiently. Because study groups schedule regular meetings, group members study in a more disciplined fashion. They also gain emotional support. The group should be large enough that different people can contribute various kinds of knowledge, but small enough so that it stays focused. Often, three to six people is a good size for the group.

Here are some ways to use this chapter as part of a study group:

Plan the group's study program. Parts of the PPST Study Plan Sheet can help structure your group's study program. By filling out the first five columns and sharing the worksheets, everyone will learn more about your group's mix of abilities and about the resources (such as textbooks) that members can share with the group. In the sixth column (Dates planned for study of content), you can create an overall schedule for your group's study program.

Plan individual group sessions. At the end of each session, the group should decide what specific topics will be covered at the next meeting and who will present each topic. Use the topic headings and subheadings to select topics. Some sessions might be based on topics from the review courses contained in these chapters, and other sessions might be based on the sample questions from the chapters.

Prepare your presentation for the group. When it's your turn to present, prepare something that's more than a lecture. If you are presenting material from the review course part of a chapter, write 5 to 10 original questions to pose to the group. Writing questions can help you better understand the topics covered on the test as well as the types of questions you will encounter on the test. It will also give other members of the group extra practice at answering questions. If you are presenting material from the sample questions, use each sample question as a model for writing at least one original question.

Take the practice test together. To simulate actual administrations of the test, schedule a test session with the group to add to the realism and help boost everyone's confidence. Use practice tests from Part III of this book.

Learn from the results of the practice test. Score one another's answer sheets. Then, plan one or more study sessions based on the questions group members got wrong. For example, each group member may be responsible for a question that he or she got wrong and can use it as a model to create an original question to pose to the group, together with an explanation of the correct answer.

Whether you study alone or with a group, remember the best way to prepare is to have an organized plan. The plan should set goals based on specific topics and skills that you need to learn, and it should commit you to realistic deadlines for meeting these goals. Then, you must discipline yourself to stick with your plan and accomplish your goals on schedule.

PPST Checklist

- Do you have your appointment for the computer-based test or your admission ticket for the paper-based test?
- Do you know the topics that will be covered in each section of the test?
- Have you reviewed any textbooks, study notes, and course readings that relate to the topics covered?
- Do you know how long the test will take and the number of questions it contains? Have you considered how you will pace your work?
- Are you familiar with the test directions and the types of questions for the test?
- If you are taking the PPST, writing the test in a paper-based format, are you aware that a pencil, not a pen, is the preferred way to write your essay?
- If you are taking a test on computer, have you familiarized yourself with the appearance of the screens and the use of the buttons?
- Are you familiar with the recommended test-taking strategies and tips?
- Have you practiced by working through the practice test questions at a pace similar to that of an actual test?
- If you are repeating a PPST, have you analyzed your previous score report to determine areas where additional study and test preparation could be useful?

PPST Study Plan Sheet

Content covered on test	How well do I know the content?	What material do I have for study-ing this content?	What material do I need for study-ing this content?	Where could I find the materials I need?	Dates planned for study of content	Dates completed

TIPS FOR TAKING THE COMPUTER VERSION

You need only a beginner's level of computer skills to take the computer-based version of a PPST. The test runs in an Internet browser. If you have spent an hour surfing the Internet, you know how to work the mouse and how to click on buttons. If you do not have experience with computers, the mouse, and the Internet, visit your public library and ask someone to help you get started. Surf around until you feel comfortable using the mouse.

What You Will See on the Screen

Most of the screens you will see when you take the computer-based version of a PPST will look like this:

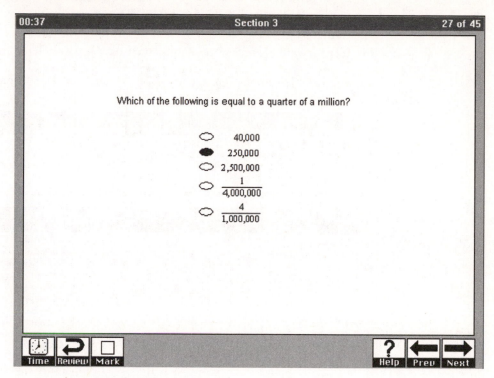

Note how the screen is laid out:

- In the upper right-hand corner, you can see which question you are now working on (question 27 of 45).
- In the upper left-hand corner, you can see how much time you have left (37 minutes). You can hide or display the clock by clicking ▣. (During the last few minutes of the test, the clock remains on continuously.)
- The test questions appear in the middle of the screen. You simply click the oval ◯ next to your answer choice, and it changes to black. You can change your answer by clicking on another oval, which then becomes blacked in, and the oval you clicked on previously will change back to white.
- When you're ready to move to the next question, click ➡. To move back to a previous question, click ⬅.
- To remind yourself of a question you want to check later, click ☐. When you return to the question, you'll see the button has changed to ☑.

- Help is always available by clicking 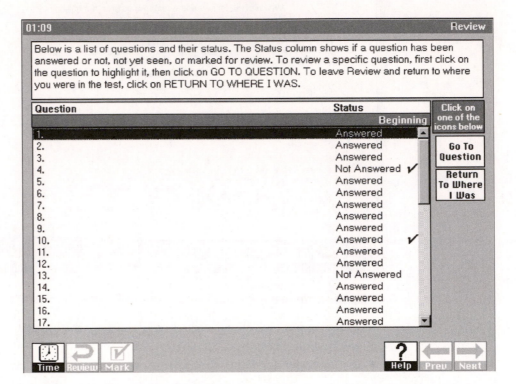 to see instructions about the PPST.
- When you reach the last question, or when time runs out, you will be able to exit the test and receive your score. Once you exit a test, you CANNOT return to it.
- If you want to review questions, such as those you have marked, or those you have left unanswered, click [Review]. You'll see a screen that looks like this:

01:09	Review

Below is a list of questions and their status. The Status column shows if a question has been answered or not, not yet seen, or marked for review. To review a specific question, first click on the question to highlight it, then click on GO TO QUESTION. To leave Review and return to where you were in the test, click on RETURN TO WHERE I WAS.

Question	Status	Click on one of the icons below
	Beginning	
1.	Answered	Go To Question
2.	Answered	
3.	Answered	Return To Where I Was
4.	Not Answered ✔	
5.	Answered	
6.	Answered	
7.	Answered	
8.	Answered	
9.	Answered	
10.	Answered ✔	
11.	Answered	
12.	Answered	
13.	Not Answered	
14.	Answered	
15.	Answered	
16.	Answered	
17.	Answered	

Time Review Mark   Help Prev Next

- Click on the question you want to review, then click [Go To Question]. To resume where you left off, click [Return To Where I Was].

In the Reading and Writing sections, when you are given a long passage of text accompanied by several questions, the screen is divided and looks like this:

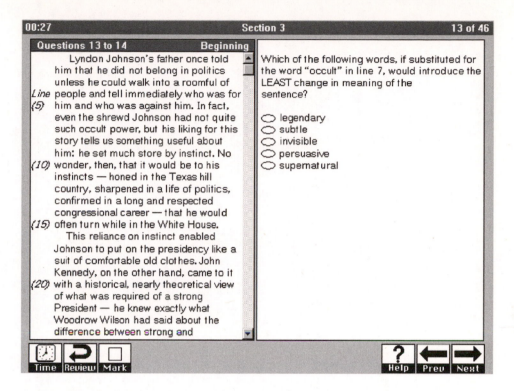

Note the heading for the passage (above on the left) indicates that two questions (13 and 14) are based on the passage. After you answer the first question and click the NEXT icon, like you did previously the right side of the screen changes to show you the next question about the passage.

After you complete the test and exit, you will be able to print your unofficial score report by using your Internet browser's Print button.

CHAPTER 5

PPST™ Reading

Paper-Based Version	Computer-Based Version
40 questions	46 questions
60 minutes	75 minutes

PURPOSE OF THE READING TEST

"Reading comprehension" refers to the ability to *understand, analyze,* and *evaluate* written material. The key to doing well on the PPST Reading test is to read carefully and make correct judgments and conclusions about what you have read. You do not need to read fast to succeed on the test, but you do need to understand what you have read. You also need to evaluate how each author presents his or her arguments and the evidence used to support them.

FORMAT OF THE READING TEST

The test consists mostly of reading passages and questions related to the passages. There are no questions that test vocabulary in isolation, such as antonyms (finding the word opposite in meaning) or analogies ("*X* is to *Y* as *Z* is to blank"). You do not have to memorize lists of hard words. Some questions may, however, require you to determine meanings of words in the context of a passage. One or more questions may be based on a visual representation, such as a graph or chart, that you will be asked to interpret. Mostly, you simply need to be able to read about 20 different selections and answer accompanying questions.

There are 40 questions on the test, and you will have 60 minutes to complete them. (If you are taking the computer version, you have 46 questions to answer in 75 minutes.) Your best preparation is to develop the ability to read *carefully*, but with strategies that help you move through the material quickly.

Reading Passages: Sources and Subject Matter

The reading passages are taken from a wide range of reading materials intended for the general public. Many passages come from magazines and journals such as *Scientific American, Smithsonian, Archaeology,* and *Psychology Today.*

Other reading passages in the PPST Reading test come from nonfiction books published for general audiences, such as biographies, histories, and books of essays. A relatively small percentage of passages is taken from newspapers, usually from lengthy feature articles in major newspapers such as the *New York Times* or the *Washington Post* and online source articles.

The subject matter of the passages varies. The passages cover a variety of subjects in the areas of social science, humanities, science, and general interest. You should expect to encounter a wide assortment of topics.

You may know a lot about some of the topics and next to nothing about others. That does not matter. *To answer the questions, you do not need to draw on any background or outside knowledge.* Everything you need to know to answer the questions is directly stated or implied in the passages.

In some cases, the information in the passage may conflict with knowledge you have about the subject. If it does, do not let your knowledge influence your choice of an answer. *Always answer each question on the basis of what is stated or implied in the given passage.*

The passages reflect various forms of writing: description, explanation, persuasion, narrative, and personal reflection. Most passages make a single central point and then back it up with supporting examples or observations. There will be a flow of logic or observation, often with transition words such as "but," "however," "therefore," and "in addition."

Reading Passages: Length

Each reading passage consists of one or more paragraphs on a single topic, followed by one or more questions.

The passages are of varying lengths:

- Long passages of roughly 200 words (with four to seven questions)
- Short passages of roughly 100 words (with two to three questions)
- Statements of a sentence or two (with one question)

Even the longest passages, of 200 words, are equivalent in length to a fairly brief newspaper article, so you can be confident that you can read each passage carefully and quickly without running out of time.

STRATEGIES FOR THE READING TEST

Once you've started a set of questions, answer all the questions in the set. When you take the reading comprehension test, work through each set of questions completely before moving on to the next set. For tests made up of discrete, unrelated questions, it might make sense to leave some questions unanswered and come back to them; however, once you have read a passage carefully, you should try to answer all the accompanying questions before going on to the next passage.

You may, however, read the passages in whatever order seems best to you. In other words, if a passage seems easy or interesting, you may prefer to begin with that one, and answer all the accompanying questions. If a passage seems difficult, you may want to save it for last.

Read through the passage once. For each passage, first read through it carefully but quickly. Then answer each question, referring to the passage as necessary.

Don't analyze the passage in great detail when you first read it. Analyze it only as needed to answer a question.

Cross out choices you think are wrong. When working on a question on the paper test, cross out choices you definitely know to be wrong. If you cross them out in your test booklet, you will not waste time rereading choices you've already decided are wrong. Once you eliminate the obviously wrong choices, you may increase the probability (improve your ability) to make an educated guess.

If it helps you focus, you may also want to mark parts of the passage that seem important. For instance, you might want to underline transition words, such as *however* or *therefore*, to call attention to the structure of the author's argument. Do not, however, spend too much time marking the passage.

Expect variety. Don't panic if you are not familiar with the topic of the passage. Even if the passage is on multicolored eels found near the New Zealand coast, don't be put off! Plunge in and read carefully. You will be given all the information you need to answer the questions.

Be prepared to shift your mindset between topics. You might encounter a dense passage describing a medical discovery and then a lighter passage about childhood memories of a hometown.

Pace yourself. Do not spend too much time on any one passage or question. If you find that a certain passage or question is taking up too much of your time, make an educated guess and move on to another question.

Answer all the questions. Be sure to answer every question. Because the test is scored according to the number of correct answers, you are not penalized for guessing. At the end of the test period, take a moment to check the answer sheet for any unanswered questions.

GUIDED PPST READING PRACTICE

The 12 Types of Questions on the PPST Reading Test

It may look as if every question on the PPST Reading test is different, but there are really only 12 question types. Below you'll see that the 12 types fall into two main categories. Read the in-depth explanation of each type and try the practice questions.

The 12 types of questions fall into two major categories:

- Literal comprehension skills (types 1–4)
- Critical and inferential comprehension skills (types 5–12)

Literal comprehension is the ability to understand accurately and completely what is explicitly stated in a passage. It also involves the ability to recognize how a passage is organized and how it uses language. To answer this kind of question, you must concentrate on what is written and how it is written. A little less than one-half of the questions measure this kind of comprehension.

The PPST Reading test assesses the following literal comprehension skills:

Type 1: Recognizing the *main idea* or primary purpose of a passage
Type 2: Recognizing a *supporting idea* or detail in a passage
Type 3: Recognizing how particular *vocabulary* words or phrases are used in a passage
Type 4: Recognizing the *organization* of a passage

Critical and inferential comprehension questions test the ability to understand aspects of a passage that are not explicitly stated. When you read critically or inferentially, you must understand implications, make predictions, analyze an author's argument, and compare situations and arguments.

To answer this kind of question, you do not need any specialized knowledge. Clear and careful thinking is sufficient. A little more than one-half of the questions measure this kind of comprehension.

The PPST Reading test assesses the following critical and inferential comprehension skills:

Type 5: Drawing an *inference* or implication from a passage
Type 6: Evaluating supporting *evidence*—its relevance or appropriateness
Type 7: Identifying an *assumption* made by the author
Type 8: Distinguishing *fact from opinion*
Type 9: Identifying the *attitude* of the author toward the topic
Type 10: *Extending and predicting* based on passage content
Type 11: Drawing a *conclusion*
Type 12: Making an *application* to another situation

In-Depth Preparation for All 12 Types of Questions

Type 1: Main Idea Questions

There are two kinds of Main Idea questions:

- Main idea
- Primary purpose

Main idea questions ask about the central point of a passage. The main idea may be explicitly stated, or you may have to figure it out. It might help first to identify the topic of the passage (in a few words) and then to identify the author's point about that topic (in a complete sentence). That will be the main idea. For example, the topic of a passage might be "the person who invented laptop computers," and the main idea might be "The person who invented laptop computers did not get support from coworkers when trying to sell the idea to the company's marketing department."

Primary purpose questions ask about the author's purpose. The author may explicitly state the purpose, or you may have to figure it out. Sometimes the question will ask you to identify a general phrase describing the purpose (using language such as "explain an event" or "refute an argument"). Sometimes the question will ask you to identify a specific statement describing the purpose (using language such as "refute a traditional theory about glaciers").

How to recognize Main Idea questions

Here are the ways in which Main Idea questions are usually asked:

- Which of the following statements best summarizes the main idea of the passage?
- Which of the following statements best expresses the main idea of the passage?
- The main idea of the passage is …

Here are the ways in which Primary Purpose questions are usually asked:

- In the passage, the author is primarily concerned with which of the following?
- The primary purpose of the passage is to …

Keep in mind that the question asks about the *main* idea and the *primary* purpose, not minor ideas and secondary purposes. For example, the way a harpsichord works might be described, but the author might do so *in order to* explain why pianos became more popular than harpsichords in the 1700s. So the primary purpose is not to describe harpsichords, but to explain the rising popularity of pianos.

Look for the choice that is a *complete* description of the main idea or primary purpose of the passage. This will require that you read the *entire* passage.

ETS TIPS for Main Idea Questions

- Don't just choose answers that are true. Some choices may be true, but they may not express the main idea of the given passage.
- Don't choose an answer just because you think the author would agree with the idea expressed; that may not be the main point the author was making in the passage.
- Don't look for the answer choice that has wording that is most similar to that used in the passage. Often, all choices will have wording similar to that used in the passage. You will have to read both the passage and the choices carefully to understand exactly what is meant by the words. Merely skimming the passage will not enable you to determine the main idea of the passage.
- For primary-purpose questions, pay attention to the specific meanings of words such as *compare, examine, explain*, and *refute*, which are often used in the answer choices.
- Be sure the choice you select does not go *beyond* the passage. Sometimes a choice may present information that is not directly given in the passage. That choice will not, therefore, be the main idea or primary purpose.

Try a Main Idea question

Shakespeare wrote four types of plays: histories, comedies, tragedies, and tragicomedies. Some scholars contend that Shakespeare's choice of three of these types of dramatic forms reflects his various psychological states. As a young man making a name for himself in London, he wrote comedies. Then, saddened by the death of his son, he turned to tragedies. Finally, seasoned by life's joys and sorrows, he produced tragicomedies. But a look at the theater scene of his day reveals that Shakespeare was not so much writing out of his heart as into his pocketbook. When comedies were the vogue, he wrote comedies; when tragedies were the rage, he wrote tragedies; and when tragicomedies dominated the stage, he produced tragicomedies.

1. The primary purpose of the passage is to

(A) examine Shakespeare's life in light of his dramatic works
(B) contest a theory that attempts to explain why Shakespeare wrote the kinds of plays he did
(C) explain the terms comedy, tragedy, and tragicomedy as they are used in discussions of Shakespeare's plays
(D) compare Shakespeare's plays with the works of other dramatists of his day
(E) discuss what is known about Shakespeare's psychological state

Explanation: The first two sentences classify Shakespeare's plays into four categories and offer a theory, endorsed by "some scholars," concerning why Shakespeare chose to write three of these four kinds of plays. The next three sentences provide support for this theory by showing correspondence between Shakespeare's likely psychological state and the plays he wrote at various times in his life. The word "But" in the next sentence indicates a change of direction in the passage: the author now suggests that the first theory may be wrong, and goes on to provide an alternate theory—that Shakespeare may well have written the kinds of plays he wrote not because they reflected a particular psychological state but because he thought they would be financially successful. The primary purpose of the passage then, is best described in choice B, which states that the author's purpose is to "contest a theory" (and choice B correctly describes the theory being contested; that is, a theory about why Shakespeare wrote the kinds of plays he did).

Choice C can be eliminated because although the terms listed in choice C are used in the passage, they are not explained.

Choice D can be eliminated because the passage is not concerned with comparing Shakespeare's plays with those of another dramatist.

While choices A and E do to some extent reflect the content of the passage, neither expresses the complete primary purpose of the passage. (And, in fact, choice A has the examination backwards: Shakespeare's works are examined in light of his life, not the other way around.)

Type 2: Supporting Idea Questions

Supporting ideas are ideas used to support or elaborate on the main idea. Supporting Idea questions can focus on facts, details, definitions, or other information presented by the author. Whereas questions about the main idea ask you to determine the meaning of a passage or a paragraph as a whole, questions about supporting ideas ask you to determine the meaning of a particular part of the passage. Think of a lawyer during a court case examining an expert medical witness on the stand. The lawyer asks specific questions about supporting details: "What are the usual symptoms of the disease?", "What medicines are typically used to combat the disease?", "Why would some people take longer to be cured than others?" These specific questions do not comprise the main argument of the lawyer's case, which may be to show a hospital's negligence in the care of a patient, but they are critical supporting facts.

How to recognize Supporting Idea questions

Here are the ways in which Supporting Idea questions are usually asked:

- According to the passage, which of the following is true of X?
- The passage mentions all the following as characteristics of X EXCEPT …
- According to the author, the kinds of data mentioned in line n are significant because they …
- The author's description of X mentions which of the following?
- The passage states that one of the consequences of X was …
- According to the passage, X is immediately followed by …

ETS TIPS for Supporting Idea Questions

- You may need to refer to the passage to find out exactly what is said about the subject of the question. Since the question is asking about a specific detail, you may not recall the detail from your first reading of the passage.
- Eliminate the choices that present information contradictory to what is presented in the passage.
- Eliminate the choices that present information not given in the passage.
- Don't just select a choice that presents information that is given in the passage; your choice must answer the specific question that is asked.

Try two Supporting Idea questions

Predominantly Black land-grant colleges in the United States have a long tradition of supporting cooperative education programs. These programs combine academic courses with work experience that carries academic credit. This tradition has made these colleges the leaders in the recent movement in American education toward career-oriented curriculums.

2. According to the passage, predominantly Black land-grant colleges in the United States are leaders in career-oriented education because they

(A) have had "cooperative education programs" as part of their curriculums for many years

(B) were among the first colleges in the United States to shift away from "career-oriented curriculums"

(C) offer their students academic credit for their work experience prior to entering college

(D) have a long tradition of cooperation with local business and community leaders

(E) provide opportunities for students to work on campus to earn money for tuition

Explanation: The first sentence tells us that Black land-grant colleges have supported cooperative education programs for a long time. The second sentence describes cooperative education programs. The final sentence tells us that it is this tradition of support for cooperative education programs that has made these colleges leaders in the career-oriented education movement. Of the five choices, choice A best states the reason that the colleges are leaders in career-related education.

Choice B can be eliminated because it contradicts information in the passage.

Choice C can be eliminated because although it may be an accurate statement about these colleges, it does not account for their leadership in career-oriented education.

The passage says nothing about local business and community leaders; therefore, choice D can be eliminated.

Although choice E may be a correct statement about these colleges, this information is not explicitly stated in the passage. Even if the information were included, it would not help explain why the colleges are *leaders* in career-oriented education. Providing students with jobs on campus would not necessarily be beneficial to them in developing skills for a future career.

The women's movement emerged in the United States in the 1830s, a period of intense reform and evangelism. Women were encouraged to speak out at religious revival meetings, and many women thus gained public speaking experience. When women sought and were denied leadership and the right to speak out in the abolitionist and temperance societies to which they belonged, they organized their own reform groups and later worked to improve their own status.

3. According to the passage, women formed their own reform societies because women

(A) were denied membership in other reform societies
(B) disagreed with the aims of the societies to which they belonged
(C) were not permitted to act as leaders of the organizations of which they were members
(D) were preoccupied with issues that pertained only to the status of women
(E) wished to challenge the existing political order by questioning the political motives of their opponents

Explanation: This question asks you to identify information that is explicitly stated in the passage. The last sentence states that women formed their own reform societies because they were "denied leadership and the right to speak out" in the societies to which they already belonged. Thus, choice C is the best answer.

Choice A can be eliminated because the passage indicates that women were members of temperance and abolitionist societies.

Choices B, D, and E can be eliminated because the passage provides no information about the specific views of the women or about a desire on their part to challenge the existing political order.

Type 3: Organization Questions

Organization refers to how the content of a reading passage is put together to achieve the author's purpose. The individual sentences and paragraphs that make up the passages have a logical and coherent relationship to one another.

Sometimes you will be asked to identify how a passage as a whole is constructed. For instance, a passage may introduce and then describe a theory. It may compare and then contrast two points of view. It may offer an idea and then refute it, and so on.

Sometimes you will be asked to identify how one paragraph is related to another. For instance, the second paragraph may give examples to support a statement offered in the first paragraph, or the second paragraph may refute a theory presented in the first paragraph. The answers may be expressed in general terms (e.g., a hypothesis is explained and then challenged) or in terms specific to the passage (e.g., how children learn one kind of activity is described and then this method is recommended for teaching children another kind of activity).

As another way of testing your ability to recognize organization, you may be asked to identify why an author mentions a particular piece of information or why an author quotes someone. For example, an author might mention a reason or an example to support an assertion. An author might quote someone to provide an example of a person who holds a certain opinion.

To answer Organization questions, pay attention to how sentences and paragraphs are connected. Sometimes certain words make the connections explicit: *for example*, *however*, *a second reason*, *furthermore*, and so on. They may tell you whether a sentence or paragraph is giving an example, offering a contrast, offering additional information, or extending a point. You may even want to underline those kinds of words as you read through the passage for the first time. However, you should keep in mind that such key words might not always be present. When you cannot find key words, simply ask yourself how one sentence or paragraph is connected to another.

How to recognize Organization questions

Here are the ways in which Organization questions are usually asked:

- Which of the following statements best describes the organization of the passage?
- Which of the following best describes the way in which the claim is presented?
- The final paragraph can best be described as …

ETS TIPS for Organization Questions

- Pay careful attention to the words used in the answer choices. They are usually the key to finding the right answer. Know the precise meanings of these terms: *definition, comparison, analogy, summary, refutation, chronological, controversial, criticism,* and *generalization.* These words are often used in the choices given for Organization questions.

Sometimes it may help to recall the main idea or primary purpose of the passage—the organization of the whole as well as of the parts should serve that idea or purpose.

Try one Organization question

One promising energy source would require sophisticated redesign of the basic windmills that have pumped water for centuries. Coupled with advanced storage batteries, large windmills might satisfy the total energy needs of rural areas and even small cities where strong and prevalent winds can be counted on. Wind power has several advantages. First, no new technology is really required. Second, the energy source is inexhaustible. Third, relatively little capital investment is needed to install or operate windmills.

But wind power has major disadvantages, too. Most obviously, it will work only in areas where wind is strong and prevalent. Furthermore, the amount of electricity that could be generated by wind power would simply be insufficient to meet major nationwide energy needs.

However, a network of sea-based windmills, placed on buoys and driven by the same prevailing winds that once powered sailing vessels, could provide a substantial fraction of the world's electrical energy—especially if the buoy-based windmills could be linked to land by superconducting power transmission cables.

4. Which of the following best describes the organization of the passage?

(A) A series of interrelated events are arranged chronologically.
(B) A controversial theory is proposed and then persuasively defended.
(C) An unforeseen problem is described and several examples are provided.
(D) A criticism is summarized, evaluated, and then dismissed.
(E) A problematical issue is discussed and a partial solution is suggested.

Explanation: Choice E is the best answer. "A problematical issue is discussed" summarizes the first two paragraphs, in which both the positive and negative aspects of a complicated situation are examined. This discussion is followed, in the third paragraph, by the suggestion of "a partial solution," which may solve some of the problems involved in using windmills to generate electricity.

Choice A can be eliminated because the passage is concerned with examining an issue from different sides rather than with narrating specific events. Nor is there any sense of chronology in the passage.

Choice B attributes a one-sided approach to the author, who actually presents different points of view. Furthermore, although the passage implies there may be disagreement about the usefulness of the windmills, it does not anywhere indicate that the issue is controversial. In addition, the passage focuses more on concrete aspects of a problem than on a theory.

Choice C can be eliminated because there is no evidence in the passage that the problems discussed in the second paragraph were unforeseen.

Choice D can be eliminated because the passage does not summarize, evaluate, or dismiss any criticism that is mentioned, nor does the entire passage deal with criticism.

Whatever their disadvantage with respect to distributing education tax dollars equally among school districts may be, in one respect at least, local property taxes are superior to state taxes as a means of funding public schools. Because local property taxes provide public schools with a direct source of revenue, these public schools are relatively free from competition with other government services for tax dollars. School administrators do not have to compete for a share of the state tax dollars, which are already being spent on health, criminal justice, public safety, and transportation. They are not placed in the position of having to argue that school programs must have priority over other public services financed by state taxes.

5. The author mentions the tax dollars spent on health, criminal justice, public safety, and transportation most likely in order to highlight the

(A) government services with which public schools do not have to compete for tax dollars
(B) unequal distribution of local property tax dollars among various public services
(C) high expense of maintaining schools as compared to other public services
(D) government services over which public schools have priority
(E) disadvantage of distributing education tax dollars among various public services

Explanation: The first sentence of this passage states that using local property taxes for schools has advantages over using state taxes. The second sentence explains this advantage: "public schools are relatively free from competition with other government services for tax dollars." The next sentence elaborates, listing some of those "other government services"—"health, criminal justice, public safety, and transportation." Thus, choice A is the best answer.

Choices B and E can be eliminated because they do not reflect the passage's content. The potentially unequal distribution of local property-tax dollars (a disadvantage) is among school districts, not among various public services.

Choice C can be eliminated because the author is not making a point about the relative cost of education.

Choice D can be eliminated with similar reasoning. The author does not say that public schools have priority over government services, merely that the freedom from competition frees school administrators from having to make that argument.

Type 4: Vocabulary Questions

Vocabulary questions require you to identify the meanings of words as they are used in the context of a reading passage. These questions not only test your understanding of the meaning of a particular word, but also test your ability to understand how the word is being used in context. Authors make choices about the language they use, and they sometimes deliberately choose unusual words or figures of speech (words not intended to be understood literally). When you are asked about an unusual word or a figure of speech, you will be given sufficient context to help you identify the meaning of the word.

How to recognize Vocabulary questions

Here are the ways in which Vocabulary questions are usually asked:

- Which of the following words could be substituted for "*Y*" in line *n* without substantially altering the meaning of the statement?
- The author most probably uses the word "*Y*" in line *n* to mean …
- In line *n*, the word "*Y*" most nearly means …

> **ETS TIPS for Vocabulary Questions**
>
> - Remember the question is not simply asking about the meaning of a specific word; it is asking about its meaning *in the context of the passage*. Therefore, do not simply choose the answer choice that provides a correct meaning; you must understand which meaning the author is using in the passage.
> - Often all the choices will offer acceptable meanings of the word. Your job is to choose which meaning makes the most sense as the word is used in the passage.
> - Reread the relevant sentence in the passage, using the word or phrase you have chosen. Confirm that the sentence makes sense in the context of the passage as a whole.

Try two Vocabulary questions

President Lyndon Johnson's father once told him that without the ability to walk into a roomful of people and tell immediately who was a supporter and who was an opponent, one did not belong in politics. In fact, even the shrewd younger Johnson never had such occult power, but his liking for this story tells us something useful about him: he set much store by instinct. No wonder, then, that it would be to his instincts—honed in the Texas hill country, sharpened in a life of politics, confirmed in a long and respected congressional career—that he would often turn while in the White House.

6. Which of the following words, if substituted for the word "occult" in line 4, would LEAST change the meaning of the sentence?

    (A) legendary
    (B) subtle
    (C) invisible
    (D) persuasive
    (E) supernatural

Explanation: The "occult" power described in the first sentence is clearly not a power that people ordinarily have. It could, therefore, best be described as "supernatural." Choice E is, therefore, the best answer.

Choices A and D can be eliminated because they are not synonyms of *occult* in any context.

Choice B can be eliminated because the process of dividing people into two categories, "for" and "against," is not "subtle," but rather a crude and direct means of dealing with others.

Choice C can be eliminated because powers of the mind are always "invisible," and there is no reason why the author would attribute a high degree of invisibility to one power when all are equally invisible.

In *Understanding Media*, Marshall McLuhan sheds a brilliant light, punctuated by occasional shadows of obscurity, on the essential nature of electronic media; the chapter on radio looks harder at that medium than anything since Arnheim's *Radio*.

7. The phrase "shadows of obscurity" most probably refers to McLuhan's

    (A) use of imagery
    (B) lack of clarity
    (C) depth of understanding
    (D) wide-ranging interests
    (E) waning reputation

Explanation: This question asks you to identify the meaning of a figure of speech (the author does not mean to suggest *real* shadows). The passage as a whole presents an evaluation of Marshall McLuhan's *Understanding Media*. The "brilliant light" shed by McLuhan is a figure of speech that can be interpreted as an illuminating discussion of electronic media. The passage states that this brilliant light is "punctuated by" something else, meaning that it is interrupted by something that contrasts with it. The "shadows of obscurity" can thus be interpreted as confusing or unclear parts of McLuhan's discussion. Thus, choice B is the best answer.

Choice A can be eliminated because the passage is discussing McLuhan's work in general and not particular aspects of his style, such as imagery.

Choice C can be eliminated because while "shadows" might refer to "depths," "understanding" is *contrary* to "obscurity."

Choice D can be eliminated because "wide-ranging interests" captures the meaning of neither "shadows" nor "obscurity."

Choice E can be eliminated because the passage is about the merits of McLuhan's book rather than about McLuhan's reputation.

Type 5: Inference Questions

An inference is a statement that is clearly suggested or implied by the author. An inference is based on information given in the passage, but it is not directly stated in the passage. To answer inference questions, you may have to carry statements made by the author one step beyond what is presented in the passage. For example, if a passage explicitly states an effect, a question could ask you to infer its cause. Be ready, therefore, to concentrate not only on the explicit meanings of the author's words, but also on the logical implications of those words.

We make inferences in conversation all the time. Consider this conversation between two students:

Sean: "Did you get an A on the quiz?"

Chris: "Didn't you hear the professor say that no one got an A?"

Sean should be able to infer that Chris did not get an A on the quiz, even though Chris did not explicitly say so.

Here's another conversation that illustrates an inference:

Lee: "This is the first year that the university is offering a course in writing poetry."

Sara: "So my sister, who graduated last year, couldn't have taken a course here in writing poetry."

Sara can make an inference about her sister's particular situation from Lee's general statement.

How to recognize Inference questions

Pay special attention when you see words such as "infer," "suggests," and "implies" in a question. These are often signals for inference questions.

Here are the ways in which Inference questions are usually asked:

- Which of the following can be inferred about *X* from the passage?
- The passage strongly suggests that *X* would happen if …
- The author of the passage implies which of the following about *X*?
- It can be inferred from the passage that *X* is effective in all of the following ways EXCEPT …

ETS TIPS for Inference Questions

- Make sure your answer doesn't contradict the main idea of the passage.
- Make sure your answer doesn't go too far and make assumptions that aren't included in the passage. (For example, in the conversation between Lee and Sara about poetry courses, Sara would have gone too far if she had said, "So all English majors will now be required to take the course in writing poetry." This cannot be inferred from Lee's statement.)
- Don't just choose a statement that sounds important or true. It must be inferable from the passage.
- You should be able to defend your selection by pointing to explicitly stated information in the passage that leads to the inference you have selected.
- Use the "if-then" test to verify your answers. To perform this test, complete the following statement: if *X* (information in the passage), then *Y* (your selected choice). Does your "if-then" statement make sense?

Try two Inference questions

Histories of the Middle East abound in stereotypes and clichés, particularly with respect to women. The position of women in the Middle East is frequently treated as though Middle Eastern societies formed a single unit that could be accurately represented in a simple description.

8. The author of the passage suggests which of the following about histories of the Middle East with regard to their treatment of women?

(A) A general problem with such histories was first noticed in their descriptions of the role of women.

(B) The experience of women in Middle Eastern societies is much more diverse than such histories have often assumed.

(C) The study of women's roles and experience has recently become a central focus in such histories.

(D) Such histories report the position of women in Middle Eastern societies has undergone a major transformation.

(E) Until recently, such histories typically neglected to discuss the position of women.

Explanation: In the first sentence, the author asserts that histories of the Middle East are filled with oversimplified generalizations, particularly with regard to women. In the second sentence, the author explains the error lies in the way historians of the Middle East discuss women as though all Middle Eastern societies were similar. By saying "as though," the author suggests that Middle Eastern societies are different and the experiences of women in the countries are different, so that it is a mistake to assume that the experiences are similar. Thus, choice B is the best answer.

Choice A can be eliminated because the author does not suggest that the problem with histories of the Middle East was discovered as a result of the way those studies treat women.

Choices C and E can be eliminated because although the passage suggests that women are discussed in studies of the Middle East, it does not suggest that such studies either typically neglected or focused on women.

Choice D can be eliminated because the passage does not report that there has been a change in the position of women in the Middle East.

In the 1960s and 1970s, electoral support for public education was strong, mainly as a result of certain trends in the U.S. population. For example, enrollments in primary and secondary schools reached their zenith in these years, when public school students constituted one out of every four members of the U.S. population. Moreover, parents of children in public schools and public school employees comprised approximately 40 percent of eligible voters in the United States.

9. The author implies that one of the results of large enrollments in public schools in the 1960s and 1970s was

(A) a deterioration in the quality of education offered by nonpublic schools

(B) an increase in the demand for higher education

(C) an increase in the number of eligible voters in the United States

(D) broad electoral support for public education programs

(E) overall improvement in the quality of higher education

Explanation: The author says that electoral support for public education was strong during the 1960s and 1970s because of certain trends in the United States population. The author then goes on to cite, as an example of those trends, the high levels of enrollment in public schools during this period. The author thus implies a cause-and-effect relationship between large enrollments in public schools and broad electoral support for education. This answer is given in choice D.

Choices A, B, C, and E can be eliminated because the passage does not suggest anything about the quality of education offered in nonpublic schools, the demand for higher education, the number of eligible voters, or the quality of higher education.

Type 6: Evidence Questions

In the questions that assess your ability to evaluate supporting evidence, you will sometimes be given hypothetical pieces of evidence and asked which of them is relevant to supporting an argument made in a passage. To answer such a question, you must have a clear understanding of the argument made in the passage and must make a judgment about what kinds of acts, statistics, reasons, examples, or expert testimony would provide strong support for that argument.

For example, if a person argued that dancers experience fewer injuries than other athletes because they are more coordinated, then evidence about the injury rates of various athletes and their relative coordination would be relevant.

Other questions of this type ask you to identify which of several pieces of evidence strengthens or weakens an argument made in a passage. Evidence that provides support for the conclusion would strengthen an argument; evidence that contradicts or casts doubt on the conclusion would weaken an argument.

For example, in the case of the argument mentioned above about injury to dancers, evidence that dancers engage in more injury-reducing warm-up exercises than other athletes would weaken the argument, as it casts doubt on the conclusion that coordination (and not warm-up) is the reason for fewer injuries.

How to recognize Evidence questions

Here are the ways in which Evidence questions are usually asked:

- Which of the following, if true, would most weaken the author's argument concerning *X*?
- The author's argument would be strengthened if it could be proved that …
- Which of the following facts, if true, would most help to explain *X*?
- Which of the following, if true, supports the conclusion drawn in the passage?
- In order to assess the claim made in the passage, it would be most useful to know which of the following?

ETS TIPS for Evidence Questions

- Remind yourself of the author's claim and the evidence used to support the claim.
- Then, test each choice to see whether it provides an example that directly affects the chain of reasoning and supporting evidence.
- Usually a new piece of evidence will strengthen the author's claim, weaken the author's claim, or be irrelevant to whether the claim is valid or not.

Try an Evidence question

In our increasing awareness of ecological health, many industrial practices have come under close examination, and mining is no exception. Though drilling is required in both cases, base-metal mining involves toxic chemical leachates for separating the metal from the rock, whereas diamond mining does not—diamonds can be separated from surrounding rock using only crushers, screens, and all-natural water. Thus, base-metal mining is environmentally destructive, but diamond mining does not harm the environment.

10. Which of the following, if true, would most weaken the author's argument concerning the effect of diamond mining on the environment?

(A) The process of drilling and getting the drill rig to and from the site destroys ecological habitats.

(B) Base metals have utilitarian value, but diamonds are functionally almost worthless.

(C) Toxic chemical leachates contaminate not only soil, but groundwater as well.

(D) There have been proposals to use abandoned mine shafts as garbage dumps.

(E) Logging can be as ecologically destructive as mining.

Explanation: The author argues that whereas base-metal mining is harmful to the environment, diamond mining is not environmentally destructive. Therefore, evidence to the contrary would weaken the argument. Since choice A provides evidence indicating that diamond mining is harmful to the environment, it is the best answer.

Choices B, C, and E may well be true, but they are irrelevant to the argument made in the passage about the impact of diamond mining on the environment.

Choice D may seem at first reading to weaken the argument, but the statement describes environmental destruction caused not by the mining process itself, but by the use of the mines subsequent to mining. Furthermore, the destruction described is merely *potential* damage. Choice D is not, therefore, the best answer.

Type 7: Assumption Questions

These questions will ask you to recognize the ideas or perspectives that underlie an author's arguments. These assumptions are unstated ideas or facts that the author accepts as true or takes for granted. Indeed, they must be accepted as true in order for the author's argument to be valid.

If a person argued, "We could increase student performance if all students got eight hours of sleep every night," then this person would be assuming that at least some students are not getting eight hours of sleep every night.

How to recognize Assumption questions

Here are the ways in which Assumption questions are usually asked:

- Which of the following assumptions is most likely made by the author of the passage?
- In arguing *X*, the author makes which of the following assumptions?
- The argument in the passage is based on which of the following assumptions?

ETS TIPS for Assumption Questions

- Ask yourself which choice would have to be true for the author's argument to be valid.
- Sometimes the assumption is something you identified as a "missing step" as you were reading the passage.

Try an Assumption question

Studying a recent exhibition of photographs representing the many extraordinary buildings that have appeared in Paris over the last four decades must have been dispiriting for New Yorkers, who have seen no radical local architecture since Frank Lloyd Wright's Guggenheim Museum was completed in 1959.

11. Which of the following assumptions is most likely made by the author of the passage?

(A) New Yorkers are unlikely to appreciate exhibitions of architectural photographs.

(B) New Yorkers do not think of the Guggenheim Museum as an example of radical architecture.

(C) New Yorkers would like to have more exciting architecture in their city.

(D) New Yorkers are not particularly interested in the architecture of their city.

(E) New Yorkers would like to see more photographs of buildings designed by Frank Lloyd Wright.

Explanation: Choice C is the best answer. The author expresses the idea that New Yorkers must have been dispirited by evidence of the contrast between Paris' exciting new buildings and the comparative absence of radical architecture in New York. This idea would not hold up if New Yorkers actually were uninterested in having more such architecture in their city. New Yorkers' desire for more radical local architecture is an idea that the author implicitly accepts and that underlies the argument in the passage, but which is not directly stated in the passage. It is therefore an assumption made by the author.

Choice A is incorrect. The passage actually implies the contrary, that its author believes New Yorkers appreciate exhibitions of architectural photographs enough to respond emotionally when such an exhibition reveals something about their city that they wish were different.

Choice B is incorrect because the statement in choice B would not have to be true for the author's argument to be valid. If New Yorkers did not think of the Guggenheim Museum as an example of radical architecture, this would tend more to strengthen than to invalidate the author's claim that New Yorkers are dispirited by the absence of such architecture in their city.

Choice D is incorrect because for New Yorkers to respond as the author supposes they did to the issue of the character of local architecture, they would have to be interested in that architecture.

Choice E states a belief that may or may not held by the author, but which has no bearing either way on the question of New Yorkers' supposed response to a comparison of their own city's recent architecture with that of Paris. Therefore, choice E is not an assumption underlying the passage content.

Type 8: Fact/Opinion Questions

Often a piece of writing will contain both facts and opinions, and you will be asked to distinguish one from the other.

Facts can be verified (as objectively true or false) and are often presented in a straightforward fashion without emotion.

Opinions are beliefs or judgments that are subjective in nature and are sometimes presented with emotion.

Here are two statements, both related to music studies. One is an opinion about the effect of music studies; the other is a presentation of facts about music study.

- Opinion: "Nothing can match the sense of accomplishment a young person feels after mastering the basics of a musical instrument and playing in a first recital."
- Fact: "Studies have shown a positive correlation between learning to play a musical instrument and achieving above-average evaluations in other subjects."

How to recognize Fact/Opinion questions

Here is the way Fact/Opinion questions are usually asked:

Which of the following statements, taken from the passage, is most clearly an expression of opinion rather than fact?

Try a Fact/Opinion question

William Bailey, an American Realist painter, studied at Yale in the 1950s. His still lifes depict smooth, rounded containers that sit in a field of uniform color. Bailey denies a close connection to Giorgio Morandi, another American Realist, but admits that they share "a belief in the power of the mute object." While Morandi painted from direct observation, Bailey painted from memory. This difference in method makes Bailey's objects superior to Morandi's for they are thus purified, immutable, and mysterious.

12. Which of the following statements, taken from the passage, is most clearly an expression of opinion rather than fact?

(A) William Bailey, an American Realist painter, studied at Yale in the 1950s.
(B) His still lifes depict smooth, rounded containers that sit in a field of uniform color.
(C) Bailey denies a close connection to Giorgio Morandi, another American Realist, but admits that they share "a belief in the power of the mute object."
(D) While Morandi painted from direct observation, Bailey painted from memory.
(E) This difference in method makes Bailey's objects superior to Morandi's for they are thus purified, immutable, and mysterious.

Explanation: Choice E is the best answer because it expresses a subjective judgment about Bailey's objects (as well as about the effect of his method). One might disagree with the statement (and claim, e.g., that Bailey's objects are not "purified, immutable, and mysterious" or that they are so but not because of his method of painting from memory).

Choices A, B, C, and D are statements of fact. Each is either objectively true or false.

Type 9: Attitude Questions

Authors often have feelings about their subjects; that is, they may feel enthusiastic, angry, critical, uncertain, and so forth. The words an author chooses help you recognize her or his attitude. If, for example, an author describes a new invention as "unfortunate" and "misguided," you can say the author's attitude toward the invention is critical or unfavorable.

How to recognize Attitude questions

Here are the ways in which Attitude questions are usually asked:

- The author's attitude toward X can best be described as …
- The author's attitude toward X is most accurately reflected in which of the following words, as they are used in the passage?

> ### ETS TIP for Attitude Questions
>
> Look for clue words in the passages. Words such as "successful," "fortunately," and "courageous" probably indicate a positive attitude toward the topic. Words or phrases such as "shortsighted," "inadequate," and "falls short" probably indicate a negative attitude toward the topic.

Try an Attitude question

Parents usually do not insist that their children learn to walk by a certain age. Parents feel confident that the children will learn to walk within a reasonable period of time, when their bodies are ready for such an undertaking. Teachers should adopt the same attitude when teaching children in school how to read. If teachers did this, children might learn to read much more quickly and experience less anxiety while doing so.

13. The author's attitude toward teachers who try to force children to learn to read once they reach a certain age can best be described as

    (A) sympathetic
    (B) accepting
    (C) disapproving
    (D) neutral
    (E) enthusiastic

Explanation: The word "should" in the third sentence indicates that the author is prescribing that, when teaching children how to read, teachers adopt the same attitude as that usually adopted by parents—not insisting that something be learned by a certain age, but rather letting the child do it when ready. The author would, therefore, disapprove of teachers who try to force children to read at a certain age, making choice C the best answer.

Choices B and E can be eliminated because they express positive attitudes toward teachers who force children to learn to read at a certain age.

Sympathy toward teachers who try to force children to learn to read at a certain age is not suggested by the author, so choice A can be eliminated.

Choice D, neutrality, is contradicted by the author's use of the word "should"—which clearly indicates an attitude of some sort.

Type 10: Extending/Predicting Questions

This type of question tests your ability to recognize ideas or situations that extend information that has been presented in the passage. For example, such questions can ask you to predict what is most likely to occur in the future if what the author says in the passage is accurate. These questions can also ask you to use information presented in the passage to determine whether the author or an individual mentioned in the passage would agree or disagree with a particular statement that has not been discussed in the passage.

This kind of extending or predicting occurs frequently in casual conversations. Consider this exchange:

Terry: "Did you like the concert last night?"

Rosalyn: "Yes, but it was much too loud for me. My ears hurt the whole time, and for hours afterward."

Terry could safely predict that Rosalyn would prefer *all* concerts she attends to be at comfortable noise levels. Terry could also generalize that Rosalyn's experience at the concert is similar to someone who attends an outdoor theater performance and finds the spotlights too bright, making his or her eyes uncomfortable. At both the concert and the outdoor theater performance, an aspect of the performance made the attendee physically uncomfortable.

To answer extending and predicting questions, you must do more than recall what you have read. You must be able to understand the essential nature or characteristics of ideas or situations appearing in the passage. You must then use that understanding to evaluate the choices in order to determine which choice is most consistent with information you have already been given in the passage.

How to recognize Extending/Predicting questions

Here are the ways in which Extending/Predicting questions are usually asked:

- On the basis of the description of X in the passage, the author would be most likely to make which of the following recommendations for future action regarding X?
- With which of the following statements about X would the author be most likely to agree?

Try an Extending/Predicting question

Carl Filtsch, composer Frederic Chopin's favorite pupil, was once asked by a visitor why he played one of Chopin's compositions so differently from his teacher. His reply delighted Chopin: "I can't play with someone else's feelings."

14. The statement above suggests that Chopin would have agreed with which of the following ideas about musical performance?

(A) The most important element of a good performance is fidelity to the composer's intentions.

(B) The quality of a musical performance can be best judged by the composer of the piece.

(C) Performances of the same composition by two different musicians should sound different.

(D) A piano teacher must teach a student not only the notes in a composition but also their emotional interpretation.

(E) A composer's interpretation of his or her own compositions is not as profound as another musician's interpretation.

Explanation: The passage indicates that Chopin was pleased to hear his student say that the student's rendition of a musical composition differed from Chopin's because the student could play only with his own feelings and not with those of his teacher. Chopin's delight in this reply suggests he would agree that each individual's rendition of a musical composition should sound different because each individual brings his or her own feelings to the piece. Thus, choice C is the best answer.

Choice A can be eliminated because the passage indicates that Chopin feels that each musician should play a piece with regard to his or her own feelings rather than with regard to the composer's intentions.

Choice B can be eliminated because the passage does not provide information from which to deduce Chopin's views on how a performance should be judged.

Choice D can be eliminated because Chopin's response to his student's remark suggests that Chopin believes it is up to each individual, not a teacher, to bring his or her own emotional interpretation to a piece.

Choice E can be eliminated because Chopin's response to the student's remark suggests that Chopin would not necessarily agree that a composer's interpretation of a piece is more profound than another musician's interpretation.

Type 11: Conclusion Questions

This type of question asks you to determine which of several conclusions can best be drawn from the information presented in a passage, assuming that information is accurate. In other words, if everything the author says is true, what is a necessary consequence that follows from what the author says?

How to recognize Conclusion questions

Here are the ways in which Conclusion questions are usually asked:

- Given the information in the passage, which of the following must be concluded about *X*?
- Which of the following conclusions is best supported by the passage?

ETS TIPS for Conclusion Questions

- Be sure to find a choice that is highly consistent with the passage. Mentally add your choice to the end of the passage—does it fit?
- For example, the passage might present the findings of research that links an audience's comprehension of an advertisement with the advertisement's effectiveness: at the normal rate of 141 words per minute, listeners comprehend 100 percent of the advertisement; at 282 words per minute, listeners comprehend 90 percent of the advertisement; at 423 words per minute, listeners comprehend 50 percent of the advertisement. One might conclude that especially if advertisers incorporate some repetition of key points into their messages, their ads will be highly effective even if read at twice the normal rate—such a sentence would indeed fit well at the end of the passage.
- Don't choose an answer choice just because it sounds related and important. It may in fact overextend the principles expressed in the passage.

Try a Conclusion question

Scientists consider both landslides and surface-creep movement instrumental in the formation of rock glaciers. Evidence of landslides can be distinguished from that of surface-creep movement because landslides leave a more definite and deeper surface of rupture, partly due to their faster rate of movement. Those studying the origins of rock glaciers have noted that some glaciers are well-defined, while others are not, that is, some show evidence of deep ruptures, while others do not.

15. Given the information in the passage, which of the following must be concluded about rock glaciers?

(A) Not all rock glaciers originate in the same way.
(B) Landslides initiate the formation of rock glaciers, then surface-creep movement follows.
(C) Neither landslides nor surface-creep movement can account for the formation of rock glaciers.
(D) While the definition and depth of rupture can be measured at rock glacier sites, the rate of movement cannot.
(E) Further study is required in order to determine the origins of rock glaciers.

Explanation: The passage suggests two possible mechanisms for the formation of rock glaciers (first sentence) and describes the effects that distinguish them (second sentence). Since observations reveal both kinds of effects (third and fourth sentences) at rock glacier sites, one can conclude that both formation mechanisms have been occurring. Thus, choice A is the best answer.

Choices C and E can be eliminated because the passage indicates scientists believe that both landslides and surface-creep movement initiate rock glaciers.

There is no evidence given to support the conclusion that landslides, rock glaciers, and surface-creep movement occur consecutively. Hence, B can be eliminated.

Choice D can be eliminated because there is nothing in the passage to suggest the rate of movement cannot be measured.

Type 12: Application Questions

This type of question requires you to recognize a general rule or idea that underlies a specific situation described in the passage and apply that rule or idea to other situations not described in the passage. Specifically, this kind of question measures your ability to discern the relationships between situations or ideas presented by the author and other situations or ideas that might parallel those described in the passage. You might consider these questions "real-life application" questions.

How to recognize Application questions

Here are the ways in which Application questions are usually asked:

- The information in the passage suggests that X would be most useful to Y in which of the following situations?
- It can be inferred from the passage's description of certain Xs that all Xs must be …

ETS TIPS for Application Questions

- Look for the most reasonable and consistent choice. The principle from the passage must be directly applicable to the new situation.
- Look for a situation that has characteristics similar to those in the passage. For example, if the passage describes the problems associated with trying to locate the remains of shipwrecks, look for a situation among the choices that has similar features (unknown locations, no eyewitnesses or maps, and some medium such as water that makes finding the object difficult).

Try an Application question

Part of the appeal of certain vacation sites is the solitude that can be experienced there. But as more people discover and visit such locations, demand for vacations at those locations will likely decrease. Paradoxically, as soon as the sites become popular, they will necessarily become unpopular.

16. If the analysis in the passage were applied to gemstones, one would expect the demand for certain gems to decrease when they became

(A) rare
(B) fashionable
(C) beautiful
(D) expensive
(E) useful

Explanation: Choice B is correct because becoming fashionable implies becoming popular, and once that happens, according to the analysis in the passage, unpopularity follows (demand will decrease).

Choice A reverses the logic of the passage. Choices C, D, and E are not relevant to the level of demand; they merely offer possible characteristics of the gems.

CHAPTER 6

PPST™ Mathematics

Paper-Based Version	Computer-Based Version
40 questions	46 questions
60 minutes	75 minutes

PURPOSE OF THE PPST™: MATHEMATICS TEST

The emphasis in the *PPST™: Mathematics* test is on interpretation rather than on computation. Thus, you will not be expected to carry out intricate calculations, but you may be asked to choose appropriate calculations or estimate answers. Many college courses involve some mathematics, but you are seldom required to do long division or add complicated fractions. More likely, you will have to compare among very large numbers (e.g., the national debts of different countries) or among very small numbers (e.g., the sizes of atomic particles), to interpret graphs, or to evaluate formulas. The categories tested in the *PPST™: Mathematics* test represent the kinds of mathematics that might be encountered in any college course, not just in mathematics courses.

The mathematical preparation expected of you is limited to the usual topics of contemporary elementary school mathematics and at least one year of high school mathematics. The questions come from four content areas—numbers and operations, algebra, geometry and measurement, and data analysis and probability—and require the kind of mathematical competence that you may need in your coursework or in everyday life.

FORMAT OF THE PPST™: MATHEMATICS TEST

You will have 60 minutes to complete the 40 questions in the paper-and-pencil test. On the computerized test you will have 75 minutes to complete 46 questions. The approximate distribution of questions across the four content areas is as follows: 32.5 percent of the questions test numbers and operations, 20 percent test algebra, 22.5 percent test geometry and measurement, and 25 percent test data analysis and probability. The test is scored on the basis of the number of correct answers; there is no penalty for incorrect answers.

STRATEGIES FOR THE PPST™: MATHEMATICS TEST

The test questions are chosen from the following four categories, but questions may fit into more than one category.

Category I: Numbers and Operations

This category includes knowledge of order, equivalence, numeration and place value, number and operation properties, computation, estimation, ratio, proportion, percent, and numerical reasoning.

Each number represents a particular value that determines its place when numbers are ordered. When we count "1, 2, 3, 4, 5, …" we follow the order of the counting numbers. You should be familiar with the order not only of the counting numbers but also of integers and fractions.

Integers   Integers consist of the counting numbers, zero, and the negatives of the counting numbers, as shown below:

$$…, -5, -4, -3, -2, -1, 0, 1, 2, 3, 4, 5, …$$

Fractions and Decimals   Fractions, sometimes called rational numbers, include not only the integers but also certain numbers between integers. A number line is a handy way to show how fractions are ordered. Here is an example:

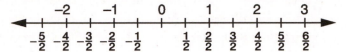

In this example, each unit has been partitioned into two equal parts, and the midpoint of each unit has been represented as a fraction with 2 as the denominator. On the number line, you can see that $\frac{5}{2}$ is between 2 and 3 and that $-\frac{1}{2}$ is between 0 and -1. When each unit is partitioned into three equal parts, the number line will look like this:

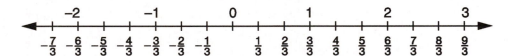

This number line shows, for example, that $\frac{5}{3}$ is between 1 and 2 and that $-\frac{4}{3}$ is less than -1. You should also notice that each integer has a fraction representation. For example:

$$-1 = -\frac{2}{2} = -\frac{3}{3} \text{ and}$$
$$3 = \frac{6}{2} = \frac{9}{3}.$$

When the units on the number line are partitioned into fourths, we can continue the sequence as follows:

$$-1 = -\frac{2}{2} = -\frac{3}{3} = -\frac{4}{4} \text{ and}$$
$$3 = \frac{6}{2} = \frac{9}{3} = \frac{12}{4}.$$

You can see that a number can have different representations. For example, $\frac{1}{2}$ (one-half) and $\frac{2}{4}$ (two-fourths) are different notations (and different names) for the same numerical value. Similarly, $\frac{3}{2}$ (three-halves) and $\frac{6}{4}$ (six-fourths) are different representations for the same numerical value. Another example, which comes from partitioning the unit on the number line into tenths, gives

$$\frac{1}{10} = \frac{10}{100} = \frac{100}{1,000},$$

which means that 1 tenth is the same as 10 hundredths, which is the same as 100 thousandths.

Number lines can be useful for showing both order and equivalence, and you might find it helpful to try some examples of your own, using various kinds of subdivisions.

We use two different systems of notation for numbers: fraction notations, such as $\frac{6}{2}$ and $\frac{5}{10}$, and decimal notations, such as 3.0 or 0.5. All numbers can be expressed in decimal form. A decimal point is used, and the place value for each digit depends on its position relative to the decimal point. For example, in the number 25.36, the part before the decimal point, 25, means $(2 \times 10) + (5 \times 1)$ and the part after the decimal point, .36, means $(3 \times \frac{1}{10}) + (6 \times \frac{1}{100})$. (For decimals less than 1, use 0 to the left of the decimal point to make it more noticeable.)

Number Properties   Number properties include knowledge of factors and multiples, primes and divisibility, even and odd numbers, and properties of zero and one.

Operation Properties   Operation properties include knowledge of the commutative, associative, and distributive principles.

Computation   Computation includes finding the solution to applied problems, determining information needed, and interpreting and adjusting results of computations.

Estimation   The ability to estimate and to determine that a problem-solving method or a solution is reasonable is also important.

Estimation skills are useful in many situations. At the supermarket, for example, you might want to estimate the total cost of your groceries as you shop; when taking a test, you might want to estimate the average amount of time you want to spend on each question. In the case of shopping, you might want to *overestimate* the cost to be sure you have enough money. On the other hand, in the case of a test, you may want to estimate how much time you need per question and then try to work under that time to give yourself a little extra time at the end. Whatever your purpose, estimating means selecting some numbers "close to" the given numbers and also numbers that will make the computation easy because a lot of estimation is done mentally.

Sometimes the answer you're looking for has to be more precise, as when you need to determine how much larger, or smaller, one number is than another, or how many times greater is one number than another. This may require computation rather than estimation, but estimation skills can help you verify your answer.

Numerical Reasoning   This subcategory deals with connectives and quantifiers, validity, and conclusions, including generalizations and counterexamples.

For example, conclusions can be arrived at using deductive reasoning. The term "deductive reasoning" may not be as familiar as some other terms we have discussed, but you have probably had quite a bit of experience with the process, since it is an integral part of mathematics. For example, knowing that

$$\frac{1}{2} = \frac{3}{6} \text{ and that}$$
$$\frac{1}{3} = \frac{2}{6},$$

you can conclude that $\frac{1}{2} + \frac{1}{3} = \frac{3}{6} + \frac{2}{6} = \frac{5}{6}$.

In school, you probably first learned to add fractions with the same denominator and then, using arguments such as that shown above, developed a way to add fractions with different denominators.

Some Symbols You Should Know

(This section contains some symbols that may be helpful when taking the *PPST™: Mathematics* test. For a more comprehensive list of symbols, consult a mathematics textbook.)

The following list shows some symbols you may see on the *PPST™: Mathematics* test.

$=$ is the symbol for "equal to." $\neq$ is the symbol for "not equal to."

$<$ is the symbol for "less than." $>$ is the symbol for "greater than."

$\leq$ is the symbol for "less than or equal to." $\geq$ is the symbol for "greater than or equal to."

Some Words and Phrases You Should Know

(This section contains some words and phrases that may be helpful when taking the *PPST™: Mathematics* test. For a more comprehensive list of words and phrases, consult a mathematics textbook.)

Integers	The numbers $\ldots, -4, -3, -2, -1, 0, 1, 2, 3, 4, \ldots$
Positive integers	The numbers $1, 2, 3, 4, \ldots$
Negative integers	The numbers $-1, -2, -3, -4, \ldots$
Whole numbers	All positive integers and zero
Zero	An integer that is neither positive nor negative
Even numbers	Integers that are divisible by 2; that is, $\ldots, -4, -2, 0, 2, 4, 6, 8, \ldots$

Odd numbers	Integers that are not divisible by 2; that is, ..., -3, -1, 1, 3, 5, 7, ...
Consecutive integers	Integers in sequence, such as 3, 4, 5 or -1, 0, 1; they can be represented in general as n, $n + 1$, $n + 2$, ... (where n is any integer)
Real numbers	All numbers, including fractions, decimals, etc., that correspond to points on the number line
Factor	A divisor of an integer; for example, 1, 3, 5, and 15 are factors of 15, but 2 is not a factor of 15. Note that -1, -3, -5, and -15 are also factors of 15. Any integer can be a factor of zero, but zero is not a factor of a nonzero integer.
Multiple of an integer n	The product of integer n and another integer; some multiples of 4 are -8, -4, 0, 4, 8, 12, and 16. Note that 2 is a factor of 4 but is not a multiple of 4. Zero is a multiple of any integer.
Prime number	A positive integer that has exactly two different positive factors, 1 and itself; for example, 2, 3, 5, 7, 11, 13 are all prime numbers.
Reciprocal	The inverse of a number; that is, one of a pair of numbers whose product is 1; the reciprocal of 5 is $\frac{1}{5}$; the reciprocal of $\frac{2}{3}$ is $\frac{3}{2}$.
Exponent	A superscript of a number that indicates the number of times to multiply the number by itself, for example, 3^4 indicates $3 \times 3 \times 3 \times 3$. In this example, 4 is the exponent and 3 is the base.
Number squared	A number multiplied by itself, for example, 5^2 or $5 \times 5 = 25$.
Number cubed	A number multiplied twice by itself, for example, 5^3 or $5 \times 5 \times 5 = 125$.
Square root of a number	A positive number that when squared produces the given number. The square root of a number n is denoted by $\sqrt{n}$. Recall that $\sqrt{2}$ is approximately 1.4; $\sqrt{3}$ is approximately 1.7; and $\sqrt{5}$ is approximately 2.2.
Fraction	A number of the form $\frac{a}{b}$, where a and b are real numbers ($b \neq 0$); in the expression $\frac{a}{b}$, number a is called the *numerator* and number b is called the *denominator*. If the numerator is larger than the denominator, the fraction is called an improper fraction.
Ratio	A comparison of two or more quantities; for example, if there are 20 women and 15 men in a classroom, the ratio of the number of women to the number of men is 20 to 15, or 20:15, or $\frac{20}{15}$.

Proportion	A statement of equality between two ratios; for example, continuing the example above, if another classroom contained 4 women and 3 men, the ratio of the number of women to the number of men in one classroom would be equivalent to the corresponding ratio in the other classroom; 20:15 = 4:3 is a proportion. Proportions can be used to solve problems such as the following: If it takes a student 2 days to read 1 book, how many days will it take the student to read 5 books at the same rate? This can be expressed as $\frac{2}{1} = \frac{x}{5}$. Using cross multiplication, we can see that if it takes 2 days to read 1 book, then it will take 10 days to read 5 books.
Percent	Amount per hundred, or number out of 100; it can be expressed as a fraction with a denominator of 100, or as a decimal. For example,

$$35\% = \frac{35}{100} = 0.35; \quad 200\% = \frac{200}{100} = 2;$$

$$0.6\% = \frac{0.6}{100} = 0.006.$$

Percent change	Change represented as the amount changed divided by the original amount, or $\frac{\text{the amount of change}}{\text{the original amount}}$. For example, the percent change for an increase from 100 to 150 is $\frac{50}{100}$, or 50%; the percent change for a decrease from 150 to 100 is $\frac{50}{100}$, or $33\frac{1}{3}\%$.
Operation properties	*Associative* (grouping): $(a+b)+c = a+(b+c)$; $(a \times b) \times c = a \times (b \times c)$ *Commutative* (order): $a+b = b+a$; $a \times b = b \times a$ *Distributive*: $a \times (b+c) = (a \times b) + (a \times c)$

Category II: Algebra

Algebra is a generalization of arithmetic in which letters (variables) often represent numbers and rules of arithmetic are followed. Using algebra, we can translate word problems into equations.

This category includes equations and inequalities, algorithmic thinking, patterns, algebraic representations, and algebraic reasoning.

Equations and Inequalities   This subcategory includes solving equations and inequalities, and predicting the outcome of changing some number or condition in a problem.

Rules to remember when solving equations

- Combine like terms.
- Isolate the unknown term on one side of the equation (e.g., x).
- When two fractions make up both sides of the equation, cross-multiply to solve the equation.
- When you multiply or divide two numbers that are both positive or both negative, the result is a positive number.
- When you multiply or divide two numbers one of which is positive and the other of which is negative, the result is a negative number.

Although you will not be expected to know many formulas for the *PPST™: Mathematics* test, you should be able to evaluate a given formula or equation or interpret one. As an example of equivalence of equations, you should recognize that each of the following is equivalent to the equation $2x = 4y + 6$:

$$x = 2y + 3$$
$$2x - 4y = 6$$
$$2x + 1 = 4y + 7$$
$$2x - 2 = 4y + 4$$

Algorithmic Thinking   This subcategory includes following or interpreting procedures, following and interpreting flowcharts, recognizing various ways to solve a problem, and identifying, completing, or analyzing a procedure.

As an example, let us look at the procedure below:

Step 1: Input an integer x.
Step 2: Multiply x by 3.
Step 3: Subtract 4.
Step 4: If the result is positive, divide by 2; otherwise, subtract 1.
Step 5: Print result.

Observe that a specific instruction was given for each step in the procedure. You have to do exactly what each instruction says, in order to obtain the correct answer. Let's use some input numbers to make this clearer.

<u>Example 1</u>
Step 1:   Input 6
Step 2: $6 \times 3 = 18$
Step 3: $18 - 4 = 14$
Step 4: $14 \div 2 = 7$
Step 5:   Print 7

<u>Example 2</u>
Step 1:   Input 1
Step 2: $1 \times 3 = 3$
Step 3: $3 - 4 = -1$
Step 4: $-1 - 1 = -2$
Step 5:   Print -2

The previous procedure can be represented more clearly using the equivalent flowchart below:

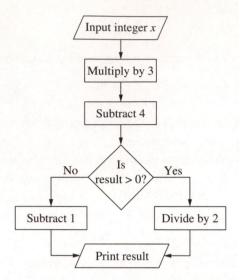

Patterns   This subcategory includes discovering patterns in a procedure, identifying and recognizing patterns in data, and understanding direct, inverse, and other kinds of variation.

Consider the following problems—problem 1 illustrates direct variation, and problem 2 illustrates inverse variation.

> Problem 1: If 1 ice-cream sundae takes 3 scoops of ice cream, how many scoops will 2 sundaes take?
> Problem 2: If 1 person takes 3 hours to do a piece of work, how long will it take 2 people to do the work?

When events happen in a very regular way so that you can predict the outcome, it is sometimes possible to write an equation that fits. In problem 1, if every sundae is made with 3 scoops of ice cream, then the number of scoops (N) will be 3 times the number of sundaes (S), and we can write

$$N = 3 \times S, \text{or just } N = 3S.$$

Note that the larger the number of sundaes made, the larger the number of scoops needed. Of course, this equation, which illustrates direct variation, would not fit problem 2. For one thing, the more people there are who work, the *less* time it should take to do the piece of work. Also, it is not likely that all the people will work at the same rate, so it is not as easy to predict how long the job will take even if you know how many workers there are. *If* everyone worked at the same rate, you would expect the job to take half as long if 2 people worked, one-third as long if 3 people worked, and so on. Assuming that each person worked at the same rate, you would expect that

$$\text{Time } (T) = \frac{3 \text{ hours}}{\text{Number of workers } (N)}, \text{ or } T = \frac{3}{N}.$$

The algebraic relation above is an example of inverse variation.

Algebraic Representation This subcategory includes understanding the relationship between verbal or symbolic expressions and graphs and understanding the use of symbolic algebra to represent situations and to solve problems.

Translating from words to symbols and from symbols to words is an important and useful skill. For example, if Ann is exactly 3 years older than Joe, she will *always* be 3 years older than Joe, and we can express the relationship by the equation

$$A = J + 3,$$

where A represents Ann's age and J represents Joe's age.

It can be reasoned that Joe will always be 3 years younger than Ann. An equivalent equation would be

$$A = J - 3.$$

Consider another example. The formula $D = 5t$ could represent the distance D, in miles, traveled by someone or something moving at a constant speed of 5 miles per hour for t hours, and $t = \frac{D}{5}$ would represent the time it takes to go D miles at 5 miles per hour.

Strategies for solving word problems

- Decide what information is included in the problem and what information is unknown.
- Substitute a variable for the unknown quantity.
- Then write an equation to express the relationship given in the problem and solve the equation.

Algebraic Reasoning This subcategory deals with connectives and quantifiers, validity, and conclusions, including generalizations and counterexamples.

Many statements are written in the form of an "if . . . then" statement. Consider the statement below:

Statement 1: If $x > 3$, then $x^2 > 9$.

One thing you could try is to check the statement for various values of x. For example, when $x = 4$, we have that $4 > 3$ and $4^2 = 16 > 9$. The example $x = 4$ is consistent with statement 1. We could try $x = 5$, for which we have $5 > 3$ and $5^2 = 25 > 9$. The example $x = 5$ is also consistent with statement 1. Checking for particular values of x is not enough to conclude that the statement is true—we would need to check the statement for *all* values of x. Of course, we cannot do this numerically—variable x can have an infinite number of values—but we could use algebra. Notice that when the value of x is positive and x increases, the value of x^2 increases as well. That is enough to conclude that statement 1 is true for all values of x.

Consider the statement below, which is obtained from statement 1 by switching the places of the two inequalities:

Statement 2: If $x^2 > 9$, then $x > 3$.

Statement 2 is false. In order to see that, we need to find at least one example that would contradict statement 2. For example, let $x = -5$. You can see that $(-5)^2 = 25 > 9$ but that $-5 < 3$. An example that contradicts a statement is called a *counterexample*. $x = -5$ is a counterexample to statement 2.

Consider the statement below, which is obtained from statement 1 by replacing each of the two inequalities by their opposites:

Statement 3: If $x \leq 3$, then $x^2 \leq 9$.

Statement 3 is false. A counterexample to statement 3 is $x = -5$. That is because $-5 \leq 3$ but $(-5)^2 = 25 > 9$.

Some Words and Phrases You Should Know

(This section contains some words and phrases that may be helpful when taking the *PPST™: Mathematics* test. For a more comprehensive list of words and phrases, consult a mathematics textbook.)

Variable	A letter, such as x or n, that is used to represent an unknown quantity.
Equation	A statement of equality between two algebraic expressions; for example, $2x - 4 = 10$ is a *linear* equation.
Sequence	An ordered list of numbers; for example, 2, 5, 8, 11, . . . Note that in this example, the first term is 2 and that each term after the first is 3 greater than the preceding term.
Counterexample	An example that would contradict a statement or a claim.

Category III: Geometry and Measurement

This category includes knowledge of the U.S. customary and the metric system of measurement; reading calibrated scales; using geometric concepts and properties, such as spatial relationships, symmetry, the Pythagorean theorem, and angles; solving measurement problems, computing perimeter, area, and volume; number line and *xy*-plane; transformations in the *xy*-plane; geometric reasoning.

There are two systems of measurement in common use: the metric system and the U.S. customary system. Many measurements today are given in the metric system, and you should know the basic units, together with the common measures that are derived from them. In the metric system, most units of measure are related to each other by powers of 10. This makes it easy to convert between units of measure. Metric Standard Units:

- meter (length)
- gram (mass)
- liter (volume)
- degree Celsius (temperature)

Common prefixes:

- milli- (one one-thousandth, or 0.001)
- centi- (one one-hundredth, or 0.01)
- kilo- (one thousand, or 1,000)

The standard units of measure in the United States are called the U.S. customary system. The U.S. customary system does not use a common factor to convert from one unit to another, so it is important to know the relationships between the units of measure.

Length:

- 12 inches = 1 foot
- 3 feet = 1 yard
- 5,280 feet = 1 mile
- 1,760 yards = 1 mile

Weight:

- 16 ounces = 1 pound (lb)
- 2,000 pounds = 1 short ton

Liquid capacity:

- 8 fluid ounces = 1 cup
- 2 cups = 1 pint
- 2 pints = 1 quart
- 4 quarts = 1 gallon

The following charts may be helpful:

Attribute Measured	U.S. Customary Units
Length or Distance	inch foot yard mile
Capacity or Volume	pint quart gallon
Weight	ounce pound short ton
Temperature	degree Fahrenheit

Attribute Measured	Metric Basic Units	Other Units
Length or Distance	meter	millimeter centimeter kilometer
Capacity or Volume	liter	milliliter
Mass	gram	milligram kilogram metric ton
Temperature	degree Celsius	

To solve measurement problems in everyday life, you need to know what characteristic or attribute to consider. If you have a square garden plot and want to know the amount of fence it will take to enclose it, you will be calculating the total *length* of the fence needed to go around the plot. But if you already have a fence and want to paint it, you will need to consider the *height* of the fence as well as its total length, in order to find out its area.

In order to select an *appropriate* unit of measure, you need to recognize the attribute that is important for the problem and know the units used to measure that attribute. Different units of measurement are used for different attributes—weight and height, for example. These are familiar examples, and you probably know many of the units used to measure each of these. You probably think of your age as being measured in years, but the ages of young children are sometimes expressed in months.

Sometimes different words are used for the same type of attribute: length, width, and height are examples. These words are used to describe the position of an object in space or to indicate relative lengths. Each of the rectangles below can be said to have length 4 and width 3; the bottom of the box is also 4 by 3, and the height of the box is 2.

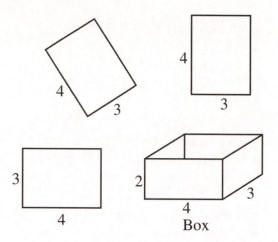

Box

Units of linear measure—inches, feet, miles, meters, kilometers, and so on—are used for length, width, and height. Units of linear measure are also used to measure distance. Distance may be measured along a path, such as a highway or sidewalk, or it may be the straight-line distance, as from point *A* to point *B* in the figure below:

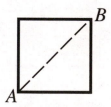

A box that is 2 feet by 3 feet by 4 feet can be thought of as a container with a certain capacity (also called volume). Capacity can be measured in units such as cubic inches, cubic feet, or cubic yards. If you had wooden blocks, each with volume 1 cubic foot (1 foot by 1 foot by 1 foot), you could cover the bottom of the box with 12 of the blocks, as shown below:

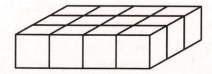

To find the capacity of the box, add another layer of blocks to fill the box, as shown below:

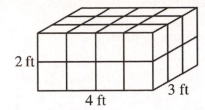

Since two layers contain 24 blocks, the volume of the box is 24 cubic feet.

The 24 blocks form a rectangular solid. If you wanted to paint it, you would need to measure the surface, not its volume. The solid pictured has a top, a bottom, and four sides. The front and back sides of the solid are alike; they are rectangular and measure 4 feet by 2 feet. The two ends are also alike; they are rectangular and measure 3 feet by 2 feet. Finally, the top and bottom are alike; they measure 3 feet by 4 feet, as shown below:

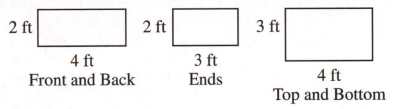

The areas of the front and the back are each 8 square feet, the area of each end is 6 square feet, and the areas of the top and the bottom are each 12 square feet. Therefore, the total area of the six surfaces is $8 + 8 + 6 + 6 + 12 + 12 = 52$ square feet.

The lengths could also be in centimeters or meters; in that case, the volume would be in cubic centimeters or cubic meters, and the surface areas in square centimeters or square meters.

Spatial relationships are often important in solving everyday problems. Have you ever had to try several times to get all your belongings into the trunk of your car? If so, and if you succeeded, you probably realize that the shape of the load can be as important as its size. Shape and arrangement may be of practical importance, as in packing the trunk of a car, or it may be important for artistic reasons. As a teacher, for example, you may want to prepare a work sheet for your students that includes charts or graphs. In this case the size of the paper will be a limiting factor, but if you do not want the layout to look too crowded, you will be concerned with arrangement as well as with size. Making patterns for projects is an example of a situation in which you may need to be able to visualize certain spatial relations.

Some of the spatial relations with which you should be familiar are those among lines. Two lines in the same plane may be parallel or they may intersect. Two intersecting lines may also be perpendicular. These relations are used to identify certain kinds of geometric figures, such as parallelograms and right triangles.

You will not be expected to know a great deal of the vocabulary of spatial relations for the *PPST™: Mathematics* test, but you will need to recognize some of these relations.

xy-Coordinate System

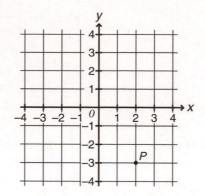

The figure above shows the *xy-coordinate system*, or the *rectangular coordinate plane*. The horizontal number line is the *x*-axis, and the vertical number line is the *y*-axis; the point of intersection of the axes is the *origin*. Each point in the plane has an *x*-coordinate and a *y*-coordinate. A point is identified by an ordered pair (x, y) of numbers in which the *x*-coordinate is the first number and the *y*-coordinate is the second number. The *x*-coordinate of point *P* represents the distance from point *P* to the *y*-axis, with a positive sign if point *P* is to the right of the *y*-axis and a negative sign if point *P* is to the left of the *y*-axis. Similarly, the *y*-coordinate represents the distance from point *P* to the *x*-axis, with a positive sign if point *P* is above the *x*-axis and a negative sign if point *P* is below the *x*-axis. In the figure above, point *P* has coordinates $(2, -3)$.

Geometric Reasoning This category deals with connectives and quantifiers, validity, and conclusions, including generalizations and counterexamples.

For example, you probably first learned you could find the area of a rectangular region by using the formula $A = lw$ and then used this to develop a formula for the area of a region enclosed by any parallelogram. The reasoning is based on this series of diagrams:

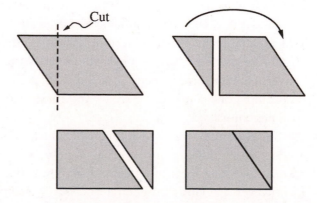

Because the region enclosed by the parallelogram in the first figure can be separated into two pieces that can be rearranged to form a rectangular region, the area can be calculated in the same way. The formula is written as $A = bh$, however, to emphasize that the measurement called the "width" of the rectangle is actually the *height* of the parallelogram and not the measurement of a side. The next step in this particular chain of reasoning would be to deduce the formula for the area of a triangular region. Many people find that following such chains of reasoning is an aid to memory because the chains show how topics are related.

You should note that certain basic assumptions were made in the example above and that the reasoning proceeded from them. These assumptions often take the form of generalizations—in the example above, the assumption was "The area of any rectangular region can be calculated by the formula $A = lw$." As the examples show, generalizations can be useful, but only if they faithfully represent the mathematical situation. Thus, it is important to be able to tell whether a general statement is, in fact, true. For example, the statement "All squares are rectangles" is true because it agrees with the definitions of "square" and "rectangle," but the statement is not true if turned around—it is *false* that "all rectangles are squares." Some general statements are true when reversed, but others are false, as the previous example shows. It is sometimes difficult to verify that a general statement is *always* true, because it would take too long to test every possible case. However, it takes only one case to show that a statement is false. For example, the figure below is a counterexample to the statement "All rectangles are squares."

Many statements are written with the words "if . . . then"; for example, the statement "All squares are rectangles" can be equivalently expressed as follows:

If a figure is a square, then it is a rectangle.

Note that the true "if . . . then" statement above is false when it is turned around—that is, the statement "If a figure is a rectangle, then it is a square" is false.
Consider the claim below:

Claim: If a figure is not a square, then it is not a rectangle.

Let us analyze this claim by looking at three examples. For each of the three examples, we will determine whether the example is consistent with, or contradicts, the claim:

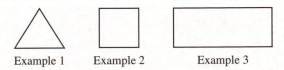

Example 1   Example 2   Example 3

Example 1 represents a triangle. A triangle is not a square, so example 1 satisfies the "if" part of the claim. A triangle is not a rectangle, so example 1 also satisfies the "then" part of the claim. We can conclude that example 1 is consistent with the claim and does not contradict it.

Example 2 represents a square. Example 2 does not satisfy the "if" part of the claim. Note that the claim makes statements only about figures that are not squares. It does not make any statements about figures that are squares. We can conclude that example 2 is consistent with the claim and does not contradict it. Recall that an example that would contradict an "if . . . then" statement will satisfy the "if" part but will not satisfy the "then" part of the "if . . . then" statement.

Example 3 represents a rectangle that is not a square. Example 3 satisfies the "if" part of the claim but does not satisfy the "then" part of the claim. Thus, example 3 is not consistent with the claim. Since example 3 is a counterexample to the claim, we can conclude that the claim is false.

As you study for the *PPST™: Mathematics* test, it can be helpful to follow the chains of reasoning and test yourself on whether the "if . . . then" statements you find are still true when the part that follows "if" and the part that follows "then" are switched or are replaced with the corresponding opposite statements.

Some Symbols You Should Know

(This section contains some symbols that may be helpful when taking the *PPST™: Mathematics* test. For a more comprehensive list of symbols, consult a mathematics textbook.)

The following list shows some symbols you may see on the *PPST™: Mathematics* test:

$\parallel$ is the symbol for "parallel to."
$\perp$ is the symbol for "perpendicular to."
$\llcorner$ is the symbol for "right angle."

Some Words and Phrases You Should Know

(This section contains some words and phrases that may be helpful when taking the *PPST™: Mathematics* test. For a more comprehensive list of words and phrases, consult a mathematics textbook.)

Line	A straight line extends infinitely in both directions.

Line segment	A segment has two endpoints. The part of line l from point P to point Q is a line segment.

Parallel lines	These are two lines in the same plane that do not intersect.
Perpendicular lines	These are two lines that intersect to form four angles of equal measure, and each angle has a measure of 90°.

Ray

A ray has a single endpoint and extends infinitely from that point.

$$\longrightarrow$$

Angles

An angle is created by the intersection of two lines, rays, or segments. The point where they intersect is called the *vertex*. When two lines intersect, the opposite angles have equal measure.

A *straight angle* measures 180° and can be represented by a straight line. A 90° angle is called a *right angle* and can be represented by ⌐ in a figure. An angle whose measure is less than 90° is called an *acute angle*, and an angle whose measure is more than 90° is called an *obtuse angle*. Two angles whose measures add up to 90° are called *complementary angles*, while two angles whose measures add up to 180° are called *supplementary angles*.

Triangles

The sum of the measures of the three angles of a triangle is 180°. *Equilateral triangles* have three equal sides, so that each angle is 60°. *Isosceles triangles* have two equal sides, giving them two angles of equal measure. *Right triangles* have a 90° angle, and the side opposite the right angle is called the *hypotenuse*. The other two sides in the right triangle are called *legs*.

Perimeter

Perimeter is a measurement of the distance around an object. To find an object's perimeter, add the measurements of all the sides.

Circumference

Circumference is the distance around a circle (its perimeter). Circumference can be found without measuring the distance around the circle if the length of the diameter or of the radius is known.

Linear units of measure

Linear units of measure are used to measure length—for example, an inch, a foot, or a centimeter.

Square units of measure

Square units of measure are used to measure the area of a two-dimensional surface (such as a triangle, square, or circle) or the surface area of a three-dimensional figure (such as a prism, cone, or sphere).

Surface area

Surface area is the total area of all outside surfaces of three-dimensional objects. For example, a box has six outside surfaces—the sides, or faces, of the box. To find the surface area, you must find the area of each face and then add these values.

Plane transformations

Examples of transformations in the plane include *translations, reflections, rotations,* and *dilations.*

Some Formulas You Should Know

(This section contains some formulas that may be helpful when taking the *PPST*™: *Mathematics* test. For a more comprehensive list of formulas, consult a mathematics textbook.)

$a^2 + b^2 = c^2$	The Pythagorean theorem: In a right triangle, the sum of the squares of the legs equals the square of the hypotenuse.
$A = \dfrac{1}{2}bh$	The area of a triangle is equal to one-half the base times the height.
$A = lw$	The area of a rectangle or square is equal to the length multiplied by the width.
$d = 2r$	The diameter of a circle is found by multiplying the radius by 2.
π	π (read "pi") represents half the circumference of a circle of radius 1. The numerical value of π is approximately 3.14 or $\dfrac{22}{7}$.
$C = \pi d = \pi 2r$	The circumference of a circle is found by multiplying the circle's diameter by π or by multiplying the circle's radius by 2π.
$A = \pi r^2$	The area of a circle is found by multiplying the square of the radius by π.
$V = lwh$	The volume of a rectangular solid is equal to the length multiplied by the width multiplied by the height.
$V = Ah = \pi r^2 h$	The volume of a cylinder is the product of the area of the base and the height of the cylinder.
Distance = Speed × Time, $\text{Time} = \dfrac{\text{Distance}}{\text{Rate}}$, $\text{Rate} = \dfrac{\text{Distance}}{\text{Time}}$	Use these formulas to solve word problems involving time, speed, and distance.

Category IV: Data Analysis and Probability

This category includes reading and interpreting visual displays of quantitative information, such as graphs, tables, and diagrams; computing the average, range, mode, or median; making comparisons, predictions, extrapolations, or inferences; applying variation; and computing probabilities.

Graphs Many college textbooks contain graphs to represent given sets of data, illustrate trends, and the like. Here are two examples—a bar graph (Figure I) and a line graph (Figure II):

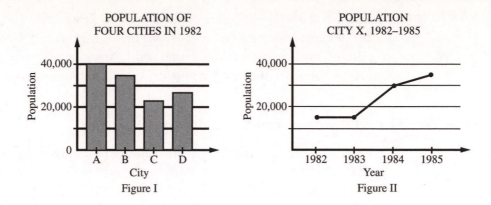

POPULATION OF
FOUR CITIES IN 1982

Figure I

POPULATION
CITY X, 1982–1985

Figure II

The same data set can be represented using different types of graphs, but, for a given data set, some types of graphs may be more appropriate than other types. In the bar graph (Figure I), you can see that the population of City B is approximately 35,000 and that the population of City C is less than the population of each of the other three cities. The bar graph does not show trends. The line graph (Figure II) does suggest that the population of City X, after showing no change from 1982 to 1983, began to increase. It can also be seen that the increase between 1983 and 1984 was greater than the increase between 1984 and 1985. Notice that the data in each graph could be presented in a table, but the visual presentation of a graph is often preferable.

Other types of graphs that you might see on the *PPST™: Mathematics* test include pie charts, scatterplots, histograms, frequency distributions, pictographs, Venn diagrams, and so on.

Average, Median, Mode, and Range   Given a list of numbers, it is possible to find the average (arithmetic mean), median, mode, and range. For example, for the list

$$2, 10, 7, 3, 3$$

the average is

$$\frac{2+10+7+3+3}{5} = 5$$

For the same list of numbers, the median is 3, since the median is the middle number when the numbers are ordered from least to greatest; the mode is 3 because 3 is the number that appears most often; and the range is 8 because the difference between the greatest number, 10, and the least number, 2, in the list is $10 - 2 = 8$.

Probability   Probability problems ask you to predict the outcome of events. The probability of a particular event is determined by dividing the number of outcomes in the event by the total number of possible outcomes. For example, when one ball is to be selected at random out of 3 yellow balls and 2 red balls in a jar, the probability that the ball selected will be red is 2 out of 5. Note that the value of a probability is always a number from 0 to 1. An event has probability 0 when the event *never* happens. An event has probability 1 when the event *always* happens.

Some Words and Phrases You Should Know

(This section contains some words and phrases that may be helpful when taking the *PPST™: Mathematics* test. For a more comprehensive list of words and phrases, consult a mathematics textbook.)

Mean	The average (arithmetic mean) of a list of numbers—that is, for a list consisting of n numbers, the average is the sum of n numbers divided by n.
Median	The middle number in a list of numbers when the numbers are ordered either in increasing order (from least to greatest) or in decreasing order (from greatest to least). For example, for the list 1, 3, 3, 4, 6, 9, 11, the median is 4. Note that when there is an even number of numbers, there is no single middle number. In such instances, the median is the average (arithmetic mean) of the *two* middle numbers. Thus, for example, for the list 1, 3, 3, 4, 6, 9, 11, 18, the median is $\frac{4+6}{2}$. Note that for a list of n numbers, the median is a number in the list when n is odd but may not be among the numbers in the list when n is even.
Mode	The number (or the numbers) that occurs (or occur) most often in a list of numbers.
Range	The greatest number minus the least number in a list of numbers.

Helpful Advice for Taking the PPST™ Mathematics Test

Review the mathematics topics, the words, phrases, and symbols you are expected to know, as listed above; work on any weaknesses you believe you have in those areas.

If you work through the practice questions carefully, you will probably find some mathematics that you already know, but you may also find some things that you need to review more closely. This should help you organize your review more efficiently.

You may need to consult some mathematics texts or other sources for assistance.

You will not be required to identify which type of question is being asked, but being aware of the different types of questions as you prepare for the test will likely help you succeed in answering the questions correctly.

As you take the test, you should do the following carefully:

- identify the specific task in each test question;
- organize the given information in order to solve the problem;

- execute each calculation carefully;
- monitor your pace in order to remain on schedule;
- use estimation as a means of checking your work.

The following suggestions may help you choose the best answer—and remember, try to answer every question.

In a question that involves both decimals and fractions, convert the decimals to fractions or the fractions to decimals. For example, converting $\frac{1}{2}$ to 0.5 may help you determine whether it is greater than or less than 0.7.

You may also wish to convert given fractions to those with common denominators in order to compare them. For example, converting $\frac{1}{2}$ to $\frac{3}{6}$ may help you determine whether it is greater than or less than $\frac{5}{6}$. Likewise, to determine whether $\frac{1}{3}$ is greater than or less than $\frac{2}{5}$, convert both numbers to fractions with 15 as the denominator—that is, $\frac{5}{15}$ and $\frac{6}{15}$.

Remember that negative numbers are less than positive numbers.

Drawing a number line often helps in solving "greater than," "less than," and "equivalent" questions.

You may not need to perform time-consuming calculations to answer a question. If, for example, you are simply asked which of the given fractions is least, you may see at a glance that all are greater than 1 except one—that one would be the correct answer. Or, if a question asks which of the given numbers is greatest, you need not calculate by how much it is greater than each of the others.

Don't be intimidated by the visual presentation of data; take some time to figure out what the chart, graph, etcetera, is saying before you read the accompanying question.

To solve irregular area measurement problems, it may help to visualize the piece that's not there—the piece that would make the area regular. Calculate the area of the missing piece and subtract it from the area as if the area were regular; the difference will be the area of the irregular piece. For example, if you have to figure out the area of a rectangle that has a corner missing, figure out the area of the missing corner (use the formula for calculating the area of triangles, $A = \frac{1}{2}bh$), and then subtract it from the area of the rectangle; you will then know the area of the rectangle with the missing corner.

For word problems asking you to calculate area measurements, draw a sketch. It does not have to be drawn to scale; the important thing is that you have a place in which to put the given numbers.

Remember that not all general statements are true when reversed. For example, it is true that "All squares are rectangles," but it is not true that "All rectangles are squares."

It is often difficult to verify that a statement is always true, because it would take too long to test every possible case; however, it takes only one case to show that a generalization is false.

Sometimes it is easier to analyze a statement when it is expressed in the "if . . . then" form. For example, "If a figure is a square, then it is a rectangle" or "If $x > 3$, then $x^2 > 9$."

To succeed on the *PPST™: Mathematics* test and many other mathematics tests, you will need to be able to apply mathematics to real-world situations. There are several things you can do to prepare for the test. You can review the mathematical skills that will be required for the test. You can work on any weaknesses you believe you have in those skills. You can study test-taking skills and practice working problems under a variety of self-imposed time limits. If you believe your performance will be hurt by a fear of tests, or some other weakness, you can seek advice from your university testing center. Finally, you will need to ensure that you arrive at the test center relaxed and rested so that you do your best on the test.

You should note that no single test can cover all of the topics listed here; rather, only a sample of the topics will be included.

DIRECTIONS FOR THE PAPER-BASED VERSION OF THE PPST™: MATHEMATICS TEST

You should familiarize yourself with the following directions before taking the test.

Directions: Each of the questions or incomplete statements below is followed by five suggested answers or completions. Select the one that is best in each case and then fill in the corresponding lettered space on the answer sheet with a heavy, dark mark so that you cannot see the letter.

Remember, try to answer every question.

Special Note: Figures that accompany problems in the test are intended to provide information useful in solving the problem. The figures are drawn as accurately as possible except when it is stated in a specific problem that its figure is not drawn to scale. Figures can be assumed to lie in a plane unless otherwise indicated. Position of points can be assumed to be in the order shown, and lines shown as straight can be assumed to be straight. The symbol ⌐ denotes a right angle.

The following questions are representative of some of the questions in the test. They are arranged by category here, but they appear in random order in the test. Some of the questions that appear in this section are not multiple-choice questions; however, all the questions on the actual test are multiple-choice questions.

Category I: Numbers and Operations

1. Which of the following is equal to a quarter of a million?

    (A)   40,000

    (B)   250,000

    (C) 2,500,000

    (D) $\dfrac{1}{4,000,000}$

    (E) $\dfrac{4}{1,000,000}$

Since one million is 1,000,000, a quarter of a million is $\frac{1}{4} \times 1,000,000 = 250,000$. The answer is B.

2. Which of the following fractions is least?

(A) $\frac{11}{10}$

(B) $\frac{99}{100}$

(C) $\frac{25}{24}$

(D) $\frac{3}{2}$

(E) $\frac{501}{500}$

It is not necessary to perform time-consuming calculations to answer the question. Of the five fractions given, four are greater than 1. Only one of the fractions, $\frac{99}{100}$, is less than 1, so it must be least. The answer is B.

3. Of the five numbers listed below, which is greatest?

(A) 0.02

(B) 0.009

(C) 0.036900

(D) 0.01078

(E) 0.0601

E is the correct answer. All five numbers are between 0 and 1. The tenths digit for all five numbers is 0. The hundredths digit varies among the five numbers. The highest hundredths digit for the five numbers is 6 (answer choice E). Therefore, the highest number is given in E. Note that the lowest hundredths digit for the five numbers is 0 (choice B). Therefore, the lowest number is given in B.

4. Which of the following numbers is between $\frac{1}{3}$ and $\frac{2}{5}$?

(A) $\frac{1}{2}$

(B) $\frac{1}{4}$

(C) $\frac{6}{15}$

(D) $\frac{11}{30}$

(E) $\frac{20}{60}$

The answer is D. If you think about the location of $\frac{1}{3}$ and $\frac{2}{3}$ on a number line, you might notice that both $\frac{1}{3}$ and $\frac{2}{5}$ are less than $\frac{1}{2}$, so answer choice A can be ruled out. Also, $\frac{1}{4}$ is less than $\frac{1}{3}$, and $\frac{20}{60} = \frac{1}{3}$, so B and E can be eliminated. To check the remaining two choices, rewrite $\frac{1}{3}$ and $\frac{2}{5}$ as fractions with the denominators 15 and 30 (or note that $\frac{6}{15} = \frac{2}{5}$, leaving only $\frac{11}{30}$).

5. In which of the following are the two numbers equivalent?

I. 0.7 and 0.70

II. $\frac{1}{3}$ and 1.3

III. 4.5 and $4\frac{1}{2}$

Examination of each of the pairs shows that I and III have two numbers that are equivalent:

I. $0.7 = 7 \times \frac{1}{10} = (7 \times \frac{1}{10}) + (0 \times \frac{1}{100}) = 0.70$, or just $0.7 = \frac{7}{10} = \frac{70}{100} = 0.70$

II. $\frac{1}{3}$ is less than 1, but $1.3 = 1 + \frac{3}{10}$, which is greater than 1, so $\frac{1}{3} < 1.3$. These are not equivalent.

III. $4.5 = 4 + \frac{5}{10} = 4 + \frac{1}{2} = 4\frac{1}{2}$

6. 1,200 is how many times 1.2?

(A) 10
(B) 100
(C) 1,000
(D) 10,000
(E) 100,000

The answer is C. You can divide 1,200 by 1.2 or multiply 1.2 by each of the answer choices. You can verify your answer by noting that since 1.2 is a little more than 1, and 1,200 is a little more than 1,000, the answer must be 1,000.

7. Which of the sales commissions shown below is greatest?

(A) 1% of $1,000
(B) 10% of $200
(C) 12.5% of $100
(D) 15% of $100
(E) 25% of $40

This problem can be solved by computing each of the commissions, but comparing them first may save some time. Since 15% of $100 (choice D) is greater than 12.5% of $100 (choice C), there is no need to consider C. Since 10% of $200 (choice B) is $20 and 15% of $100 (choice D) is $15, there is no need to consider choice D. That leaves 1% of $1,000 (choice A) and $\frac{1}{4}$ of $40 (choice E) to consider, both of which equal $10. The answer is B.

8. Two executives, Ms. Smith and Ms. Grambling, arrived at a restaurant, ordered, and were served their meal. A little later, Mr. Lucia, an important client of Ms. Smith's walked into the dining room. The women invited Mr. Lucia to join them. As they prepared to leave, the waiter brought two checks: one for the earlier order, in the amount of $13.57, and one for Mr. Lucia's order, in the amount of $7.62. Ms. Smith planned to pay for all three meals and wanted to include a tip of about 15%. Approximately how much should she leave?

The problem involves both percent and estimation. The approximate cost of the three meals is $21—about $13.50 for the first two and $7.50 for the third. If Ms. Smith wants to leave about a 15% tip, the tip can be computed mentally as

$$10\% \text{ of } \$21 \text{ is } \$2.10$$

$$\underline{\text{so } 5\% \text{ of } \$21 \text{ is } \$1.05,}$$

$$\text{therefore } 15\% \text{ of } \$21 \text{ is } \$3.15.$$

We can conclude that the price of the meals plus tip is approximately $25.

9. In a class of 25 students, 15 are girls. What percent of the students in the class are girls?

(A) 10%
(B) 15%
(C) 25%
(D) 30%
(E) 60%

The answer is E. "Percent" means per hundred, and $\frac{15}{25} = \frac{60}{100}$, or 60%.

10. In a certain class, there are 15 girls and 10 boys. What percent of the students in the class are girls?

(A) 10%
(B) 15%
(C) 60%
(D) $66\frac{2}{3}\%$
(E) 150%

The answer is C. This problem is the same as the previous one, except that here you must first determine the number of students in the class. But the ratio of the number of girls to the number of students is still 15:25, which is 60:100, or 60%.

11. Which of the following is closest to 34×987?

(A) 25,000
(B) 27,000
(C) 30,000
(D) 34,000
(E) 40,000

The answer is D. 34×987 is a little less than $34 \times 1,000$, or approximately 34,000.

12. Which of the following is closest to 0.053×21?

(A)   0.1
(B)   1
(C)   10
(D) 100
(E) 1,000

The answer is B. Since 0.053 is about $\frac{50}{1,000}$, which equals $\frac{5}{100}$, or $\frac{1}{20}$, and 21 is close to 20, we can estimate the product by $\frac{1}{20} \times 20 = 1$.

13. Mr. Jones discovered that his heating bill for December 2007 was $9.15 higher than his bill for December 2006. If the bill for December 2006 was $50.00, what was the percent increase of his heating bill?

According to the problem, the bill for December 2006 was $50.00. The bill went up by $9.15. Thus, the problem is to compare $9.15 to $50.00 and express that ratio as a percent:

$$\frac{9.15}{50.00} = \frac{18.30}{100.00}, \text{ which is } 18.3\%.$$

14. (a) How many 10-foot lengths of rope can be cut from a coil of rope that is 42 feet long?
(b) How many boxes are needed to transport 42 plants if no more than 10 plants can be placed in a box?
(c) If 10 people share equally in the cost of a gift, what is each person's share for a gift costing $42?
(d) If a 42-foot length of rope is cut into 10 pieces of equal length, how long is each of the pieces?

Notice that the *computation* $42 \div 10$ is appropriate for each of these examples. However, a different interpretation of the *answer* is needed for each of the situations:

(a) At most 4 pieces of rope 10 feet long can be cut from a 42-foot length.
(b) At least 5 boxes are needed to transport the 42 plants if no more than 10 can be placed in a box.
(c) Each of 10 people should pay $4.20 to cover the cost of a $42 gift.
(d) Each of the 10 pieces of rope cut from a 42-foot length would be $4\frac{1}{5}$ feet long.

These examples illustrate the fact that in a real-life setting, the "answer" to "$42 \div 10$" may be 4 or 5 or 4.20 or $4\frac{1}{5}$, depending on the context.

> **Some values of x are less than 100.**

15. All of the following are consistent with the sentence above EXCEPT:

    (A) 5 is not a value of x.
    (B) 95 is a value of x.
    (C) Some values of x are greater than 100.
    (D) All values of x are less than 100.
    (E) No numbers less than 100 are values of x.

The sentence says that *some* values of x are less than 100, which means that there is *at least one* value of x that is less than 100. This value can be 5, but it does not have to be, or it can be 95, so choices A and B both are consistent with the boxed sentence. While at least one value of x must be less than 100, some values can be greater than 100, or all values can be less than 100 without contradicting the sentence. Thus, choices C and D are consistent with the boxed sentence. If no numbers less than 100 are values of x, then no value of x will be less than 100, so choice E is not consistent with the boxed sentence. The answer is E.

Category II: Algebra

16. If $P \div 5 = Q$, then $P \div 10 =$

    (A) $10Q$
    (B) $2Q$
    (C) $Q \div 2$
    (D) $Q \div 10$
    (E) $Q \div 20$

$P \div 5 = Q$ can be expressed as $P = 5Q$. Since we are trying to determine what $P \div 10$ equals, we can divide both sides of the equation $P = 5Q$ by 10, as follows:

$$P \div 10 = \frac{P}{10} = \frac{5Q}{10}.$$

Simplifying $\frac{5Q}{10}$ results in $\frac{Q}{2}$, and therefore $P \div 10 = \frac{P}{10} = \frac{5Q}{10} = \frac{Q}{2} = Q \div 2$. The answer is C.

x	y
0	5
2	11
6	23
7	26
10	35

17. Which of the following equations expresses the relationship between x and y in the table above?

(A) $y = x + 5$
(B) $y = x + 6$
(C) $y = 3x + 5$
(D) $y = 4x - 1$
(E) $y = 4x - 5$

Although it is possible to see the relationship between x and y by carefully examining the values in the table, a more systematic approach may be helpful. The correct equation must hold when each of the pairs of values from the table is substituted for x and y in the equations given. Choice A holds for $x = 0, y = 5$, but not for $x = 2, y = 11$. Choices B, D, and E do not hold for $x = 0, y = 5$. Choice C holds for all of the values given:

if $x = 0$, then $y = 3(0) + 5 = 5$,
if $x = 2$, then $y = 3(2) + 5 = 11$,
if $x = 6$, then $y = 3(6) + 5 = 23$, and so on.

The answer is C.

18. Correct methods for multiplying 399 by 19 include which of the following?

I.

$$
\begin{array}{r}
399 \\
\times 19 \\
\hline
3591 \\
+399 \\
\hline
\end{array}
$$

II.

$$
\begin{array}{r}
19 \\
\times 400 \\
\hline
7600 \\
-19 \\
\hline
\end{array}
$$

III.

Step 1.
$400 \times 10 = 4,000$
$400 \times 9 = 3,600$
Step 2.
$4,000 + 3,600 = 7,600$
Step 3.
$7,600 - 19 =$

(A) I only
(B) III only
(C) I and II only
(D) II and III only
(E) I, II, and III

The answer is E. All of the procedures are correct, and it is not necessary to complete each computation to determine this. Procedure I is the familiar procedure for multiplication.

For II, the procedure is $19 \times 399 = 19 \times (400 - 1) = (19 \times 400) - (19 \times 1)$.

The procedure for III looks a bit more complicated because it includes extra steps for calculating 19×400.

19. If $A = 6s^2$ and $s = 3$, then $A =$

    (A) 12
    (B) 15
    (C) 36
    (D) 54
    (E) 324

The answer is D because if $s = 3$, then $s^2 = 9$, and so $6s^2$ is 6×9, or 54.

20. If $D = 5t$ and $D = 20$, then $t =$

    (A) $\dfrac{1}{4}$
    (B)   4
    (C) 15
    (D) 25
    (E) 100

The answer is B because 5 must be multiplied by 4 to get 20.

Category III: Geometry and Measurement

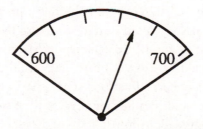

21. On the scale above, the arrow most likely indicates

    (A) $630\dfrac{1}{2}$
    (B) 635
    (C) $630\dfrac{1}{2}$
    (D) 670
    (E) 685

The scale given in the problem shows the numbers 600 and 700, which means that the interval between them represents 100 units. The interval is marked off in fifths, so each subdivision represents 20 units, and the reading at each mark can be written on the scale as follows:

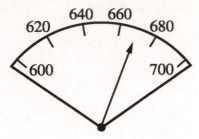

The arrow marks a point approximately halfway between 660 and 680, or 670. The best answer is D.

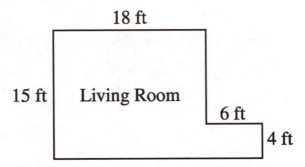

22. The de Falco family wanted to replace the carpet in their living room. The room was shaped as shown in the diagram above. The carpet they liked was available in 12-inch-square carpet tiles that were sold in cartons of 12 per carton. How many cartons of carpet did they need to buy?

The first thing to note, because the room dimensions are in feet, is that the carpet tiles are 1 foot square. You also need to recognize that the floor space can be separated into two rectangular parts. The main part of the living room is a rectangle 15 feet by 18 feet that would require 15 × 18, or 270, carpet tiles to completely cover the floor. The area in the lower right of the diagram is 4 feet by 6 feet and requires another 24 tiles; so the de Falcos need a total of 294 tiles. Because the tiles come in units of 12 tiles per carton, you must divide 294 by 12 to determine the number of cartons needed. Since the answer is 24.5, the de Falcos must buy 25 cartons.

23. On a trip from Chicago to Seattle, the Bergen family drove westward on Interstate Route I-90. At a rest area just before Spearfish, Ms. Bergen examined the route from Spearfish to Billings on the map. This is what she saw:

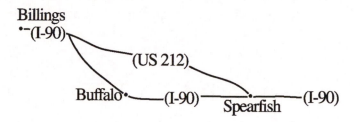

What could Ms. Bergen conclude from the map about the relative distances along US 212 and I-90 from Spearfish to Billings?

An important relation in a triangle is that any one of its sides is always shorter than the sum of the other two. Since the routes shown here form a rough triangle, the route along US 212 is shorter than the route along I-90.

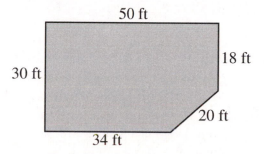

24. Suppose you want to buy sod to make a lawn on the plot of ground pictured above. How much sod would you need?

This is an example of a measurement problem you might encounter in everyday life. To solve it, you must first recognize that it is the *area* of the plot that is to be found. The plot is an odd shape, one for which you did not learn a formula in school, so a bit of work needs to be done. The plot is almost rectangular, but it has a corner missing. This is where spatial visualization comes in, because the missing corner is in the shape of a right triangle:

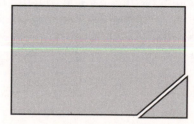

That is, the area of the plot can be found by calculating the area of a rectangular plot and then subtracting the area of the triangular piece. The area of a rectangular plot 50 feet by 30 feet is 1,500 square feet, but what is the area of the corner? You need to recall that the formula for the area of a triangular region is $A = \frac{1}{2}bh$, so all that is needed now is to determine the base and the height of the piece. It is a right triangle, so its base and height can be considered to be as shown here:

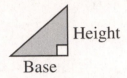

The completed rectangle is 50 by 30, and we know some other measurements:

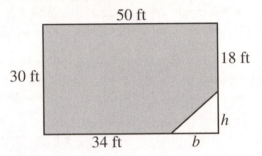

Thus, $h = 30 - 18 = 12$ feet and $b = 50 - 34 = 16$ feet.

The area of the missing right triangle is $\frac{1}{2}(12)(16) = 96$. Therefore, the area of the plot to be sodded is $1,500 - 96$, which is 1,404 square feet. You should notice that to solve the problem you need spatial skills to visualize the missing piece, and also knowledge of formulas and how to evaluate them. Also notice that the measurement of 20 feet given in the problem was not needed for the solution.

25. Ramon wants to buy fabric for drapes in his den. He has one window 60 inches wide. The top of the window is 6 feet 8 inches above the floor. He wants the drapes to hang from 2 inches above the window to 1 inch from the floor. He also wants the drapes to extend outward 4 inches on either side of the window. He needs to allow 6 inches at the top and the bottom for hems, and he plans to add 50% to the width to allow for pleats and side hems. What are the dimensions of the piece of fabric needed before it is hemmed and pleated?

Without a picture to guide you, this may seem like a jumble of numbers, and making a sketch might be the most helpful thing to do first. The sketch does not need to be drawn to scale; the important thing is that you have a place to put in the numbers given. Beginning with the figure on the left, we can see what some of these numbers represent:

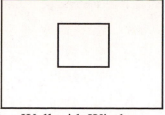 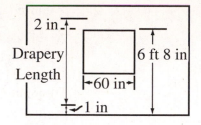

Wall with Window

With the help of the sketch, you see that the height of the piece of fabric would be 6 feet 8 inches plus 2 inches (extra at the top) less 1 inch (height from the floor), but also plus 12 inches (hem allowance). So the vertical dimension is 7 feet 9 inches. The horizontal dimension is 60 inches + 8 inches (in order to allow for the extra coverage), or 68 inches. However, we must increase this by 50% to allow for pleats and side hems. That is, the width must be 68 inches $+ \frac{1}{2}$(68 inches), which is 102 inches, or 8 feet 6 inches. Thus, the dimensions of the piece of fabric to be bought are 7 feet 9 inches by 8 feet 6 inches.

26. About how many <u>cubic</u> yards of coal can be stored in a silo 20 feet in diameter and 40 feet high? (A silo is a storage tower having the shape of a cylinder.)

In this problem you need to use the formula for the *volume* of a cylinder, $V = Ah$, where A represents the area of the base and h represents the height of the cylinder. The base is circular, and the formula for the area of a circular region is $A = \pi r^2$, where r represents the radius. You are given that the diameter is 20 feet, so you need to recall that the diameter is twice the radius. You also need to recall that π is approximately 3.14. You should also notice that the problem asks, "How many cubic yards?" while the dimensions of the silo are given in feet. Before you substitute into the formula, convert the dimensions from feet to yards as shown below, recalling that 3 feet = 1 yard.

$$\text{Diameter} = 20 \text{ feet} = \frac{20}{3} \text{ yards}$$

$$\text{Radius} = \frac{1}{2}(\text{Diameter}) = \frac{1}{2}\left(\frac{20}{3} \text{ yards}\right) = \frac{10}{3} \text{ yards}$$

$$\text{Height} = 40 \text{ feet} = \frac{40}{3} \text{ yards}$$

The area of the base of the silo is approximately 3.14 × the square of the radius, or $3.14 \times \frac{100}{9} = \frac{314}{9}$ square yards. The silo is $\frac{40}{3}$ yards tall, so the volume is approximately $\frac{314}{9}$ square yards × $\frac{40}{3}$ yards, or approximately $\frac{315}{9} \times \frac{40}{3} = 35 \times \frac{40}{3} = \frac{1400}{3}$, or approximately 467 cubic yards.

27. To convert centimeters to millimeters, you should

    (A) divide by 10
    (B) multiply by 10
    (C) divide by 100
    (D) multiply by 100
    (E) multiply by 1,000

      The answer is B. Since 100 centimeters = 1 meter and 1,000 millimeters = 1 meter, you can see that 100 centimeters = 1,000 millimeters, or 1 centimeter = 10 millimeters. Therefore, x centimeters = $10x$ millimeters.

28. If pesos are exchanged for dollars at a rate of 11 pesos for one dollar, how do you convert pesos to dollars?

    (A) Divide by 0.1
    (B) Multiply by 0.1
    (C) Divide by 11
    (D) Multiply by 11
    (E) Multiply by 1

      The answer is C. Since 11 pesos = 1 dollar, you can see that 1 peso = $\frac{1}{11}$ dollar.

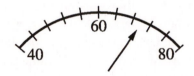

29. On the scale above, the arrow most likely points to

    (A) $60\frac{1}{2}$

    (B) $62\frac{1}{2}$

    (C) $63\frac{1}{2}$

    (D) 65
    (E) 70

      The answer is E. The arrow points to a number that is about halfway between 60 and 80. Alternatively, each subinterval on the scale represents 4 units, so the arrow is pointing halfway between 68 and 72, or 70.

30. If the scale used on a scale drawing of a room is such that 1 inch on the drawing represents an actual distance of 4 feet, and if the drawing of the room is $3\frac{1}{2}$ inches wide, how wide is the room?

(A) $7\frac{1}{2}$ ft

(B) $12\frac{1}{2}$ ft

(C) 14 ft

(D) 15 ft

(E) $15\frac{1}{2}$ ft

The answer is C. Each inch represents 4 feet, so 3 inches would represent 12 feet, and the $\frac{1}{2}$ inch would represent another 2 feet. The total width of the room is $12 + 2 = 14$ feet.

31. On a scale drawing of a room, 1 inch on the drawing represents an actual distance of 4 feet. If the room is 20 feet long, how long should the drawing be?

(A)   5 in
(B) 16 in
(C) 20 in
(D) 24 in
(E) 80 in

The answer is A. If 1 inch represents 4 feet, then the proportion $\frac{1}{4} = \frac{x}{20}$ can be solved for x. By cross-multiplication, $4x = 20$, and $x = 5$.

32. Carlos left Dallas with a full tank of gasoline and drove to Little Rock before stopping for fuel. He purchased 11.2 gallons of gas, refilling his tank. Since he had forgotten to write down the mileage on his odometer when he left Dallas, he consulted his map and found that the distance was reported as 330 miles. Using this information, he estimated his fuel consumption in miles per gallon. What would be a good estimate?

Without carrying out the actual computation, you can probably see that the Carlos' car averaged a little less than 30 miles per gallon. If he had used exactly 11 gallons of gasoline and gone 330 miles, that would have represented a rate of 30 miles per gallon. Because he used a little more than 11 gallons, his car must have averaged a little less than 30 miles per gallon.

33. What if Carlos plans to drive 660 miles farther than he has traveled so far? What is the easiest way to calculate the amount of gas he will use?

There is no need for lengthy calculation; simply doubling what he used for 330 miles (11.2 gallons) will result in the approximate amount he will need to go 660 miles (22.4 gallons).

34. As Carlos was completing his purchase in Little Rock, another motorist asked how far it was to Dallas. Carlos told her the distance was 330 miles, and the motorist wondered how much gas she would use getting there. Since the motorist said her pickup truck used a gallon of fuel every 15 miles, Carlos estimated her consumption to be 22 gallons. What method might he have used?

Because the pickup truck gets 15 miles per gallon, it must use twice as much gas as Carlos' car, which gets about 30 miles per gallon. So, if Carlos' car required 11.2 gallons on the Dallas-Little Rock trip, the pickup should use about twice as much.

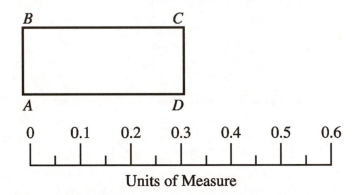

Units of Measure

35. According to the scale shown above, approximately what is the length of side *AD*?

(A) 0.225 unit
(B) 0.300 unit
(C) 0.325 unit
(D) 0.350 unit
(E) 3.25 units

The answer is C. Each subinterval on the scale represents 0.05 unit. *AD* extends from 0 to about halfway between 0.30 and 0.35, or 0.325.

Category IV: Data Analysis and Probability

Car Model	Frequency
K	7
X	9
W	7
J	8

36. The chart above gives data about the distribution of four compact-car models in a company parking lot. Which of the following figures best represents the data given?

(A)
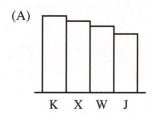

(B)
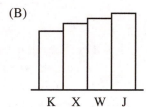

(C)
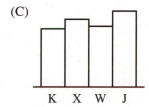

(D)
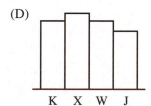

(E)
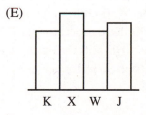

 The chart shows that one frequency is greater than all the others and that two frequencies are equal. A quick look at the choices shows that only C, D, and E have both one bar that is taller than the others and two bars of equal height. According to the chart, the frequency of model X is greatest, which eliminates choice C. Car model J is second greatest, which eliminates choice D. Only choice E shows bars whose relative heights all agree with the information in the chart. The best answer is E.

WIND-CHILL CHART

Temp. (F)	Wind Speed (m.p.h.)							
	5	10	15	20	25	30	35	40
50°	48	40	36	32	30	28	27	26
40°	37	28	22	18	16	13	11	10
30°	27	16	9	4	0	–2	–4	–6
20°	16	4	–5	–10	–15	–18	–20	–21
10°	6	–9	–18	–25	–29	–33	–35	–37
0°	–5	–21	–36	–39	–44	–48	–49	–53
–10°	–15	–33	–45	–53	–59	–63	–67	–69
–20°	–26	–46	–58	–67	–74	–79	–82	–85
–30°	–36	–58	–72	–82	–88	–94	–98	–100
–40°	–47	–70	–85	–96	–104	–109	–113	–116
–50°	–57	–83	–99	–110	–118	–125	–129	–132

37. The temperature today is 10°F, but it feels as cold as it did last week when the temperature was −10°F and the wind speed was 10 miles per hour. According to the chart above, what is the wind speed today?

(A) 10 miles per hour
(B) 15 miles per hour
(C) 20 miles per hour
(D) 25 miles per hour
(E) 30 miles per hour

According to the chart, if the temperature is −10°F and the wind speed is 10 miles per hour, then the wind-chill factor is −33. The problem states that it feels this cold today although the temperature is 10°F. To solve this problem, look at the row of the chart for 10°F and find the wind-chill factor −33. This factor corresponds to a wind speed of 30 miles per hour. The answer is E.

CHILDREN'S FAVORITE
CARTOONS

Billy Beagle	😊 😊 😊
Sergeant Starch	😊 😊 ◖
Kitty Kitty	😊 😊 😊 😊

Each 😊 represents 10 children.

38. According to the graph above, how many children chose "Sergeant Starch" as their favorite?

(A) $2\frac{1}{2}$

(B) 3

(C) $20\frac{1}{2}$

(D) 25

(E) 30

The answer is D. If each face in the pictograph represents 10 children, then half a face represents 5 children. There are $2\frac{1}{2}$ faces for Sergeant Starch, and $2\frac{1}{2} \times 10 = 25$.

MARKET SHARE

39. Based on the graph above, if Acme's share of the market is $2,519,900, approximately what is Beta's share?

(A) $3,000,000
(B) $4,000,000
(C) $5,000,000
(D) $6,000,000
(E) $7,000,000

The answer is C. This is a circle graph, or pie chart. Because the sector for Beta is about double that for Acme, you can double $2,500,000 for an estimate of Beta's share.

40. For a certain board game, two number cubes are thrown to determine the number of spaces a player should move. One player throws the two number cubes, and the same number comes up on each of the cubes. What is the probability that the sum of the two numbers is 9?

(A) 0

(B) $\frac{1}{6}$

(C) $\frac{2}{9}$

(D) $\frac{1}{2}$

(E) 1

If two number cubes are thrown and the same number appears on both, the sum will always be 2 times the number thrown on either of the cubes and thus, must be an even number. Since 9 is an odd number, the sum cannot be 9; therefore, the probability is zero. The answer is A.

41. Susan says that the probability that a certain traffic light will be green when she gets to it is 0.20. What is her best prediction of the number of times the light will be green for the next 30 times she gets to it?

(A) 5

(B) 6

(C) 7

(D) 10

(E) 15

The answer is B. A probability of 0.20 means that she would expect a green light 20 out of every 100 times, or $\frac{1}{5}$ of the time. Since $\frac{1}{5}$ of 30 is 6, the light would probably be green 6 times out of the next 30 times she gets to it.

42. There are 3 red marbles, 4 yellow marbles, and 3 blue marbles in a bag. If one of these marbles is to be selected at random, what is the probability that the marble chosen will be yellow?

(A) $\frac{1}{10}$

(B) $\frac{1}{4}$

(C) $\frac{1}{3}$

(D) $\frac{2}{5}$

(E) $\frac{2}{3}$

The answer is D. There are 10 marbles in the bag, and 4 of them are yellow. Therefore, there are 4 out of 10 chances of selecting a yellow one, and $\frac{4}{10} = \frac{2}{5}$.

CHAPTER 7

PPST™ Writing: The Multiple-Choice Section

Paper-Based Version	Computer-Based Version
38 questions	44 questions
30 minutes	38 minutes

PURPOSE OF THE WRITING MULTIPLE-CHOICE SECTION

The multiple-choice section of the PPST Writing test is designed to measure your ability to recognize correct standard written English, which is the language of most college textbooks and the language you will be expected to use as a professional. You will not need to define grammatical terminology or label particular elements of grammar. You will simply need to recognize what is correct and what is incorrect.

This chapter contains a review course on basic grammar and sentence construction, a close-up examination of the two types of questions (**Usage** and **Sentence Correction**), and practice questions with explanatory answers.

FORMAT OF THE WRITING MULTIPLE-CHOICE SECTION

The multiple-choice section of the test consists entirely of individual sentences. There are no essays or long paragraphs.

There are 38 sentences, and each is the basis of a single multiple-choice question. You have 30 minutes to complete these 38 questions. (If you are taking the computer-based version, you have 38 minutes in which to answer 44 questions.) You will need to develop the ability to work carefully and confidently, at a fairly quick pace.

Sentences: Sources and Subject Matter

The sentences used in the PPST Writing test are rarely written from scratch by the question writers. The vast majority are taken from college-level books, magazines, and newspapers.

The sentences cover a wide variety of topics, ranging from science, history, and social sciences to literature and the arts. You should not be worried about or intimidated by their content. Each sentence makes a statement or presents an idea that you can understand without having any specialized knowledge. Do not be put off by subjects that seem foreign to you or names that are unfamiliar. Your task is to understand how the different parts of the sentence work together.

The Two Types of Questions

The multiple-choice section of the test consists of two subsections.

- The first subsection (**Usage**) consists of sentences that contain four underlined parts. Appearing after each sentence is a fifth underlined choice, "No error." For each sentence, you have to determine which underlined part, if any, contains an error. Some of the sentences will not contain any errors; that is, all the underlined parts will be correct. If this is the case, you should select the fifth choice, "No error," as your answer.
- The second subsection (**Sentence Correction**) gives you sentences in which some of or all of the words have been underlined. Each sentence is followed by five choices. The first choice is the same as the underlined part, and the other choices are rewrites. Your job is to decide whether the original is the best way to express the meaning of the sentence or whether one of the other four choices would be better.

An in-depth look at each question type, with specific ETS TIPS for each, can be found after the review course.

STRATEGIES FOR THE WRITING MULTIPLE-CHOICE SECTION

It is important to know what's being tested in the Writing multiple-choice section. The two question types, **Usage** and **Sentence Correction**, are the basis for assessing a whole range of skills and knowledge in standard written English.

The following list indicates the major areas covered by the questions. Each element in the list is covered in the review course that follows. Study the review course to refresh your knowledge of the basics of English grammar, usage, and mechanics.

Parts of speech:
- Noun
- Verb
- Adjective
- Adverb
- Pronoun
- Preposition
- Conjunction
- Interjection

Parts of sentences:
- Subject
- Predicate
- Phrases and clauses

Grammar:
- Forms of adjectives and adverbs
- Comparisons
- Subject–verb agreement

- Verb tense
- Parallelism
- Noun–pronoun agreement
- Negation
- Modification

Sentence fragments and run-on sentences

Punctuation:
- Comma usage
- Colon usage
- Semicolon usage
- Apostrophe usage

Capitalization

Word usage (diction)

Idiomatic expressions

Clarity of expression:
- Wordiness
- Redundancy

It is also important to know what is **not** tested on the multiple-choice section of the test.

- Spelling is not tested. Everything on the test is spelled correctly. Don't be tempted to choose an answer based on what you think is a spelling error.
- Extremely subtle and often-ignored distinctions, such as the difference between "shall" and "will" or the difference between "due to" and "because," are not tested.

You cannot study for the multiple-choice section of the PPST Writing test, but you can use these strategies to help improve your score.

- "Say" test sentences in your head as you read them. Often, you will notice errors more readily by "hearing" them than by seeing them.
- Use the English Grammar Review below to assess your knowledge. If you find terms or concepts you do not know, practice on exercises from a grammar handbook until you are comfortable with those concepts.
- Edit your own written work, using the rules listed in the English Grammar Review. Decide whether most problems in your writing occur in the area of grammar, punctuation, capitalization, or diction. Recognizing your own errors will help you identify sentence errors on the test.

ENGLISH GRAMMAR REVIEW

This review course covers many of the common elements of grammar and sentence construction you must know to do well on this test. The review course may use some grammar terms that are new to you. You do **not** need to know these terms to do well on the PPST Writing test. These terms are mentioned in case you want to consult a grammar handbook for more help.

Parts of Speech

Every word in a sentence can be classified as a part of speech. There are eight parts of speech:

- Noun
- Verb
- Adjective
- Adverb
- Pronoun
- Preposition
- Conjunction
- Interjection

In the PPST Writing test, you will need to know how to identify the first six parts of speech on this list (you will not need to know how to identify conjunctions or interjections). However, it is helpful to recognize conjunctions and interjections because they often serve as signals for particular kinds of punctuation. Let's review the parts of speech and how to recognize them.

Noun   A **common noun** is a word that names a person, place, thing, or concept. Examples of nouns include "nurse" (person), "office" (place), "book" (thing), and "happiness" (concept).

A **proper noun** is a noun that names a specific person, place, thing, or concept; it is always capitalized. Examples of proper nouns include "Ellen" (person), the "Grand Canyon" (place), the "Washington Monument" (thing), and "Buddhism" (concept).

You will need to know when a noun should be a proper noun, and when it should not. For example, "judge," when used by itself, is a common noun and should not be capitalized. However, if "judge" is used as a part of someone's title, as in "Judge Harry Jones," it then becomes a proper noun and should be capitalized.

Verb   A **verb** is a word that tells what a subject does or is. Examples of verbs include "walk," "feel," "led," "is running," and "had eaten." The base, or infinitive, form of a verb is the phrase "to + verb": "to show," "to fall," "to seek," "to read." From this base form, the verb can change its form for one of several purposes. These include the following:

A verb can show time through its tense.

Example:	to <u>learn</u>	Present tense:	Tammy <u>learns</u>.
		Past tense:	Tammy <u>learned</u>.
		Past perfect tense:	Tammy <u>has learned</u>.
		Future tense:	Tammy <u>will learn</u>.

An **irregular verb** does not follow this pattern; the base form changes in different ways. Here are some common irregular verbs you should know for the PPST Writing test:

Present	Past	Past Participle
be	was/were	(have/had) been
do	did	(have/had) done
go	went	(have/had) gone
lay	laid	(have/had) laid
lie	lay	(have/had) lain
rise	rose	(have/had) risen
swim	swam	(have/had) swum

The following verb pairs are often confused. The difference between those in each pair is that the first one takes a direct object and the second one does not.

Present	Past	Past Participle	
set (put)	set	set	*Set the glass down.*
sit (be seated)	sat	sat	*Please sit down.*
lay (put)	laid	laid	*She laid the papers down.*
lie (recline)	lay	lain	*An hour ago I lay down for a nap.*
raise (lift)	raised	raised	*The glasses have been raised.*
rise (get up)	rose	risen	*The sun has risen.*

A verb can indicate the number of the nouns engaging in the action—singular (one) or plural (more than one).

Example: to sprint Singular: The runner sprints to the finish line.

Plural: The runners sprint to the finish line.

Adjective An **adjective** is a word that describes a noun or pronoun. Adjectives are said to *modify* nouns and pronouns because they help change a reader's understanding of a noun. Notice how your image of the dog changes in the following sentences:

Examples: A <u>tired</u> dog sat on the porch next to the door.

An <u>angry</u> dog sat on the porch next to the door.

A <u>happy</u> dog sat on the porch next to the door.

Adverb An **adverb** is a word that modifies a verb, an adjective, another adverb, or a clause. Adverbs are used to add detail and specificity to the action of a sentence.

Examples:	The adverb modifies a verb:	Dan finished his dessert <u>quickly</u>.
	The adverb modifies an adjective:	The puzzle left him <u>completely</u> confused.
	The adverb modifies another adverb:	The cat climbed the tree <u>very</u> quickly.

Most adverbs end in -ly. They are often formed by adding -ly to an adjective.

Pronoun   A **pronoun** is a word that stands in for or refers to a noun. A pronoun can be personal (stands in for a noun) or possessive (refers to a noun).

Examples: <u>He</u> baked a cake. (The pronoun "he" stands in for a noun, so it is a personal pronoun.)
Leticia fixed <u>her</u> car. (The pronoun "her" shows Leticia's possession of her car, so it is a possessive pronoun.)

Personal pronouns usually change their form depending on whether they are used as the subject (the person or thing performing the action) or object (the person or thing receiving the action) of a sentence.

Personal pronouns to use as subjects: *I, we, you, he, she, it, they*

Personal pronouns to use as objects: *me, us, you, him, her, it, them*

Examples: <u>He</u> fell out of the boat. ("He" is the subject of the sentence.)
Alice gave <u>me</u> the extra ticket. ("Me" is an object of the sentence.)

Possessive pronouns usually change form depending on whether they are used as adjectives or stand alone.

Possessive pronouns to use as adjectives: *my, our, your, his, her, its, their*

Possessive pronouns to use standing alone: *mine, ours, yours, his, hers, its* (rarely used), *theirs*

Examples: <u>Her</u> book won the Pulitzer Prize. ("Her" modifies *book* and thus acts as an adjective.)
Alice took my sandwich and gave me <u>hers</u>. ("Hers" stands alone; it is an object of the sentence and is being used in place of the phrase "her sandwich.")

Pronouns must agree in number with the noun they are replacing or to which they are referring. If a pronoun is used to replace "the students," it should be a plural pronoun (e.g., "they" or "them") because it is referring to more than one student.

Example: General Motors is one of our biggest companies. <u>It</u> has about 365,000 employees. ("It" refers to "General Motors," which is a single company even though the name ends with the letter s. Therefore the singular pronoun "it" is used, rather than the plural pronoun "they.")

Pronouns must also agree in gender with the noun for which they are standing in or to which they refer. If a pronoun is used to replace the male name "Mark," it should be a masculine pronoun, "he" or "him."

Following is an explanation of the most often confused pronouns.

"Who" and "whoever" are used as subjects.
Who is it?

"Whom" and "whomever" are used as objects.
Whom did you invite?

"Its" is a possessive pronoun.
The dog ate its dinner.

"It's" is not a pronoun, but a contraction.
It's not my dog.

Anytime you encounter the word "it's," substitute "it is" and check whether that makes sense.

Pronouns are often used to introduce information about the nouns to which they refer. We call such words **restrictive** and **nonrestrictive pronouns**.

Examples: Bring me the pear <u>that</u> looks ripest.

I do not like *Romeo and Juliet*, <u>which</u> is too sad for me to enjoy.

In the first example, the sentence does not make much sense without the information that follows the pronoun. "Bring me the pear" does not explain <u>which</u> pear is desired. The information "that looks ripest" limits or restricts the reader's understanding of the "pear" being referred to; therefore, the pronoun is **restrictive**.

By contrast, note that in the second example, *Romeo and Juliet* is very clearly a particular play, and the information that follows ("which is too sad for me to enjoy") is nice to know, but not necessary. (The fact that "which is too sad for me to enjoy" is set off by a comma is another clue that it is extra information.) *Romeo and Juliet* does not need any additional restrictive information, so the pronoun that follows is **nonrestrictive**.

Most pronouns can be either restrictive or nonrestrictive without any change in form.

Examples: My cousin <u>who</u> lives in Dallas called me last week. ("Who" is restrictive, because we assume that the writer has more than one cousin and is giving the information to indicate which cousin is being discussed.)

Charles Dickens, <u>who</u> wrote *David Copperfield*, was born in 1814. ("Who" is nonrestrictive, because the famous name indicates exactly which person is being discussed.)

On the other hand, with "that" (restrictive) and "which" (nonrestrictive), you do need to be careful to use the correct pronoun.

Preposition   A preposition is a word used most often in front of a noun or pronoun to identify a relationship such as time or space. Prepositions help provide more details about an action.

Examples: Portia drove <u>to</u> the bank. (The preposition "to" helps to show *where* Portia was driving.)

Josh hasn't seen Ken <u>since</u> Friday. (The preposition "since" helps to indicate *when* Josh last saw Ken.)

Common prepositions include "about," "at," "before," "for," "in," "like," "of," "on," "to," and "with." Consult a grammar handbook for a more detailed list of prepositions.

Conjunction   There are three types of conjunctions: **coordinate, subordinate** and **correlative**.

Coordinate conjunctions join two coordinate elements—for example, two independent nouns, verbs, phrases, or clauses. Coordinate conjunctions include "and," "but," "or," "nor," "for," and "also."

Example: I brought a notebook <u>and</u> a pen.

Subordinate conjunctions join subordinate elements to the principal elements of sentences.

Example: I will go <u>because</u> you asked.

Correlative conjunctions are conjunctions that are used in pairs. Correlative conjunctions include "either … or," "neither … nor," etc.

Example: <u>Either</u> he <u>or</u> I must go.

Interjection   An **interjection** is a word that expresses emotion. It is inserted into a sentence or stands alone. Interjections are usually punctuated by exclamation points.

Examples: <u>Wow!</u> Dante received an A on his research paper.

Trina lost control of her sled—<u>look out</u>!

Examples of interjections include "*wow!*," "*oh my!*," "*ha!*," and "*neat!*"

Parts of Sentences

Subject and Predicate   Every complete sentence needs two essential parts to be a complete sentence: a **subject** (a person, place, or thing that is performing an action) and a **predicate** (what the subject does or is).

For example, in the sentence

Raoul has been working in his garden.

"Raoul" is the **subject** of the sentence. Raoul is performing an action (he *has been working* in his garden).

"… has been working in his garden" is the **complete predicate**. It tells what Raoul does. As a complete predicate, it includes both the main verb ("has been working") and any modifiers of the action, or anyone or anything receiving the action of the verb. In this case "in his garden" modifies the action by saying where it happened.

"… has been working …" is the **simple predicate**. It consists only of the main and auxiliary verbs in the sentence.

The subject of a sentence may be a common noun ("book," "table," "lamp"); a proper noun ("Reggie," "Janet," "the Secretary of Education"); or a pronoun ("I," "you," "they"). It may consist of a word, phrase, clause, or combination of nouns ("Tyrone and Laura," "the first person who comes into the room," "the woman wearing the baseball cap"). The **simple subject** is the noun or pronoun about whom the sentence is written. The **complete subject** is the simple subject plus any descriptive or related words, phrases, or clauses.

Phrases and Clauses   Phrases and clauses are both parts of sentences. A **phrase** is a group of words that does not contain a subject and a predicate. "According to Susan" is a phrase.

A **clause** is a group of words that contains both a subject and predicate and that is used as part of a sentence.

Example: If she is late, we will miss the movie.

The example is made up of two clauses. The first clause ("If she is late") is grammatically and logically incomplete on its own. This is called a **dependent**, or **subordinate**, clause. The second clause ("we will miss the movie") is an **independent**, or **principal**, clause. It could stand alone as a sentence, but the sentence would not have the same meaning as in the example, which requires the dependent clause to express a complete thought.

The dependent, or subordinate, clause is introduced by a subordinating word that relates it to another clause. "She is late" would be an independent clause or a simple sentence. Adding the word "if" makes the clause subordinate to the second part of the sentence.

Grammar

Grammar is a system of rules that governs how words are used to form sentences. Grammar can be intimidating because it is often discussed using a highly specialized vocabulary. However, you do not need to know all the grammar rules and vocabulary to identify and correct grammar mistakes effectively. Here are some of the aspects of grammar that are most important for students who are learning how to write and speak effectively.

Forms of Adjectives and Adverbs   Adjectives and adverbs usually have three forms: the **positive**, the **comparative**, and the **superlative**. The comparative form is used to compare two things, and the superlative is used to compare three or more.

Positive	*Comparative*	*Superlative*
big	bigger	biggest
interesting	more interesting	most interesting
good	better	best
badly	worse	worst

Examples: She was <u>good</u> at tennis.
Of the two, she was the <u>better</u> player.
She is the <u>best</u> tennis player on the team.

The used car ran <u>badly</u>.
The ancient truck ran even <u>worse</u>.
The beat-up van ran <u>worst</u> of all.

Subject–Verb Agreement   Subjects and verbs have to indicate the same number. If a noun names a single thing, then the verb that goes with the noun must also be in singular form. A sentence has a **subject–verb agreement error** when one word in a subject–verb pair is singular and the other word is plural.

Incorrect: Birds flies.   This sentence is incorrect because the subject, "Birds," is in a plural form while the verb, "flies," is in singular form.

You can correct sentences by changing the form of one of the words to make both words singular or both words plural.

Correct: Birds fly.   (Both the subject and the verb are plural.)

A bird flies.   (Both the subject and the verb are singular.)

For the most part, English speakers have internalized this grammar point, and subject–verb agreement just "sounds" right. Speakers tend to make subject–verb agreement errors when the subject and verb are separated by a clause.

Example: Many employees at the law firm take long lunches.

Even though "law firm" is the noun next to the verb, "employees" is the subject, and "take" agrees with the plural subject.

Compound subjects are sometimes tricky. When two subjects are joined by "and," the subject is generally plural.

Example: Coffee and tea are available.

On the other hand, some words and phrases, such as "plus," "as well as," or "in addition to," do not make true compound subjects.

Example: Coffee, as well as tea, is available.

The commas around the phrase "as well as tea" are another hint that only "coffee" is the subject of the verb.

When compound subjects are joined by "or" or "nor," the verb agrees with the closest subject.

Example: Neither cookies nor tea is available.

Verb Tense Each verb in a sentence must be in the proper tense. If two or more actions in a sentence occur at the same time, the verbs that indicate those actions must be in the same tense. Both verbs may be past-tense verbs, or both verbs may be present-tense verbs, but they must be consistent. A sentence has a **verb tense error** if a verb in the sentence is in the wrong tense. Keeping all the verbs in the same tense clarifies when the action in a sentence is taking place.

Incorrect: During the committee meeting last week, Jessie <u>suggested</u> going to the beach, while Tracy <u>votes</u> for going to a museum. (Both underlined verbs should be in the past tense because the phrase "During the committee meeting last week" indicates that both actions occurred in the past.)

You can correct the sentence by changing "votes" to the past tense.

Correct: During the committee meeting last week, Jessie <u>suggested</u> going to the beach, while Tracy <u>voted</u> for going to a museum. (Both verbs are now in the past tense. Verbs in the past tense often end in -ed.)

Parallelism When a sentence contains a series of items, all the items should be in parallel form. Keeping all phrases and clauses in the same form creates **parallelism** by clarifying the relationship among the parts of the sentence.

Incorrect: Nadia enjoys <u>traveling</u> and <u>to visit</u> friends. (This sentence is not parallel because "traveling" and "to visit" are not in the same form.)

You can correct sentences by putting both expressions in the same form.

Correct: Nadia enjoys <u>traveling</u> and <u>visiting</u> friends. (Both words are now in an -ing form.)

Parallel grammatical structure is crucial for clear and concise sentences.

Incorrect: He was good at English, history, and playing soccer.
Correct: He was good at English, history, and soccer.

Noun–Pronoun Agreement All pronouns and the nouns to which they refer must have the same number; both words must be singular or both words must be plural. If both words do not have the same number, the sentence has a **noun–pronoun agreement** error.

> Example: I tried to go to the <u>supermarket</u> near my house, but <u>they</u> were closed.
> (The sentence is incorrect because the noun "supermarket" is singular, and the pronoun "they" is plural.)

You can correct the sentence by making the pronoun singular.

> Example: I tried to go to the <u>supermarket</u> near my house, but <u>it</u> was closed.
> (Both noun and pronoun are singular. Note that the verb "were" also had to become singular to agree with the pronoun.)

Negation The negative particles are "not" and "no." The negative particle is placed after the auxiliary verb in a sentence.

> Example: The dog **will** *not* **come** when called.

"Come" is the verb, "will" is the **auxiliary verb** (it helps the verb "come" by putting it into the future tense), and "not" is the negative particle.

A form of the verb "to do" often performs an auxiliary function in forming the negative.

> Example: I **do** *not* **want** dessert.

"Never" can be used with the main verb.

> Example: I *never* **want** dessert.

Contractions are common in negation: "don't," "haven't," "isn't," "can't." In English, only one negative is allowed per sentence.

> Example: I *don't* **go** to school.

If a double negative is used, the expression becomes affirmative.

> Example: I *never don't* **go** to school.

"I never don't go to school" means "I always go to school."

Modification *Adjectives* modify nouns, and *adverbs* modify verbs.

> Examples: Her smile looked happy. (adjective)
> She smiled happily. (adverb)

Speakers often confuse the pairs of modifiers "good" (adjective) and "well" (adverb), and "bad" (adjective) and "badly" (adverb).

Examples: Peach cobbler tastes so good. (adjective)

She throws the ball well. (adverb)

He played tennis badly. (adverb)

I feel bad for his partner. (adjective)

A modifier should be placed as close as possible to the word it modifies. It should be clear which word in the sentence the modifier is modifying.

Examples: The copyeditor only found two errors.

The copyeditor found only two errors.

The first sentence suggests that the copyeditor did nothing with the errors except to find them. The second sentence suggests that there were only two errors to be found.

Adjectives usually precede the nouns they modify.

Example: I heard a loud noise.

If a modifier does not have a clear subject, it is called a **dangling modifier**.

Incorrect: As an adult, childhood was a happy memory.

It is not clear what or who the phrase "As an adult" modifies. The sentence seems to imply a subject.

Correct: As an adult, Marty remembered his childhood fondly.

Sentence Fragments and Run-On Sentences

Run-on sentences and **sentence fragments** are punctuated as sentences, but they have either too much or too little information to be a single sentence. Run-on sentences should be split into two or more sentences. Sentence fragments need to have their missing elements added in order to form complete sentences.

Incorrect: A new blender. Absolutely free!

These two sentence fragments can be made into a sentence with the addition of a verb:

Correct: Customers will receive a new blender absolutely free.

Run-on sentences occur when two independent clauses are joined with no connecting word or punctuation between them.

Incorrect: She called he didn't answer.
Correct: She called, but he didn't answer.

Comma splices occur when two independent clauses are joined by a comma. The two clauses must be separated by a semicolon.

Incorrect: He wasn't at home, therefore he didn't answer the phone.

Correct: He wasn't at home; therefore, he didn't answer the phone.

Punctuation

Punctuation separates the different parts of a sentence and distinguishes between sentences. While there are many rules for punctuation, we will concentrate on three of the most common punctuation errors: comma usage, colon and semicolon usage, and use of apostrophes to show possession.

Comma Usage Commas are used to separate elements of a sentence. For example, they may be used to separate a series of words in a list or two separate clauses. A **clause** is a group of words that contains both a subject and a verb. The following are the four most common ways to use commas.

1. Use commas between two independent clauses that are connected by a **conjunction** such as "and," "but," "yet," "or," "nor," "so," or "for." An **independent clause** is a clause that can stand alone as a complete sentence.

    Incorrect: Gemma won the election for student body president but Dana has more experience in leadership roles.

    Correct: Gemma won the election for student body president, but Dana has more experience in leadership roles.

The sentence above should have a comma because it contains two independent clauses connected by the word "but" (a coordinating conjunction). You can tell that it has two independent clauses because each clause has a subject paired with its own verb: The independent clause "Gemma won the election for student body president" has a subject ("Gemma") paired with a verb ("won"), and the independent clause "Dana has more experience in leadership roles" also has a subject ("Dana") paired with a verb ("has").

A good test to determine whether a sentence requires a comma is to break it into two sentences where you think the comma might need to go (before the coordinating conjunction). If you end up with two complete sentences ("Gemma won the election for student body president." "Dana has more experience in leadership roles."), then you need a comma. Make sure you don't forget about the coordinating conjunction; a sentence of this type with a comma but no coordinating conjunction is incorrect.

Note: In very short sentences, the comma may be omitted, but it is not incorrect to put a comma as long as there are two independent clauses connected by a coordinating conjunction.

2. Use commas after an introductory element for a sentence when that element appears before the subject of the sentence.

> Incorrect: Before the race started Cliff stretched his muscles.
>
> Correct: Before the race started, Cliff stretched his muscles.

Some writers do not use a comma after very short introductory elements. However, you should use a comma if the introductory element is long or if the comma would help clarify the meaning of the sentence.

3. Use commas before and after a clause or phrase that provides additional information that is not essential to the meaning of the sentence.

> Incorrect: My cousin an experienced pilot landed the plane safely.
>
> Correct: My cousin, an experienced pilot, landed the plane safely.

Since the phrase "an experienced pilot" is not essential to understanding that the speaker's cousin landed the plane safely, it should be surrounded by commas.

4. Use commas to separate items in a series. When three or more items are used in a series, commas should separate the items.

> Incorrect: Seth has traveled to France Italy and the Czech Republic.
>
> Correct: Seth has traveled to France, Italy, and the Czech Republic.

Some writers omit the comma before the last item in a series (before "and the Czech Republic"), but it is not incorrect to use a comma there.

Colon Usage   The **colon** (:) means "as follows." The colon is used to introduce a list or to anticipate a statement. It is also used after the salutation of a business letter: "Dear Madam or Sir:"

> Example: There is one main challenge for the new dog owner: house-breaking.

Semicolon Usage   The **semicolon** (;) is used to separate two independent clauses that are closely related in subject matter. (Remember, an **independent**

clause is a clause with a subject and verb that does not depend on another part of the sentence to clarify its meaning. It can stand alone as a complete sentence.)

Incorrect:	Darrell wanted to wear his lucky tie for his job interview, unfortunately, the tie was at the cleaners.
Correct:	Darrell wanted to wear his lucky tie for his job interview; unfortunately, the tie was at the cleaners.

The sentence contains two complete independent clauses: "Darrell wanted to wear his lucky tie for his job interview" and "unfortunately, the tie was at the cleaners." You can tell that they are independent clauses because either clause could stand alone as a sentence. Therefore, they should be separated by a semicolon, not a comma.

Apostrophe Usage The **apostrophe** (') can be used to show that a noun belongs to someone or something.

Use apostrophes in the following situations:

1. To show possession for singular nouns: add '*s*.

> Example: the bird's wing, the host's party

2. To show possession for plural nouns that do not end in s: add 's.

> Example: men's shoes, the mice's cheese

3. To show possession for plural nouns that end in s: add '.

> Example: the dogs' howling, the players' rivalry

Do not use apostrophes in the following situations:

1. *Do not* use apostrophes for possessive pronouns:

> Example: Use "yours," not "your's," to show possession: *This coat must be yours.*

2. *Do not* use apostrophes to make nouns plural:

> Example: Use "ten fingers," not "ten finger's."

Capitalization

Capitalization is used to mark the beginning of a sentence. The first letter of the first word of a sentence is capitalized. A quoted sentence within a sentence also begins with a capital letter.

Capitalization is also used to distinguish proper nouns and titles. A proper noun is the individual title of a person, place, or thing.

> Examples: United States
> Rutgers University

Nathaniel Hawthorne
The Scarlet Letter
Lake Erie
the Victorian Age
The New York Times

Word Usage (Diction)

Word usage refers to using words with meanings and forms that are appropriate for the context and structure of a sentence. A common error in word usage occurs when a word's meaning does not fit the context of the sentence. This often occurs with homophones (words that sound alike but have different meanings).

Incorrect:	Mark likes candy better then gum.
Correct:	Mark likes candy better than gum.
Incorrect:	The dog chased it's tail.
Correct:	The dog chased its tail.

In addition to "than/then" and "it's/its," some other commonly misused words include "they/their/they're," "your/you're," "except/accept," and "affect/effect." For contractions ("it's," "they're," "you're"), you can spell out the contraction to make sure you are using the correct word ("it's" = "it is"; "they're" = "they are"; "you're" = "you are"). For other words, however, you will need to learn the correct usage by looking up the word in the dictionary to find out its meaning.

Idiomatic Expressions

Some words take particular prepositions in idiomatic usage. To English speakers, the correct form should "sound" right.

Incorrect:	similar as
Correct:	similar to

You should be able to identify when a certain preposition should be used. For example, dinner is *in* the oven, but *on* the table. A person is *in* love, but *at* home.

Clarity of Expression

Wordiness, redundancy, and awkwardness impede clarity of expression.

Wordiness Always express your meaning in the clearest way possible. Omit unnecessary words. Wordy phrases should be simplified or eliminated.

Incorrect:	We missed our appointment due to the fact that the train was late.
Correct:	We missed our appointment because the train was late.
Incorrect:	at that point in time for the purpose of
Correct:	then for

Vague nouns and modifiers such as "factor," "situation," "really," and "very" can simply be deleted from most sentences in which they are used.

Redundancy

Incorrect:	I was very exhausted.
Correct:	I was exhausted.

"Very exhausted" is redundant because "exhausted" is already an extreme state.

Incorrect:	Combine the butter and sugar together in a bowl.
Correct:	Combine the butter and sugar in a bowl.

"Combine" already means to mix together.

GUIDED PPST WRITING MULTIPLE-CHOICE PRACTICE

Type 1: Usage Questions

In each **Usage** question, four elements of the sentence are underlined. Here is an example:

The larger fireflies of eastern <u>North</u> America belong, <u>for the most part</u>,
                        A   B
to the genus *Photurus*, a group <u>in which</u> the males show much more vari-
                                     C
ation in flash pattern <u>as</u> in body structure and color. <u>No error</u>
                           D   E

To answer the question, you have to determine whether there is an error and, if so, where it is. You are not required to specify what the error is, nor do you have to suggest a way to fix it. You just have to identify where the error is, if an error exists.

Note that choice E is "No error." You should choose E if you think the sentence is correct as shown. In every **Usage** question, E is the "No error" choice.

In the question about fireflies above, choice A tests capitalization: Is the continent correctly referred to as "North America" or "north America?" Choice B tests diction—is the phrase used correctly? Choice C tests subordination—does the wording "in which" correctly link the idea "group" to the following information about males in that group? Choice D tests a comparative construction: Should the phrase beginning with "more" be completed by a phrase beginning with "as" or "than?" The error is in choice D. Substituting "than" for "as" at D would make the sentence grammatically correct ("… the males show much greater variation in flash pattern *than* in body structure and color"). Choice D is the answer.

Usage questions typically present specific, discrete errors rather than expressions that may be ineffective. Stylistic problems, such as wordiness and vagueness, are generally tested in **Sentence Correction** questions.

ETS TIPS for Usage Questions

- Before you choose an answer, look at all parts of the sentence to see how they fit together.
- If you see a line under a blank space, it means that you must decide whether a punctuation mark is needed there.
- If you see a line under a single punctuation mark, you must consider three possibilities: (a) no punctuation mark is needed in that spot, so the mark shown is an error; (b) a punctuation mark is needed, but not the one shown; and (c) the punctuation mark is correct.
- The underlined part may consist of a single word or more than one word. Remember, where an underlined part is several words long, not all the underlined elements need be wrong for that part to be incorrect. The error may depend on only one word or element.
- The "No error" answer choice is always E in a Usage question. Do not be afraid to choose E if, after careful consideration, you think the sentence looks and sounds correct. Not every sentence has an error; there are some E answers in every Usage section.
- If you think that an answer choice contains an error, you should be able to correct the error mentally in one of the following ways.
  —You can delete an element, such as one of the words in an underlined phrase.
  —You can change the form of an element that is already there, such as changing *it's* to *its*.
  —You can replace an element, such as changing *than* to *then*.
  —You can add an element, such as a comma.

Try Usage Questions

1. The club members <u>agreed</u> that <u>each would contribute</u> ten days of

                  A   B

volunteer work <u>annually each year</u> at the <u>local hospital</u>. <u>No error</u>

                  C   D   E

The error in this sentence occurs at choice C. The phrase "annually each year" is redundant, because "annually" and "each year" convey the same information. The sentence would be correct with either "annually" or "each year" at choice C. The error is one of redundancy.

2. Tennis players <u>have complained</u> for years <u>about</u> the surly crowds and

                  A   B

the raucous noise at matches <u>,</u> distractions that seriously affect their ability

                             C

to concentrate and <u>for playing</u> well. <u>No error</u>

                    D   E

The error occurs at choice D. The phrases "to concentrate" and "for playing" are connected by "and"; therefore, they should be parallel verb forms. The correct phrase at choice D is "to play."

3. Anesthesiologists are in <u>so short supply</u> that operating rooms <u>are used</u>

                          A   B

<u>only three or four days</u> a week in <u>some</u> hospitals. <u>No error</u>

             C   D   E

The error in this sentence occurs at choice A. The correct modifier for the noun phrase "short supply" is "such." "Such" is used to modify nouns or noun phrases, which may include nouns that are modified by adjectives (for example, "such tall trees"), whereas *so* is used to modify adjectives alone (for example, "so tall").

4. The school magazine will print <u>those who win</u> prizes for poetry, short

                                    A

stories, and drama <u>;</u> nonfiction, however, <u>will not</u> be <u>accepted for</u>

                    B   C   D

publication. <u>No error</u>

           E

The error occurs at choice A. In the phrase "those who win," the pronoun "those" indicates the people who win prizes. But the magazine will not print the *people* who win; it will print what the winners have written, or the names or submissions of those who win prizes. The error in this question is the illogical use of a pronoun.

---

5. Fireworks_, which were probably <u>first created</u> in ancient China in
        A   B

order to frighten off devils, were not used <u>as</u> entertainment purposes
                                           C

<u>until around</u> A.D. 1500. <u>No error</u>
    D   E

The error occurs at choice C. The phrase "used as … purposes" is unidiomatic. The correct word at choice C is "for."

---

6. If <u>smaller amounts</u> of pesticide <u>would have</u> been used by the farmers,
         A   B

the streams <u>around</u> Merchantville would not now be <u>so polluted</u>. <u>No error</u>
        C   D   E

The error in this sentence occurs at choice B. The conditional "would," when used as it is here with "if," suggests that a specific action can still be performed ("if only the farmers would use smaller amounts of pesticide"). But the actions of the farmers were completed in the past and cannot be changed. Consequently, "would" is incorrect here. The correct verb form here is "had been used."

---

7. <u>Plagued by</u> robbers, Paris in 1524 passed an ordinance <u>requiring citizens</u>
   A   B   C

to burn candles _ in windows fronting on the streets. <u>No error</u>
         D   E

Because this sentence contains no grammatical, idiomatic, logical, or structural errors, the best answer is choice E. Note that at choice B a single letter is underlined in order to test whether that letter should be a capital. In this case a capital letter is incorrect. Also note that at D the underline of a blank space is designed to test the need for a mark of punctuation at that point. In this particular case no punctuation is needed.

---

8. Diabetes mellitus is <u>a disorder of</u> carbohydrate metabolism that
                          A

<u>inflicts</u> <u>approximately</u> 3 percent <u>of the population</u>. <u>No error</u>
  B   C   D   E

The error in this sentence occurs at choice B. The verb "inflict" means "to cause to be suffered" and is used to describe a step that is *actively* taken by a person or similar agent. (Example: "He inflicted punishment on the prisoners.") Diabetes mellitus, however, does not cause something to be suffered in this way; rather, it is a disease that *is* suffered. The correct word here is "afflicts," which means "distresses" or "affects." The error in this question is one of diction.

---

9. For a writer, the <u>rarest</u> privilege <u>is not merely</u> <u>to describe</u> her country
             A   B   C

and time but to help shape <u>it</u>. <u>No error</u>
                  D   E

The error in this sentence occurs at choice D. The pronoun "it" is wrongly used to refer to two nouns, "country" and "time." The pronoun required here is the plural "them."

---

10. Researchers in the United States say _ that a diet rich in fish oils
                                   A

<u>reduces</u> the <u>amount</u> of fat in the blood as <u>effective</u> as a diet rich in
   B   C   D

vegetable oils. <u>No error</u>
            E

The error in this sentence occurs at choice D. The word at choice D describes (or modifies) the verb "reduces," and because verbs are modified by adverbs, the word at choice D should be in the form of an adverb. In this sentence, the correct word would be "effectively."

---

11. The company is under pressure to sell <u>its</u> assets <u>to avoid</u> difficulties
                                 A   B

<u>in making</u> future interest payments <u>on</u> outstanding loans. <u>No error</u>
   C   D   E

This sentence contains no grammatical, idiomatic, logical, or structural errors, so the best answer is choice E, "No error."

---

12. The famous portraitist ‿ John Singer Sargent <u>learned</u> the art
                      A   B

<u>of sketching</u> from his mother ‿ an enthusiastic amateur. <u>No error</u>
   C   D   E

The comma at choice A is incorrect. The name "John Singer Sargent" is necessary to identify *which* "famous portraitist" is referred to in the preceding phrase. Elements that are necessary to the sentence in this way are **restrictive** and are not set off by commas. At choice D, the comma is correct because the phrase that follows "mother" is not needed to identify who his mother is.

---

13. The oldest remains <u>of cultivated</u> rice, <u>dating from</u> about 5000 B.C.E.,
                        A   B
<u>has been found</u> in eastern China _ and northern India. <u>No error</u>
       C   D   E

This sentence presents a problem in subject–verb agreement. The plural subject "remains" requires a plural form of the conjugated verb at choice C. The phrase "have been found" would be correct.

---

14. <u>No one</u> is quite sure where the Moon came from _, but it is clear that
       A   B
the Apollo lunar samples <u>are</u> very similar <u>with the rocks</u> of the Earth's
                          C   D
outer mantle. <u>No error</u>
                   E

Choice D presents an error of idiom. The correct expression for the sentence would be "to the rocks."

---

15. The town council is applying <u>for funds</u> from the agency that
                                  A
<u>has been established</u> two years ago <u>to coordinate</u> environmental
       B   C
projects in the <u>state</u>. <u>No error</u>
                    D   E

The error in this sentence occurs at choice B. The tense of the verb should indicate that the action of establishing the agency was completed at a definite time in the past (two years ago). You could correct the sentence by changing choice B to "was established."

---

16. Movies, <u>like</u> fairy tales, <u>embody</u> powerful myths <u>that help</u> children
             A   B   C
<u>struggle against</u> unexpected difficulties. <u>No error</u>
       D   E

This sentence contains no grammatical, idiomatic, logical, or structural errors, so the best answer is choice E, "No error."

Type 2: Sentence Correction Questions

In **Sentence Correction** questions, you will not evaluate the underlined choices for a discrete grammatical error; instead, you will look at an entire portion of a sentence to determine how it should best be worded. **Sentence Correction** questions look different from **Usage** questions. One or more words in the sentence are underlined, as shown in this example:

By analyzing the wood used in its construction, <u>the settlement was dated by scientists to the seventh century</u>.

(A) the settlement was dated by scientists to the seventh century

(B) the dating of the settlement by scientists has been to the seventh century

(C) scientists dated the settlement to the seventh century

(D) the seventh century was the date of the settlement by scientists

(E) the settlement has been dated to the seventh century by scientists

---

The five choices provide five different ways that the underlined portion could be expressed. Your job is to decide whether the sentence is correct as is or whether one of the other four choices is the correct way to express the meaning of the underlined portion.

Note that choice A is the same as the original underlined portion. This is true for all **Sentence Correction** questions. If the sentence is correct as is, you should select choice A.

In the example about old wood above, the original sentence is not correct. The introductory phrase of the sentence, "By analyzing the wood used in its construction," should modify "scientists" because they do the analyzing; therefore, "scientists" should immediately follow the phrase. Choice C, the best answer, is the only choice in which "scientists" appears in this position.

The underlined portion of a **Sentence Correction** question may be as short as one or two words or as long as the entire sentence. It is important to read each of the choices carefully. More than one element may change from choice to choice, and if you do not read all choices carefully, you may miss some of these changes.

ETS TIPS for Sentence Correction Questions

- Choice A always repeats the underlined portion of the original sentence. Do not be reluctant to select choice A if you think that the original is better than any of the variations, but do not choose any answer until you have read every choice.
- If you detect one or more errors in the original sentence, you should be able to correct the sentence mentally, and, in most cases, you should find your corrections among the answer choices.

Do not spend more than a few seconds trying to make the corrections before you start reading the choices; you may very well recognize the corrections when you see them, even if you cannot come up with them yourself.

- Don't be alarmed if you mentally correct the sentence but then fail to find an answer choice that would correct it in exactly the same way. Sometimes there are several possibilities for correcting a faulty sentence; however, only one will appear among the answer choices. As long as you can recognize what is correct, you should still be able to answer the question.

- Read all the way through each answer choice. Don't stop at the first corrected element. Individual choices may correct some errors while also introducing new errors that do not appear in the original sentence.

- Remember that the answer you choose not only should be error-free but also should fit correctly and logically with the part of the original sentence that is not underlined.

- Don't be tempted into thinking that you can answer a question by looking at the relative lengths of the choices. A long choice does not necessarily signal a sophisticated statement. It may in fact be less effective than other possibilities because of wordiness or awkwardness. Conversely, don't assume that the shortest answer is as correct as it is concise.

- Once again, be sure to read all the choices before you choose an answer. It frequently happens that a version strikes you as being correct until something in another choice makes you realize that you have overlooked an error.

Try Sentence Correction Questions

1. <u>To try and appeal</u> to consumers who prefer no additives, some food companies are making unneeded changes in products.

   (A) To try and appeal

   (B) With the intention to appeal

   (C) In an effort to appeal

   (D) Because they made an effort to try appealing

   (E) In that they made an effort to be appealing

The original sentence is incorrect because it includes the phrase "try and appeal" instead of "try to appeal." Choice B is incorrect, because "intention to appeal" should be "intention of appealing." Choices D and E are wordy and present an action, "made an effort," that took place in the past—incorrect in this sentence, because both parts of the sentence need to be in the same tense. Only choice C, the best answer, creates a logical and idiomatic statement.

---

2. Shunning astrologers and fortune-tellers, she insisted that life would be less interesting <u>were we in the possession of knowledge of the future</u>.

(A) were we in the possession of knowledge of the future

(B) were we to possess knowledge of the future

(C) if we were to possess the future's knowledge

(D) if we possess future knowledge

(E) if we can possess knowledge of the future

The original sentence is incorrect because the phrase "in the possession of knowledge of the future" is an awkward string of prepositional phrases and because it permits an ambiguous reading—that the people ("we") would be "possessed" *by* the knowledge. Choices C and D inaccurately replace "knowledge of the future" (knowledge *about* the future) with "the future's knowledge" (knowledge that the future possesses) and "future knowledge" (knowledge that exists in the future). Choices D and E are wrong because "we possess" and "we can possess" fail to indicate that the discussion is hypothetical. Choice B, the best answer, is both clear and grammatically correct.

---

3. Conservationists want to preserve stretches of "wild" rivers, those whose banks are still unobstructed by buildings and <u>uncontaminated by wastes in their waters</u>.

(A) uncontaminated by wastes in their waters

(B) whose waters are uncontaminated by wastes

(C) whose waters are without wastes contaminating them

(D) by wastes contaminated their waters

(E) wastes contaminating their waters

The problem in this sentence is faulty parallelism. Two attributes of "wild" rivers are named in the clause beginning with "those whose." Both parts of the clause should have the same grammatical structure. Choices B and C are therefore the only possibilities. Choice C is awkward, and "them" does not have a clear referent (it could refer to "waters" or "banks"). Choice B, "whose waters are uncontaminated by wastes," has the same grammatical structure as the first part of the clause, "whose banks are still unobstructed by buildings," and is clear and correct.

4. The fact that some mushrooms are perfectly safe for one person <u>but not for another</u> probably accounts for differences of opinion as to which species are edible and which are not.

(A) but not for another

(B) but not for the other

(C) and not for the other

(D) and unsafe for some other

(E) and some are unsafe for others

The original sentence is clear and grammatically correct. Therefore choice A is the correct answer. Choices B, C, and D change "another" to "the other" or "some other," suggesting incorrectly that one particular person is being discussed. In choices C, D, and E the appropriate conjunction "but" is changed to "and."

5. In the celery fields of Florida, <u>chameleons are welcome by the growers: they</u> feed upon caterpillars and moths.

(A) chameleons are welcome by the growers, they

(B) the chameleon is welcome to the growers, since they

(C) the chameleons are welcomed by the growers, since they

(D) the growers are welcoming of chameleons, which

(E) the growers welcome chameleons, which

The original sentence is incorrect and confusing. The phrase "are welcome by" is wrong (it should be "are welcomed by"). In addition, it is not clear whether the pronoun "they" refers to the chameleons or the growers. Choices B and C are wrong because the noun referent of the pronoun "they" is still "growers" instead of "chameleons." Choices D and E are correct with regard to the referent, but D uses an unidiomatic form of "welcome." Choice E, the best answer, is clear, idiomatic, and grammatically correct.

6. Martin Luther King, Jr., <u>spoke out passionately</u> for the poor of all races.

(A) spoke out passionately

(B) spoke out passionate

(C) did speak out passionate

(D) has spoke out passionately

(E) had spoken out passionate

This sentence presents no problem of structure or logic. The verb tense is correct, and the use of the adverb "passionately" is also correct in this context. In choices

B, C, and E, the adjective "passionate" is incorrectly used instead of the adverb. Choice D, while it uses the correct adverb, introduces an incorrect verb form, "has spoke out." Thus, the best answer is choice A.

---

7. The king preferred accepting the republican flag <u>than giving</u> up the throne altogether.

(A) than giving

(B) than to giving

(C) than to give

(D) rather than give

(E) to giving

The correct form for this kind of comparative statement is "preferred X to Y." Choices B, C, and E have the correct "to," but choices B and C can be eliminated because they add "than" before the "to." Only choice E, the best answer, presents the correct construction.

---

8. <u>The agent, passing through the crowd without being noticed by hardly anyone.</u>

(A) The agent, passing through the crowd without being noticed by hardly anyone.

(B) The agent passed through the crowd without hardly being noticed by anyone.

(C) The agent's passing through the crowd was not hardly noticed by anyone.

(D) No one hardly noticed how the agent passed through the crowd.

(E) The agent was hardly noticed as she passed through the crowd.

This sentence presents two major problems: it is not a complete sentence and the phrase "without … hardly" is not idiomatic. Although choices B, C, and D are complete sentences, each retains the problem of using "hardly" in an unidiomatic construction. The best correction is choice E.

---

9. <u>As a consumer, one can accept</u> the goods offered to us or we can reject them, but we cannot determine their quality or change the system's priorities.

(A) As a consumer, one can accept

(B) We the consumer either can accept

(C) The consumer can accept

(D) Either the consumer accepts

(E) As consumers, we can accept

The main problem in this sentence concerns agreement in pronoun number. In the portion of the sentence that is not underlined, the first person plural, "we," is used as the subject of the second part of the compound sentence. The underlined portion of the sentence is therefore wrong in the original, since it uses the singular "consumer" and the singular pronoun "one." To create a sentence free of agreement faults, you must look for a choice that contains "we" and the plural of "consumer." Choice E is the only one that corrects the agreement problem and has a phrase parallel to "we can reject them."

---

10. Since 1977, Mexico has <u>had a building code comparable to California</u>.

(A) had a building code comparable to California

(B) had a building code comparable to that of California

(C) had a building code that is similar to California

(D) a building code comparable to California's

(E) a building code comparable to that of California's

This sentence is correct in its verb tense (present perfect tense, "has had"), but it illogically compares Mexico's building code to the whole state of California rather than to California's building code. Choices D and E are wrong because they use the simple present tense, "has," alone. Choice C preserves the illogical comparison. Choice B correctly uses "has had" and creates a logical comparison.

---

11. <u>That its collection of ancient manuscripts can be preserved</u>, the museum keeps them in a room where temperature and humidity are carefully controlled.

(A) That its collection of ancient manuscripts can be preserved

(B) So they can preserve the collection of ancient manuscripts

(C) For preserving its collection of ancient manuscripts

(D) In order that they can preserve the collection of ancient manuscripts

(E) To preserve its collection of ancient manuscripts

This sentence presents an awkward and unidiomatic expression but is correct in that the pronoun "its" agrees with the singular noun "museum." Choices B and D have pronoun reference agreement problems: the plural pronoun "they" doesn't match the singular noun "museum." Between choices C and E, choice E presents the clearer and more idiomatic expression.

12. The flow of the Hudson River was so reduced by the drought of 1985 that salt water borne on ocean tides moved upstream to within six miles of Poughkeepsie, New York.

(A) The flow of the Hudson River was so reduced by the drought of 1985 that

(B) So reduced was the flow of the Hudson River by the drought of 1985 as to make

(C) The drought of 1985 made such a reduction of the flow of the Hudson River that

(D) Of such a reduction was the flow of the Hudson River by the drought of 1985 that

(E) There was such a reduction of the flow of the Hudson River by the drought of 1985 as to make

The original sentence is correct; therefore, choice A is the answer. Choices B, C, D, and E are unidiomatic, wordy, and awkward.

13. Neon glows red-orange upon placing it in a glass tube and charged with electricity.

(A) upon placing it

(B) when placed

(C) as placed

(D) on its placement

(E) after placement

This sentence suffers from lack of parallelism. Both verbs in the sentence ("place" and "charge") should be in the same form. Choices B and C use correct forms of "place," but the "as" in choice C is unidiomatic. Choice B is best.

14. The conflict between somatic and psychological interpretations of mental disorder rage as noisily as ever, and each side make tragic errors of diagnosis and treatment.

(A) rage as noisily as ever, and each side make

(B) rage as noisily as ever, and each side makes

(C) rages as noisily as ever, and each side make

(D) rages as noisily as ever, with each side making

(E) have raged as noisily as ever, with each side making

There are two subject–verb agreement errors in the original sentence. The subject of the first part of the sentence is "conflict," a singular noun. The correct form of the conjugated verb is "rages." Therefore, "rage" in choices A and B and "have raged" in choice E (which also inappropriately changes the tense of the verb) are all wrong. The second part of choice C contains a second subject–verb agreement error (it should be "each side *makes*"). Only choice D avoids errors in subject–verb agreement in both parts of the sentence. Therefore, choice D is the best answer.

---

15. Jazz is a rigorous and <u>technical demanding music, deeply affecting such composers like Stravinsky and Gershwin</u>.

(A) technical demanding music, deeply affecting such composers like Stravinsky and Gershwin

(B) technical demanding music, one that deeply affected such composers like Stravinsky and Gershwin

(C) technically demanding music, which deeply affected such composers like Stravinsky and Gershwin

(D) technically demanding music, and such composers as Stravinsky and Gershwin were being deeply affected by it

(E) technically demanding music, one that deeply affected such composers as Stravinsky and Gershwin

---

In the original sentence there are two errors. The first is the word "technical": since it modifies an adjective ("demanding"), it should be in adverbial form ("technically," as in choices C, D, and E). The second error is "like" (preceded by "such"): the correct modifier is "as." Choices D and E use "as," but choice D is awkward and also uses the past progressive tense unidiomatically. Choice E, which is clear as well as grammatically and idiomatically correct, is the best answer.

CHAPTER 8

PPST™ Writing—The Essay

PURPOSE AND FORMAT OF THE ESSAY

The essay section comprises one-half of your total test score on the *PPST Writing* test, so it is crucial that you maximize your success on this part. The purpose of the examination is to test your ability to write effectively within a limited period of time. The term "writing sample" is often used to describe the kind of writing you will be asked to produce, and it is useful to think of your response in this way; if you were trying out for a part in a play or for a sports team, you might be asked to read a small section of dialogue or to demonstrate some aspect of your athletic skills. Your overall ability would be evaluated on the basis of samples of what you can do. The writing sample works in the same way. You are not expected to turn out a well-researched, comprehensive essay about a highly specific, specialized topic.

This chapter discusses the scoring criteria and offers some strategies for using your time effectively during the test. The chapter also includes a list of 71 sample essay topics that show the kind of topic you will encounter when you take the test.

OVERVIEW OF THE ESSAY SECTION

In the essay section of the *PPST Writing* test, you are given 30 minutes to write on an assigned topic. Thirty minutes should allow you sufficient time to read the topic carefully, organize your thoughts prior to writing, write a draft with reasonable care and precision, and briefly check over your response. Note that the result is considered a *draft*, not the kind of highly polished document you would be expected to produce if you were given the assignment to do as homework.

After your draft essay is returned to ETS, it will be evaluated by experienced teachers of writing. Every essay is graded by at least two scorers, neither of whom knows what score the other has given. Each scorer gives a score ranging from 1 (low) to 6 (high). (Essays that do not respond to the specified topic are given a score of 0, regardless of the quality of the writing.) If the two scorers differ by more than one point in the score they assign, the essay is scored *independently* by a third scorer, who is not given any information about what other scores the essay has received. Your essay score is then combined with your multiple-choice Writing score to give you a total *PPST Writing* test score.

HOW THE ESSAY IS SCORED

The easiest way to find out what skills are being tested in the essay section of the test is to look at the *PPST Writing* scoring guide, which scorers use in assigning a score of 1 to 6 to each essay. You should also look at the sample question and sample responses included at the end of this chapter.

The ETS Scoring Guide

Here is the official ETS scoring guide used by the *PPST Writing* essay scorers:

---

6 A 6 essay demonstrates a *high degree of competence* in response to the assignment but may have a few minor errors.

An essay in this category:
- states or clearly implies the writer's position or thesis
- organizes and develops ideas logically, making insightful connections between them
- clearly explains key ideas, supporting them with well-chosen reasons, examples, or details
- displays effective sentence variety
- clearly displays facility in the use of language
- is generally free from errors in grammar, usage, and mechanics

5 A 5 essay demonstrates *clear competence* in response to the assignment but may have minor errors.

An essay in this category:
- states or clearly implies the writer's position or thesis
- organizes and develops ideas clearly, making connections between them
- explains key ideas, supporting them with relevant reasons, examples, or details
- displays some sentence variety
- displays facility in the use of language
- is generally free from errors in grammar, usage, and mechanics

4 A 4 essay demonstrates *competence* in response to the assignment.

An essay in this category:
- states or implies the writer's position or thesis
- shows control in the organization and development of ideas
- explains some key ideas, supporting them with adequate reasons, examples, or details
- displays adequate use of language
- shows control of grammar, usage, and mechanics, but may display errors

---

3 A 3 essay demonstrates *some competence* in response to the assignment but is obviously flawed. An essay in this category reveals *one or more* of the following weaknesses:
- limited in stating or implying a position or thesis
- limited control in the organization and development of ideas
- inadequate reasons, examples, or details to explain key ideas
- an accumulation of errors in the use of language
- an accumulation of errors in grammar, usage, and mechanics

2 A 2 essay is *seriously flawed.* An essay in this category reveals *one or more* of the following weaknesses:
- no clear position or thesis
- weak organization or very little development
- few or no relevant reasons, examples, or details
- frequent serious errors in the use of language
- frequent serious errors in grammar, usage, and mechanics

1 A 1 essay demonstrates *fundamental deficiencies* in writing skills.

An essay in this category:
- contains serious and persistent writing errors, or
- is incoherent, or
- is undeveloped

0 A 0 essay is off topic; that is, it is not a response to the topic specified.

STRATEGIES FOR WRITING YOUR ESSAY

While preparing for the test, you should maximize your chances for success by focusing on the same characteristics that the scorers look for when scoring the essays. To help you do this, let's closely dissect the scoring guide; that's where the strategies for success lie.

Strategy 1: Respond to the Specific Topic

Note that in the scoring guide, the degree of competence the writer shows in *responding to the assignment* is reflected in the characteristics of the scores from 6 through 3. A response that does not directly address the question but is still on topic may be scored as low as a 2. A response written to something other than the given topic will receive no credit. This is the goal of Strategy 1: staying focused on the exact question being asked. It sounds simple, but this focus is critical for success.

Strategy 2: State Your Position Clearly

The first bullet under the description of each score-point, from 6 to 2, makes it clear that responses with higher scores *state their position or thesis clearly*. As you will see in the next section of this chapter, the essay assignment in the *PPST Writing* test always involves stating to what extent you agree or disagree with a given statement. The scoring guide specifies that it is critical to make sure you communicate clearly whether or to what extent you agree or disagree; don't leave the reader guessing.

Strategy 3: Plan Your Essay Before You Write, So that It Is Organized

The second bullet under the description of each score-point addresses *organization* and *development*. You should strive for logical organization and flow, not just a loose collection of ideas. You might consider taking a few minutes to make an outline or notes before you write.

Strategy 4: Create a Logical Flow from Idea to Idea

In addition, when you are writing your draft, think about the logical flow from idea to idea. You should consider using transition phrases to link ideas both within and between paragraphs.

Strategy 5: Develop Each Key Idea with One Or More Examples Or Clarifying Statements

The third bullet under the description of each score-point mentions the use of reasons, examples, or details. Depending on the topic you're given and the arguments you're making, this could take the form of particular examples (such as, "For example, there are literally thousands of species of spiders") or clarifying explanations (such as, "The enforcement of such a policy would put an undue burden on teachers, who already have a great many responsibilities to attend to during the school day"). Be alert for opportunities to expand your key ideas or provide specific details or examples.

Strategy 6: Use Variety in Sentence Construction

The fourth bullet under the two highest score points refers to "sentence variety." This means that in high-scoring papers, the sentences are not all structured in the same way as one another. You should try to vary the length and type of sentences. For example, don't start every sentence with "There is . . . " Use transitions and, perhaps, begin some sentences with modifying phrases (such as, "Remaining true to their profession, teachers often …"). Higher-scoring papers also display facility in the use of language. Consider occasionally combining simple sentences in order to vary the length and rhythm of your sentences.

Strategy 7: Follow The Rules of Standard Written English

The remaining bullets encompass the large territory known as standard written English. This means correct subject–verb agreement, correct use of modifiers, correct parallelism, correct idiomatic expressions, and so on—all the elements discussed in the multiple-choice section of the test. Try to leave time to review these elements and correct any errors before submitting your test. However, do not sacrifice organization, development, details, and sentence variety by spending all of your time thinking about the mechanics.

Now that you have considered the strategies, let's examine the types of topics you'll apply the strategies to.

THE ESSAY TOPICS

ETS has published the list of topics that is printed below. One of these topics, or a similar topic, will be presented to you when you take the test. This is the official ETS list of essay topics, so it makes sense to examine it carefully.

The format for every essay question is the same: you will be asked to discuss the extent to which you *agree* or *disagree* with the opinion presented in the topic and to *support your position* with specific reasons and examples from your own experience, observations, or reading.

It does not matter whether you agree or disagree with the topic, the scorers are trained to accept all varieties of opinions. What matters are the skills we've discussed in the previous section: taking a clear stand that responds directly to the question and writing a draft essay that is characterized by good organization, complete development, sentence variety, and standard written English.

None of the topics requires specialized academic knowledge. Most topics are general and are based on common educational experiences or issues of public concern. Don't be intimidated by the topic. Just decide quickly whether or to what extent you agree or disagree with the statement, and then begin working on your essay.

What should you do with this list of 71 topics? To prepare for the essay portion of the test, you should practice writing essays in response to these topics. Try to make your practice conditions as much like the actual testing conditions as possible. Make sure to time yourself, giving yourself 30 minutes to read a question and write a response. After completing an essay, read it over and compare it with the scoring guide. Better yet, have a friend, professor, or teacher evaluate the essay against the scoring criteria and give you feedback. Identify the skills with which you have trouble, and try to practice them in future writing. Composition professors and staff at college writing labs can also recommend useful textbooks on how to improve your writing.

Here are the official directions that precede each topic in the test:

Read the opinion stated below. Discuss the extent to which you agree or disagree with this point of view. Support your position with specific reasons and examples from your own experience, observations, or reading.

Each of the following 71 topics is an opinion statement. You will be asked to agree or disagree with one of them (or a statement like one of them) when you take the *PPST Writing* test.

1. "Celebrities have a tremendous influence on the young, and for that reason, they have a responsibility to act as role models."
2. "Our society is overly materialistic. We center our lives on acquiring material things at the expense of such traditional values as family and education."
3. "Censorship of song lyrics, television shows, and offensive speech is necessary in order to protect the rights of all members of society."
4. "Young people who attend college immediately after high school often lack a clear sense of direction and seriousness about learning. Before hurrying into college, it's better to get a taste of the real world by working or serving in the military for a few years."
5. "Although routines may seem to put us in a rut and stifle creativity, in fact routines make us more efficient and allow creativity to blossom."
6. "An effective leader of any organization—from the military to businesses to social organizations—is someone who is decisive, acts quickly, and remains committed to certain key principles."
7. "Advances in computer technology have made the classroom unnecessary, since students and teachers are able to communicate with each other from computer terminals at home or at work."
8. "Schools should be open for classes all year long."
9. "Schools should focus more on preparing students for specific careers and vocations, and less on teaching subjects such as literature, art, and history."
10. "Although the marvels of technology surround us every day, there are moments when we all would give anything to be freed from that technology."
11. "Colleges should require all students, regardless of their individual majors, to take a common set of required courses."
12. "Schools should require all students to participate in field trips since these outings are an essential part of the curriculum for all grade levels."
13. "In order to prepare students to live in a culturally diverse society, schools should formally require all students to study other cultures and societies in depth."

14. "One clear sign that our society has improved over the past 100 years is the development of disposable products whose convenience has made our lives easier."

15. "The best way to understand the true nature of a society is to study its dominant trends in art, music, and fashion."

16. "Because the traditional grading scale of A through F fosters needless competition and pressure, colleges and universities should use a simple pass/fail system."

17. "To address the problem of chronic truancy, schools should fine the parents of students who are frequently absent from school."

18. "Studying a foreign language should be a college requirement for anyone planning to be a teacher."

19. "We are constantly bombarded by advertisements—on television and radio, in newspapers and magazines, on highway signs and the sides of buses. They have become too pervasive. It's time to put limits on advertising."

20. "In order to understand other societies, all college students should be required to spend at least one of their undergraduate years studying or working in a foreign country."

21. "Every member of society should be required before the age of twenty-one to perform at least one year of community or government service, such as in the Peace Corps, AmeriCorps, USA Freedom."

22. "Citizens of the United States should be allowed to designate how a portion of their tax dollars should be spent."

23. "The only important criterion by which to judge a prospective teacher is his or her ability to get along with the widest possible variety of students."

24. "Rather than relying on taxes, communities should be directly responsible for raising any required funds to pay for all extracurricular public school activities, including after-school sports."

25. "School activities not directly related to course work, such as assemblies and pep rallies, should not be part of the regular school day."

26. "School children should be required to participate in a variety of extracurricular activities so that they can become well-rounded individuals."

27. "All schools should have student dress codes."

28. "It is well within the capability of society to guarantee that all public schools are entirely drug-free."

29. "Opinion polls should not play an important role in the political decision-making process, because they indicate only what is popular, not what is the right or wrong position for our leaders to take."

30. "Childhood is a time for studying and playing, not working. Parents should not force their children to do chores."

31. "We are all influenced in lasting ways—whether positive or negative—by the particular kind of community in which we grow up."

32. "Television has had an overwhelmingly negative impact on society."

33. "Grading systems should be replaced with some other method of measuring students' performance because giving grades to students puts too much emphasis on competition and not enough emphasis on learning for its own sake."

34. "Political candidates should not be allowed to use popular actors in their advertising campaigns. Candidates too often win elections because they have actors for friends rather than because they are honestly qualified to represent the public interest."

35. "Television programming should be limited and strictly monitored for offensive content by a governmental supervising agency."

36. "Although we say we value freedom of expression, most of us are not really very tolerant of people who express unpopular ideas or act in nonconforming ways."

37. "Job satisfaction is more important in a career than a high salary and fringe benefits."

38. "College students should not have to decide on a major until after they have taken several classes and examined the various career fields the school has to offer."

39. "Schools should make a greater effort to teach ethics and moral values to students."

40. "Colleges and universities should ban alcoholic beverages on campus, even for students who are of legal drinking age."

41. "Teachers and parents should be more concerned than they are about the gradual trend among high school students toward part-time employment and away from participation in school sponsored extracurricular activities."

42. "It is the responsibility of the government rather than the individual citizen to find a solution to the growing problem of homelessness in the United States."

43. "Federal regulations should entirely ban all advertising of alcoholic beverages in all media, including television, radio, and magazines."

44. "Schools should put as much emphasis on such subjects as music, physical education, and visual arts as they do on traditional academic courses such as English or math."

45. "Materialism and consumerism have gone too far in American society. We often buy things that we do not need, and we even buy things that we do not especially enjoy."

46. "The failure of public schools is not ruining society. The failure of society has ruined the public schools."

47. "Honesty is universally valued, at least in principle. In practice, however, there are many cases in which governments, businesses, and individuals should not be completely honest."

48. "All employers should institute mandatory drug testing for employees."

49. "All high school students should be required to take some classes in vocational education."

50. "School administrators should regulate student speech in school-sponsored publications."

51. "Computer training should be mandatory for anyone planning to become a teacher, no matter what subject the person will teach."

52. "The world offers us abundant places to learn. We should not expect all of our most important lessons to be learned in the buildings we call schools."

53. "Many public buildings and transportation systems in the United States prohibit or restrict smoking. These restrictions are unfair, because they deny smokers their individual rights."

54. "Public schools should be required to offer socially oriented courses, such as sex education and personal finance, because such courses help students cope with problems in society."

55. "Our lives today are too complicated. We try to do too much and, as a result, do few things well."

56. "The United States government has become so corrupt that people who vote in national elections are wasting their time."

57. "The increasing involvement of businesses in the schools, ranging from the establishment of apprenticeships and grants to the donation of equipment and facilities, is a cause for concern because this involvement gives the businesses too much influence over school policy and curriculum."

58. "One of the biggest troubles with colleges is that there are too many distractions."

59. "The best way to improve the quality of public schools in the United States is to institute a national curriculum with national standards so that students, parents, and teachers all across the country know exactly what is expected at each grade level."

60. "Instead of making our lives simpler, computers cause more problems than they solve."

61. "Children learn responsibility and the value of work by being required to do household chores such as making beds, washing dishes, and taking care of pets."

62. "We should ban any speech—whether on the radio, in the movies, on television, or in public places such as college campuses—that encourages violent behavior."

63. "In today's society, the only real function of a college education is to prepare students for a career."

64. "Students suffer from participating in highly competitive extracurricular activities such as debate and sports."

65. "We live in a passive society in which few people take a stand or become involved in social issues."

66. "Students should be required to meet certain academic standards, such as passing all courses or maintaining a C average, in order to participate in extracurricular activities."

67. "Increasing reliance on the use of new technologies in the classroom has distracted from, rather than contributed to, the learning process."

68. "We find comfort among those who agree with us—growth among those who don't."

69. "Film and television studios in the United States nearly always want to dish up a sunny view of life because American audiences would rather not be reminded of problems in society."

70. "Competition is a destructive force in society."

71. "All 18–21 year olds should be required to perform government or community service."

Using Your 30 Minutes—Planning and Writing
Planning Your Essay—Take Five Minutes

After you have carefully read the topic, you may find it helpful to jot down notes about the points you plan to cover or even to make a brief outline. Space for notes is provided in the test booklet, or for those taking the computer-based version, on scratch paper; these notes will not be considered when your essay is evaluated. The space is for your own use, and the kind of outline you write or the kind of notes you make is up to you. You do not have time to make an elaborate outline, but it is important to take time to plan what you are going to write. Skilled writers typically plan first; even when time is an issue, as it is in timed writing tests, spending five minutes on some kind of outline or notes is often a good investment. A simple list of the major points (and supporting examples or reasons) you want to cover can be very helpful as you write your essay. Suppose that you are writing on Topic 71 from the list, "All 18–21 year olds should be required to perform government or community service," your notes might look like this:

I. Agree
1. Chief reason #1: gets them into the community-service habit for life
2. Chief reason #2: might help career choice; might help meet people in area of interest
3. Chief reason #3: the high numbers of volunteers would really help relieve poverty and other problems

II. Examples: Habitat for Humanity; friend who became literacy volunteer in college

III. Other reasons:
1. could get school or college credit for their work
2. could choose type of service based on college major

This kind of outline might be all you need to jog your memory as you write.

WRITING YOUR ESSAY

On the paper-based version of the test, some people try to write out their essays in the section for notes and then copy them over into the designated answer area. In these cases, the writers usually run out of time before they can complete the copying, and they are forced to turn in incomplete essays. It is usually best to use the answer area to write out your essay once, writing as legibly as you can. You might plan to give yourself five minutes near the end of the allotted time period for editing and proofreading your essay. Such editing might include checking that the essay is organized and that it proceeds from one point to another in a way that your readers can follow—that your sentences are clearly stated, and that your spelling and punctuation are correct.

The people who evaluate your essay need to be able to read your handwriting, but neatness, as such, does not count. It is expected that you might cross out words and make insertions. Also, it is not necessary for papers to be mechanically perfect: a misspelled word or a forgotten comma in an otherwise well-written paper will not lower your score. Still, careless mistakes can be corrected if you use your time well; you do not want to give your readers the impression that you do not understand the rules that govern written English when, in fact, you just have not taken the time to make corrections.

SAMPLE SCORED ESSAYS

Let's return to Topic 71 in the list of ETS topics, "All 18–21 year olds should be required to perform government or community service," and look at actual test-taker responses at each score level, from a high score of 6 to a low score of 1.

Response That Received a Score of 6

Essay	Explanation of Score
It has been suggested that to improve communities in the United States and to solve the problem of too few workers for government services such as the Peace Corps or the military, or community services such as enovironmental groups or schools, people aged 18 to 21 should be required to perform one year of service to these organizations. Many good things could come from an idea such as this. However, some unforseen problems may crush some of our freedoms in the process. Requiring one year of community or government service would transform organizations' needs from not having enough help to being flooded with workers. This could bring about huge changes in the community by giving organizations the man power to fulfill all of their charitable deeds. Society would benefit greatly from this program by having more role models in the schools, more people on clean-up crews for environmental groups, and extra help in hospitals so doctors	This paper begins by paraphrasing the prompt and concludes the introductory paragraph with a clear thesis that addresses both sides of the argument yet still clearly takes a position, that "some unforseen problems may crush some of our freedoms in the process." Subsequent paragraphs touch on the benefits of such mandatory service but also explain in even more detail the drawbacks of requiring such service. There are several well-chosen examples that provide details to support the writer's main idea

(Continued)

Essay	Explanation of Score

and nurses can take care of those who need it while the volunteers do the more menial work. The United States would not be the only country to gain from this program. The Peace Corps could send hundreds of people to countries in need around the globe to help the natives of those countries learn how to grow better crops and prevent disease.

Requiring people to perform a year of service could work as job training for some. They could find that they enjoy the particular organization they work for and could eventually become a permanent worker with a salary. It would also help students decide what school to attend or what major to pursue. They would have an extra year to "experience the real world" to see what they enjoy doing and to just have more time to think about the direction they would like to choose. I found that it would have been an advantage for me to postpone college for a while. After one year I changed my major and had to change my schedule for the semester as well as for the rest of my academic career.

However, a program such as this would require a large price: individual freedom. Some people between the ages of 18 and 21 are responsible enough to decide whether or not they want to help a community or government service, and they already have their academic or career future decided. A program that ignores liberty such as this is reminiscent of the Soviet Union forcing every male to serve a certain length of time in the military. Jobs are already scarce in some areas, and a one year, service requirement would delay entrance into the already overcrowded job market. The people involved in this program would also have their income postponed one year, setting back the purchase of everything in the economy from clothes to houses. It would also cause a break in between high school and college for some students, increasing the burden of changing to a new school and trying to continue learning from where it was interrupted the year before. The final mark against a one year service requirement would be the apathy of workers forced to help an organization when they do not want to be there. They would hinder rather than help the community by being lazy and incompetent on purpose so they could be relieved from their duties.

At first mention, requiring people aged 18 to 21 to give a year of service to the government or community sounds like a good idea. It could change our entire world for the better, but it could have some bad effects. People would have to give up some of their most cherished beliefs like freedom and liberty, and would have to postpone their life for a year, setting back their education, financial well-being, and career.

---

that such required service would provide "man power." These examples include allowing doctors and nurses to "take care of those who need it while the volunteers do the more menial work," having volunteers do work to benefit the environment, and helping countries beyond the United States through groups such as the Peace Corps. The following paragraph discusses the benefits accruing to those who provide such services, and the support is strengthened by concluding the paragraph with a brief personal experience.

In the next paragraph, however, the writer changes direction to build a stronger argument against mandatory service, which "would require a large price: individual freedom." Mandatory service for 18–21 year olds, asserts the writer, is "reminiscent of the Soviet Union forcing every male to serve a certain length of time in the military." The writer insightfully extends this discussion of personal rights by explaining several drawbacks to required service: loss of income, difficulties in returning to school after a one-year break and how "the apathy of workers forced to... be there" would "hinder rather than help the community."

Concluding the paper by once again recognizing that such service might be a good idea, the writer reiterates the drawbacks and continues the organizational scheme present in the balance of the paper, thus demonstrating a strong control of organization. The sentence variety and language facility clearly demonstrate control of the language, and the paper is generally free from errors, as is required to earn a score of 6.

Response That Received a Score of 5

Essay	Explanation of Score
I believe that enforcing a government or community service requirement for all individuals 18–21 years old would be very beneficial to the individual involved and to the community as a whole. Community service provides the opportunity for young people to see what the real would can be like for a select group of society, of which they may not be familiar. Take for example a rural or inner-city school, a child who has grown up and attended elementary and highschool at a school located in a growing and wealthy suburban community probably has no idea of the obstacles and daily problems that children face at an inner-city school. By performing community service at a school which is not as fortunate, students can learn about appreciation of their own life experiences and also learn about economic differences in society. What is readily available in one community may be almost scarce in another. Appreciation for education would also be gained by these individuals. Resources at an inner-city school may be out of date or limited in quantity where as resources at a suburban school are unlimited. Children may be exposed for the first time to a society that is not as fortunate as the one they are familiar with. Children of inner-city schools may dress differently act differently, or even speak differently. This can be an eye-opener to an 18–21 year old student. It is very easy for the youth to take advantage of what they have been given, almost as if they deserve it. By involving oneself in community service in an area which is unknown, one can learn and grow and appreciate what they have been provided. One can learn to be accepting and understanding of those who may not be as fortunate as them. There are numerouse opportunities for community service within a hospital. This is another place where I believe 18–21 year olds would benefit greatly by becoming involved in the community. A hospital is where sick people go and where often times you see unhappy people. People who are admitted to hospitals normally are there because they have a medical condition which requires help. The families of the sick are there for support and encouragement. The sick people in a hospital are real people, with real lives, with real families and jobs to attend to. Nobody asks to get sick, but one must deal with real life situations as they anse. Young people sometimes think that they are immune to everything negative or bad, or have the attitude that "it can't happen to me." Well by volunteering in a hospital, one can learn that bad illnesses or negative things can happen to anyone. A better appreciation of life and all that life has to offer would be gained. One would realize that anything negative can happen at anytime and would realize not to waste time or one's life away. Numerous opportunities and experiences are awating today's youth. I believe that by requiring some form of community service, such as the two ideas I described above, the youth would gain invaluable insight and increased appreciation of what is available to them.	The writer begins this paper with a clearly stated thesis: "I believe that enforcing a government or community service requirement for all individuals 18–21 years old would be very beneficial to the individual involved and to the community as a whole." The primary benefit, as the writer sees it, is "the opportunity for young people to see what the real world can be like for a select group of society..." The writer supports this idea in two well-developed paragraphs about service in different settings: schools in the inner city or rural areas and hospitals. Not only does the writer explain what young people may encounter in such settings, but each paragraph also concludes with a comment making a connection between the young adult's experiences in these settings and the far-reaching consequences of these experiences. Working in schools, for example, young people "can learn and grow and appreciate what they have been provided," and they can also "learn to be accepting and understanding of those who may not be as fortunate as them." Working in hospitals can help young people learn that "anything negative can happen at anytime and would realize not to waste time or one's life away." Despite the distracting lack of parallel structure present in this sentence, the writer demonstrates the ability to go beyond a simple listing of what happens in the schools or the hospitals by providing the connections for the reader among experiences, benefits, and ultimate lessons learned.

(Continued)

Essay	Explanation of Score
	The writer concludes the paper with a comment that pulls together the paragraphs and contributes to the clear control of organization: "I believe that by requiring some form of community service, such as the two ideas I described above, the youth would gain invaluable insight and increased appreciation of what is available to them." While the writer keeps the focus of this paper somewhat narrow—the benefits to the young adult of serving others less fortunate or less healthy rather than 18–21 year olds in general—the writer does so with details and reasons that are better than adequate. The paper's development and language facility, despite a few errors, place this paper in the 5 range.

Response That Received a Score of 4

Essay	Explanation of Score
Government or community service would be beneficial for those 18–21 year olds who have not made a decision as to what to do after graduating from high school. High school graduates and even young adults that didn't graduate from high school have very tough decisions to make. Many 18–21 year olds do not know what career paths to choose or even if they want to pursue careers. Government or community service would be a wonderful opportunity for three types of people. The Peace Corps would be a tremendous opportunity for those who may wish to travel abroad to see what opportunities are in other countries. Two of my friends were enrolled in Peace Corps programs; both requiring teaching in other countries. One friend lived on a island in Japan and taught Japanese students how to speak English. The other lived in Mexico and taught first grade at a private English school. Both were glad they had these opportunities and are now back in the States. One is a professor of a college in Boston and the other is working with learning disabled kids in the public school setting. In this case, my friends confirmed that they truly enjoy the teaching profession and their opportunities with the Peace Corps helped them to know that.	This writer does not initially take a strong position for or against mandatory service in general, although it is clear that the writer finds government or community service "beneficial for those 18–21 year olds who have not made a decision as to what to do after graduating from high school." As a result, this paper shows neither the clear competence in response to the task required for a 5 paper nor the high degree of competence required of a 6. The following paragraphs provide examples of three types of community service and how each opportunity for service will benefit the young adult. However, these

(Continued)

Essay	Explanation of Score
Many young adults also work for environmental organizations. Many take these jobs in the summer time and go door to door asking people to support certain environmental issues. This would be a good opportunity for a person to know whether or not they enjoy communicating with people on issues important to them. If this did become an interest, it could lead to careers in politics, sales, and telemarketing. Working for an environmental agency for the summer could be very beneficial in making a career choice for the future. Volunteering in public schools would also be beneficial for young adults. Young adults who volunteer in schools have a variety of choices; from being a reading buddy to helping teachers with class room projects. Volunteering can also be done at home or in the school. If you are someone who enjoys crafts or art, you could help teachers with new bulletin board ideas. If you enjoy reading to students, maybe being a reading buddy would be fun for you. Either way, volunteering in schools is a great opportunity to give people additional help and feel good about doing it. Young adults who are having difficulty making career choices should be encouraged to pursue government or community service. It will give them an idea of what opportunities are out there and best suited for them. I think this idea of government or community service is a great idea for certain types of people.	opportunities—working for the Peace Corps, for an environmental organization, and for public schools—all appear to be volunteer services. While the writer uses an effective combination of friends' experiences as well as speculation about the benefits of such activities to support the thesis, these examples provide no more than adequate evidence to support an argument for the benefits of mandatory government or community service. The three examples simply reiterate the same main idea: that the young adult will benefit from serving others. A stronger paper may have explained the connection between beneficial volunteer activities and what may be the writer's assumption—that what benefits volunteers, who choose their own activities, will also benefit young adults who are required to choose some sort of service. The connection, however, is not clear, and this lack of clarity contributes to the paper's score. Language facility is appropriate for a 4-level paper. The paper demonstrates some variety of sentence types, including some subordination, as well as some range of vocabulary, with control of grammar usage, and mechanics, in general. The few errors that appear are acceptable in a 4-level paper.

Response That Received a Score of 3

Essay	Explanation of Score
Requiring 18–21 year olds to participate in government or community service for one year is an excellent idea. However, this type of a program may not be suitable for all young adults, it may only be beneficial to those that plan to continue on to college or some sort of specialty school. This would provide these young adults with a broad experience of different cultures in the world, help to prepare them for making future career choices, and also help them to develop into better young adults by learning to relate to others. Today many students who have graduated from high school and are continuing on to college are not prepared to decide on a particular field of study. In many cases we as seventeen year olds do not have the experience or foresight to make a decision on our future. I did not make a final decision on my field of study until late into my sophomore year. As I look back on my college experience I feel I could have learned more by having that extra year and a half of time dedicated to my major field of study. The more an individual can experience in life, the better off he or she will be in the long run. Our life experiences can help us to see things from many perspectives instead of strictly one perspective and this makes life a little easier. With this type of experience in community or government service, the young adults will be more well rounded in their view of the world in which we live. I think this idea will help the world to be a better place as well as save much money on wasted college tuition.	This essay presents a strong opening by stating that mandatory community service "is an excellent idea," but qualifies that it may be best suited for those who "plan to continue on to college or some sort of specialty school." The essay defends that position by citing several benefits these young adults could gain, such as "a broad experience of different cultures in the world, help to prepare them for making future career choices, and also help them to develop into better young adults by learning to relate to others." The essay, however, does not follow through in developing these benefits in support of the argument. The second paragraph does pick up the issue of career choice, but rather than indicating how mandatory government or community service would help students who are not prepared to decide about a field of study the essay indicates that the writer would have preferred to use "that extra year and a half of time dedicated to my major field of study." The following paragraph provides vague references to the benefits of expanded experiences and developing multiple perspectives. These benefits are tenuously connected to government or community service, but there are no specific details or examples. The essay's position in support of the idea is reinforced in the last sentence, but again the idea is not developed. While there are a few errors in language use in this essay, it does not exhibit the types of language, grammar, and mechanics errors that are often found in a paper scored a 3. Its limited development and inadequate details keep it from receiving a higher score.

Response That Received a Score of 2

Essay	Explanation of Score
Developing a community outreach or government service for young adults for one year. I think is a great idea. If organized well it could only make the United States a better country. Young people could learn responsibility, accountability, and character. Since we live in a democracy something like this could not be enforced, but it could be highly encouraged. For example if from the time they start school until they finish they are taught the opportunities and benefits of doing an outreach project. The government could provide financial assistance for the young adults. They could provide an opportunity for the student to do one year of community service and in return one full year of school. This kind of community service would not have to mean leaving the country or state; although this could be an option. It could be done right in their own community. I also think that there could be options of the length of time the student would put in.	While this essay takes the position that "Developing a community outreach or government service ... is a great idea," and provides some rationale for that position, it does not directly address the issue of required service. What may initially appear to be support for the idea of required service is negated in the second paragraph, which indicates that required service cannot be enforced in a democracy. The balance of the essay provides some brief examples of how such a program might work, but it does not develop an argument to support whether or not a program requiring government or community service should be adopted. The failure of the essay to present relevant reasons and examples in support of an argument places it at the score of 2. Problems with organization, sentence structure, and language usage also weaken this essay and contribute to the 2 score.

Response That Received a Score of 1

Essay	Explanation of Score
The government already tell too much what should and shouldn't do. They shouldn't tell how much we have to help that something we should to decide on our own. What good if the government decide, we should be good people if we don't feel like it. They can't make laws tell people to be nice, that crazy. Weather or not, people are nice is gonna be there choice, not the Presidents or anyone else. If people want to do good thing they ought but not someone making them do it.	This essay does appear to take a stance against required community service, but approaches it only from the perspective that people need to be able to make that decision and government should not tell people what to do. This sentiment is repeated but never explained with any reasons or examples, leaving it without development. Throughout this very brief essay, there are serious and persistent problems with sentence structure, language usage, and mechanics that also support the score of 1.

NOW THAT YOU'VE PREPARED

Now that you have worked through the strategy for writing your essay and have seen examples of essays at different score points, you are ready to put your preparation to work.

PART III

Real PPSTs for Practice

Your Goals for This Part:

- Take real PPSTs under actual testing conditions.
- Read explanations for all test questions, focusing especially on those you answered incorrectly.
- Use your scores to help determine your test readiness.

CHAPTER 9

PPST™: Reading Test

Professional Assessments for Beginning Teachers ®

TEST NAME:
Pre-Professional Skills Test in Reading

Time—60 minutes

40 Questions

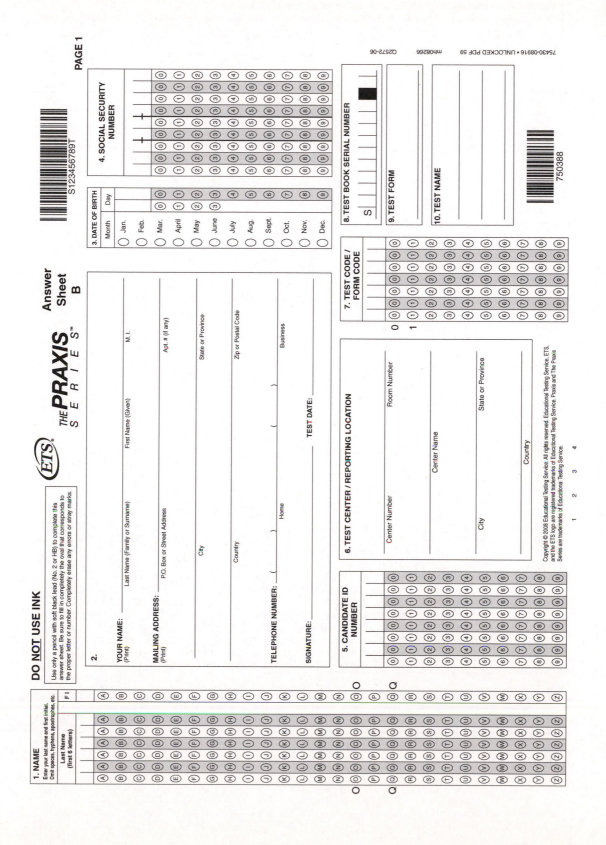

CERTIFICATION STATEMENT: (Please write the following statement below. DO NOT PRINT.)

"I hereby agree to the conditions set forth in the *Registration Bulletin* and certify that I am the person whose name and address appear on this answer sheet."

_____

_____

_____

SIGNATURE: _____ DATE: ___ / ___ / ___

Month   Day   Year

BE SURE EACH MARK IS DARK AND COMPLETELY FILLS THE INTENDED SPACE AS ILLUSTRATED HERE: ●

1 Ⓐ Ⓑ Ⓒ Ⓓ Ⓔ	41 Ⓐ Ⓑ Ⓒ Ⓓ Ⓔ	81 Ⓐ Ⓑ Ⓒ Ⓓ Ⓔ	121 Ⓐ Ⓑ Ⓒ Ⓓ Ⓔ
2 Ⓐ Ⓑ Ⓒ Ⓓ Ⓔ	42 Ⓐ Ⓑ Ⓒ Ⓓ Ⓔ	82 Ⓐ Ⓑ Ⓒ Ⓓ Ⓔ	122 Ⓐ Ⓑ Ⓒ Ⓓ Ⓔ
3 Ⓐ Ⓑ Ⓒ Ⓓ Ⓔ	43 Ⓐ Ⓑ Ⓒ Ⓓ Ⓔ	83 Ⓐ Ⓑ Ⓒ Ⓓ Ⓔ	123 Ⓐ Ⓑ Ⓒ Ⓓ Ⓔ
4 Ⓐ Ⓑ Ⓒ Ⓓ Ⓔ	44 Ⓐ Ⓑ Ⓒ Ⓓ Ⓔ	84 Ⓐ Ⓑ Ⓒ Ⓓ Ⓔ	124 Ⓐ Ⓑ Ⓒ Ⓓ Ⓔ
5 Ⓐ Ⓑ Ⓒ Ⓓ Ⓔ	45 Ⓐ Ⓑ Ⓒ Ⓓ Ⓔ	85 Ⓐ Ⓑ Ⓒ Ⓓ Ⓔ	125 Ⓐ Ⓑ Ⓒ Ⓓ Ⓔ
6 Ⓐ Ⓑ Ⓒ Ⓓ Ⓔ	46 Ⓐ Ⓑ Ⓒ Ⓓ Ⓔ	86 Ⓐ Ⓑ Ⓒ Ⓓ Ⓔ	126 Ⓐ Ⓑ Ⓒ Ⓓ Ⓔ
7 Ⓐ Ⓑ Ⓒ Ⓓ Ⓔ	47 Ⓐ Ⓑ Ⓒ Ⓓ Ⓔ	87 Ⓐ Ⓑ Ⓒ Ⓓ Ⓔ	127 Ⓐ Ⓑ Ⓒ Ⓓ Ⓔ
8 Ⓐ Ⓑ Ⓒ Ⓓ Ⓔ	48 Ⓐ Ⓑ Ⓒ Ⓓ Ⓔ	88 Ⓐ Ⓑ Ⓒ Ⓓ Ⓔ	128 Ⓐ Ⓑ Ⓒ Ⓓ Ⓔ
9 Ⓐ Ⓑ Ⓒ Ⓓ Ⓔ	49 Ⓐ Ⓑ Ⓒ Ⓓ Ⓔ	89 Ⓐ Ⓑ Ⓒ Ⓓ Ⓔ	129 Ⓐ Ⓑ Ⓒ Ⓓ Ⓔ
10 Ⓐ Ⓑ Ⓒ Ⓓ Ⓔ	50 Ⓐ Ⓑ Ⓒ Ⓓ Ⓔ	90 Ⓐ Ⓑ Ⓒ Ⓓ Ⓔ	130 Ⓐ Ⓑ Ⓒ Ⓓ Ⓔ
11 Ⓐ Ⓑ Ⓒ Ⓓ Ⓔ	51 Ⓐ Ⓑ Ⓒ Ⓓ Ⓔ	91 Ⓐ Ⓑ Ⓒ Ⓓ Ⓔ	131 Ⓐ Ⓑ Ⓒ Ⓓ Ⓔ
12 Ⓐ Ⓑ Ⓒ Ⓓ Ⓔ	52 Ⓐ Ⓑ Ⓒ Ⓓ Ⓔ	92 Ⓐ Ⓑ Ⓒ Ⓓ Ⓔ	132 Ⓐ Ⓑ Ⓒ Ⓓ Ⓔ
13 Ⓐ Ⓑ Ⓒ Ⓓ Ⓔ	53 Ⓐ Ⓑ Ⓒ Ⓓ Ⓔ	93 Ⓐ Ⓑ Ⓒ Ⓓ Ⓔ	133 Ⓐ Ⓑ Ⓒ Ⓓ Ⓔ
14 Ⓐ Ⓑ Ⓒ Ⓓ Ⓔ	54 Ⓐ Ⓑ Ⓒ Ⓓ Ⓔ	94 Ⓐ Ⓑ Ⓒ Ⓓ Ⓔ	134 Ⓐ Ⓑ Ⓒ Ⓓ Ⓔ
15 Ⓐ Ⓑ Ⓒ Ⓓ Ⓔ	55 Ⓐ Ⓑ Ⓒ Ⓓ Ⓔ	95 Ⓐ Ⓑ Ⓒ Ⓓ Ⓔ	135 Ⓐ Ⓑ Ⓒ Ⓓ Ⓔ
16 Ⓐ Ⓑ Ⓒ Ⓓ Ⓔ	56 Ⓐ Ⓑ Ⓒ Ⓓ Ⓔ	96 Ⓐ Ⓑ Ⓒ Ⓓ Ⓔ	136 Ⓐ Ⓑ Ⓒ Ⓓ Ⓔ
17 Ⓐ Ⓑ Ⓒ Ⓓ Ⓔ	57 Ⓐ Ⓑ Ⓒ Ⓓ Ⓔ	97 Ⓐ Ⓑ Ⓒ Ⓓ Ⓔ	137 Ⓐ Ⓑ Ⓒ Ⓓ Ⓔ
18 Ⓐ Ⓑ Ⓒ Ⓓ Ⓔ	58 Ⓐ Ⓑ Ⓒ Ⓓ Ⓔ	98 Ⓐ Ⓑ Ⓒ Ⓓ Ⓔ	138 Ⓐ Ⓑ Ⓒ Ⓓ Ⓔ
19 Ⓐ Ⓑ Ⓒ Ⓓ Ⓔ	59 Ⓐ Ⓑ Ⓒ Ⓓ Ⓔ	99 Ⓐ Ⓑ Ⓒ Ⓓ Ⓔ	139 Ⓐ Ⓑ Ⓒ Ⓓ Ⓔ
20 Ⓐ Ⓑ Ⓒ Ⓓ Ⓔ	60 Ⓐ Ⓑ Ⓒ Ⓓ Ⓔ	100 Ⓐ Ⓑ Ⓒ Ⓓ Ⓔ	140 Ⓐ Ⓑ Ⓒ Ⓓ Ⓔ
21 Ⓐ Ⓑ Ⓒ Ⓓ Ⓔ	61 Ⓐ Ⓑ Ⓒ Ⓓ Ⓔ	101 Ⓐ Ⓑ Ⓒ Ⓓ Ⓔ	141 Ⓐ Ⓑ Ⓒ Ⓓ Ⓔ
22 Ⓐ Ⓑ Ⓒ Ⓓ Ⓔ	62 Ⓐ Ⓑ Ⓒ Ⓓ Ⓔ	102 Ⓐ Ⓑ Ⓒ Ⓓ Ⓔ	142 Ⓐ Ⓑ Ⓒ Ⓓ Ⓔ
23 Ⓐ Ⓑ Ⓒ Ⓓ Ⓔ	63 Ⓐ Ⓑ Ⓒ Ⓓ Ⓔ	103 Ⓐ Ⓑ Ⓒ Ⓓ Ⓔ	143 Ⓐ Ⓑ Ⓒ Ⓓ Ⓔ
24 Ⓐ Ⓑ Ⓒ Ⓓ Ⓔ	64 Ⓐ Ⓑ Ⓒ Ⓓ Ⓔ	104 Ⓐ Ⓑ Ⓒ Ⓓ Ⓔ	144 Ⓐ Ⓑ Ⓒ Ⓓ Ⓔ
25 Ⓐ Ⓑ Ⓒ Ⓓ Ⓔ	65 Ⓐ Ⓑ Ⓒ Ⓓ Ⓔ	105 Ⓐ Ⓑ Ⓒ Ⓓ Ⓔ	145 Ⓐ Ⓑ Ⓒ Ⓓ Ⓔ
26 Ⓐ Ⓑ Ⓒ Ⓓ Ⓔ	66 Ⓐ Ⓑ Ⓒ Ⓓ Ⓔ	106 Ⓐ Ⓑ Ⓒ Ⓓ Ⓔ	146 Ⓐ Ⓑ Ⓒ Ⓓ Ⓔ
27 Ⓐ Ⓑ Ⓒ Ⓓ Ⓔ	67 Ⓐ Ⓑ Ⓒ Ⓓ Ⓔ	107 Ⓐ Ⓑ Ⓒ Ⓓ Ⓔ	147 Ⓐ Ⓑ Ⓒ Ⓓ Ⓔ
28 Ⓐ Ⓑ Ⓒ Ⓓ Ⓔ	68 Ⓐ Ⓑ Ⓒ Ⓓ Ⓔ	108 Ⓐ Ⓑ Ⓒ Ⓓ Ⓔ	148 Ⓐ Ⓑ Ⓒ Ⓓ Ⓔ
29 Ⓐ Ⓑ Ⓒ Ⓓ Ⓔ	69 Ⓐ Ⓑ Ⓒ Ⓓ Ⓔ	109 Ⓐ Ⓑ Ⓒ Ⓓ Ⓔ	149 Ⓐ Ⓑ Ⓒ Ⓓ Ⓔ
30 Ⓐ Ⓑ Ⓒ Ⓓ Ⓔ	70 Ⓐ Ⓑ Ⓒ Ⓓ Ⓔ	110 Ⓐ Ⓑ Ⓒ Ⓓ Ⓔ	150 Ⓐ Ⓑ Ⓒ Ⓓ Ⓔ
31 Ⓐ Ⓑ Ⓒ Ⓓ Ⓔ	71 Ⓐ Ⓑ Ⓒ Ⓓ Ⓔ	111 Ⓐ Ⓑ Ⓒ Ⓓ Ⓔ	151 Ⓐ Ⓑ Ⓒ Ⓓ Ⓔ
32 Ⓐ Ⓑ Ⓒ Ⓓ Ⓔ	72 Ⓐ Ⓑ Ⓒ Ⓓ Ⓔ	112 Ⓐ Ⓑ Ⓒ Ⓓ Ⓔ	152 Ⓐ Ⓑ Ⓒ Ⓓ Ⓔ
33 Ⓐ Ⓑ Ⓒ Ⓓ Ⓔ	73 Ⓐ Ⓑ Ⓒ Ⓓ Ⓔ	113 Ⓐ Ⓑ Ⓒ Ⓓ Ⓔ	153 Ⓐ Ⓑ Ⓒ Ⓓ Ⓔ
34 Ⓐ Ⓑ Ⓒ Ⓓ Ⓔ	74 Ⓐ Ⓑ Ⓒ Ⓓ Ⓔ	114 Ⓐ Ⓑ Ⓒ Ⓓ Ⓔ	154 Ⓐ Ⓑ Ⓒ Ⓓ Ⓔ
35 Ⓐ Ⓑ Ⓒ Ⓓ Ⓔ	75 Ⓐ Ⓑ Ⓒ Ⓓ Ⓔ	115 Ⓐ Ⓑ Ⓒ Ⓓ Ⓔ	155 Ⓐ Ⓑ Ⓒ Ⓓ Ⓔ
36 Ⓐ Ⓑ Ⓒ Ⓓ Ⓔ	76 Ⓐ Ⓑ Ⓒ Ⓓ Ⓔ	116 Ⓐ Ⓑ Ⓒ Ⓓ Ⓔ	156 Ⓐ Ⓑ Ⓒ Ⓓ Ⓔ
37 Ⓐ Ⓑ Ⓒ Ⓓ Ⓔ	77 Ⓐ Ⓑ Ⓒ Ⓓ Ⓔ	117 Ⓐ Ⓑ Ⓒ Ⓓ Ⓔ	157 Ⓐ Ⓑ Ⓒ Ⓓ Ⓔ
38 Ⓐ Ⓑ Ⓒ Ⓓ Ⓔ	78 Ⓐ Ⓑ Ⓒ Ⓓ Ⓔ	118 Ⓐ Ⓑ Ⓒ Ⓓ Ⓔ	158 Ⓐ Ⓑ Ⓒ Ⓓ Ⓔ
39 Ⓐ Ⓑ Ⓒ Ⓓ Ⓔ	79 Ⓐ Ⓑ Ⓒ Ⓓ Ⓔ	119 Ⓐ Ⓑ Ⓒ Ⓓ Ⓔ	159 Ⓐ Ⓑ Ⓒ Ⓓ Ⓔ
40 Ⓐ Ⓑ Ⓒ Ⓓ Ⓔ	80 Ⓐ Ⓑ Ⓒ Ⓓ Ⓔ	120 Ⓐ Ⓑ Ⓒ Ⓓ Ⓔ	160 Ⓐ Ⓑ Ⓒ Ⓓ Ⓔ

FOR ETS USE ONLY	R1	R2	R3	R4	R5	R6	R7	R8	TR	CS

READING
Time—60 minutes
40 Questions

Directions: Each statement or passage in this test is followed by a question or questions based on its content. After reading a statement or passage, choose the best answer to each question from among the five choices given. Answer all questions following a statement or passage on the basis of what is <u>stated</u> or <u>implied</u> in that statement or passage; you are not expected to have any previous knowledge of the topics treated in the statements and passages.

Be sure to mark all your answers on your answer sheet and completely fill in the lettered space with a heavy, dark mark so that you cannot see the letter.

Remember, try to answer every question.

1. In *A Vindication of the Rights of Woman* (1792), British philosopher Mary Wollstonecraft argued that women should have access to the same educational and professional opportunities as men, and legal equality as well. She was not the first writer to be angered by the stifling of female potential, but she was the first to turn her frustration into a critique of polite society. She prosecuted its hypocrisies with high rhetoric, liberating sarcasm, and a firm late-eighteenth-century respect for reason as the anchor of individual rights.

   According to the passage, Mary Wollstonecraft differed from others who were angered by the oppression of women in that she was the first to

   (A) present her arguments for women's rights in writing
   (B) focus on educational and professional opportunities for women
   (C) express concern about the stifling of female potential
   (D) present a written critique of polite society
   (E) rely on reason in making her arguments for women's rights

2. In the United States, surfing became popular because of movies. Although *he'e nalu* (wave sliding) existed in Hawaii before the 1500s, surfing was first brought to the public's attention by 1920s screen idols. Teen movies and music gave the sport another boost in the 1960s. Today the surfing world is hoping another entertainment medium, television, will again increase the sport's popularity so that televised surfing meets can be staged in remote places like Indonesia, where surfing conditions are ideal.

The author would probably agree with which of the following statements about surfing?

(A) The entertainment industry has been crucial to the popularity of surfing in the United States.
(B) Surfing was not recognized as a true sport until it was popularized in the 1920s by movie idols.
(C) Surfing is more accurately defined as a form of entertainment than as a competitive athletic sport.
(D) Surfing had a profound effect on teen movies and music in the 1960s.
(E) It is unlikely that televised surfing will generate the same interest in surfing that surf movies and music once did.

3. The 550-mile highway between Daly Waters and Alice Springs boasts just one small town, an old gold-mining community called Tennant Creek, comprising three or four clustered habitations that made Daly Waters look cosmopolitan, and a roadhouse perhaps once every eighty miles. And that was it. I had never been out in such a boundless blank.

The passage suggests that the author is most impressed by which aspect of the drive between Daly Waters and Alice Springs?

(A) Its apparent danger
(B) Its rugged terrain
(C) Its sense of desolation
(D) Its tranquil setting
(E) Its winding highways

Questions 4–5

After landing in Mexico in 1519, the Spanish explorer Hernando Cortez depended on an Aztec woman named Malinche to act as his interpreter and to guide him from the coast to Tenochtitlán, the inland capital of the
Line
Aztec empire. Because of her knowledge of the various Mexican cultures
5
and languages, however, her role surpassed that of mere interpreter or guide: she became his chief negotiator and strategist, welding together a coalition of dissatisfied Indian nations that, along with Cortez' troops, defeated the emperor Montezuma and destroyed the Aztec empire.

4. The primary purpose of the passage is to

   (A) contrast the roles of Cortez and Malinche in the destruction of the Aztec empire
   (B) explain the historical importance of Malinche
   (C) describe the defeat of Montezuma
   (D) identify the reasons for dissatisfaction among the Indian nations in Mexico circa 1519
   (E) discuss Malinche's reasons for helping Cortez to defeat Montezuma

5. According to the passage, which of the following contributed to Malinche's role in the defeat of Montezuma?

   (A) Her knowledge of Spanish culture
   (B) Her connections with influential people in various Indian nations
   (C) Her knowledge of military strategy
   (D) Her resistance to the coalition of Indian nations
   (E) Her ability to speak many Mexican languages

Questions 6–9

Not too long ago, dinosaurs were believed to have been sluggish reptilian creatures. Their relationship to creatures living today was only vaguely understood, though crocodiles and lizards provided some inspiration for ideas about what dinosaurs must have been like. Indeed, many science-fiction filmmakers recruited lizards and attached horns or spikes to them when they wanted live-action dinosaurs. They then filmed the embellished lizards attacking other lizards or even cavemen. Even as a kid I knew the juxtaposition of these faux dinosaurs with modern humans was absurd—modern humans after all appeared on Earth more than 60 million years after the dinosaurs disappeared. In the late 1950s, though, neither I nor paleontological experts knew many things that we know today. For one thing, we did not know that some dinosaurs survived the massive extinction event at the end of the Cretaceous period, the last chapter in the age of the dinosaurs. The survivors were of course birds. We have strong evidence that birds likely evolved from a subgroup of dinosaurs, including active, predatory, and probably very intelligent forms like *Tyrannosaurus* and *Velociraptor*. Today a few scientists still question this connection between birds and dinosaurs, but they do so in denial of a mass of accumulating paleontological data.

6. The primary purpose of the passage is to

   (A) provide evidence that birds evolved from a subgroup of dinosaurs
   (B) describe the dinosaurs that flourished during the Cretaceous period
   (C) suggest that a great variety of dinosaur species once lived on Earth
   (D) discuss the appeal of movies in the 1950s that featured dinosaurs
   (E) give an example of how scientific understanding of dinosaurs has changed since the 1950s

7. It can be inferred from the passage that the author as a "kid" (line 7) was

   (A) impressionable
   (B) perceptive
   (C) adventurous
   (D) combative
   (E) squeamish

8. According to the passage, which of the following was true of pale-ontologists in the 1950s?

    (A) They possessed a clear understanding of the relationship between dinosaurs and modern-day creatures.

    (B) They were not in agreement about what caused the extinctions of the Cretaceous period.

    (C) They refuted the notion that dinosaurs were sluggish reptilian creatures.

    (D) They were unaware of the existence of the *Tyrannosaurus* and *Velociraptor*.

    (E) They were unaware that possible descendents of some dinosaurs survived the extinctions of the Cretaceous period.

9. The author's comment in the last sentence of the passage suggests that the "scientists" (line 17) are

    (A) fanatical

    (B) egotistical

    (C) misguided

    (D) pessimistic

    (E) ill-prepared

Questions 10–11

In the English speaking world, it is a mistake to promote the learning of a foreign language primarily on the basis of that language's usefulness. Computers can translate material at the stroke of a key, even if the translation is not perfectly idiomatic; research data originally published in a foreign language are available almost instantly in English; many people in other countries speak English. The main reasons for studying a foreign language are not practical ones. Rather, the study of language is a humanistic enterprise, a way to deepen our understanding of what it means to be human.

Line

5

10. The primary purpose of the passage is to

    (A) suggest that there are many more ways to teach languages than are commonly used

    (B) argue that people should learn languages for reasons other than utilitarian ones

    (C) explain why English has become one of the most widely spoken languages on Earth

    (D) express regret that scientists have created computers that can translate human languages

    (E) describe the different kinds of careers open to people who master languages

11. The sentence in lines 3–6 ("Computers can translate . . . countries speak English") lists

    (A) suggestions for new and interesting methods of learning a foreign language

    (B) activities that one might pursue after having mastered a foreign language

    (C) difficulties experienced by many people who attempt to learn a foreign language

    (D) objections to the view that learning a foreign language is a waste of time for most people

    (E) reasons that undermine a particular rationale for learning a foreign language

12. Journalism is like gardening. Its most successful practitioners are those best able to detect nuances, to discern trends from skimpy evidence. The good gardener is the one who can tell from a single sniff of the air that the weather is right for transplanting cauliflowers, or that this is the exact time to boost tomatoes with a drop of water or a spot of fertilizer.

The passage suggests that an important quality shared by good journalists and good gardeners is the ability to

(A) focus clearly on a single objective
(B) think creatively in pursuit of a goal
(C) perceive subtle indicators
(D) plan for any eventuality
(E) work hard day after day

13. Thomas Edison, an inventor with over 1,000 patents, often worked closely with artists in various fields. One of his objects in inventing the first recording machine, or phonograph, was to hand down to posterity the voices of great singers and instrumentalists, and his improvements in electric lighting were of immense help to dramatists.

What does the passage suggest about Thomas Edison?

(A) He wanted to make a positive contribution to furthering the arts.
(B) He might have been a musician or an actor if he had not become an inventor.
(C) He insisted that his collaborators receive credit for some of his patents.
(D) As an inventor, he was more widely known for his artistic innovations than for his scientific ones.
(E) As an amateur musician, he wanted others to experience music firsthand.

14. Although Sir Arthur Conan Doyle, the creator of Sherlock Holmes, ranks among the most famous of all Victorian writers, his life is shrouded in as much mystery as one of his tales. Countless biographers have simply rehearsed what little is known about Doyle's life. Why has this been the case? Largely because no researchers have ever had unhampered access to Doyle's personal papers.

In line 4 of the passage, the word "rehearsed" most nearly means

(A) practiced
(B) repeated
(C) imitated
(D) criticized
(E) perfected

15. The United States entered the twentieth century with a youthful confidence about its place in the world. The growth of big cities, spurred by the shift of populations from rural areas to urban centers and from Europe to the United States, along with the advent of modern industry and transportation, served to transform the country into a complex, diverse, and cosmopolitan nation.

The passage mentions each of the following as serving to transform the United States into a diverse and cosmopolitan nation EXCEPT

(A) urban growth
(B) population shifts
(C) industrial modernization
(D) expansion of education
(E) improvements in transportation

Questions 16–17

Today's automobiles contain between 20 and 80 microprocessors which control everything from the running of the engine to the locking of doors. Over the next several years, the numbers of microprocessors in cars are expected to grow dramatically. Interestingly, these microprocessors are rarely self-contained; instead, almost all interact with other microprocessors in the automobile through a network.

Line
5

In fact, there are generally two distinct networks in today's automobiles. The first is the network of safety-critical components, such as those that control the braking system. The second network controls nonsafety-critical functions, such as the entertainment system. These two networks are completely separate, ensuring that the safety-critical functions cannot be compromised by the nonessential functions.

10

16. The passage suggests that "two distinct networks" (line 7), rather than one, exist because

(A) it is difficult to build one large microprocessor network
(B) having only one network might put essential functions at risk
(C) it is less expensive to repair two networks than one large network
(D) having only one network would reduce drivers' entertainment experience
(E) it is difficult to get safety-critical components to interact with nonessential components

17. The second paragraph can best be described as

(A) highlighting an unforeseen problem
(B) defining a technical term
(C) offering an explanation
(D) critiquing a decision
(E) evaluating the feasibility of a suggestion

Questions 18–21

There is a wealth of scholarship on the economic value of unpaid housework. Glenna Matthews has argued that as domesticity has diminished in social importance since the mid-nineteenth century, women's
Line
5 household skills have lost cultural currency. I seek to restore value and depth to a discounted form of "women's work" by examining home sewing during the early decades of the twentieth century—a time when social and economic changes rendered it less central to many women's lives. Clothing a family took considerable time, effort, and skill. Unlike cooking and cleaning, its tangible results were long lasting
10 and traveled outside the home. Dress was vital to presenting an image of upward mobility or of preserving class status. Some women earned cash making clothing for others, but most did not. However, as a way to save money, home dressmaking played a major economic role in a household. Sewing skills gave women the ability to avoid and reduce
15 cash expenditures whether or not they earned money themselves.

But if sewing was work, it was also an escape from drudgery and a tool for self-definition. Home sewing often moved beyond its functional role as housework to become a way to express personal tastes and challenge assumptions about femininity, class, and race. The ability to dress
20 well on a budget, reinterpret styles according to personal taste, or test the boundaries of modesty was a form of power.

18. The primary purpose of the passage is to

   (A) critique the scholarship of a particular author
   (B) point out the value of a particular form of housework
   (C) examine the history of the fashion design industry
   (D) analyze the motivations for women's working outside the home
   (E) discuss the various household responsibilities of women

19. Information in the passage suggests that the author would be most likely to agree with which of the following statements about sewing that occurred at home in the early decades of the twentieth century?

   (A) It was one of the more taxing of women's chores.
   (B) It was one of the more lucrative ways for women to earn an income.
   (C) It was done primarily as a way to counter the boredom of other forms of housework.
   (D) It had a greater significance than might initially be thought.
   (E) It was done solely for practical, rather than creative, purposes.

20. The passage indicates which of the following about women who sewed at home in the early decades of the twentieth century?

    (A) They had little interest in influencing fashion.
    (B) They were well compensated for their sewing skills.
    (C) They preferred sewing to jobs outside the home.
    (D) They sewed primarily out of a desire to earn an income.
    (E) They helped their households save money.

21. In line 18, "express" most nearly means

    (A) exude
    (B) convey
    (C) broach
    (D) vent
    (E) extract

Questions 22–23

From the 1970s to the 1990s, there were no fundamental changes in the relationship between television viewer demographics (such as age and gender) and amounts of viewing time; there was, however, an
Line overall increase in television viewing among United States adults. This
5 should come as no surprise. First, the cost of a television set continued to drop despite inflation; at the same time, the minimum wage continued to increase. Second, the development of cable and satellite transmission of television programs not only made television more accessible but also improved its reception. Third, new technologies such as the videocas-
10 sette recorder and the remote control device made television viewing more convenient.

22. Which of the following best describes the organization of the passage?

    (A) A phenomenon is described and then factors contributing to it are presented.

    (B) A theory is advanced and then arguments in its favor are put forth.

    (C) A problem is introduced and then possible solutions to it are provided.

    (D) A research study is summarized and then its conclusion is stated.

    (E) A claim is presented and then evidence undermining it is offered.

23. Which of the following statements, if true, would most clearly weaken the importance of the "new technologies" (line 9) to the author's argument?

    (A) They were most popular among younger television viewers.

    (B) They were used to watch rented movies as well as taped television shows.

    (C) They often were purchased at the same time as new television sets were purchased.

    (D) They tended to be used more often by men than by women.

    (E) They were not affordable to the majority of television viewers.

24. Once a standing ovation achieves a certain critical mass, anyone who stays seated feels like a spoilsport. One's dissent becomes painfully obvious in a way it never does when one is simply not clapping as loudly as everyone else. To keep one's seat seems to convey a distinctly negative judgment rather than a merely less positive one. However loudly one may clap, cheer, or whistle, one's very failure to stand acts as the equivalent of a boo.

The passage is primarily concerned with

(A) discussing how an audience member who remains seated during a standing ovation may be perceived
(B) recounting an incident that changed the author's mind about the advisability of participating in a standing ovation
(C) arguing that most performances do not merit the applause they receive
(D) describing the effect of a standing ovation on performers onstage
(E) denouncing the hypocrisy of most people who participate in standing ovations

25. Robert Louis Stevenson (1850–1894) was a ham-handed playwright, a less than minor poet, a fitful journalist, and the author of several awful novels. What might have been his crowning masterpiece was never finished: only a scrap of his most ambitious project was ever published, and he died young. Yet Stevenson also wrote a timeless classic of young-adult fiction (*Treasure Island*), two other novels of the first rank, a classic children's book of poems, and an exceptional travel book.

The passage best supports which of the following conclusions?

(A) Stevenson had little interest in commercial literary success.
(B) Stevenson did not combine his talent with a sufficient degree of work.
(C) Stevenson remains greatly misunderstood.
(D) The quality of Stevenson's writing varied tremendously.
(E) Critics' estimation of Stevenson's work has changed dramatically.

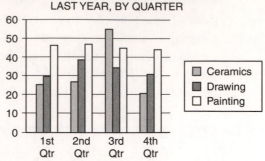

JUNIORS AND SENIORS ENROLLED IN THE
ART COURSES AT WARNER HIGH SCHOOL
LAST YEAR, BY QUARTER

26. Assuming that only juniors and seniors can enroll in art courses, that no student can enroll in the same art course twice, and that each art course lasts one quarter of the school year, each of the following can be determined from the graph above EXCEPT the art course

(A) that had the greatest number of students enrolled in the third quarter
(B) for which the greatest number of students enrolled last year
(C) for which the fewest number of students enrolled last year
(D) for which the greatest number of juniors enrolled last year
(E) that experienced the greatest decrease in the number of students enrolled from the third to the fourth quarter

27. Archeologists have found at Paleo-Eskimo sites many carvings of bears that are very realistic, complete with claws and bared teeth. However, at Neo-Eskimo sites, they have found not carvings of bears, but the teeth of bears, extracted and drilled to be worn as personal decoration. One possible conclusion is that the Paleo-Eskimos considered the bear a threat whereas the Neo-Eskimos considered it a trophy.

The author mentions the bear teeth found at Neo-Eskimo sites most likely in order to

(A) indicate the prevalence of bears in the Neo-Eskimo period
(B) demonstrate that the Neo-Eskimos used animal teeth as tools
(C) provide reasoning for the opinion that Neo-Eskimos saw the bear as a trophy
(D) suggest that Neo-Eskimos were less skilled at bear hunting than were Paleo-Eskimos
(E) emphasize the danger posed by bears to Neo-Eskimos

Questions 28–32

Before 1957 much of the creative energy of science fiction writers went into visions of space and space travel. A wave of euphoria broke over the science fiction community late that year when the Russians launched *Line* Sputnik, the first artificial satellite, into space. Finally, it's real! Now every-
5 one will know that we were right all along. We were the ones who had faith, and now the world will give us the respect and attention we deserve.

Within a few weeks, the horrible truths began to pile up. The world did not care that science fiction writers and readers had been right. Aside from a few newspaper articles about science fiction becoming science
10 fact, no one paid any more attention to science fiction than they ever had. In fact, it soon became clear that fewer and fewer people were buying and reading science fiction books and magazines.

As the Russian and American space programs gathered steam in the 1950s and 1960s, science fiction enthusiasts found it increasingly diffi-
15 cult to retain the romance of space travel when faced with the boring facts of the real thing. The classic space-travel stories of science fiction were now no better than fantasies and lacked interest for readers who had embraced the notion that science fiction was about "predicting the future." Yet as these older fans turned away, a new crop emerged who
20 embraced the fantastic, rather than the predictive, aspect of science fiction. Within a decade, science fiction was more popular than it had ever been, and its sway continues to expand.

28. The primary purpose of the passage is to

   (A) present the views of one science fiction author on the impor-
       tance of Sputnik
   (B) explore how science fiction authors incorporated Sputnik into
       their work
   (C) outline the effects of Sputnik on Russian and American space
       programs
   (D) characterize the response of the American public to the Sputnik
       launch
   (E) describe the effects of the Sputnik launch on the science fiction
       community

29. The perspective expressed in lines 4–6 ("Finally . . . we deserve")
    is that of

    (A) would-be astronauts
    (B) science fiction enthusiasts
    (C) newspaper columnists writing about Sputnik
    (D) Russian scientists who launched Sputnik
    (E) politicians who supported the American space program

30. The phrase "horrible truths" (line 7) most likely refers to

    (A) the public's lack of interest in the predictions of science fiction
    (B) the realization that America was losing the space race
    (C) Americans' rapidly declining interest in space travel
    (D) revelations about the dangers of traveling to outer space
    (E) information detailing Russian scientific superiority

31. The third paragraph suggests which of the following about "older
    fans" (line 19)?

    (A) They were far more fascinated by actual space travel than by
        fiction about space travel.
    (B) They became frustrated by America's slow advancements in
        space travel.
    (C) They became disillusioned with science fiction as a genre.
    (D) They became dismayed by the ever-increasing number of
        science fiction fans.
    (E) They were irritated by the response of science fiction authors
        to Sputnik.

32. Lines 19–22 ("Yet . . . expand") serve primarily to

    (A) support a criticism
    (B) summarize a position
    (C) elaborate on an example
    (D) describe a shifting trend
    (E) predict a likely outcome

Questions 33–36

    In 1916 a Black writer named Freeman Henry Morris Murray
published *Emancipation and the Freed in American Sculpture*, a work
full of passion, informed by an intelligence that took images seriously.
Line Writing in a period when the cultural elite insisted on the study of "art
5 for art's sake," Murray maintained that "the most important feature
of art is *what* is portrayed." Indeed, the subtitle of his text, "A Study
in Interpretation," hints at his aim to reawaken numbed perception to

the immediacy of art's effects in the real world. Murray declared that "when we look at a work of art, especially when 'we' look at one in which Black Folk appear—or do not appear when they should—we should ask: What does it mean? . . . What impression is it likely to make on those who view it?"

10

Murray took on the professional critics and art historians, challenging their elitist assumptions with the studied sobriety of someone coming to the sudden realization of the links between cultural practice and political power. He sought to establish the criteria for "reading" sculptural "text," asserting that, in the nineteenth century, art generally had been used as a kind of propaganda.

15

33. The passage is primarily concerned with

(A) contrasting Murray's views of art with the views of established critics and art historians
(B) discussing a variety of criticisms of Murray's views regarding art
(C) assessing the impact of Murray's views on the art world
(D) comparing Murray's views regarding art to those of more modern thinkers
(E) correcting a misconception about Murray's views regarding art

34. The passage suggests that which of the following is a view held by Murray?

(A) Artistic expression should not be limited by social concerns.
(B) Sculptural art can be a reflection of social and political attitudes.
(C) Most critics are not qualified to critique sculptural art.
(D) Sculptors have a greater impact on society than do other artists.
(E) Few sculptors understand the power of the sculptural art they produce.

35. In lines 6–7, the author refers to Murray's choice of subtitle primarily to

(A) point out the similarities between Murray's views of art and those of Murray's contemporaries
(B) emphasize the ultimate goal that Murray had in writing about art
(C) explain why Murray showed such great concern for sculpture in particular
(D) illustrate that Murray's views of the arts were met with enthusiasm
(E) highlight that Murray wished to establish himself as a major nineteenth-century art critic

36. The passage suggests that Murray would have been most likely to ask which of the following questions about a sculpture that portrays a Black person?

(A) What is the background of the person portrayed in the sculpture?
(B) What are the artistic principles that were most important to the sculptor?
(C) What are the views of art critics regarding the artistic merits of the sculpture?
(D) What motivated the person to model for the sculpture?
(E) What message does the sculpture send about the person depicted?

37. The reputation of Marcus Tullius Cicero (106–43 B.C.) has varied more than that of any other figure in ancient history. He has often been denounced as an opportunist or a weakling. Without Cicero's writings, however, we would hear no unguarded voice from the great days of Rome. Nor would the Renaissance have had access to the Greek culture of which he was an admirer and popularizer.

The author suggests that Cicero's writings stand apart from other surviving ancient Roman writings because of their

(A) candor
(B) precision
(C) beauty
(D) unusual style
(E) humor

38. The first silent-film star was Florence Lawrence, who emerged as a star around 1908. When she first appeared in movies for the film-making company Biograph, she was not identified by name, and when audiences began asking, "Who is that girl?" Biograph was unwilling to answer. Biograph's policy was not to allow players to become known, since revealing their identity might give actors bargaining power in salary negotiations. Undeterred, the public called Lawrence "the Biograph girl," bestowing on her a popularity that catapulted her into stardom.

According to the passage, Biograph's policy regarding actors' identities was

(A) calculated to create publicity that would attract viewers
(B) intended to limit the amount of power actors could wield
(C) embraced by all the successful filmmaking companies
(D) designed to protect the privacy of the actors
(E) based on established theatrical precedents

39. In the past two decades, there has been a boom in rail construction in the United States. However, unless such construction is coordinated with existing residential and commercial development, as well as with existing road development, the new railway systems are likely to be underutilized. For example, rail lines that pass through residential areas already designed for high automobile use are unlikely to attract many rail transit riders.

Which of the following, if true, would most clearly weaken the author's argument about railway use?

(A) Many people find the idea of rail transit appealing but are leery of being tied to a rail schedule.

(B) Many people who currently live in neighborhoods specifically designed for high automobile use are opposed to rail construction in their area.

(C) Many people who currently use automobiles on a regular basis do so only because no other mode of transportation is available to them.

(D) The fact that certain neighborhoods have been specifically designed for high automobile use is not widely known.

(E) The boom in rail construction in the last two decades in the United States is not unprecedented.

40. Spanish painter Francisco Goya (1746–1828) lived at a time when the role of women in urban and affluent society began to change. Many women emerged from their homes to gather in squares and promenades, sometimes joining organizations that cared for the sick and disadvantaged. Influential women such as the Duchess of Alba hosted salons where both men and women could discuss literature. While Goya portrayed the more liberated women of his time, he was more ironic commentator than feminist.

The passage suggests which of the following about Goya's attitude toward the liberated women of his time?

(A) He encouraged the women's actions and used his art to foster their goals.

(B) He was more supportive of the women's charitable activities than of their efforts in the arts.

(C) He did not understand fully the purpose of the organizations and salons that the women favored.

(D) He depicted liberated women in his art but was not entirely sympathetic to the feminist cause.

(E) He was generally pleased that women were interested in literature and used his art to show their interest.

Reading Test

Answers and Explanations

1. **Choice D is the best answer.** The second sentence of the passage explains that Wollstonecraft "was the first to turn her frustration into a critique of polite society." Choices A and C are incorrect because the second sentence also implies that other writers had previously discussed women's rights and expressed concern about the stifling of female potential. If other writers had done this, they certainly must have had to "rely on reason," and the mention of "late-eighteenth-century respect for reason" further suggests that other writers would have relied on it, making choice E incorrect. Choice B can be eliminated since no mention is made of whether other writers had already focused on educational and professional opportunities for women.

2. **Choice A is the best answer.** The passage discusses the role played by movies and music in popularizing surfing and suggests the potential importance of television. Since "wave sliding" existed before the 1500s, it is going too far to say that surfing was not recognized as a true sport until it was popularized by movie idols (choice B) or that it is better defined as a form of entertainment (choice C). Choice D is incorrect because it suggests that surfing affected movies and music, while the passage describes only how those media affected surfing. The author never comments on the likelihood that televised surfing would generate interest, so there is no support for choice E.

3. **Choice C is the best answer.** The passage describes the emptiness of a highway that features "one small town," "four clustered habitations," and "a roadhouse perhaps once every eighty miles." The author ends the passage with the observation, "I had never been out in such a boundless blank." These images emphasize the sense of desolation of the drive rather than any apparent danger (choice A), rugged terrain (choice B), tranquil setting (choice D), or winding highways (choice E).

4. **Choice B is the best answer.** By describing Malinche's role as an interpreter, guide, negotiator, and strategist, the author explains her historical importance. This explanation does not contrast Malinche with Cortez (choice A) but rather shows how they cooperated. Choice C is incorrect because the defeat of Montezuma is mentioned only briefly in the passage. Choices D and E are incorrect because neither the reasons for the Indian nations' dissatisfaction nor Malinche's reasons for helping Cortez are ever mentioned.

5. **Choice E is the best answer.** The passage explains that Malinche was able to help Cortez principally "Because of her knowledge of the various Mexican cultures and languages" (lines 4–5). There is no mention of her knowledge of Spanish culture (choice A), her connections to influential people in various Indian nations (choice B), her knowledge of military strategy (choice C), or her resistance to the Indian coalition (choice D).

6. **Choice E is the best answer.** The first half of the passage describes various mistaken views of dinosaurs, while the information beginning in line 10 works to show how scientific understanding of the dinosaurs has changed since the 1950s. The passage does not provide specific evidence that birds evolved from dinosaurs (choice A) or describe Cretaceous dinosaurs (choice B); nor does it focus on the variety of dinosaur species (choice C) or the appeal of movies in the 1950s (choice D).

7. **Choice B is the best answer.** The fact the author "knew the juxtapositions of these faux dinosaurs with modern humans was absurd" shows that the author was perceptive. None of the qualities in choices A, C, D, and E is suggested by the author's observation.

8. **Choice E is the best answer.** Lines 10–13 reveal that paleontologists in the 1950s were unaware that possible descendents of some dinosaurs had survived the Cretaceous extinctions. The passage does not support the idea that paleontologists in the 1950s possessed an understanding of the relationship between dinosaurs and modern-day creatures (choice A), that they were not in agreement about the cause of extinctions (choice B), that they refuted the notion of dinosaurs as sluggish (choice C), or that they were unaware of the existence of certain dinosaurs (choice D).

9. **Choice C is the best answer.** The final sentence of the passage reveals that the "scientists" (line 17) are misguided in that they question the connection between birds and dinosaurs "in denial of a mass of accumulating paleontological data." There is not enough information in the passage to determine whether the scientists are necessarily fanatical (choice A), egotistical (choice B), pessimistic (choice D), or ill-prepared (choice E).

10. **Choice B is the best answer.** The passage concludes with the observation that the "main reasons for studying a foreign language are not practical ones. Rather, the study of language is a humanistic enterprise ..." (lines 6–8). This comment supports the idea that people should learn languages for reasons other than utilitarian (useful) ones. The passage does not discuss ways to teach languages (choice A), explain why English is widely spoken (choice C), express regret about computers that translate (choice D), or describe different careers (choice E).

11. Choice E is the best answer. The sentence in lines 3–6 provides specific reasons why the rationale identified in the first sentence (studying a foreign language on the basis of its usefulness) is a mistake. The sentence does not list new methods of learning (choice A), activities to be pursued following the mastery of a language (choice B), difficulties experienced by those attempting to learn a foreign language (choice C), or objections to a view about learning a foreign language (choice D).

12. Choice C is the best answer. The passage says that journalists and gardeners are alike in that the most successful journalists and gardeners "are those best able to detect nuances, to discern trends from skimpy evidence." The passage does not focus on the gardeners' or journalists' ability to focus clearly (choice A), think creatively (choice B), plan for any eventuality (choice D), or work hard (choice E).

13. Choice A is the best answer. The passage explains that one of Edison's aims in inventing the phonograph was "to hand down to posterity the voices of great singers and instrumentalists," suggesting that he wished to contribute positively to the arts. The passage does not offer any evidence that Edison might have been a musician or actor (choice B), that he insisted his collaborators receive credit (choice C), that he was more widely known for his artistic innovations (choice D), or that he was an amateur musician (choice E).

14. Choice B is the best answer. In the context of the passage as a whole, the idea that biographers simply repeated known facts about Doyle's life makes most sense, as we are told that Doyle's life is shrouded in mystery and that no researchers have been given full access to Doyle's personal papers. It does not make sense to say that biographers have practiced (choice A), imitated (choice C), criticized (choice D), or perfected (choice E) the little that is known about Doyle's life.

15. Choice D is the best answer. Expansion of education is not mentioned in the passage. The second sentence of the passage does mention urban growth (choice A), population shifts (choice B), industrial modernization (choice C), and improvements in transportation (choice E) as forces that served to transform the United States.

16. Choice B is the best answer. The final sentence of the passage explains that two distinct networks exist to ensure that "the safety-critical functions cannot be compromised by the nonessential functions." The passage never states or implies the difficulty of building one large network (choice A) or of getting safety-critical components to interact with nonessential components (choice E).

Nor does it suggest anything about the expense of repairing two networks (choice C) or reducing drivers' entertainment experience (choice D).

17. Choice C is the best answer. The second paragraph offers an explanation of how the two automobile networks function. It does not highlight a problem (choice A), define a technical term (choice B), critique a decision (choice D), or evaluate a suggestion (choice E).

18. Choice B is the best answer. In lines 4–6, the author explains, "I seek to restore value and depth to a discounted form of 'women's work' by examining home sewing during the early decades of the twentieth century." The author does not critique scholarship (choice A), examine the history of the fashion design industry (choice C), analyze women's motivations for working outside the home (choice D), or discuss various responsibilities (choice E).

19. Choice D is the best answer. The fact that the author seeks to "restore value and depth" to sewing, a "discounted form" of work, suggests that home sewing had a greater significance than might initially be thought. Choice A is incorrect because sewing is not discussed as merely a chore throughout the passage, especially in the second paragraph. Similarly, choice (C) is incorrect because sewing was a form of work as well as a way to counter boredom. Choice B is incorrect since the passage mentions that most women did not earn income from sewing (lines 11–12). Choice E is incorrect since the second paragraph explains that sewing "often moved beyond its functional role as housework to become a way to express personal tastes."

20. Choice E is the best answer. Lines 12–14 explain that "as a way to save money, home dressmaking played a major economic role in a household." The passage does not indicate that women who sewed had little interest in influencing fashion (choice A), that they were well compensated (choice B), preferred sewing to other jobs (choice C), or sewed primarily to earn income (choice D).

21. Choice B is the best answer. In the context of the second paragraph, "express" most nearly means convey, since the women sought to convey (to communicate or make known) their personal tastes. Choice A is incorrect because it is going too far to say that sewing had become a way to exude, or conspicuously display, personal taste. It makes no sense to say that sewing had become a way to broach, vent, or extract personal taste; therefore, choices C, D, and E are incorrect.

22. Choice A is the best answer. Lines 3–4 describe a phenomenon: the fact that there was an overall increase in television viewing among United States adults from the 1970s to the 1990s. The rest of the passage describes economic and technological factors that contributed to this phenomenon. The passage does not advance a theory (choice B), introduce a problem (choice C), summarize a study (choice D), or offer evidence to undermine a claim (choice E).

23. **Choice E is the best answer.** The author argues that the "new technologies" made television viewing more convenient. Certainly, if these technologies were "not affordable to the majority of television viewers," as choice E suggests, the argument about the importance of these technologies would be weakened. Choices A, B, C, and D are incorrect because if any of these statements were true, the author's argument would be either strengthened or unaffected, but not weakened.

24. **Choice A is the best answer.** The passage states that to "keep one's seat seems to convey a distinctly negative judgment rather than a merely less positive one," an example of how one who remains seated during a standing ovation may be perceived. The passage does not recount an incident (choice B), argue that most performances do not merit applause (choice C), describe an effect on performers (choice D), or denounce hypocrisy (choice E).

25. **Choice D is the best answer.** The first half of the passage focuses on Stevenson's failures, while the second half focuses on his successes, demonstrating that the quality of his writing varied tremendously. In discussing Stevenson's failures, the passage does not speculate on what might have caused them; therefore, choices A and B are incorrect. Choice C is incorrect because the passage does not state or imply that Stevenson is misunderstood. Choice E is incorrect because the passage deals only with the author's point of view, not the views of other critics.

26. **Choice D is the best answer.** Since the chart does not separate the juniors from the seniors, there is no way to tell the art course for which the greatest number of juniors enrolled last year. Choices A, B, C, and E deal simply with numbers of students—be they juniors or seniors—who participated in a given course for a given time period; therefore, all of these values can be determined from the graph.

27. **Choice C is the best answer.** After mentioning bear teeth, the author says, "One possible conclusion is that the Paleo-Eskimos considered the bear a threat whereas the Neo-Eskimos considered it a trophy." Clearly, mentioning the archeological record of bear teeth for the two groups is intended to provide reasoning for this conclusion about the Neo-Eskimos. Choice A is incorrect; since the passage does not specify the number of teeth found at Neo-Eskimo sites, there is no basis for judging the prevalence of bears.

Choice B is incorrect because the passage speculates that the Neo-Eskimos considered the teeth a trophy, not a tool. Choices D and E are incorrect because the passage does not compare the skill levels of the Neo- and Paleo-Eskimos or emphasize the danger posed by bears.

28. **Choice E is the best answer.** The passage describes the effects of the Sputnik launch and the space programs generally on the science fiction community. The passage does not present the views of one author (choice A), explore how writers incorporated Sputnik into their work (choice B), outline the effects of Sputnik on space programs (choice C), or characterize the American response to Sputnik (choice D).

29. **Choice B is the best answer.** Within the context of the paragraph, lines 4–6 provide an illustration of the observation that a "wave of euphoria broke over the science fiction community" (lines 2–3). Therefore, it makes sense that these lines are intended to express this perspective of science fiction enthusiasts. Further, given this observation, it does not make sense that the perspective expressed in lines 4–6 would be that of would-be astronauts (choice A), newspaper columnists (choice C), Russian scientists (choice D), or politicians (choice E).

30. **Choice A is the best answer.** The phrase "horrible truths" is followed by the observation, "The world did not care that science fiction writers and readers had been right," indicating the public's lack of interest. The passage does not state or imply that America was losing the space race (choice B) or that interest in space travel was declining (choice C). Choices D and E are incorrect because neither the dangers of space travel nor information detailing Russian scientific superiority is mentioned in the passage.

31. **Choice C is the best answer.** The third paragraph explains that classic space-travel stories "lacked interest for readers who had embraced the notion that science fiction was about 'predicting the future,'" suggesting that these older fans became disillusioned with, or lost interest in, science fiction as a genre. The passage does not state or imply that older fans were fascinated by actual space travel (choice A), that they were frustrated by America's slow advancements (choice B), that they became dismayed by increasing numbers of fans (choice D), or that they were irritated by authors' response to Sputnik.

32. **Choice D is the best answer.** Lines 19–21 describe a shifting trend in science fiction's readership: as older fans turned away, a new group of younger fans emerged. Choice A is incorrect because no criticism appears in the lines. The lines do not summarize a

position (choice B), elaborate an example (choice C), or predict an outcome (choice E).

33. **Choice A is the best answer.** Lines 4–6 explain that critics during the period in which Murray was writing insisted on the study of "'art for art's sake,'" while Murray believed that "'the most important feature of art is *what* is portrayed,'" and line 13 states that Murray took on critics and art historians. The passage does not discuss criticisms of Murray's views (choice B), assess the impact of those views (choice C), or correct a misconception about them (choice E). Choice D is incorrect because the passage compares Murray's views with those of other thinkers living in his time, not with the views of more modern thinkers.

34. **Choice B is the best answer.** Lines 14–16 explain that Murray challenged the art establishment as "someone coming to the sudden realization of the links between cultural practice and political power." This suggests that Murray viewed sculptural art (a cultural practice) as something that can reflect social and political attitudes. While Murray may have believed that artistic expression should not be limited by social concerns (choice A), the passage does not state or imply this belief on his part. Neither does the passage imply that Murray believed that critics are unqualified (choice C), that sculptors have greater impact than other artists (choice D), or that few sculptors understand the power of their art (choice E).

35. **Choice B is the best answer.** Lines 7–8 explain that Murray's subtitle "hints at his aim to reawaken numbed perception to the immediacy of art's effects in the real world." This suggests that the subtitle is mentioned primarily to emphasize Murray's ultimate goal. Choice A is incorrect because the passage points out the differences rather than the similarities between Murray's views and the views of others. Choice C is incorrect since Murray's subtitle does not explain his concern for sculpture. Choices D and E are incorrect because Murray's views were not met with enthusiasm and because Murray is not talked about as wishing to establish himself as a critic.

36. **Choice E is the best answer.** Lines 9–12 explain that Murray believed that "when we look at a work of art, especially when 'we' look at one in which Black Folk appear—or do not appear when they should—we should ask: What does it mean?. . . What impression is it likely to make on those who view it?" This suggests that Murray would want to know what message a sculpture that portrays a Black person sends about the person depicted. Choices A and D are incorrect because Murray does not indicate interest in the background or motivations of those modeled in sculptures. Similarly, choices B and C

are incorrect because Murray is not concerned with the intentions of particular sculptors or the views of art critics.

37. Choice A is the best answer. The passage describes Cicero's writings as "unguarded," suggesting his candor, or honesty. Nothing in the passage suggests that Cicero's writings can be characterized as having precision (choice B), beauty (choice C), unusual style (choice D), or humor (choice E).

38. Choice B is the best answer. The passage specifies, "Biograph's policy was not to allow players to become known, since revealing their identity might give actors bargaining power in salary negotiations." The passage does not state or imply that Biograph's policy was calculated to create publicity (choice A), that it was embraced by other companies (choice C), designed to protect actors' privacy (choice D), or based on theatrical precedents (choice E).

39. Choice C is the best answer. The author argues that "rail lines that pass through residential areas already designed for high automobile use are unlikely to attract many rail transit riders." If it is true that many people who currently use automobiles regularly do so only because they have no other mode of transportation available, then even people who live in residential areas designed for automobile use may be attracted to rail transit. Choices A and B present situations involving people skeptical of rail transit and rail construction; these choices would strengthen, rather than weaken, the author's argument. Choices D and E present situations that are irrelevant to the author's argument.

40. Choice D is the best answer. The final sentence of the passage explains, "While Goya portrayed the more liberated women of his time, he was more ironic commentator than feminist," suggesting that Goya was not entirely sympathetic to the feminist cause. The passage does not state or imply that Goya encouraged the women's actions (choice A), that he was supportive of women's charitable activities (choice B), that he did not understand the purpose of organizations and salons (choice C), or that he was pleased that women were interested in literature (choice E).

CALCULATING YOUR SCORE

To score your PPST: Reading sample test:

- Count the number of questions you answered correctly. The correct answers are in Table 1.
- Use Table 2 to find the scaled score corresponding to the number of questions answered correctly. You can compare your scaled score to the passing score required by your state or institution. (Passing state scores are available on the Praxis Web site at www.ets.org/praxis.)
- Score report category R-1 contains 19 questions measuring literal comprehension. The 21 questions in category R-2 assess reading skills in critical and inferential comprehension. Count the number of questions you answered correctly in each of these categories. This may give you some idea of your strengths and weaknesses.

Table 1—PPST: Reading Sample Test

*Answers to Practice Test Questions and Percentages of Examinees
Answering Each Question Correctly*

Sequence Number	Score Report Category	Correct Answer	Percentage of Examinees Choosing Correct Answer
1	R-1	D	83%
2	R-2	A	76%
3	R-2	C	82%
4	R-1	B	78%
5	R-1	E	48%
6	R-1	E	68%
7	R-2	B	80%
8	R-1	E	92%
9	R-2	C	35%
10	R-1	B	82%
11	R-1	E	68%
12	R-2	C	85%
13	R-2	A	83%
14	R-1	B	70%
15	R-1	D	97%
16	R-2	B	73%
17	R-1	C	81%
18	R-1	B	87%
19	R-2	D	76%
20	R-1	E	88%
21	R-1	B	84%
22	R-1	A	57%
23	R-2	E	64%
24	R-1	A	91%
25	R-2	D	77%
26	R-1	D	74%
27	R-2	C	84%
28	R-1	E	79%
29	R-2	B	81%
30	R-2	A	83%

(Continued)

Table 1—PPST: Reading Sample Test (*Continued*)

*Answers to Practice Test Questions and Percentages of Examinees
Answering Each Question Correctly*

Sequence Number	Score Report Category	Correct Answer	Percentage of Examinees Choosing Correct Answer
31	R-2	C	52%
32	R-2	D	86%
33	R-1	A	48%
34	R-2	B	51%
35	R-2	B	72%
36	R-2	E	77%
37	R-2	A	46%
38	R-1	B	84%
39	R-2	C	46%
40	R-2	D	77%

NOTE: Percentages are based on the test records of 3,276 examinees who took the 60-minute version of the PPST: Reading test in July 2008.

In general, questions may be considered as easy, average, or difficult based on the following percentages:

Easy questions = 75% or more answered correctly

Average questions = 55%–74% answered correctly

Difficult questions = less than 55% answered correctly

Table 2—PPST: Reading Sample Test

Score Conversion Table

Number Right	Scaled Score
40	185
39	184
38	183
37	183
36	182
35	181
34	180
33	179
32	179
31	178
30	177

(Continued)

Table 2—PPST: Reading Sample Test (*Continued*)

Score Conversion Table

Number Right	Scaled Score
29	176
28	175
27	175
26	174
25	173
24	171
23	170
22	169
21	168
20	166
19	165
18	164
17	163
16	162
15	161
14	160
13	159
12	158
11	157
10	156
9	156
8	155
7	155
6	154
5	154
4	153
3	153
2	152
1	152
0	151

CHAPTER 10

PPST™: Mathematics Test

THE **PRAXIS**™
S E R I E S
Professional Assessments for Beginning Teachers ®

TEST NAME:
Pre-Professional Skills Test **Mathematics**

Time—60 minutes

40 Questions

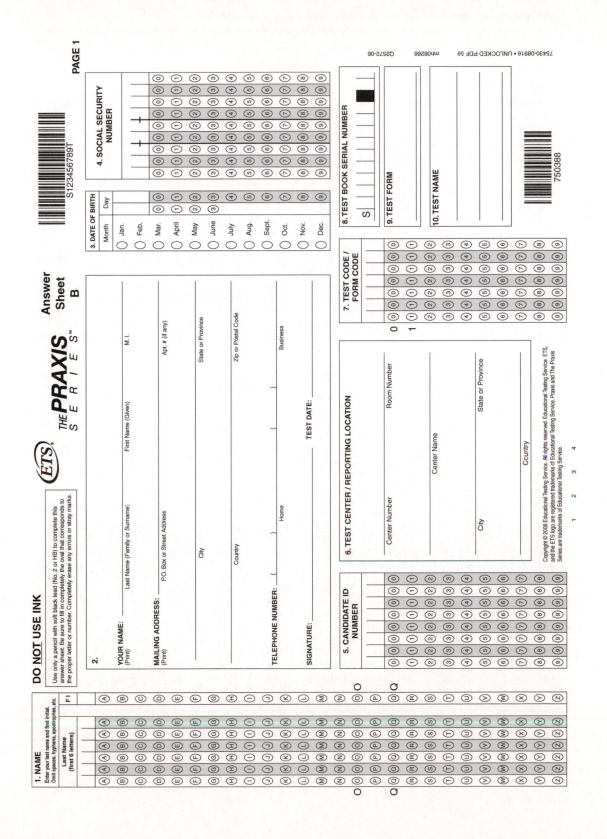

CERTIFICATION STATEMENT: (Please write the following statement below. DO NOT PRINT.)

"I hereby agree to the conditions set forth in the *Registration Bulletin* and certify that I am the person whose name and address appear on this answer sheet."

_____

_____

_____

SIGNATURE: _____   DATE: _____ / _____ / _____

Month   Day   Year

BE SURE EACH MARK IS DARK AND COMPLETELY FILLS THE INTENDED SPACE AS ILLUSTRATED HERE: ●

1 Ⓐ Ⓑ Ⓒ Ⓓ Ⓔ	41 Ⓐ Ⓑ Ⓒ Ⓓ Ⓔ	81 Ⓐ Ⓑ Ⓒ Ⓓ Ⓔ	121 Ⓐ Ⓑ Ⓒ Ⓓ Ⓔ
2 Ⓐ Ⓑ Ⓒ Ⓓ Ⓔ	42 Ⓐ Ⓑ Ⓒ Ⓓ Ⓔ	82 Ⓐ Ⓑ Ⓒ Ⓓ Ⓔ	122 Ⓐ Ⓑ Ⓒ Ⓓ Ⓔ
3 Ⓐ Ⓑ Ⓒ Ⓓ Ⓔ	43 Ⓐ Ⓑ Ⓒ Ⓓ Ⓔ	83 Ⓐ Ⓑ Ⓒ Ⓓ Ⓔ	123 Ⓐ Ⓑ Ⓒ Ⓓ Ⓔ
4 Ⓐ Ⓑ Ⓒ Ⓓ Ⓔ	44 Ⓐ Ⓑ Ⓒ Ⓓ Ⓔ	84 Ⓐ Ⓑ Ⓒ Ⓓ Ⓔ	124 Ⓐ Ⓑ Ⓒ Ⓓ Ⓔ
5 Ⓐ Ⓑ Ⓒ Ⓓ Ⓔ	45 Ⓐ Ⓑ Ⓒ Ⓓ Ⓔ	85 Ⓐ Ⓑ Ⓒ Ⓓ Ⓔ	125 Ⓐ Ⓑ Ⓒ Ⓓ Ⓔ
6 Ⓐ Ⓑ Ⓒ Ⓓ Ⓔ	46 Ⓐ Ⓑ Ⓒ Ⓓ Ⓔ	86 Ⓐ Ⓑ Ⓒ Ⓓ Ⓔ	126 Ⓐ Ⓑ Ⓒ Ⓓ Ⓔ
7 Ⓐ Ⓑ Ⓒ Ⓓ Ⓔ	47 Ⓐ Ⓑ Ⓒ Ⓓ Ⓔ	87 Ⓐ Ⓑ Ⓒ Ⓓ Ⓔ	127 Ⓐ Ⓑ Ⓒ Ⓓ Ⓔ
8 Ⓐ Ⓑ Ⓒ Ⓓ Ⓔ	48 Ⓐ Ⓑ Ⓒ Ⓓ Ⓔ	88 Ⓐ Ⓑ Ⓒ Ⓓ Ⓔ	128 Ⓐ Ⓑ Ⓒ Ⓓ Ⓔ
9 Ⓐ Ⓑ Ⓒ Ⓓ Ⓔ	49 Ⓐ Ⓑ Ⓒ Ⓓ Ⓔ	89 Ⓐ Ⓑ Ⓒ Ⓓ Ⓔ	129 Ⓐ Ⓑ Ⓒ Ⓓ Ⓔ
10 Ⓐ Ⓑ Ⓒ Ⓓ Ⓔ	50 Ⓐ Ⓑ Ⓒ Ⓓ Ⓔ	90 Ⓐ Ⓑ Ⓒ Ⓓ Ⓔ	130 Ⓐ Ⓑ Ⓒ Ⓓ Ⓔ
11 Ⓐ Ⓑ Ⓒ Ⓓ Ⓔ	51 Ⓐ Ⓑ Ⓒ Ⓓ Ⓔ	91 Ⓐ Ⓑ Ⓒ Ⓓ Ⓔ	131 Ⓐ Ⓑ Ⓒ Ⓓ Ⓔ
12 Ⓐ Ⓑ Ⓒ Ⓓ Ⓔ	52 Ⓐ Ⓑ Ⓒ Ⓓ Ⓔ	92 Ⓐ Ⓑ Ⓒ Ⓓ Ⓔ	132 Ⓐ Ⓑ Ⓒ Ⓓ Ⓔ
13 Ⓐ Ⓑ Ⓒ Ⓓ Ⓔ	53 Ⓐ Ⓑ Ⓒ Ⓓ Ⓔ	93 Ⓐ Ⓑ Ⓒ Ⓓ Ⓔ	133 Ⓐ Ⓑ Ⓒ Ⓓ Ⓔ
14 Ⓐ Ⓑ Ⓒ Ⓓ Ⓔ	54 Ⓐ Ⓑ Ⓒ Ⓓ Ⓔ	94 Ⓐ Ⓑ Ⓒ Ⓓ Ⓔ	134 Ⓐ Ⓑ Ⓒ Ⓓ Ⓔ
15 Ⓐ Ⓑ Ⓒ Ⓓ Ⓔ	55 Ⓐ Ⓑ Ⓒ Ⓓ Ⓔ	95 Ⓐ Ⓑ Ⓒ Ⓓ Ⓔ	135 Ⓐ Ⓑ Ⓒ Ⓓ Ⓔ
16 Ⓐ Ⓑ Ⓒ Ⓓ Ⓔ	56 Ⓐ Ⓑ Ⓒ Ⓓ Ⓔ	96 Ⓐ Ⓑ Ⓒ Ⓓ Ⓔ	136 Ⓐ Ⓑ Ⓒ Ⓓ Ⓔ
17 Ⓐ Ⓑ Ⓒ Ⓓ Ⓔ	57 Ⓐ Ⓑ Ⓒ Ⓓ Ⓔ	97 Ⓐ Ⓑ Ⓒ Ⓓ Ⓔ	137 Ⓐ Ⓑ Ⓒ Ⓓ Ⓔ
18 Ⓐ Ⓑ Ⓒ Ⓓ Ⓔ	58 Ⓐ Ⓑ Ⓒ Ⓓ Ⓔ	98 Ⓐ Ⓑ Ⓒ Ⓓ Ⓔ	138 Ⓐ Ⓑ Ⓒ Ⓓ Ⓔ
19 Ⓐ Ⓑ Ⓒ Ⓓ Ⓔ	59 Ⓐ Ⓑ Ⓒ Ⓓ Ⓔ	99 Ⓐ Ⓑ Ⓒ Ⓓ Ⓔ	139 Ⓐ Ⓑ Ⓒ Ⓓ Ⓔ
20 Ⓐ Ⓑ Ⓒ Ⓓ Ⓔ	60 Ⓐ Ⓑ Ⓒ Ⓓ Ⓔ	100 Ⓐ Ⓑ Ⓒ Ⓓ Ⓔ	140 Ⓐ Ⓑ Ⓒ Ⓓ Ⓔ
21 Ⓐ Ⓑ Ⓒ Ⓓ Ⓔ	61 Ⓐ Ⓑ Ⓒ Ⓓ Ⓔ	101 Ⓐ Ⓑ Ⓒ Ⓓ Ⓔ	141 Ⓐ Ⓑ Ⓒ Ⓓ Ⓔ
22 Ⓐ Ⓑ Ⓒ Ⓓ Ⓔ	62 Ⓐ Ⓑ Ⓒ Ⓓ Ⓔ	102 Ⓐ Ⓑ Ⓒ Ⓓ Ⓔ	142 Ⓐ Ⓑ Ⓒ Ⓓ Ⓔ
23 Ⓐ Ⓑ Ⓒ Ⓓ Ⓔ	63 Ⓐ Ⓑ Ⓒ Ⓓ Ⓔ	103 Ⓐ Ⓑ Ⓒ Ⓓ Ⓔ	143 Ⓐ Ⓑ Ⓒ Ⓓ Ⓔ
24 Ⓐ Ⓑ Ⓒ Ⓓ Ⓔ	64 Ⓐ Ⓑ Ⓒ Ⓓ Ⓔ	104 Ⓐ Ⓑ Ⓒ Ⓓ Ⓔ	144 Ⓐ Ⓑ Ⓒ Ⓓ Ⓔ
25 Ⓐ Ⓑ Ⓒ Ⓓ Ⓔ	65 Ⓐ Ⓑ Ⓒ Ⓓ Ⓔ	105 Ⓐ Ⓑ Ⓒ Ⓓ Ⓔ	145 Ⓐ Ⓑ Ⓒ Ⓓ Ⓔ
26 Ⓐ Ⓑ Ⓒ Ⓓ Ⓔ	66 Ⓐ Ⓑ Ⓒ Ⓓ Ⓔ	106 Ⓐ Ⓑ Ⓒ Ⓓ Ⓔ	146 Ⓐ Ⓑ Ⓒ Ⓓ Ⓔ
27 Ⓐ Ⓑ Ⓒ Ⓓ Ⓔ	67 Ⓐ Ⓑ Ⓒ Ⓓ Ⓔ	107 Ⓐ Ⓑ Ⓒ Ⓓ Ⓔ	147 Ⓐ Ⓑ Ⓒ Ⓓ Ⓔ
28 Ⓐ Ⓑ Ⓒ Ⓓ Ⓔ	68 Ⓐ Ⓑ Ⓒ Ⓓ Ⓔ	108 Ⓐ Ⓑ Ⓒ Ⓓ Ⓔ	148 Ⓐ Ⓑ Ⓒ Ⓓ Ⓔ
29 Ⓐ Ⓑ Ⓒ Ⓓ Ⓔ	69 Ⓐ Ⓑ Ⓒ Ⓓ Ⓔ	109 Ⓐ Ⓑ Ⓒ Ⓓ Ⓔ	149 Ⓐ Ⓑ Ⓒ Ⓓ Ⓔ
30 Ⓐ Ⓑ Ⓒ Ⓓ Ⓔ	70 Ⓐ Ⓑ Ⓒ Ⓓ Ⓔ	110 Ⓐ Ⓑ Ⓒ Ⓓ Ⓔ	150 Ⓐ Ⓑ Ⓒ Ⓓ Ⓔ
31 Ⓐ Ⓑ Ⓒ Ⓓ Ⓔ	71 Ⓐ Ⓑ Ⓒ Ⓓ Ⓔ	111 Ⓐ Ⓑ Ⓒ Ⓓ Ⓔ	151 Ⓐ Ⓑ Ⓒ Ⓓ Ⓔ
32 Ⓐ Ⓑ Ⓒ Ⓓ Ⓔ	72 Ⓐ Ⓑ Ⓒ Ⓓ Ⓔ	112 Ⓐ Ⓑ Ⓒ Ⓓ Ⓔ	152 Ⓐ Ⓑ Ⓒ Ⓓ Ⓔ
33 Ⓐ Ⓑ Ⓒ Ⓓ Ⓔ	73 Ⓐ Ⓑ Ⓒ Ⓓ Ⓔ	113 Ⓐ Ⓑ Ⓒ Ⓓ Ⓔ	153 Ⓐ Ⓑ Ⓒ Ⓓ Ⓔ
34 Ⓐ Ⓑ Ⓒ Ⓓ Ⓔ	74 Ⓐ Ⓑ Ⓒ Ⓓ Ⓔ	114 Ⓐ Ⓑ Ⓒ Ⓓ Ⓔ	154 Ⓐ Ⓑ Ⓒ Ⓓ Ⓔ
35 Ⓐ Ⓑ Ⓒ Ⓓ Ⓔ	75 Ⓐ Ⓑ Ⓒ Ⓓ Ⓔ	115 Ⓐ Ⓑ Ⓒ Ⓓ Ⓔ	155 Ⓐ Ⓑ Ⓒ Ⓓ Ⓔ
36 Ⓐ Ⓑ Ⓒ Ⓓ Ⓔ	76 Ⓐ Ⓑ Ⓒ Ⓓ Ⓔ	116 Ⓐ Ⓑ Ⓒ Ⓓ Ⓔ	156 Ⓐ Ⓑ Ⓒ Ⓓ Ⓔ
37 Ⓐ Ⓑ Ⓒ Ⓓ Ⓔ	77 Ⓐ Ⓑ Ⓒ Ⓓ Ⓔ	117 Ⓐ Ⓑ Ⓒ Ⓓ Ⓔ	157 Ⓐ Ⓑ Ⓒ Ⓓ Ⓔ
38 Ⓐ Ⓑ Ⓒ Ⓓ Ⓔ	78 Ⓐ Ⓑ Ⓒ Ⓓ Ⓔ	118 Ⓐ Ⓑ Ⓒ Ⓓ Ⓔ	158 Ⓐ Ⓑ Ⓒ Ⓓ Ⓔ
39 Ⓐ Ⓑ Ⓒ Ⓓ Ⓔ	79 Ⓐ Ⓑ Ⓒ Ⓓ Ⓔ	119 Ⓐ Ⓑ Ⓒ Ⓓ Ⓔ	159 Ⓐ Ⓑ Ⓒ Ⓓ Ⓔ
40 Ⓐ Ⓑ Ⓒ Ⓓ Ⓔ	80 Ⓐ Ⓑ Ⓒ Ⓓ Ⓔ	120 Ⓐ Ⓑ Ⓒ Ⓓ Ⓔ	160 Ⓐ Ⓑ Ⓒ Ⓓ Ⓔ

FOR ETS USE ONLY	R1	R2	R3	R4	R5	R6	R7	R8	TR	CS

Directions: Each of the questions or incomplete statements below is followed by five suggested answers or completions. Select the one that is best in each case and then fill in the corresponding lettered space on the answer sheet with a heavy, dark mark so that you cannot see the letter.

Remember, try to answer every question.

Special Note: Figures that accompany problems in the test are intended to provide information useful in solving the problem. The figures are drawn as accurately as possible except when it is stated in a specific problem that its figure is not drawn to scale. Figures can be assumed to lie in a plane unless otherwise indicated. Position of points can be assumed to be in the order shown, and lines shown as straight can be assumed to be straight. The symbol ∟ denotes a right angle.

NUMBER OF STUDENTS STUDYING
FOREIGN LANGUAGES

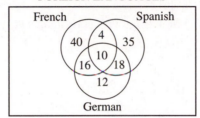

1. According to the Venn diagram above, how many students are studying all three of the languages?

   (A) 10
   (B) 14
   (C) 28
   (D) 38
   (E) 48

| 53,184.905 | 35,640.178 | 20,539.541 |
| 6,218.059 | 4,153.342 | 3,805.725 |

2. How many of the six numbers shown in the table above have 5 in either the hundredths place or the thousandths place?

   (A) Six
   (B) Five
   (C) Four
   (D) Three
   (E) Two

3. It took Meghan 4 days to write a certain paper. She wrote 11 pages on the first day, 15 pages on the second day, and 7 pages on the third day. If Meghan wrote an average (arithmetic mean) of 12 pages per day, how many pages did she write on the fourth day?

(A) 13
(B) 14
(C) 15
(D) 26
(E) 27

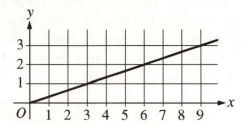

4. For a point with coordinates (x, y) on the line shown, x and y, respectively, could represent

(A) feet and yards
(B) inches and feet
(C) seconds and minutes
(D) days and weeks
(E) minutes and hours

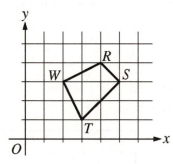

5. In the graph above, vertex S of figure $RSTW$ has the coordinates $(15, 9)$. If $RSTW$ is reflected across the x-axis, what are the coordinates of the image of vertex W?

(A) $(2, -1)$
(B) $(4, -3)$
(C) $(6, -3)$
(D) $(6, -6)$
(E) $(6, -9)$

6. If $\frac{2}{9}x - 1 = 1$, what is the value of x?

(A) 0
(B) 4
(C) 5
(D) 9
(E) 10

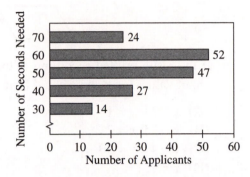

7. A dexterity test was given to 164 job applicants. The bar graph above summarizes the time needed for each applicant to complete the test. Approximately what percent of the applicants took at least 60 seconds to complete the test?

(A) 40%
(B) 45%
(C) 55%
(D) 65%
(E) 75%

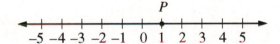

8. On the number line above, point Q (not shown) is located 3 units from point P, and point R (not shown) is located 1 unit from point Q. Which of the following could be the coordinate of point R?

(A) −5
(B) −2
(C) −1
(D) 2
(E) 4

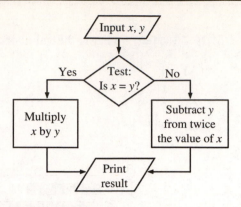

9. If the result printed according to the flowchart above was 49, the input values for x and y could have been which of the following?

(A) $x = 24$; $y = 1$
(B) $x = 25$; $y = 2$
(C) $x = 49$; $y = 50$
(D) $x = 7$; $y = 7$
(E) $x = 9$; $y = 9$

All odd integers are prime numbers.

10. Which of the following numbers is a counterexample to the statement above?

(A) 2
(B) 3
(C) 3.5
(D) 9
(E) 17

A new animated movie had a premiere showing at a certain theater. The admission price was

$9 for an adults' ticket and

$5 for a children's ticket.

There was a total of 650 tickets sold to the premiere showing.

11. Together with the information above, which of the following pieces of information about the premiere could be used to determine the number of adults' tickets sold?

(A) It was on a Saturday afternoon.
(B) Some adults bought more than 1 children's ticket.
(C) Of the children for whom tickets were bought, 108 were less than 9 years old.
(D) Of the adults for whom tickets were bought, $\frac{3}{5}$ were over 25 years old.
(E) The total revenue from ticket sales was $4,150.

PIZZAS SOLD ON FRIDAY, SATURDAY, AND SUNDAY

Friday	◯◯◯◯
Saturday	◯◯◯◯◖
Sunday	◯◯◯◖

Each ◖ represents half the number of pizzas represented by ◯.

12. The pictograph above shows the number of pizzas sold at a pizzeria during three days. If a total of 240 pizzas were sold during the three days, how many pizzas were sold on Saturday?

(A) 45
(B) 70
(C) 85
(D) 90
(E) 99

13. $\sqrt{8 \times 72} =$

(A) $8\sqrt{2}$

(B) $8\sqrt{3}$

(C) $12\sqrt{2}$

(D) 24

(E) 36

14. The figure above is a parallelogram. If $58 < t < 70$, which of the following could be the value of k?

(A) 108

(B) 118

(C) 128

(D) 138

(E) 148

15. If 26 is r percent of 65, what is r percent of 95?

(A) 29

(B) 38

(C) 40

(D) 47

(E) 49

16. Of the following, which number is greatest?

(A) 0.1025

(B) 0.101

(C) 0.1

(D) 0.1026

(E) 0.103

17. A solid rectangular block is 5 feet long, 2 feet wide, and 8 feet high. What is the volume of the block, in cubic feet?

(A) 15

(B) 20

(C) 70

(D) 80

(E) 90

18. On a certain day, the temperature was 37°F at 10 A.M. and 49°F at 1 P.M. If the temperature rose at a constant rate from 10 A.M. to 1 P.M. on that day, what was the temperature at 11 A.M.?

(A) 39°F
(B) 40°F
(C) 41°F
(D) 42°F
(E) 43°F

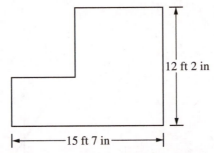

19. The figure above is a floor plan in which all adjacent sides meet at right angles. What is the perimeter of the floor? (12 inches = 1 foot)

(A) 27 ft 9 in
(B) 32 ft 9 in
(C) 45 ft 6 in
(D) 55 ft 6 in
(E) 65 ft 3 in

Sept.	Oct.	Nov.	Dec.	Jan.	Feb.	Mar.
65	82	76	93	62	97	84

20. Steven's scores on the 7 monthly vocabulary quizzes he took in his English class are shown above. In which month was Steven's vocabulary quiz score equal to the median of his 7 vocabulary quiz scores? (When n is an odd positive integer, the median of n numbers is the middle number when the numbers are ordered from least to greatest.)

(A) October
(B) November
(C) December
(D) February
(E) March

21. Which of the following is equivalent to $\dfrac{3}{xk} \div \dfrac{k}{4}$ if $xk \neq 0$?

(A) $\dfrac{12}{x}$

(B) $\dfrac{12}{k}$

(C) $\dfrac{3}{4x}$

(D) $\dfrac{4}{3k}$

(E) $\dfrac{12}{xk^2}$

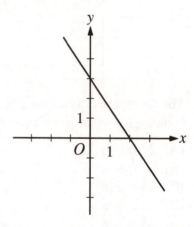

22. The line in the xy-plane above is the graph of which of the following equations?

(A) $2x + 3y = 4$

(B) $2x + 3y = 6$

(C) $3x + 2y = 4$

(D) $3x + 2y = 6$

(E) $3x - 2y = 6$

23. Derren will drive 42.3 miles from home to his doctor's office. Then he plans to drive 24.4 miles from the doctor's office to a department store. Finally, he will drive 48.5 miles from the department store to home. If Derren's car gets 22 miles per gallon of gasoline, then the total amount of gasoline his car will use during these three trips is

(A) between 3 and 4 gallons
(B) between 4 and 5 gallons
(C) between 5 and 6 gallons
(D) between 6 and 7 gallons
(E) between 7 and 8 gallons

24. Which of the following scatterplots best illustrates the trend that as x decreases, y becomes larger and larger?

(A)

(B)

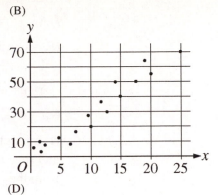

(C)

(D)

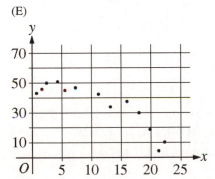
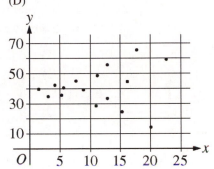

(E)

25. If $x = \dfrac{1}{5}$, which of the following lists x, $\sqrt{x}$, and x^2 in order from least to greatest?

(A) $\sqrt{x}, x, x^2$

(B) $\sqrt{x}, x^2, x$

(C) $x, x^2, \sqrt{x}$

(D) $x^2, x, \sqrt{x}$

(E) $x^2, \sqrt{x}, x$

26. A committee of a state senate consists of 9 Democrats, 6 Republicans, and several Independents. If one person is to be selected at random from the members of the committee, the probability that the person selected will be a Democrat is $\dfrac{3}{8}$. How many of the members of the committee are Independents?

(A) 6

(B) 7

(C) 8

(D) 9

(E) 10

27. $(1{,}275 \times 0.6) + (0.6 \times 725) =$

(A) 330

(B) 600

(C) 900

(D) 1,000

(E) 1,200

28. Elena plans to randomly select 2 different letters from the 6 letters in the word BURDEN. If her first selection is either E or U, what is the probability that her second selection will be either E or U?

(A) $\dfrac{1}{2}$

(B) $\dfrac{1}{3}$

(C) $\dfrac{1}{4}$

(D) $\dfrac{1}{5}$

(E) $\dfrac{1}{6}$

29. Nassim goes to the gym to work out once every 2 days, and Louisa goes to the same gym to work out once every 3 days. If both Nassim and Louisa go to the gym today, on how many of the next 100 days will Nassim and Louisa go to the gym on the same day?

(A) 12
(B) 15
(C) 16
(D) 18
(E) 20

1 foot = 12 inches

1 inch = 2.54 centimeters

100 centimeters = 1 meter

30. The speed of an object is 32 feet per second. Which of the following computations gives the speed of the object in meters per second?

(A) $32\left(\dfrac{1}{12}\right)(2.54)$

(B) $32\left(\dfrac{1}{12}\right)\left(\dfrac{1}{2.54}\right)$

(C) $32(12)\left(\dfrac{1}{2.54}\right)(100)$

(D) $32(12)(2.54)\left(\dfrac{1}{100}\right)$

(E) $32(12)(2.54)(100)$

31. In a certain company, the ratio of the number of female employees to the number of male employees is exactly 3 to 4. Which of the following could be the total number of employees in the company?

(A) 81
(B) 87
(C) 91
(D) 95
(E) 101

32. Last year a company spent $15 million on employee salaries. On a circle graph of the company's total expenses last year, the sector representing employee salaries has a central angle of 100°. Which of the following is the amount of the company's total expenses last year, in millions of dollars?

(A) $50
(B) $51
(C) $52
(D) $53
(E) $54

33. Each of the following is equivalent to 75% of 60 EXCEPT

(A) 0.75×60

(B) 0.6×75

(C) $\dfrac{60 \times 15}{20}$

(D) $\dfrac{75 \times 6}{100}$

(E) $60 \times \dfrac{3}{4}$

$$c = \frac{a^2 + b^2}{ab}$$

34. In the equation above, a and b are positive numbers. If the values of a and b are each multiplied by 10, what is the corresponding change in the value of c?

(A) It will be multiplied by 10.

(B) It will be multiplied by 100.

(C) It will remain unchanged.

(D) It will be divided by 10.

(E) It will be divided by 100.

35. Ned divided a given number by 3 and then added 2. If he should have multiplied the number by 3 and then subtracted 2, which of the following two steps can he do next to get the correct answer?

(A) Subtract 4 and then multiply by 9.

(B) Subtract 12 and then multiply by 3.

(C) Multiply by 3 and then subtract 4.

(D) Multiply by 6 and then subtract 14.

(E) Multiply by 9 and then subtract 20.

Class	This Year's Enrollment as a Percent of Last Year's Enrollment
Freshman	103%
Sophomore	95%
Junior	98%
Senior	112%

36. The table above shows this year's enrollment in each of the four classes at a high school as a percent of the number of students enrolled last year in that class. Based on the information in the table, which of the following statements is true?

(A) There are 12 more students enrolled in this year's senior class than in last year's senior class.
(B) The number of students enrolled in this year's freshman class is less than the number of students enrolled in last year's freshman class.
(C) The number of seniors enrolled increased from last year to this year.
(D) The total student enrollment increased from last year to this year.
(E) This year, the junior class has 3% more students enrolled than does the sophomore class.

$$\frac{x}{3} = \frac{y}{5}$$
$$3 + y = z$$

37. Which of the following equations, together with the two equations above, will form a system of three equations such that there is only one value of x that satisfies all three equations?

(A) $z + y = 5$
(B) $y = z - 3$
(C) $5x = 3y$
(D) $z - y = 3$
(E) $x = \frac{3}{5}y$

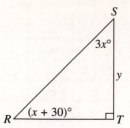

Note: Figure not drawn to scale.

38. In terms of y, what is the area of right triangle RST above?

(A) $\dfrac{y^2}{3}$

(B) $\dfrac{y^2}{2}$

(C) y^2

(D) $2y^2$

(E) $3y^2$

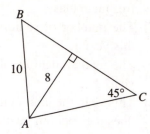

39. In triangle ABC above, what is the length of side BC?

(A) 12
(B) 13
(C) 14
(D) 15
(E) 16

40. Five people plan to buy a present, sharing the cost equally. If one person decided not to participate, the cost per person for the other 4 people would increase by $16. What is the cost of the present?

(A) $160
(B) $210
(C) $240
(D) $280
(E) $320

PPST: Mathematics Test
Answers and Explanations

1. **Choice A is the best answer.**

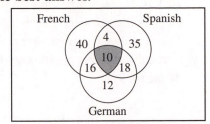

The shaded region in the figure above is inside each of the three circles representing French, Spanish, and German, respectively. Therefore, the shaded region represents the students that are studying all three languages. Since the number corresponding to the shaded region is 10, we can conclude that there are 10 students studying all three languages.

2. **Choice D is the best answer.** In a decimal number, the hundredths digit is the second digit to the right of the decimal dot, and the thousandths digit is the third digit to the right of the decimal dot.

   A careful look at the table shows that there are only three numbers that have 5 in either the hundredths or the thousandths place. The number 53,184.905 has 5 in its thousandths place, the number 6,218.059 has 5 in its hundredths place, and the number 3,805.725 has 5 in its thousandths place. None of the remaining numbers has 5 in either the hundredths or the thousandths place.

3. **Choice C is the best answer.** The total number of the pages Meghan wrote in the first 3 days is $11 + 15 + 7 = 33$. Meghan wrote an average (arithmetic mean) of 12 pages per day in the 4 days, so the total number of pages Meghan wrote in the 4 days is $12 \times 4 = 48$. The number of pages Meghan wrote on the fourth day is the total number for the 4 days minus the total number for the first 3 days. Therefore, Meghan wrote $48 - 33 = 15$ pages on the fourth day.

4. **Choice A is the best answer.** Note that the line passes through the points with coordinates (0, 0), (3, 1), (6, 2), and (9, 3), which means that one coordinate is 3 times the other coordinate.

   Recall that

$$1 \text{ yard} = 3 \text{ feet},$$

$$1 \text{ foot} = 12 \text{ inches},$$

$$1 \text{ minute} = 60 \text{ seconds},$$

$$1 \text{ week} = 7 \text{ days, and}$$

$$1 \text{ hour} = 24 \text{ hours}.$$

Of the pairs of units given in the choices, only feet and yards have this property that one unit is 3 times the other unit.

5. Choice E is the best answer. Note that the horizontal and vertical grid lines in the graph are equally spaced, so the graph has been covered by identical little squares. Note that the coordinates of the horizontal and vertical tickmarks are not indicated. The x-coordinate of S is 15, or 5 times the length of a side of the little square. That implies that the size of each little square must be $\frac{15}{5} = 3$. The figure below shows the graph when the coordinates of the horizontal and vertical tickmarks are indicated. Note that the coordinates of vertex W are $(6, 9)$.

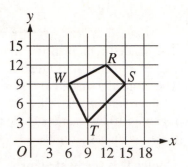

Recall how the coordinates of a point change after a reflection across the x-axis: the x-coordinate remains the same, but the y-coordinate changes its sign. This means that the reflection across the x-axis transforms $W(6, 9)$ into $W'(6, -9)$.

Graphically, the reflection across the x-axis transforms quadrilateral $RSTW$ into quadrilateral $R'S'T'W'$, as shown in the figure below. Again, vertex W', the image of vertex W under this transformation, has coordinates $(6, -9)$.

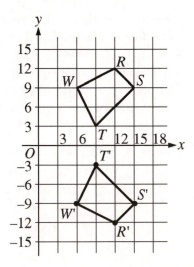

6. **Choice D is the best answer.** The problem can be solved as follows.

$$\frac{2x}{9} - 1 = 1$$

$$\frac{2x}{9} = 1 + 1 \quad \text{(by adding 1 on both sides)}$$

$$\frac{2x}{9} = 2$$

$$2x = 2 \times 9 \quad \text{(by multiplying both sides by 9)}$$

$$2x = 18$$

$$x = \frac{18}{2} \quad \text{(by dividing both sides by 2)}$$

$$x = 9$$

Therefore, the value of x is 9.

7. **Choice B is the best answer.** Recall that "at least" means "greater than or equal to." The question is about the group of applicants who took 60 or more seconds to complete the test, which is represented by the two horizontal bars corresponding to 60 seconds and 70 seconds. The total number of applicants who took 60 or more seconds to complete the test is $52 + 24 = 76$. Since there are 164 job applicants altogether, the percent of applicants who took 60 or more seconds to complete the test is $\frac{76}{164}$ or approximately 45%.

8. **Choice C is the best answer.** First, locate point Q on the number line. Since it is not stated whether Q is on the left side or the right side of P, the coordinate of Q could be either 4 or −2. Next, locate point R on the number line. Since point R could be either on the left side or the right side of point Q, the possible coordinates of R are 5, 3, −1 or −3. Of these numbers, only −1 is among the numbers in the given options.

9. **Choice D is the best answer.** The Yes-No test inside the diamond shape has a Yes branch and a No branch. The operation in the Yes branch is "Multiply x by y," which is represented by the expression xy. The operation in the No branch is "Subtract y from twice the value of x," which is represented by the expression $2x - y$.

When $x = 24$ and $y = 1$, the test "Is $x = y$?" is negative, so we need to follow the No branch, and the result is $2x - y = 2 \times 24 - 1 = 48 - 1 = 47$.

When $x = 25$ and $y = 2$, the test "Is $x = y$?" is negative, so we need to follow the No branch, and the result is $2x - y = 2 \times 25 - 2 = 50 - 2 = 48$.

When $x = 49$ and $y = 50$, the test "Is $x = y$?" is negative, so we need to follow the No branch, and the result is $2x - y = 2 \times 49 - 50 = 98 - 50 = 48$.

When $x = 7$ and $y = 7$, the test "Is $x = y$?" is positive, so we need to follow the Yes branch, and the result is $xy = 7 \times 7 = 49$.

When $x = 9$ and $y = 9$, the test "Is $x = y$?" is positive, so we need to follow the Yes branch, and the result is $xy = 9 \times 9 = 81$.

Of the given options, only the input values in option D produce a result of 49.

10. Choice D is the best answer. We need to consider the statement for each number in the options.

- 2 is not an odd integer, so the statement does not apply to this number. Therefore, 2 is not a counterexample for the statement.
- 3 is an odd integer, but it is also a prime number. Therefore, 3 is a number that confirms the statement, and it's not a counterexample.
- 3.5 is not an integer, so the statement does not apply to this number. Therefore, 3.5 is not a counterexample for the statement.
- 9 is an odd integer, but it is not prime. Therefore, 9 is a number that contradicts the statement, so 9 is a counterexample for the statement.
- 17 is odd, but it is also a prime number. Therefore, 17 is a number that confirms the statement, and it's not a counterexample.

11. Choice E is the best answer. Knowing the total revenue from ticket sales is enough to determine the number of adults' tickets sold. For example, if the total revenue was \$4,150, let x be the number of adults' tickets sold. Then, the number of children's tickets sold is $650 - x$. The total revenue, in dollars, from ticket sales is $9x + 5(650 - x)$ which is equivalent to $9x + 5 \times 650 - 5x$, and can be simplified to $4x + 3250$. Given that the total revenue was \$4,150, we get the equation $4x + 3250 = 4150$, with solution $x = 225$. Therefore, the number of adults' tickets sold is 225.

None of the information in the other choices is sufficient to determine the number of adults' tickets sold.

12. Choice D is the best answer. Counting the number of symbols in the pictograph, the total number of pizzas sold during the three days is $11 \times \bigcirc + 2 \times \mathbb{C}$. The information in the pictograph legend implies that $2 \times \mathbb{C} = \bigcirc$, so the total number of pizzas sold during the three days is $12 \times \bigcirc$. Given that the total number of pizzas sold is 240, each $\bigcirc$ symbol represents $\frac{240}{12} = 20$ pizzas and each $\mathbb{C}$ symbol represents $\frac{20}{2} = 10$ pizzas. The number of pizzas sold on Saturday is $4 \times \bigcirc + 1 \times \mathbb{C} = 4 \times 20 + 1 \times 10 = 90$.

13. Choice D is the best answer. The problem can be solved as follows.

$$\sqrt{8 \times 72} = \sqrt{8 \times (8 \times 9)}$$
$$= \sqrt{(8 \times 8) \times 9} \quad \text{(by associativity)}$$
$$= \sqrt{8^2 \times 9}$$
$$= \sqrt{8^2 \times 3^2}$$
$$= \sqrt{(8 \times 3)^2}$$
$$= \sqrt{(24)^2}$$
$$= 24$$

14. Choice B is the best answer. Recall that adjacent angles in a parallelogram are supplementary (their measures add up to 180°). Therefore, $t + k = 180$, or equivalently $k = 180 - t$. Given that $58 < t < 70$, we get that $180 - 70 < t < 180 - 58$, or equivalently $110 < t < 122$. Of the values given in the options, only 118 is between 110 and 122.

15. Choice B is the best answer. One way to solve this problem is to set up a proportion (one ratio equals another ratio). Let x stand for the number that is r percent of 95. Since r percent of 65 is 26 and r percent of 95 is x, then $\frac{65}{95} = \frac{26}{x}$. Cross-multiplying, we get $65x = 95 \times 26$, which implies that $x = \frac{95 \times 26}{65} = 38$.

Another way to solve the problem is to find first the value of the r. Given that r percent of 65 is 26, we get the equation $\frac{r}{100} \times 65 = 26$, with solution $r = \frac{26}{65} \times 100 = 40$. Then, r percent of 95 is $\frac{40}{100} \times 95 = 38$.

16. Choice E is the best answer. To find the greatest number, we need to compare the corresponding digits in the five options. The number to the left of the decimal dot is 0 for all options. The tenths digit (the first digit to the right of the decimal dot) is 1 for all options. The hundredths digit (the second digit to the right of the decimal dot) is 0 for all options. The thousandths digit (the third digit to the right of the decimal dot) is 0 for option C, is 1 for option B, is 2 for options A and D, and is 3 for option E. We can conclude that option E is the greatest of the numbers given.

17. Choice D is the best answer. The volume of a solid rectangular block is the product of its length, width, and height. Therefore, the volume is $5 \times 2 \times 8 = 80$ cubic feet.

18. Choice C is the best answer. From 10 A.M. to 1 P.M., there are 3 hours and the temperature increased by $49 - 37 = 12$ degrees Fahrenheit. During this time interval, the temperature increased by an average (arithmetic mean) of $\frac{12}{3} = 4$ degrees Fahrenheit per hour. At this constant rate, the temperature at 11 A.M. is the sum of 37°F (the temperature at 10 A.M.) and 4°F (the temperature increase in 1 hour). Therefore, the temperature at 11 A.M. is $37 + 4$, or 41 degrees Fahrenheit.

19. Choice D is the best answer.

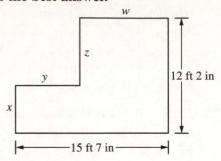

The lengths of only two sides are given. Let x, y, z, and w be the lengths, in feet, of the other 4 sides, as shown in the figure above. The perimeter of the floor is the sum of x feet, y feet, z feet, w feet, 12 feet 2 inches, and 15 feet 7 inches.

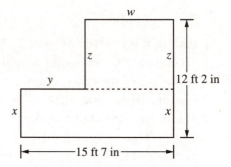

Recall that the lengths of opposite sides of a rectangle are equal. In the figure above, the dashed horizontal line divides the floor into 2 rectangles. Considering the length of the rightmost vertical side, we can infer that the sum of x feet and z feet is 12 feet 2 inches.

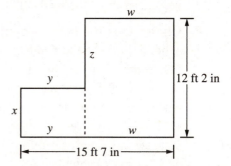

Similarly, the dashed line in the figure above divides the floor into 2 rectangles. Considering the length of the bottom horizontal side, we can infer that the sum of y feet and w feet is 15 feet 7 inches.

Putting these results together, the perimeter of the floor is twice the sum of 15 feet 7 inches and 12 feet 2 inches. We can conclude that the perimeter of the floor is 55 feet 6 inches.

A different approach is to enclose the floor inside a rectangle as shown in the figure below.

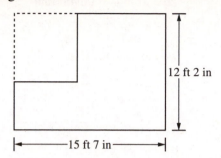

12 ft 2 in

15 ft 7 in

Arguing as above, the perimeter of the floor is the same as the perimeter of the enclosing rectangle. Because twice the sum of 15 feet 7 inches and 12 feet 2 inches is 55 feet 6 inches, we can conclude that the perimeter of the floor is 55 feet 6 inches.

20. **Choice A is the best answer.** The 7 vocabulary quiz scores, ordered from least to greatest, are

$$62, 65, 76, 82, 84, 93, 97.$$

The middle number is the 4th leftmost number in the list above, so the median is 82, which corresponds to the month of October.

21. **Choice E is the best answer.** Recall that dividing by a fraction is the same as multiplying with the reciprocal of the fraction.

$$\frac{3}{xk} \div \frac{k}{4} = \frac{3}{xk} \times \frac{4}{k} = \frac{12}{xk^2}$$

Therefore, E is the best answer.

22. **Choice D is the best answer.** Note that the line in the graph passes through the points (2, 0) and (0, 3). Plugging $x = 2$ and $y = 0$ in the options, we can see that only the equations in options A, D, and E hold. Plugging $x = 0$ and $y = 3$ in the options, we can see that only the equation in option D holds. Therefore, D is the best answer.

23. **Choice C is the best answer.** The total distance that Derren drove is $42.3 + 24.4 + 48.5 = 115.2$ miles. Given that Derren's car gets 22 miles per gallon of gasoline, the total amount of gasoline used is $\frac{115.2}{22}$, or approximately 5.2 gallons. Therefore, C is the best answer.

24. **Choice C is the best answer.** The phrase "as x decreases, y becomes larger and larger" means that, as you inspect the dots in a graph from right to left, the dots should be higher and higher in the graph. A careful inspection of all graphs shows that only the graph in option C has this property. Note that in the graph in option E, as you inspect the dots from right to left, the dots start increasing but at the very end (near $x = 0$) the dots are getting lower and lower, so the graph in option E does not satisfy the property. Therefore, C is the best answer.

25. Choice D is the best answer. Note that if $x = \frac{1}{5}$, then $\sqrt{x} = \frac{1}{\sqrt{5}}$ and $x^2 = \frac{1}{25}$. Given that

$$\sqrt{5} < 5 < 25,$$

we can deduce that

$$\frac{1}{\sqrt{5}} > \frac{1}{5} > \frac{1}{25}.$$

Therefore, we can conclude that the order of the three numbers, from least to greatest, is $x^2, x, \sqrt{x}$.

26. Choice D is the best answer. Let x be the number of Independents in the committee. The total number of committee members is $15 + x$. If one person is to be selected at random from the members of the committee, the probability that the person selected will be a Democrat is $\frac{9}{15+x}$. Given that this probability is $\frac{3}{8}$, we get the equation below.

$$\frac{9}{15+x} = \frac{3}{8}$$

$$3(x+15) = 9 \times 8 \qquad \text{(by cross multiplication)}$$

$$3x + 45 = 72$$

$$3x = 72 - 45 \qquad \text{(by subtracting 45 from both sides)}$$

$$3x = 27$$

$$x = \frac{27}{3} \qquad \text{(by dividing both sides by 3)}$$

$$x = 9$$

Therefore, 9 members of the committee are Independents.

27. Choice E is the best answer. The problem can be solved as follows.

$$(1,275 \times 0.6) + (0.6 \times 725) = (0.6 \times 1,275) + (0.6 \times 725)$$

$$\text{(by commutativity)}$$

$$= 0.6 \times (1,275 + 725) \quad \text{(by distributivity)}$$

$$= 0.6 \times (2,000)$$

$$= 1,200$$

28. Choice D is the best answer. Assume that the first selection is either letter E or U. If the first selection is E, the letters left are B, U, R, D, and N. If the first selection is letter U, the letters left are B, R, D, E, and N. In either case, after the first selection, there will be only 5 letters left and exactly 1 of these 5 letters is E or U. That means that the probability that the second selection will be either E or U is $\frac{1}{5}$.

29. Choice C is the best answer. Nassim goes to the gym every 2 days, and he went to the gym today. Therefore, Nassim will go to the gym on the following number of days after today.

$$2, 4, 6, 8, 10, 12, 14, 16, 18, 20, \ldots$$

Louisa goes to the same gym every 3 days, and she went to the gym today. Therefore, Louisa will go to the gym on the following number of days after today.

$$3, 6, 9, 12, 15, 18, 21, \ldots$$

Note that Nassim and Louisa will go to the gym on the same day 6 days from today, 12 days from today, 18 days from today, and so on, on all days that are multiplies of 6. The problem is now asking for the number of integers from 1 to 100 that are multiples of 6. Given that $\frac{100}{6}$ is approximately 16.6, we can conclude that Nassim and Louisa go to the gym on the same day on 16 days in the next 100 days.

30. Choice D is the best answer. The first two equations in the problem are shown below.

$$1 \text{ foot} = 12 \text{ inches} \quad (\text{equation 1})$$
$$1 \text{ inch} = 2.54 \text{ centimeters} \quad (\text{equation 2})$$

The third equation in the problem is equivalent to the equation below.

$$1 \text{ centimeter} = \frac{1}{100} \text{ meter} \quad (\text{equation 3})$$

The problem can be solved as follows.

$$32 \text{ feet} = (32)(12) \text{ inches} \quad (\text{by equation 1})$$
$$= (32)(12)(2.54) \text{ centimeters} \quad (\text{by equation 2})$$
$$= (32)(12)(2.54)\left(\frac{1}{100}\right) \text{ meters} \quad (\text{by equation 3})$$

Therefore, D is the best answer.

31. Choice C is the best answer. Given that the ratio of the number of female employees to the number of male employees is 3 to 4, the numbers of female employees and male employee must be $3n$ and $4n$, respectively, for some integer n. The total number of employees in the company is $3n + 4n = 7n$, which implies that the total number of employees in the company must be divisible by 7. A careful inspection of the numbers in the options shows that only 91, the number in option C, is divisible by 7.

32. Choice E is the best answer. To solve this problem, set up a proportion. Recall that the whole circle graph corresponds to a sector with central angle of 360°. Let x be the amount of the company's total expenses last year, in millions of dollars. Given that a sector with a central angle of 100° represents 15 million dollars and a sector with a central angle of 360° represents x million dollars, we get the proportion $\frac{100}{360} = \frac{15}{x}$. Cross-multiplying, we get $100x = 360 \times 15$, which implies that $x = \frac{360 \times 15}{100} = 54$. Therefore, the company's total expenses last year was $54 million.

33. Choice D is the best answer. Recall that $75\% = \frac{75}{100} = 0.75 = \frac{3}{4}$. We need to consider each option separately and determine if the corresponding expression is equivalent to 75% of 60.

Option A: $0.75 \times 60 = 75\% \times 60 = 75\%$ of 60

Option B: $0.6 \times 75 = \frac{60}{100} \times 75 = 60 \times \frac{75}{100} = \frac{75}{100} \times 60$

$= 75\% \times 60 = 75\%$ of 60

Option C: $\frac{60 \times 15}{20} = 60 \times \frac{15}{20} = 60 \times \frac{3}{4} = \frac{3}{4} \times 60$

$= 75\% \times 60 = 75\%$ of 60

Option D: $\frac{75 \times 6}{100} = \frac{75}{100} \times 6 = \frac{3}{4} \times 6 = 75\% \times 6$

$= 75\%$ of 6

Option E: $60 \times \frac{3}{4} = \frac{3}{4} \times 60 = 75\% \times 60 = 75\%$ of 60

Therefore, all options except option D are equivalent to 75% of 60. Therefore, D is the best answer.

34. Choice C is the best answer. One way to solve this problem is to think of what numbers can be factored out of the numerator and denominator after the values of a and b are each multiplied by 10. Since the numerator is $a^2 + b^2$, the number $100 = 10^2$ could be factored out of the numerator. Since the denominator is ab, the number $100 = 10^2$ could be also factored out of the denominator. Since the two 100 factors in the numerator and denominator cancel out, the expression remains unchanged.

Another way to solve the problem is to replace a and b by $10a$ and $10b$, respectively, and simplify the resulting expression.

$$\frac{(10a)^2 + (10b)^2}{(10a)(10b)} = \frac{100a^2 + 100b^2}{100ab}$$

$$= \frac{100(a^2 + b^2)}{100ab}$$

$$= \frac{a^2 + b^2}{ab} \quad \text{(by canceling out 100)}$$

Therefore, the value of c will remain unchanged after the values of a and b are each multiplied by 10.

35. Choice E is the best answer. A good way to solve this problem is to write out exactly what Ned did, as an algebraic expression. Let x represent the number that Ned started with. Ned obtained $\frac{x}{3}+2$ (expression 1) instead of $3x-2$ (expression 2). The problem is now to determine the operations that will change expression 1 into expression 2. Note that the coefficient of x needs to change from $\frac{1}{3}$ to 3, so any options (such as options A or E) that contain a multiplication by 9 will be a good starting point. It turns out that option E is correct, as shown by the computation below.

$$
\begin{aligned}
\text{Option E: } 9(\text{expression 1}) - 20 &= 9\left(\frac{x}{3}+2\right) - 20 \\
&= 9\left(\frac{x}{3}\right) + 9(2) - 20 \\
&= 3x + 18 - 20 \\
&= 3x - 2 \\
&= \text{expression 2}
\end{aligned}
$$

Similar computations show that all the other options are incorrect (that is, the operations in options A, B, C, and D do not transform expression 2 into expression 1).

$$
\begin{aligned}
\text{Option A: } 9(\text{expression } 1 - 4) &= 9\left(\frac{x}{3}+2-4\right) \\
&= 9\left(\frac{x}{3}-2\right) \\
&= 9\left(\frac{x}{3}\right) - 9(2) \\
&= 3x - 18
\end{aligned}
$$

$$
\begin{aligned}
\text{Option B: } 3(\text{expression } 1 - 12) &= 3\left(\frac{x}{3}+2-12\right) \\
&= 3\left(\frac{x}{3}-10\right) \\
&= 3\left(\frac{x}{3}\right) - 3(10) \\
&= x - 30
\end{aligned}
$$

$$
\begin{aligned}
\text{Option C: } 3(\text{expression 1}) - 4 &= 3\left(\frac{x}{3}+2\right) - 4 \\
&= 3\left(\frac{x}{3}\right) + 3(2) - 4 \\
&= x + 6 - 4 \\
&= x + 2
\end{aligned}
$$

$$\text{Option D: } 6(\text{expression 1}) - 14 = 6\left(\frac{x}{3} + 2\right) - 14$$

$$= 6\left(\frac{x}{3}\right) + 6(2) - 14$$

$$= 2x + 12 - 14$$

$$= 2x - 2$$

Therefore, E is the best answer.

36. **Choice C is the best answer.** You need to consider each option separately. Be aware of the fact that the numbers in the table are percents, not whole numbers.

Option A: An increase of 112% does not imply that there are 12 more students in the senior class.
Option B is false: Since the percent change 103% is greater than 100%, there are more freshmen is this year's class than in last year's class.
Option C is true: Since the percent change 112% is greater than 100%, there are more seniors is this year's class than in last year's class.
Option D: There is not enough information to infer that there is an increase in total student enrollment from last year to this year.
Option E: The table values for the sophomores and juniors, which are 95% and 98%, respectively, are percents out of the numbers of sophomores and juniors enrolled last year, respectively. Since these two numbers may be different, the difference of 98% and 95% has no meaning.

37. **Choice A is the best answer.** All other options are variations of the two given equations, so they don't add any new information. In particular, none of these options will allow us to conclude that there is a unique value of x.

Option B: $y = z - 3$ is equivalent to $3 + y = z$ (second given equation).

Option C: $5x = 3y$ is equivalent to $\frac{x}{3} = \frac{y}{5}$ (first given equation).

Option D: $z - y = 3$ is equivalent to $3 + y = z$ (second given equation).

Option E: $x = \frac{3}{5}y$ is equivalent to $\frac{x}{3} = \frac{y}{5}$ (first given equation).

Only option A, together with the two given equations, will form a system of three equations with only one value of x satisfying all three equations. For example, $z + y = 5$ (the equation in option A) is equivalent to $z = 5 - y$. Plugging this value of z in $3 + y = z$ (second given equation), we get $3 + y = 5 - y$, which is equivalent to $2y = 5 - 3$, which gives $y = 1$. Plugging this value of y in $\frac{x}{3} = \frac{y}{5}$ (first given equation), we get that $\frac{x}{3} = \frac{1}{5}$, or equivalently that $x = \frac{3}{5}$.

38. Choice B is the best answer. First, calculate the value of x. Given that RST is a right triangle, the sum of the measures of angles R and S is 90.

$$(x+30)+3x=90$$
$$4x+30=90$$
$$4x=90-30$$
$$x=\frac{60}{4}$$
$$x=15$$

If $x=15$, then $x+30=45$ and $3x=45$. This means that right triangle RST is an isosceles triangle, and so $RT=ST=y$. The area of the triangle RST can be computed as follows.

$$\text{Area}=\frac{\text{base}\times\text{height}}{2}=\frac{y\times y}{2}=\frac{y^2}{2}$$

Therefore, B is the best answer.

39. Choice C is the best answer.

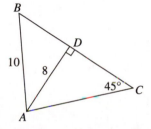

Note that triangle ABC is made up of two right triangles: ADB and ADC. Triangle ADB is a right triangle with a hypotenuse of 10 and a leg of 8. Since one of the Pythagorean triples is 6, 8, 10, we can conclude that $BD=6$. Triangle ADC is a right triangle and the measure of angle ACD is 45°. This implies that the measure of the other angle DAC must also be 45°, allowing us to infer that triangle ADC is a right isosceles triangle. Given that $AD=8$, we obtain that $DC=8$. Since $BD=6$ and $DC=8$, we can conclude that $BC=6+8=14$.

40. Choice E is the best answer. Let x be the cost, in dollars, of the present. When 5 people share the cost, the cost per person is $\frac{x}{5}$ dollars. When 4 people share the cost, the cost per person is $\frac{x}{4}$ dollars. Given that the cost per person increased by \$16, we get the equation below.

$$\frac{x}{4} - \frac{x}{5} = 16$$

$$20\left(\frac{x}{4} - \frac{x}{5}\right) = 20 \times 16$$

$$20\left(\frac{x}{4}\right) - 20\left(\frac{x}{5}\right) = 320$$

$$5x - 4x = 320$$

$$x = 320$$

Therefore, the cost of the present is \$320.

CALCULATING YOUR SCORE

To score your Mathematics sample test:

- Count the number of questions you answered correctly. The correct answers are in Table 1.
- Use Table 2 to find the scaled score corresponding to the number of questions answered correctly. You can compare your scaled score to the passing score required by your state or institution. (Passing state scores are available on the Praxis Web site at www.ets.org/praxis.)
- Score report category M-1 contains 13 questions measuring knowledge of number and operations; category M-2 contains 8 questions measuring understanding Algebra, category M-3 contains 9 questions measuring knowledge of geometry and measurement, and category M-4 contains 10 questions measuring understanding and use of data analysis and probability.
- Count the number of questions you answered correctly in each of the categories. This may give you some idea of your strengths and weaknesses.

Table 1—PPST: Mathematics Sample Test
Answers to Practice Test Questions and Percentages of Examinees Answering Each Question Correctly

Sequence Number	Score Report Category	Correct Answer	Percentage of Examinees Choosing Correct Answer
1	M-4	A	91%
2	M-1	D	63%
3	M-4	C	76%
4	M-3	A	65%
5	M-3	E	62%
6	M-2	D	69%
7	M-4	B	33%
8	M-3	C	76%
9	M-2	D	87%
10	M-1	D	55%
11	M-2	E	68%
12	M-4	D	67%
13	M-1	D	49%
14	M-3	B	53%
15	M-1	B	51%
16	M-1	E	56%
17	M-3	D	89%
18	M-4	C	78%

(Continued)

Table 1—PPST: Mathematics Sample Test (*Continued*)
Answers to Practice Test Questions and Percentages of Examinees Answering Each Question Correctly

Sequence Number	Score Report Category	Correct Answer	Percentage of Examinees Choosing Correct Answer
19	M-3	D	48%
20	M-4	A	82%
21	M-1	E	61%
22	M-2	D	20%
23	M-1	C	82%
24	M-2	C	48%
25	M-1	D	23%
26	M-4	D	54%
27	M-1	E	80%
28	M-4	D	42%
29	M-1	C	33%
30	M-3	D	43%
31	M-1	C	41%
32	M-4	E	27%
33	M-1	D	22%
34	M-2	C	39%
35	M-1	E	23%
36	M-4	C	45%
37	M-2	A	14%
38	M-3	B	36%
39	M-3	C	30%
40	M-2	E	50%

NOTE: Percentages are based on the test records of 2,520 examinees who took the 60-minute version of the PPST: Mathematics test in June 2008.

In general, questions may be considered as easy, average, or difficult based on the following percentages:

Easy questions = 75% or more answered correctly.

Average questions = 55%–74% answered correctly.

Difficult questions = less than 55% answered correctly.

Table 2—PPST: Mathematics Sample Test
Score Conversion Table

Number Right	Scaled Score
40	189
39	189
38	189
37	189
36	188
35	188
34	188
33	187
32	187
31	186
30	186
29	185
28	184
27	184
26	183
25	182
24	181
23	180
22	179
21	178
20	177
19	175
18	174
17	172
16	171
15	169
14	168
13	166
12	165
11	164
10	162

(*Continued*)

Table 2—PPST: Mathematics Sample Test (*Continued*)

Score Conversion Table

Number Right	Scaled Score
9	161
8	160
7	158
6	157
5	156
4	155
3	153
2	152
1	151
0	150

CHAPTER 11

PPST™: Writing Test

THE **PRAXIS**™
S E R I E S
Professional Assessments for Beginning Teachers ®

TEST NAME:
Pre-Professional Skills Test **Writing**

Time—60 minutes

38 Multiple-Choice Questions

1 Essay

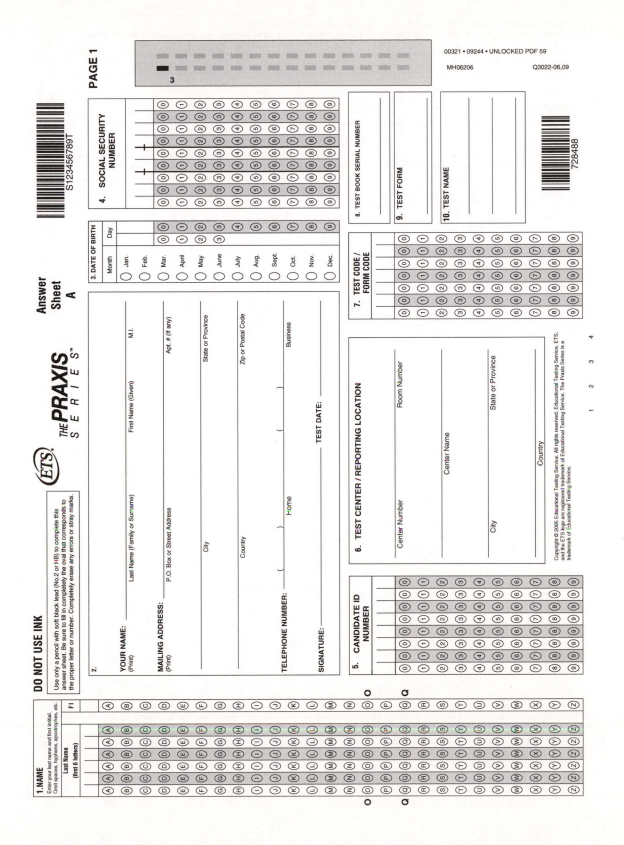

CERTIFICATION STATEMENT: (Please write the following statement below. DO NOT PRINT.)
"I hereby agree to the conditions set forth in the *Registration Bulletin* and certify that I am the person whose name and address appear on this answer sheet."

_____

_____

_____

SIGNATURE: _____ DATE: _____ / _____ / _____
                                                                                                                  Month   Day   Year

---

BE SURE EACH MARK IS DARK AND COMPLETELY FILLS THE INTENDED SPACE AS ILLUSTRATED HERE : ●

1 Ⓐ Ⓑ Ⓒ Ⓓ Ⓔ	13 Ⓐ Ⓑ Ⓒ Ⓓ Ⓔ	25 Ⓐ Ⓑ Ⓒ Ⓓ Ⓔ	37 Ⓐ Ⓑ Ⓒ Ⓓ Ⓔ
2 Ⓐ Ⓑ Ⓒ Ⓓ Ⓔ	14 Ⓐ Ⓑ Ⓒ Ⓓ Ⓔ	26 Ⓐ Ⓑ Ⓒ Ⓓ Ⓔ	38 Ⓐ Ⓑ Ⓒ Ⓓ Ⓔ
3 Ⓐ Ⓑ Ⓒ Ⓓ Ⓔ	15 Ⓐ Ⓑ Ⓒ Ⓓ Ⓔ	27 Ⓐ Ⓑ Ⓒ Ⓓ Ⓔ	39 Ⓐ Ⓑ Ⓒ Ⓓ Ⓔ
4 Ⓐ Ⓑ Ⓒ Ⓓ Ⓔ	16 Ⓐ Ⓑ Ⓒ Ⓓ Ⓔ	28 Ⓐ Ⓑ Ⓒ Ⓓ Ⓔ	40 Ⓐ Ⓑ Ⓒ Ⓓ Ⓔ
5 Ⓐ Ⓑ Ⓒ Ⓓ Ⓔ	17 Ⓐ Ⓑ Ⓒ Ⓓ Ⓔ	29 Ⓐ Ⓑ Ⓒ Ⓓ Ⓔ	41 Ⓐ Ⓑ Ⓒ Ⓓ Ⓔ
6 Ⓐ Ⓑ Ⓒ Ⓓ Ⓔ	18 Ⓐ Ⓑ Ⓒ Ⓓ Ⓔ	30 Ⓐ Ⓑ Ⓒ Ⓓ Ⓔ	42 Ⓐ Ⓑ Ⓒ Ⓓ Ⓔ
7 Ⓐ Ⓑ Ⓒ Ⓓ Ⓔ	19 Ⓐ Ⓑ Ⓒ Ⓓ Ⓔ	31 Ⓐ Ⓑ Ⓒ Ⓓ Ⓔ	43 Ⓐ Ⓑ Ⓒ Ⓓ Ⓔ
8 Ⓐ Ⓑ Ⓒ Ⓓ Ⓔ	20 Ⓐ Ⓑ Ⓒ Ⓓ Ⓔ	32 Ⓐ Ⓑ Ⓒ Ⓓ Ⓔ	44 Ⓐ Ⓑ Ⓒ Ⓓ Ⓔ
9 Ⓐ Ⓑ Ⓒ Ⓓ Ⓔ	21 Ⓐ Ⓑ Ⓒ Ⓓ Ⓔ	33 Ⓐ Ⓑ Ⓒ Ⓓ Ⓔ	45 Ⓐ Ⓑ Ⓒ Ⓓ Ⓔ
10 Ⓐ Ⓑ Ⓒ Ⓓ Ⓔ	22 Ⓐ Ⓑ Ⓒ Ⓓ Ⓔ	34 Ⓐ Ⓑ Ⓒ Ⓓ Ⓔ	
11 Ⓐ Ⓑ Ⓒ Ⓓ Ⓔ	23 Ⓐ Ⓑ Ⓒ Ⓓ Ⓔ	35 Ⓐ Ⓑ Ⓒ Ⓓ Ⓔ	
12 Ⓐ Ⓑ Ⓒ Ⓓ Ⓔ	24 Ⓐ Ⓑ Ⓒ Ⓓ Ⓔ	36 Ⓐ Ⓑ Ⓒ Ⓓ Ⓔ	

FOR ETS USE ONLY	R	ESSAY	R/ESSAY	CS

LAST NAME (first two letters) [ ] [ ]   FIRST INITIAL [ ]   DATE OF BIRTH (month and day only)   MONTH [ ] [ ]   DAY [ ] [ ]

TEST DATE: ___ / ___ / ___   CANDIDATE ID NUMBER: _____   TEST BOOK SERIAL NUMBER: _____   TEST CODE / FORM CODE: _____
MO. DAY YEAR

I agree to give Educational Testing Service permission to use my responses anonymously in its educational research and for instructional purposes. I understand that I am free to mark "No," with no effect on my score or its reporting.

○ Yes   ○ No

(ESSAY) Begin your essay on this page. If you need more space, continue on page 4.

_____
_____
_____
_____
_____
_____
_____
_____
_____
_____
_____
_____
_____
_____
_____
_____
_____
_____
_____
_____
_____
_____
_____
_____
_____

Continuation of essay from page 3. Write below only if you need more space.

_____

_____

_____

_____

_____

_____

_____

_____

_____

_____

_____

_____

_____

_____

_____

_____

_____

_____

_____

_____

_____

_____

_____

_____

_____

_____

_____

_____

_____

Section 1
Multiple-Choice
Time—30 minutes
38 Questions

Directions: In each of the sentences below four portions are underlined and lettered. Read each sentence and decide whether any of the underlined parts contains a grammatical construction, a word use, or an instance of incorrect or omitted punctuation or capitalization that would be inappropriate in carefully written English. If so, note the letter printed beneath the underlined portion and completely fill in the corresponding lettered space on the answer sheet with a heavy, dark mark so that you cannot see the letter.

If there are no errors in any of the underlined portions, fill in space E. <u>No sentence has more than one error.</u>

Remember, try to answer every question.

Examples:

1. He spoke <u>bluntly</u> and <u>angrily</u>
            A   B
   to <u>we</u> <u>spectators</u>. <u>No error</u>
     C   D   E

2. Margaret <u>insists</u> <u>that</u> this hat <u>,</u>
            A   B   C
   coat, and scarf <u>,</u> are hers.
               D
   <u>No error</u>
     E

Sample Answers:

1. (A) (B) ● (D) (E)

2. (A) (B) (C) ● (E)

1. The thousands <u>of glacier</u> studded <u>across</u> 1,500 miles of the
                     A   B
   Himalayas are a major source of South Asia's water <u>supply</u>, feeding
                                                     C
   more than a dozen major rivers and <u>sustaining</u> a billion people
                                              D
   downstream. <u>No error</u>
                E

2. Some high schools <u>have found that</u> when they reschedule their
                             A
   first classes from 7:30 A.M. <u>to</u> an hour or so <u>later</u>, both attendance
                                B   C
   and academic performance immediately <u>improves</u>. <u>No error</u>
                                       D   E

3. The health of tropical forests is very important <u>both to</u> the peoples
                                            A
   of tropical countries and to future trends in biodiversity and global
   <u>climate</u>, experts, therefore, <u>are advocating</u> international support
     B   C
   for a program <u>to monitor</u> forests worldwide. <u>No error</u>
                   D   E

4. Eagles are <u>differentiated with</u> other birds of prey <u>mainly by</u>
                     A   B
   <u>their</u> larger size, <u>more powerful</u> build, and heavier head and
     C   D
   bill. <u>No error</u>
        E

5. The growth and <u>continued</u> health of any plant <u>requiring</u>
                     A   B
   adequate supplies of nitrogen, phosphorus, and potassium, but
   the optimal <u>amount</u> of each chemical nutrient varies greatly
                C
   <u>from species to species</u>. <u>No error</u>
             D   E

6. Cargo ships take on and transport ballast water in order

for maintaining   stability,   but subsequent   discharge
    A   B

into foreign waters of ballast that contains bacteria and other
       C

organisms often causes ecological damage. No error
         D   E

7. After moving from the Northeast to southern California, I

found that I missed seeing snow in winter, so I often took
   A   B   C

a week in February to visit my sister in snow-covered Buffalo.
              D

No error
 E

8. Although aluminum is the most plentiful metallic element in
                         A

Earths crust, pure aluminum was once almost as costly as gold
    B   C

because early refining processes were so difficult. No error
        D   E

9. A recent study suggests that giving people the means to moni-
               A

tor their electricity usage help them to lower their monthly
                  B   C

bills and potentially reduces the need to build new power plants.
                                       D

No error
 E

10. A galley, a type of ancient ship, was propelled principally by
                       A   B

a crew at oars, but their sail could augment human power by
                C

harnessing the force of the wind. No error
     D   E

11. The Seventeenth-century poet Anne Bradstreet was an unusually
            A   B

well educated woman for her time, having been tutored in
                 C   D

history, several languages, and literature. No error
                               E

12. A number of organizations <u>have expressed</u> concern that biofuels
                              A

    <u>could</u> do more harm <u>than good</u> by taking large areas of arable
    B   C

    land out of food production and <u>inflate</u> crop prices. <u>No error</u>
                                    D   E

13. In initiation ceremonies that were observed by <u>many traditional</u>
                                                    A

    societies, adolescent boys left the safety of their homes and

    <u>underwent</u> various tests <u>of prowess</u> before being accepted as
    B   C

    <u>an adult</u>. <u>No error</u>
    D   E

14. Journalist and photographer Margaret Bourke-White<u>_</u> who
                                                       A

    <u>achieved prominence</u> during the Second World War as America's
            B

    first female war correspondent, also served on the original staff of

    Life magazine, <u>in which</u> her photographs <u>frequently</u> appeared.
                     C   D

    <u>No error</u>
    E

15. Growing up in California, novelist Maxine Hong Kingston was

    <u>surrounded by</u> immigrants from her <u>father's</u> village in China,
         A   B

    and <u>their</u> storytelling influenced her <u>strong</u> when she started to
        C   D

    write. <u>No error</u>
           E

16. In 2002 the <u>amount</u> of United States residents <u>who</u> could claim
                A   B

    descent <u>from</u> the original *Mayflower* passengers who settled at
            C

    Plymouth was <u>approximately</u> 35 million. <u>No error</u>
                 D   E

17. Many animals are <u>extremely</u> sensitive <u>to</u> high-frequency sounds
                     A   B

    that are all but imperceptible to <u>the adult</u> human ear. <u>No error</u>
              C   D   E

18. Before synthetic fertilizer was developed, a farmer's
    <u>A</u>

    <u>most effective means</u> of increasing the soil's nitrogen content had
    <u>B</u>

    been <u>regular intervals of periodic</u> cultivation of nitrogen-fixing
    <u>C</u>

    legumes <u>such as</u> peas. <u>No error</u>
    <u>D</u>   <u>E</u>

19. Brittany occupies a <u>large</u> peninsula in the <u>northwest</u> of France,
    <u>A</u>   <u>B</u>

    <u>laying between</u> the English <u>Channel</u> to the north and the Bay of
    <u>C</u>   <u>D</u>

    Biscay to the south. <u>No error</u>
    <u>E</u>

20. The <u>recent</u> production of the play seemed disjointed, partly
    <u>A</u>

    <u>because</u> the lead actress's style was so much more flamboyant
    <u>B</u>

    than <u>the lead actor</u> who played <u>opposite her</u>. <u>No error</u>
    <u>C</u>   <u>D</u>   <u>E</u>

21. Some people <u>advocate</u> abolishing the penny, <u>pointing out</u> that
    <u>A</u>   <u>B</u>

    due to inflation, the <u>value of</u> the copper used to make a penny
    <u>C</u>

    sometimes exceeds <u>their</u> face value. <u>No error</u>
    <u>D</u>   <u>E</u>

Part B
17 Questions
(Suggested time—20 minutes)

Directions: In each of the following sentences some part of the sentence or the entire sentence is underlined. Beneath each sentence you will find five ways of writing the underlined part. The first of these repeats the original, but the other four are all different. If you think the original sentence is better than any of the suggested changes, you should choose answer A; otherwise you should mark one of the other choices. Select the best answer and completely fill in the corresponding lettered space on the answer sheet with a heavy, dark mark so that you cannot see the letter.

This is a test of correctness and effectiveness of expression. In choosing answers, follow the requirements of standard written English; that is, pay attention to acceptable usage in grammar, diction (choice of words), sentence construction, and punctuation. Choose the answer that expresses most effectively what is presented in the original sentence; this answer should be clear and exact, without awkwardness, ambiguity, or redundancy.

Remember, try to answer every question.

Examples:

Sample Answers:

1. <u>While waving</u> goodbye to our friends, the airplane took off, and we watched it disappear in the sky.

   1.

   (A) While waving
   (B) Waving
   (C) As we were waving
   (D) While we are waving
   (E) During waving

2. Modern travelers seem to prefer speed <u>to comfort</u>.

   2.

   (A) to comfort
   (B) than comfort
   (C) rather than being comfortable
   (D) instead of being comfortable
   (E) more than comfort

22. After the discovery of King Tutankhamen's tomb by archaeologist Howard Carter in 1922, public interest in ancient Egyptian art and architecture had reached a peak and remained high even now.

    (A) had reached a peak and remained
    (B) reached a peak and remains
    (C) has reached a peak and remains
    (D) reached a peak and remaining
    (E) would reach a peak and remain

23. Like many other ancient Chinese philosophers, Lao-tzu, author of the *Tao Te Ching*, often explained his ideas by way of paradox, analogy, and he appropriated ancient sayings.

    (A) paradox, analogy, and he appropriated ancient sayings
    (B) paradox, using analogy, and he appropriated ancient sayings
    (C) paradox, using analogy, and the appropriation of ancient sayings
    (D) paradox and analogy, and he appropriated ancient sayings
    (E) paradox, analogy, and the appropriation of ancient sayings

24. During his long tenure as president, Franklin Roosevelt delivered many important speeches, and in his most famous, the first inaugural address, assuring Americans that they had nothing to fear but fear itself.

    (A) and in his most famous, the first inaugural address, assuring
    (B) but the most famous was his first inaugural address, in which he assured
    (C) but his first inaugural address, his most famous speech, has assured
    (D) but the first inaugural address, his most famous speech, was because it assured
    (E) of which his most famous, the first inaugural address, assuring

25. When a voting district is gerrymandered, its boundaries are unfairly manipulated to increase the number of voters within a particular group while the total number of voters stays about equally to what it was originally.

    (A) equally to what it was
    (B) equally to what they were
    (C) equal to what it was
    (D) equal to what they were
    (E) equalling what it was

26. In *Robinson Crusoe*, the title character's fortunes fluctuate dramatically from <u>success as a merchant to capture by pirates, from prosperity as a Brazilian planter to isolation on a remote island</u>.

(A) success as a merchant to capture by pirates, from prosperity as a Brazilian planter to isolation on a remote island

(B) success as a merchant to being captured by pirates, from Brazil as a prosperous planter to being isolated on a remote island

(C) succeeding as a merchant to capture by pirates, from prospering as a Brazilian planter to isolation on a remote island

(D) successful merchant to capture by pirates, from prosperity as a Brazilian planter to being isolated on a remote island

(E) a merchant's success to being captured by pirates, from prosperity as a Brazilian planter to a remote island's isolation

27. The ancient ice dome cloaking <u>Greenland is so vast and pilots have mistaken it for a cloud bank spanning</u> the horizon.

(A) Greenland is so vast and pilots have mistaken it for a cloud bank spanning

(B) Greenland is so vast that pilots have mistaken it for a cloud bank spanning

(C) Greenland was so vast and pilots have mistook it to be a cloud bank that spanned

(D) Greenland, so vast as pilots have mistaken it for a cloud bank spanning

(E) Greenland, it is so vast, pilots have mistook it as a cloud bank that spans

28. <u>Being skeptical about our cab driver's ability to get us to the airport on time, then we called</u> the airport from the cab to find out about later flights.

(A) Being skeptical about our cab driver's ability to get us to the airport on time, then we called

(B) We were skeptical about our cab driver's ability to get us to the airport on time, by calling

(C) Skeptical as we were about our cab driver's ability to get us to the airport on time, so we called

(D) Skeptical about our cab driver's ability to get us to the airport on time, so we were calling

(E) Skeptical about our cab driver's ability to get us to the airport on time, we called

29. <u>Though they are different from one another in style, tone, and as far as plot,</u> Shakespeare's comedy *Much Ado About Nothing* and his tragedy *Othello* both explore the susceptibility of lovers to manipulation by other people.

   (A) Though they are different from one another in style, tone, and as far as plot,
   (B) Though one being different from the other in style, tone, and their plot,
   (C) Being different from one another in style, their tone, and plot,
   (D) Different as they are from one another in style, tone, and plot,
   (E) They differ from one another in style, tone, and plot,

30. <u>The first exhibition of work by sculptor Louise Bourgeois was a success in 1947 as it was not</u> until the 1970s that she achieved widespread recognition in the art world.

   (A) The first exhibition of work by sculptor Louise Bourgeois was a success in 1947 as it was not
   (B) The first exhibition of work by sculptor Louise Bourgeois was a success in 1947, but it was not
   (C) The first exhibition of sculptor Louise Bourgeois' work being successful in 1947; it was not
   (D) Successful as sculptor Louise Bourgeois' first exhibition of her work was in 1947, not
   (E) Despite the success of sculptor Louise Bourgeois' first exhibition of her work in 1947, then it was not

31. Trained to see for the blind, hear for the deaf, and move for the immobilized, <u>for people with disabilities dogs have become indispensable companions.</u>

   (A) for people with disabilities dogs have become indispensable companions
   (B) people with disabilities find dogs have become indispensable companions
   (C) dogs, to people with disabilities, they have become indispensable companions
   (D) dogs having become indispensable companions to people with disabilities
   (E) dogs have become indispensable companions for people with disabilities

32. Often labeled a muckraker, author Ida Tarbell not only exposed unfair business practices of large corporations like Standard Oil <u>and even inspired</u> legislation that would eventually control such abuses.

(A) and even inspired
(B) and thereby inspired
(C) but also inspired
(D) but as a result inspired
(E) thus inspiring

33. In an effort to save money and to appeal to environmentally conscious customers, <u>energy-saving measures are being instituted in many hotels</u>.

(A) energy-saving measures are being instituted in many hotels
(B) energy-saving measures in many hotels have been instituted
(C) they have instituted in many hotels energy-saving measures
(D) many hotels are having energy-saving measures instituted in them
(E) many hotels are instituting energy-saving measures

34. Used primarily as a pain reliever, ordinary aspirin can also serve <u>as a treatment for inflammation of body tissues, to reduce fever, and to prevent blood clots</u> that might cause strokes.

(A) as a treatment for inflammation of body tissues, to reduce fever, and to prevent blood clots
(B) as a treatment for body tissue inflammation, in reduction of fever, and for blood clot prevention
(C) to treat inflammation of body tissues, to reduce fever, and to prevent blood clots
(D) in treating inflammation of body tissues, reducing fever, and for prevention of blood clots
(E) in treatment of inflamed body tissues, for reduction of fever, and in blood clot prevention

35. Consisting mostly of salted meat and hardtack, a hard biscuit made of flour and water, the typical diet of eighteenth-century sailors was not <u>hardly adequate to prevent diseases caused by vitamin deficiencies</u>.

(A) hardly adequate to prevent diseases caused by vitamin deficiencies
(B) hardly adequate in its vitamin content to prevent deficiency diseases
(C) hardly adequate in their vitamin content to prevent deficiency diseases
(D) adequate to prevent diseases caused by vitamin deficiencies
(E) adequate in their vitamin content to prevent deficiency diseases

36. When Queen Anne died in 1714 without a direct heir to the British throne, her cousin George <u>became king, even though he had previously lived only in Germany and spoke</u> little English.

(A) became king, even though he had previously lived only in Germany and spoke
(B) had become king, even though he had previously lived only in Germany and had spoken
(C) had become king, even though he previously lived only in Germany and spoke
(D) has become king, even though he has previously lived only in Germany and has spoken
(E) becomes king, even though he had previously lived only in Germany and speaks

37. Lacking confidence that any movie could do justice to a great literary work, <u>film adaptations of books they have loved are studiously avoided by many people</u>.

(A) film adaptations of books they have loved are studiously avoided by many people
(B) film adaptations, when they are of books that people have loved, are studiously avoided by many
(C) many people studiously avoid film adaptations of books they have loved
(D) many people will have been studiously avoiding film adaptations of books they loved
(E) many people had studiously avoided film adaptations of books they will have loved

38. While the total area of the United States is about the same as that of China, China's population of 1.33 billion is more than four times <u>what the United States is</u>.

(A) what the United States is
(B) what this number in the United States is
(C) that of the United States
(D) those in the United States
(E) the people in the United States

Section 2
Essay
Time—30 minutes

Directions: You will have 30 minutes to plan and write an essay on the topic presented on page 238. Read the topic carefully. You will probably find it best to spend a little time considering the topic and organizing your thoughts before you begin writing. DO NOT WRITE ON A TOPIC OTHER THAN THE ONE SPECIFIED. An essay on a topic of your own choice will not be acceptable. In order for your test to be scored, your response must be in English.

An essay question is included in this test to give you an opportunity to demonstrate how well you can write. You should, therefore, take care to write clearly and effectively, using specific examples where appropriate. Remember that how well you write is much more important than how much you write, but to cover the topic adequately, you will probably need to write more than a paragraph.

Your essay will be scored on the basis of its total quality—i.e., holistically. Each essay score is the sum of points (0–6) given by two readers. When your total writing score is computed, your essay score will be combined with your score for the multiple-choice section of the test.

You are to write your essay on the answer sheet; you will receive no other paper on which to write. Please write neatly and legibly. To be certain you have enough space on the answer sheet for your entire essay, please do NOT skip lines, do NOT write in excessively large letters, and do NOT leave wide margins. You may use the bottom of page 238 for any notes you may wish to make before you begin writing.

Section 2
(Essay)
Time—30 minutes

Read the opinion stated below.

"Advances in computer technology have made the classroom unnecessary, since students and teachers are able to communicate with each other from computer terminals at home or at work."

Discuss the extent to which you agree or disagree with this point of view. Support your position with specific reasons and examples from your own experience, observations, or reading.

1. **Choice A is the correct answer.** The error occurs at choice A, where the singular noun "glacier" does not logically agree with the earlier plural noun "thousands"; the correct form is "glaciers." At choice B the preposition "across" is aptly chosen to indicate a wide geographic expanse; at choice C a comma correctly separates the sentence's main clause from the nonessential modifying phrase that follows; and at choice D the participle "sustaining" is parallel with the earlier participle "feeding."

2. **Choice D is the correct answer.** An error in subject/verb agreement occurs at choice D. Since the clause has a compound subject ("both attendance and academic performance"), the verb should also be plural ("improve"). At choice A the present perfect verb tense is correct to describe a condition that began in the past but continues into the present. At choice B the preposition "to" is the proper idiom (when used along with the earlier preposition "from") to introduce the new starting time. At choice C "later" functions correctly as an adverb telling when.

3. **Choice B is the correct answer.** The error at choice B is a comma splice. Since both clauses are independent, a semicolon rather than a comma should separate them. At choice A the phrase "both to" functions correctly to introduce two parallel prepositional phrases. At choice C the progressive verb form "are advocating" correctly indicates ongoing action, and its plural number agrees with the plural subject "experts." At choice D the infinitive "to monitor" correctly introduces an adjective phrase that describes the monitoring program.

4. **Choice A is the correct answer.** An incorrect idiom at choice A is the error in this sentence. Here the verb "differentiated" should be followed by the preposition "from" (suggesting separation) rather than the preposition "with" (suggesting connection). At choice B the adverb "mainly" correctly modifies the earlier verb, and the preposition "by" correctly introduces a phrase listing features that make eagles different. The plural possessive adjective "their" at choice C agrees with its plural antecedent "Eagles," and at choice D the comparative form of the adjective ("more powerful") is correct when contrasting two groups (eagles versus all other birds of prey).

5. **Choice B is the correct answer.** This construction is an error in verb form, because it contains, at choice B, the verbal "requiring" rather than the verb "require," which would have satisfied the need

for a predicate. At A the verbal "continued" functions correctly as an adjective modifying "health"; at choice C the singular subject "amount" agrees with the singular verb "varies"; and the two prepositional phrases at choice D are appropriately chosen to indicate a range among species.

6. **Choice A is the correct answer.** An incorrect idiom occurs at choice A. After the phrase "in order," the appropriate idiom is the infinitive form "to maintain" rather than the gerund phrase "for maintaining." At choice B "but" is an appropriate conjunction to introduce a contrasting idea, and the adjective "subsequent" correctly modifies the noun "discharge." The prepositional phrase "into foreign waters" at choice C serves correctly as an adjective that modifies the noun immediately before it. At choice D the singular verb "causes" agrees with the singular subject "discharge," and the adverb "often" functions correctly to tell when damage occurs.

7. **Choice E is the correct answer.** There are no grammatical, idiomatic, logical, or structural errors in this sentence.

8. **Choice B is the correct answer.** The error at choice B is omission of a necessary apostrophe. The correct form to show possession is "Earth's" instead of "Earths." At choice A the superlative form of the adjective is correct. The phrase at choice C correctly combines an adverb meaning to the same degree ("as"), an apt adjective ("costly"), and the appropriate preposition "as" to complete the comparison. At choice D both "early" and "refining" serve correctly as adjectives modifying the noun "processes."

9. **Choice B is the correct answer.** An error in subject/verb agreement occurs at choice B, where the correct form should be the singular verb "helps." The plural verb "help" does not agree with the singular gerund phrase "giving people the means to monitor their electricity usage" that functions as the subject of the dependent clause. At choice A "that" is the correct conjunction to link the main clause "A recent study suggests" with the dependent clause that makes up the rest of the sentence. At choice C the adjective "monthly" appropriately describes the noun "bills," and at choice D the noun phrase "power plants" functions correctly as the object of the infinitive "to build."

10. **Choice C is the correct answer.** At choice C the plural possessive adjective "their" does not agree with the singular noun to which it refers, "galley." The proper adjective form is "its." At choice A, a comma is used correctly to set off a nonessential appositive ("a type of ancient ship") that merely supplies additional information; at choice B the adverb "principally" modifies the verb immediately

before it ("propelled"); and at choice D the verbal "harnessing" functions correctly as the object of the preposition "by."

11. **Choice A is the correct answer.** The error at choice A is inappropriate use of a capital letter. Since the adjective "Seventeenth-century" is not derived from a proper noun, it should begin with a lowercase letter. At choice B the adverb "unusually" correctly modifies the adjective phrase "well educated." At choice C the preposition "for" is appropriate for the context, and at choice D the helping verbs "having been" correctly introduce a participial phrase that describes Anne Bradstreet.

12. **Choice D is the correct answer.** The verbal form at choice D violates the need to maintain parallelism in expressing closely related ideas. Since the first object of the preposition "by" is a gerund ("taking"), the second object at D should take that same form ("inflating"). At choice A the verb, in present perfect tense, correctly describes action that began in the past but is continuing, and it agrees with the collective noun phrase "A number," which functions as a plural subject. At choice B the helping verb "could" is used correctly to indicate a possible future action. At choice C the phrase "than good" is idiomatically correct to complete the comparison begun by the earlier phrase "more harm."

13. **Choice D is the correct answer.** The singular noun "adult" at choice D produces an error in logical agreement. Since several boys do not become, after their tests of prowess, a single adult, the logically correct form should be "adults." The two adjectives at choice A ("many" and "traditional") work together as appropriate modifiers of the noun "societies." At choice B the past tense of the verb is correct to describe action already completed. At choice C the prepositional phrase "of prowess" functions correctly as an adjective to describe the preceding noun "tests."

14. **Choice A is the correct answer.** The error at choice A is omission of a comma needed to indicate the beginning of a nonrestrictive clause. Since the clause starting with "who" and ending with "correspondent" provides nonessential information, it should be set off by commas. At choice B the verb "achieved" is correct to describe action already completed, and the noun "prominence" functions correctly as the object of that verb. At choice C the phrase "in which" appropriately connects the subsequent clause ("her . . . appeared") to the earlier noun "magazine." The adverb "frequently" at choice D correctly modifies the verb "appeared."

15. **Choice D is the correct answer.** The error in this sentence is use of an adjective when the context requires an adverb. To modify the verb "influenced" and thus tell how, the correct adverb should

be "strongly." At choice A the past participle form of the verb ("surrounded") is correct for use after the helping verb "was," and the preposition "by" correctly begins an adverbial phrase. The apostrophe at choice B is used correctly to indicate possession by one person, and the plural possessive adjective "their" at choice C agrees with the plural noun "immigrants" to which it refers.

16. **Choice A is the correct answer.** In this sentence the error is an incorrect word choice at choice A. Since individual residents can be counted, the appropriate noun for this context is "number" rather than "amount." At choice B the relative pronoun "who" functions correctly to introduce a restrictive adjective clause; at choice C the preposition "from" is aptly chosen to indicate a source; and at choice D the adverb "approximately" correctly modifies the preceding verb.

17. **Choice E is the correct answer.** There are no grammatical, idiomatic, logical, or structural errors in this sentence.

18. **Choice C is the correct answer.** Wordiness at choice C is the error in this sentence. Since "regular intervals of" and "periodic" convey the same meaning, the sentence would be correct with either but not with both. The connecting word "Before" is used correctly at choice A to introduce an adverb clause that tells when. In the phrase at choice B, the noun "means" serves correctly as subject of the main clause, and the superlative form of the adjective ("most effective") is appropriate for comparing one method with all others. At choice D the phrase beginning with "such as" functions correctly to supply a specific example of legumes.

19. **Choice C is the correct answer.** The error in this sentence is an incorrect word choice at choice C. Instead of "laying," which means "putting in place," the proper verb is "lying," which means "staying in a particular place." At choice A the adjective "large" is an appropriate adjective to modify the noun "peninsula." The geographic term "northwest" at choice B functions correctly as the object of the preposition "in," and the capitalization at choice D is correct, since "Channel" is part of a proper noun.

20. **Choice C is the correct answer.** The phrasing at choice C produces an illogical comparison error, since an actor is being compared to a style of acting. The logically correct phrasing should be "that of the lead actor." The adjective "recent" at choice A serves aptly to describe the noun "production." At choice B the conjunction "because" correctly introduces a clause that explains why, and the prepositional phrase at choice D functions properly as an adverb telling where.

21. Choice D is the correct answer. The error is at choice D, where the plural possessive adjective "their" does not agree with the singular noun ("penny") to which it refers; the correct form is "its." The plural verb ("advocate") at choice A agrees with its plural subject ("people"), and the present tense of the verb is appropriate to describe current action. At choice B the participle "pointing out" introduces a lengthy phrase that correctly modifies "people." At choice C the singular noun "value" serves correctly as subject of the singular verb "exceeds," and "of" is the appropriate preposition to introduce the adjective phrase that follows.

Part B

22. Choice B is the best answer. Choice A contains two errors in verb tense; the past perfect tense ("had reached") illogically implies that the peak of interest was even earlier than the 1922 discovery, and the past tense ("remained") is inconsistent with the adverb clue "now." Choice B corrects both of these errors, since "reached" correctly refers to a time in the past but after 1922, and "remains" is the proper tense to describe a current condition. In choice C the second verb is correct, but the present perfect tense ("has reached") incorrectly suggests an action continuing up to the present. In choice D the first verb is correct, but the verbal "remaining" cannot function as a predicate without a helping verb. In choice E the use of "would" to imply future developments is incorrect, since the sentence refers to actions only in the past and the present.

23. Choice E is the best answer. The three strategies for explanation listed in choice A are not grammatically parallel, since the first two are nouns and the third is an independent clause. In choice B the lack of parallelism is even more pronounced, since the second item in the list is now a gerund phrase ("using analogy"). Choice C uses two parallel nouns ("paradox" and "appropriation"), but the gerund phrase still violates parallelism. Choice D adds the conjunction "and" but retains the error present in choice A. Since choice E uses three parallel nouns ("paradox," "analogy," and "appropriation"), it is the best version.

24. Choice B is the best answer. Choice A produces a fragmentary construction because the verbal "assuring," without a helping verb, cannot function as a predicate. Choice B is the best option, since "but" serves as an appropriate connecting word, the verb "was" functions as a necessary predicate, and the phrase "in which" introduces a grammatically correct dependent clause. The error in choice C is the present perfect verb tense ("has assured"), which incorrectly implies action continuing up to now. In choice D word order is garbled, since context requires that the linking verb "was" be placed immediately after "address." Choice E exhibits the same error as choice A even though wording is slightly different.

25. **Choice C is the best answer.** Choices A and B use the adverb "equally" when the context requires an adjective ("equal") to modify the noun "number." Choice B also introduces an additional problem, since the plural pronoun "they" does not agree with the singular noun "number," to which it should refer. Since choice C avoids both of these errors, it is the best option. Choice D uses the correct adjective but retains the incorrect pronoun. In choice E the verbal "equalling" is idiomatically inappropriate for use after the verb "stays."

26. **Choice A is the best answer.** Choice A is the best version, because it uses four key nouns ("success," "capture," "prosperity," and "isolation") to maintain grammatical parallelism in describing Crusoe's changing status. All the other choices violate parallelism in some way. Choice B substitutes verbal phrases ("being captured" and "being isolated") for two simpler nouns and also uses a place name ("Brazil") that is not logically parallel to the other words that describe Crusoe's condition. Choice C also mixes two verbal forms ("succeeding" and "prospering") with two nouns ("capture" and "isolation"). Choice D retains one verbal form ("being isolated") and illogically compares a person, "successful merchant," to a condition, "capture by pirates." Choice E uses one verbal ("being captured") along with three nouns and introduces still another logical problem, since it mentions not Crusoe's isolation but that of an island.

27. **Choice B is the correct answer.** Choice A uses a coordinating conjunction ("and"), even though the phrase "so vast" should be followed by the subordinating conjunction "that." Since choice B provides the correct connecting word to introduce the dependent clause, it is the best choice. Choice C retains the error in choice A and adds two more: a verb in past tense ("was" instead of "is") and the incorrect form of another verb ("mistook" instead of "mistaken"). Choice D produces a sentence fragment, since it has no clause that can stand alone. The most glaring error in choice E is the incorrect verb form ("mistook") seen earlier in choice C.

28. **Choice E is the correct answer.** Choice E is best, because it eliminates wordiness and establishes a clear connection between the initial modifying phrase ("Skeptical . . . on time") and the sentence's main clause ("we called . . . flights"). Choices A and C contain unnecessary words ("Being" and "then" in A; "as we were" and "so" in C). In choice B the sentence structure is garbled, as the phrase that begins with "by calling" has no clear grammatical

or logical relationship to the rest of the sentence. In choice D the connecting word "so" is redundant, and the progressive verb "were calling" should be reduced to the simpler past tense form "called."

29. **Choice D is the correct answer.** Choice D is best, because it maintains perfect parallelism by using three nouns ("style," "tone," and "plot") as objects of the preposition "in." Choices A, B, and C destroy parallelism by including unnecessary words or phrases: in A the phrase "as far as" is redundant, and in both B and C the possessive adjective "their" is not needed. Although choice E displays the correct parallelism, it introduces a different error by placing a comma, rather than a semicolon, between two independent clauses ("They . . . plot" and "Shakespeare's . . . people").

30. **Choice B is the correct answer.** Choice B is best, because the conjunction "but" correctly indicates a contrast between conditions at the two different times (1947 and 1970s). In choice A the connecting word "as" is not appropriate for the context. In choice C a semicolon is used incorrectly to separate a phrase ("The first . . . 1947") from an independent clause ("it . . . world"). Choice D produces a sentence fragment, since it contains no predicate. In choice E the adverb "then" is redundant, since two specific times are already clearly indicated.

31. **Choice E is the correct answer.** In choices A and B the major problem is a dangling or misplaced modifier, since the phrase beginning with "Trained" should describe "dogs" rather than "people." Choices C and D alter the word order to correct the modification problem, but in C the pronoun "they" is redundant, and D is a sentence fragment, because it provides no predicate. Choice E displays correct placement of the modifying phrase and also avoids any other errors.

32. **Choice C is the correct answer.** All choices except choice C introduce errors in correlation. To complete the idea introduced by the phrase "not only," the one idiomatically correct connecting phrase is "but also." Thus, only choice C correctly completes the sentence.

33. **Choice E is the best answer.** Choices A and B produce dangling modifiers, since the phrase that begins with "In an effort" does not logically agree with "energy-saving measures." Choice C contains the pronoun "they" but no noun to which this pronoun can refer. Choice D uses "many hotels" as the appropriate subject of the sentence, but the final phrase "in them" is redundant. Choice E is best, because it uses the correct subject ("many hotels") and avoids unnecessary words.

34. **Choice C is the best answer.** Choice C is best, because it uses three perfectly parallel infinitive phrases ("to treat," "to reduce," and "to prevent") in listing the three additional uses for aspirin. Neither choice A nor choice D provides a parallel structure: choice A starts with a long prepositional phrase and concludes with two infinitive phrases, while choice D mixes two verbal forms ("treating" and "reducing") with the noun "prevention." Both choices B and E end with the noun phrase "blood clot prevention," which does not logically agree with the modifying phrase ("that might cause strokes") that follows it.

35. **Choice D is the best answer.** The major error in choices A, B, and C is the illogical use of a double negative, since both "not" and "hardly" express negation. Choice C introduces an additional error because the plural possessive adjective "their" does not agree with the singular noun "diet." Choice E omits the superfluous negative word but also displays this error in agreement. In avoiding both errors, choice D becomes the only correct version.

36. **Choice A is the best answer.** All choices except choice A display errors in verb tense. In choice A the past tense "became" is correct to describe action that took place in 1714, and the past perfect "had . . . lived" correctly indicates action at an even earlier time. In choice B the first use of past perfect tense ("had become") is incorrect, because George did not rule before 1714. Choice C incorporates this same error and also uses incorrect past tense ("lived") to indicate George's residence before 1714. In choice D all three present perfect verb forms ("has become," "has . . . lived," and "has spoken") are incorrect, because these actions do not continue to the present time. In choice E two uses of present tense ("becomes" and "speaks") are incorrect, because the actions described were obviously in the past.

37. **Choice C is the best answer.** Choices A and B produce dangling modifiers, since the phrase that begins with "Lacking confidence" does not logically describe "film adaptations." Choice C corrects this error by placing the noun "people" in its proper position immediately after the end of the modifying phrase. Choices D and E also correct the error in modification, but both introduce errors in verb tense. The future perfect tense ("will have") in both choices D and E, and the past perfect tense ("had . . . avoided") in choice E are all inappropriate for describing current action.

38. **Choice C is the best answer.** Choice A presents an illogical or incomplete comparison, since it compares a population number ("1.33 billion") with a country ("the United States"). In choice B logic is improved, but phrasing is verbose and indirect. Choice C

is the best version, since it avoids wordiness and also supplies the proper pronoun ("that") to insure that like things (the population numbers of two different countries) are being compared. Choice D apparently attempts to correct the logic problem, but its plural pronoun "those" does not agree with the singular noun "population." In choice E logic is again flawed, since a number is compared with the people themselves.

Essay	Explanation of Score
Advancements in computer technology today have made society a close network of people—making it easier to get wired and access vast amounts of information than ever before. Some colleges and universities have taken advantage of this and have created networked classrooms, allowing students and teachers to communicate via computer terminals, thus eliminating much classroom time. However, I disagree with the statement that this new technology will completely make the classroom unnecessary, for three reasons. First, eliminating the classroom would eradicate interaction between student and teacher, creating a steril learning environment. Secondly, students who learn best via kinesthetic or audio methods would be disadvantaged. Finally, individuals who choose not to "get wired" would miss out on opportunities to advance their education because instruction is overed only on the Internet.	This well-written essay begins with a strong thesis disagreeing with the statement for three reasons: computer learning would "eradicate interaction between student and teacher," "students who learn best via kinesthetic or audio methods would be disadvantaged," and those without computers would "miss out on opportunities to advance their education." Listing these three reasons leads to natural organization. However, this essay has more logical connections than an essay earning a score of 5.
Humans are social beings—we thrive on interaction with one another. If students and teachers interacted via only the computer screen, it would eliminate the social aspect so important to the learning process. One strategy of educators is to generate response from the students. Discussions allow students to actively process information given, vocalize what they are learning, and gain additional insight from the educator by asking questions. This interaction cannot take place through a computer screen; even live chats are void of the face-to-face contact that makes learning interactive and interesting.	The second paragraph begins with a discussion of the "social aspect so important to the learning process." The essay uses well-chosen reasons to support the idea, including a description of educational strategy.
We as humans also learn and process information very differently. Some learn best through audio instruction, others visually, and others through kinesthetic methods. Computer-based teaching would cater best to those who learn visually. Audio-students might cope, if the on-line classroom included some audio downloads. However, kinesthetic learners would be put to a complete disadvantage; the only hands-on interaction that would take place would	Transitioning from the "face-to-face contact" of the preceding paragraph to how people "learn and process information very differently," the essay describes how some students learn "through audio instruction, others visually, and others through kinesthetic methods." Each of these methods is explained clearly, with a description of "kinesthetic" learning as "hands-on" learning, which the writer has used personally in a classroom.

(Continued)

Essay	Explanation of Score
be on their keyboard. I have personally witnessed in my tutoring experiences that kinesthetic learners, especially younger ones, need to classroom to interact hands-on in the learning process—taking what they have learned to create something in order to better understand the implications of the lesson. Finally, regardless of how dependent our society becomes on technology, not everyone will jump at the opportunity to "get wired." My mother works in the healthcare profession, and is constantly surrounded by technology. However, she utilizes it just enough to "get by," and simply checking her e-mail is not an easy task. Though the younger generation is quick to catch on and take advantages of the opportunities posed by technology, the older generation is being left behind; many will not take the initiative to get acquainted with technology unless their occupation demands it. If classrooms were eliminated, many would-be, older, nontraditional students not familiar or interested in technology, would not have the opportunity to continue their education, because they would be discouraged at the prospect of taking courses online. Technology today is fascinating, and has created numerous opportunities for people to get wired and reach out to the world in new ways. Though I agree that computer-based learning adds to the dimensions of a classroom, it can not totally replace the classroom. Complete computer-based learning would eliminate student-teacher interaction, and would put to disadvantage students of alternative learning styles, and non-traditional students not familiar with technology. Students learn best by utilizing a variety of educational sources, but one should not completely replace the other.	Moving to society as a whole, the essay mentions that not everyone has the inclination to use a computer and that "if classrooms were eliminated, many would-be, older, nontraditional students not familiar or interested in technology, would not have the opportunity to continue their education." Again, this idea is explained clearly with examples. The concluding paragraph distills the various arguments and logically states, "Students learn best by utilizing a variety of educational sources, but one should not completely replace the other." Because this essay shows a high degree of competence, organizes and develops ideas logically, supports ideas with details and examples, uses a variety of sentence structures, and shows a high degree of language facility, this essay is appropriately given a score of 6.

Essay	Explanation of Score
The opinion that advances in computer technology have made the classroom obsolete is one that I strongly disagree with. Although technology has helped to connect people in ways unheard of previously and provides new opportunities for supplementing learning in and out of the classroom, it will never replace the benefits of a real rather than virtual classroom. A real classroom provides important social interaction, real-time and personal interaction in the progress of our students, and acts as a baseline for social equity for the students who lack the resources and comfort of other students.	This essay starts with a clear thesis disagreeing with the statement. It then proceeds to list the benefits of a classroom: "important social interaction, real-time and personal interaction in the progress of our students" and its function "as a baseline for social equity."
One goal of universal education is to create responsible and intelligent citizens in our democracy. If this is the case, which I believe it is, then the social interaction our students receive is invaluable. Students learn how to live with one another and accept differences in appearance, as well opinion. This social interaction also helps to fulfill our own need for personal touch and personal connection that a computer will never be able to satisfy.	That leads to a natural organization to develop ideas as well as clear transitions. In the second paragraph, the essay states, "One goal of universal education is to create responsible and intelligent citizens in our democracy" and supports this idea with examples of how social interaction in schools helps students develop into such citizens. The essay then links to the thesis with: "This social interaction also helps to fulfill our own need for personal touch and personal connection that a computer will never be able to satisfy."
I also believe that the Benet of the real classroom really revolves around our being able to be involved in the minute by minute and second by second progress of our students. From the moment that our students begin math examples, the writing process and reading, we are able to monitor the process they're using and the progress they're making. This happens in real time and we can work with small groups and individuals. We can switch fluidly from student to student in a way that may be impossible for a technology such as computers.	The next paragraph is developed well as the essay moves from "minute by minute" to "second by second" to "real time" and finally to "fluidly" in the description of how a teacher may watch the progress of students. Those transitions in the description of time draw the reader in and are persuasive, as the essay then states,
Lastly, schools are the one place where students are all equal for 8 hours of their day. As many in the government and media have pointed out, there is a digital divide. How can we ensure that all students have the very same equiptment? Even if we exclude equiptment issues from this discussion, school is the one place	

(Continued)

Essay	Explanation of Score
where all students are provided a safe place. Some children live in tumultous or even dangerous places that can make it impossible for schoolwork to be completed and learning to take place. Additionally, all students have access to the same learning materials when they walk into a real classroom; they all have access to the same school or classroom library, supplemental materials, and the teacher's attention. This is perhaps the best reason to allow the real classroom to endure. It is the one place where all children are treated equally and given access to the same materials. In conclusion, despite the many benefits new computer technologies over us, they will never truly replace the benefits that our country and our children derive from a real classroom. The social interactions and the personal attention and equal access given to students are factors that can never be replaced by a virtual classroom. Our children deserve the best and most personalized curriculum we can give them. We can do that best together in the real classroom.	"We can switch fluidly from student to student in a way that may be impossible for a technology such as computers." The fourth paragraph discusses how schools can be a basis for equality in society. The support of this statement is well explained, starting with, "schools are the one place where students are all equal for 8 hours of their day" and "they all have access to the same school or classroom library, supplemental materials, and the teacher's attention." It is also explained that it would be difficult to achieve parity of computer equipment and access. In the conclusion, the essay effectively reexamines the key ideas and provides a clear conclusion: "despite the many benefits new computer technologies offer us, they will never truly replace the benefits that our country and our children derive from a real classroom." Though lacking the language facility and sentence variety of an essay earning a score of 6, this essay shows clear competence in addressing the prompt and develops ideas clearly, earning it a score of 5.

Response That Received a Score of 4

Essay	Explanation of Score
In my opinion no amount of computer technology could make the classroom unnecesary. All of the technological advances should make the teachers' and students' jobs easier but not eliminate them altogether. Students still need structure and teaching. They need someone there when they have a question about a subject. Children also need the positive reinforcement from their teacher to do well in school. A computer may be able to do many things but it is not able to extrinsically motivate a child the way a teacher can. School provides many essential things that meet childrens' needs. Without school, children would not be able to have as much social interaction. Social interaction is what the class-room is all about. Teachers have started to stray away from paper-pencil assesments and are moving more towards cooperative learning. In cooperative learning the students are able to teach each other and in return their knowledge about the subject material is enhanced. Sitting at home on a computer will not manufacture the same results. Also teachers are incorporating Garner's Eight Intelligences into their curriculum. All children learn in different ways and excel indifferent areas. Learning material through a computer would only blind them from the true potential that they have. However, I do feel that computers should be integrated into the classroom. The most recent school that I have observed at incorporated computers into their language arts program. The program was called Accelerated Reader. The students loved reading books because they got to use the computer when they were finished and take a quiz. For every book they read and passed, they recieved a prize. Computers also allow the children to research material at a much faster pace and they make communication between faculty and parents much easier.	This essay, which shows competence in response to the assignment, has the clear thesis: "no amount of computer technology could make the classroom unnecesary." The essay shows control of development when describing various things that children need: "structure and teaching," "someone there when they have a question," and "positive reinforcement." In a stronger essay these needs would have been gathered together in one sentence, rather than placed individually in simple staccato sentences. Continuing, the essay mentions "social interaction" but only states, "Social interaction is what the classroom is all about," which is not very informative. However, the essay explains the cooperative-learning technique effectively. The strongest part of the essay is where the writer describes how the "most recent school that I have observed at incorporated computers into their language arts program." The program is described in detail, especially how it inspired students to read. The writer then comes to the conclusion that computers should be integrated into school programs but should not replace them.

(Continued)

Essay	Explanation of Score
Using computers in this way is imperative but replacing the classroom is ignorant as well as unethical. Children need to be around children on a daily basis and actually experience childhood.	Despite the lack of para-graphing, the essay still shows control of organiza-tion and development, and it generally supports the thesis. The essay lacks the overall language facility, however, which would lift this essay above the 4 level.

Response That Received a Score of 3

Essay	Explanation of Score
I have to agree with the point that technol-ogy has made the classroom unnecessary. Although the classroom has become unnes-sary it will not be done away with. Children still have to have a place to go in order to learn and the classroom will always be there. Given that subject teacher may not be there any more. There will always be a supervising teacher in the room to maintain order with in the classroom. I think if you take the class room away then children will no longer want to learn or have a place to go to learn that is familiar to them. Using the technology to allow different teacher to teach more students the subject they, the teachers, are most inter-ested in will allow the students to gain better knowledge of each subject. With in my old high school we had a distance learning room where students from all over the area where linked together in order to learn one subject for a qualified teacher. I guess one of the biggest fears of taking the teacher out of the classroom will be the disruption of the student culture. Every student has to come to the norm where a classroom is taught by a teacher who stands up front as teaches. By taking out that teacher up front and placing a television set or computer there, students may not pay attention to the subject matter.	This essay shows some compe-tence, starting with the thesis that even though technology has advanced so that "the class-room has become unnecessary" it will not be done away with."

The essay offers some devel-opment of the thesis, explaining why the classroom is impor-tant and explaining the need for supervised learning stating, "if you take the classroom away then children will no longer want to learn," however, there is no further support of this idea. Later in the essay is the statement that "students may not pay attention to the subject matter" if the teacher is on television.

The writer does have some personal experience with distance learning for a specialized subject but doesn't expand on that idea to support the thesis. Continuing, the essay talks of the "disruption of the students culture" but just states that students are used to having a teacher in the classroom, rather than describing the impotance of |

(Continued)

Essay	Explanation of Score
I think that there are limitations to the using technology in the classroom, and using it so teachers can teach from home is crossing those limitations. Use the technology to help students further their education, but do it with the teacher in the room.	student culture and learning, as a stronger essay would. While the essay does have a logical conclusion, the lack of development and connections in this essay keep this essay to a score of 3.

Response That Received a Score of 2

Essay	Explanation of Score
I agree that computer technology has advanced. However, I do not feel that the classroom is unnecessary. The classroom is a very important part of a student's learning. Students need to have personal communication with their teachers. I think they would learn much more through oral communication, than reading a lesson on of the computer. Besides, what would happen if the student had a question about the lesson? Sure he/she could write back to the teacher and ask the question, but how long would it take to receive the reply? Also, not all students own a personal computer or have the transportation to get to one. In conclusion, I think it would be much more elective, for the student, to keep the classroom communication alive.	This essay starts with a clear thesis disagreeing with the statement. It continues with some support of the thesis, stating that students "need to have personal communication with their teachers" and that students "would learn much more through oral communication, than reading a lesson off of the computer." However, the essay does little more than list these positions, rather than providing supporting examples and details, as in a stronger essay. While the essay poses interesting questions concerning interaction between students and teachers, the essay provides only limited development of the main ideas, and therefore limited support of the thesis, keeping the essay to a score of 2.

Response That Received a Score of 1

Essay	Explanation of Score
Computer technology has advanced drastically within the last decade. Society has gotten a custom to handling everyday transactions and interacting with computerized machines all the time. Schools have taken advantage of the new information age.	This essay has a promising start with a description of advancing technology and the acceptance of computers by society. However, the essay only states, "Schools have taken advantage of the new information age" and does not address the topic of whether computers "have made the classroom unnecessary." Because of this lack of development, this essay is given a score of 1.

CALCULATING YOUR SCORE

Follow these instructions to score the PPST: Writing test. When you actually take the test, you will have questions that are very similar to the questions in the sample tests in this book, but they will not be identical. Because of the difference in questions, the tests you actually take may be slightly more or less difficult than the tests printed in this book. Therefore, you may not get the same number of questions right on an actual test, as on the sample tests.

NOTE: The **data** in Tables 1 and 2 apply to only the PPST: Writing test. The actual test you take will have a different answer table and a different conversion table.

To score the PPST: Writing test:

- Count the number of questions you answered correctly in the multiple-choice section of the test. The correct answers are in Table 1. Score report category W-1 contains 11 questions measuring knowledge of grammatical relationships; category W-2 contains 15 questions assessing understanding of structural relationships; and category W-3 contains 12 questions assessing understanding of idiom and word choice, mechanics, and correct usage. Count the number of questions you answered correctly in each of these categories. This may give you some idea of your strengths and weaknesses.

- Essays from actual administrations of the PPST: Writing test are read and rated by at least two writing experts. The readers use a rating scale of 1 to 6, where 6 is best. (Zero is used for "off-topic" essays.) The essay score is the sum of the two ratings and can therefore range from 2 to 12. Because it is impossible for you to score your own essay, you might want to try using three different values of essay scores, in combination with your score on the multiple-choice section, to see how your overall score would vary depending on how well you did on the essay. A score of 8 would be about average. You might also want to try a low score of 3 or 4, for example, and a high score, say, of 11 or 12.

- Use Table 2 to find your possible scaled scores. In the column on the left, find the number of questions you answered correctly on the multiple-choice section. Look across the top of Table 2 to the column with the essay score you are using. Go across the row and down the column to find the scaled scores for different combinations of multiple-choice section and essay scores. You can compare your scaled score to the passing score required by your state or institution. (Passing state scores are available on the Praxis website at www.ets.org/praxis.)

Table 1—PPST: Writing Test

Answers to Practice Test Questions and Percentages of
Examinees Answering Each Question Correctly

Sequence Number	Score Report Category	Correct Answer	Percentage of Examinees Choosing Correct Answer
1	W-1	A	81%
2	W-1	D	43%
3	W-3	B	69%
4	W-3	A	47%
5	W-1	B	60%
6	W-1	A	61%
7	W-3	E	48%
8	W-3	B	69%
9	W-1	B	78%
10	W-1	C	35%
11	W-3	A	37%
12	W-2	D	45%
13	W-1	D	16%
14	W-3	A	83%
15	W-1	D	93%
16	W-3	A	31%
17	W-3	E	36%
18	W-3	C	30%
19	W-3	C	59%
20	W-2	C	29%
21	W-1	D	59%
22	W-1	B	64%
23	W-2	E	75%
24	W-2	B	75%
25	W-1	C	64%
26	W-3	A	19%
27	W-2	B	87%
28	W-2	E	87%
29	W-2	D	57%
30	W-2	B	83%

(Continued)

Table 1—PPST: Writing Test (*Continued*)

Sequence Number	Score Report Category	Correct Answer	Percentage of Examinees Choosing Correct Answer
31	W-2	E	73%
32	W-2	C	70%
33	W-2	E	42%
34	W-2	C	37%
35	W-2	D	70%
36	W-3	A	56%
37	W-2	C	74%
38	W-2	C	83%

NOTE: Percentages are based on the test records of 3,221 examinees who took the 60-minute version of the PPST: Writing test in July 2008.

In general, questions may be considered as easy, average, or difficult based on the following percentages:

Easy questions   = 75% or more answered correctly.

Average questions = 55%–74% answered correctly.

Difficult questions = less than 55% answered correctly.

Multiple Choice Section (#Right)	Essay Score (Sum of Two Readings)												
	0	1	2	3	4	5	6	7	8	9	10	11	12
0	152	153	155	157	158	160	161	163	164	166	168	169	171
1	152	154	155	157	159	160	162	163	165	167	168	170	171
2	153	154	156	158	159	161	162	164	165	167	169	170	172
3	153	155	156	158	160	161	163	164	166	168	169	171	172
4	154	155	157	159	160	162	163	165	166	168	170	171	173
5	154	156	157	159	161	162	164	165	167	169	170	172	173
6	155	156	158	160	161	163	164	166	167	169	171	172	174
7	155	157	158	160	162	163	165	166	168	170	171	173	174
8	156	157	159	161	162	164	165	167	168	170	172	173	175
9	156	158	159	161	163	164	166	167	169	171	172	174	175
10	157	158	160	162	163	165	166	168	169	171	173	174	176
11	157	159	160	162	164	165	167	168	170	172	173	175	176
12	158	159	161	163	164	166	167	169	170	172	174	175	177
13	158	160	161	163	165	166	168	169	171	173	174	176	177
14	159	160	162	164	165	167	168	170	171	173	175	176	178
15	159	161	162	164	166	167	169	170	172	174	175	177	178
16	160	161	163	165	166	168	169	171	172	174	176	177	179
17	160	162	163	165	167	168	170	171	173	175	176	178	179
18	161	162	164	166	167	169	170	172	173	175	177	178	180
19	161	163	164	166	168	169	171	172	174	176	177	179	180
20	162	163	165	167	168	170	171	173	174	176	178	179	181
21	162	164	165	167	169	170	172	173	175	177	178	180	181
22	163	164	166	168	169	171	172	174	175	177	179	180	182
23	163	165	166	168	170	171	173	174	176	178	179	181	182
24	164	165	167	169	170	172	173	175	176	178	180	181	183
25	164	166	167	169	171	172	174	175	177	179	180	182	183
26	165	166	168	170	171	173	174	176	177	179	181	182	184
27	165	167	168	170	172	173	175	176	178	180	181	183	184
28	166	167	169	171	172	174	175	177	178	180	182	183	184
29	166	168	169	171	173	174	176	177	179	181	182	184	185
30	167	168	170	172	173	175	176	178	179	181	183	184	185

(*Continued*)

Multiple Choice Section (#Right)	Essay Score (Sum of Two Readings)												
	0	1	2	3	4	5	6	7	8	9	10	11	12
31	167	169	170	172	174	175	177	178	180	182	183	184	186
32	168	169	171	173	174	176	177	179	180	182	184	185	186
33	168	170	171	173	175	176	178	179	181	183	184	185	187
34	169	170	172	174	175	177	178	180	181	183	184	186	187
35	169	171	172	174	176	177	179	180	182	184	185	186	188
36	170	171	173	175	176	178	179	181	182	184	185	187	188
37	170	172	173	175	177	178	180	181	183	184	186	187	189
38	171	172	174	176	177	179	180	182	183	185	186	188	189

Praxis™ II: Principles of Learning and Teaching (PLT)

Your Goals for This Part

- Identify the purpose and format of the PLT tests.
- Review PLT study topics.
- Learn how to read a case study and how to answer constructed-response questions.
- Practice answering PLT questions.

CHAPTER 12

All About the PLT Tests

This chapter will give you instruction and test-taking advice to help you prepare for the Principles of Learning and Teaching (PLT) tests. Here you'll find an overview of the tests and a comprehensive outline of the areas of knowledge covered to guide your study. You'll learn how to read a case study, and you'll explore two expert strategies for answering questions based on case studies. Then, in the chapter that follows, you'll be able to test yourself with 12 sample short-answer questions just like the ones on the actual test. Sample answers and scoring guides will help you understand just what it takes to succeed on the PLT tests.

PURPOSE AND FORMAT OF THE PLT TESTS

The Principles of Learning and Teaching (PLT) tests are designed to assess a prospective teacher's knowledge of a variety of job-related topics. Students typically obtain such knowledge through undergraduate courses in educational psychology, human growth and development, classroom management, instructional design and delivery techniques, evaluation and assessment, and other areas of professional preparation.

There are four PLT tests:

PLT: Early Childhood
PLT: Grades K–6
PLT: Grades 5–9
PLT: Grades 7–12

While the four tests cover the same fundamental topics and concepts, each test differs from the others by featuring developmentally appropriate cases and scenarios.

The PLT Tests at a Glance

Format	4 case histories, each followed by 3 short-answer questions 24 multiple-choice questions in 2 sections of 12 questions each

Contents	Students as Learners (approximately 35% of total score)
	   • Student development and the learning process
	   • Students as diverse learners
	   • Student motivation and the learning environment
	Instruction and Assessment (approximately 35% of total score)
	   • Instructional analysis
	   • Planning instruction
	   • Assessment strategies
	Communication Techniques (approximately 15% of total score)
	   • Effective verbal and nonverbal communication
	   • Cultural and gender differences
	   • Stimulating discussion and responses in the classroom
	Teacher Professionalism (approximately 15% of total score)
	   • The reflective practitioner
	   • The larger community

Time	2 hours Plan on 25 minutes per case study and 10 minutes per multiple-choice section

PREPARING FOR THE PLT TESTS

You will probably want to begin with the following step:

Become familiar with the test content. Learn what will be tested, as covered in the study topics. Assess your knowledge in each area. How well do you know the material? In which areas do you need to learn more before you take the test?

In addition, you will probably want to end with these two steps:

Familiarize yourself with test taking. You can simulate the experience of the test by answering the practice questions within specified time limits. Choose a time and a place where you will not be interrupted or distracted. When you have completed the test, check the sample responses to the constructed-response questions and learn how they were scored. Plan any additional studying according to what you've learned about your understanding of the topics.

Register for the test and consider last-minute tips. See the section in Part I on how to register for the test, and review the Checklist on page 266 to make sure you are ready for the test.

What you do between the first step and these last steps depends on whether you intend to use this book to prepare on your own or as part of a study group.

Preparing on Your Own

If you are working by yourself to prepare for a Principles of Learning and Teaching test, you may find it helpful to use the following approach:

Fill out the Study Plan Sheet. This worksheet will help you to focus on what topics you need to study most, identify materials that will help you study, and set a schedule for doing the studying.

Identify study materials. Most of the material covered by the test is contained in standard introductory textbooks in the field. If you do not own introductory texts, borrow the texts from friends or from a library. Don't rely heavily on information provided by friends or from searching the Web. Neither of these sources is as uniformly reliable as textbooks.

Work through your study plan. Work through the topics and questions. Be able to define and discuss the topics in your own words rather than memorizing definitions from books.

Preparing as Part of a Study Group

Sometimes it is helpful to form a study group with others who are preparing for the same test. Study groups give members opportunities to ask questions and get detailed answers. In a group, some members usually have a better understanding of certain topics, while others in the group may be better at other topics. As members take turns explaining concepts to one another, everyone builds self-confidence. If the group encounters a question that none of the members can answer well, the members can go as a group to a teacher or other expert and get answers efficiently. Because study groups schedule regular meetings, group members study in a more disciplined fashion. They also gain emotional support. The group should be large enough that different people can contribute various kinds of knowledge but small enough so that it stays focused. Often, three to six people is a good size.

Here are some ways to use this chapter as part of a study group:

Plan the group's study program. Parts of the Study Plan Sheet can help to structure your group's study program. By filling out the first five columns and sharing the work sheets, everyone will learn more about your group's mix of abilities and about the resources (such as textbooks) that members can share with the group. In the sixth column ("Dates planned for study of content"), you can create an overall schedule for your group's study program.

Plan individual group sessions. At the end of each session, the group should decide what specific topics will be covered at the next meeting and who will present each topic. Use the topic headings and subheadings in the study topics section to select topics.

Prepare your presentation for the group. When it's your turn to present, prepare something that's more than a lecture. Write five to ten original questions to pose to the group. Practicing writing actual questions can help you better understand the topics covered on the test as well as the types of questions you will encounter on the test. It will also give other members of the group extra practice at answering questions. If you are presenting material from the sample questions, use each sample question as a model for writing at least one original question.

Take a practice test together. Scheduling a test session with the group will add to the realism and boost everyone's confidence. Practice questions are available in this study guide and online at the *Praxis* Web site (www.ets. org/praxis).

Learn from the results of the practice test. Use a scoring matrix to score one another's tests. Then plan one or more study sessions based on the questions that group members got wrong or on the constructed-response questions that members did not answer well. For example, each group member might be responsible for a question that he or she got wrong and could use it as a model to create an original question to pose to the group, together with an explanation of the correct answer.

Whether you decide to study alone or with a group, remember that the best way to prepare is to have an organized plan. The plan should set goals based on specific topics and skills that you need to learn, and it should commit you to realistic deadlines for meeting those goals. Then if you stick to your plan, you will accomplish your goals on schedule.

What's the best way to use the section on case studies?

Become familiar with case studies. Learn what a case study is and how to read one carefully and analytically in preparation for answering questions about it. Think about possible applications of situations and issues in the case studies to your own teaching experience. What information does your own teaching background provide for answering the questions?

Sharpen your skills on short-answer questions. Understand how short-answer questions are scored and how to write high-scoring responses.

Decide whether you need more review. After you have looked at your results, decide if there are areas that you need to brush up on before taking the actual tests. Go back to your textbooks and reference materials to see if the topics are covered there. You might also want to go over your questions with a friend or teacher who is familiar with the subjects.

Assess your readiness. Do you feel confident about your level of understanding in each of the subject areas? If not, where do you need more work? If you feel ready, complete the Checklist to double-check that you've thought through the details.

PLT Checklist

- Do you know the testing requirements for your teaching field in the state(s) where you plan to teach?
- Have you followed all the test registration procedures?
- Do you know how long the test will take and the number of questions it contains? Have you considered how you will pace your work?
- Are you familiar with the test directions and the types of questions for the test?

- Are you familiar with the recommended test-taking strategies and tips?
- Have you practiced by working through the practice test questions at a pace similar to that of an actual test?
- If you are repeating a *Praxis* Series Assessment, have you analyzed your previous score report to determine areas in which additional study and test preparation could be useful?

PLT Study Plan Sheet

Content covered on test.	How well do I know the content?	What materials do I have for studying this content?	What materials do I need for studying this content?	Where could I find the materials I need?	Dates planned for study of content.	Dates completed.

PLT STUDY TOPICS

Here is an overview of the areas of knowledge covered in the Principles of Learning and Teaching tests:

Students as Learners

- Student development and the learning process
- Students as diverse leaders
- Student motivation and the learning environment

Instruction and Assessment

- Instructional strategies
- Planning instruction
- Assessment strategies

Communication Techniques

- Effective verbal and nonverbal communication
- Cultural and gender differences in communication
- Stimulating discussion and responses in the classroom

Profession and Community

- The reflective practitioner
- The larger community

Using the topic lists that follow. You are not expected to be an expert on the topics that follow. But you should understand the major characteristics or aspects of each topic and be able to relate the topic to various situations presented in the test questions. For instance, here is one of the topic lists in "Instructional Strategies," under the "Instruction and Assessment" category:

Major categories of instructional strategies, including

- Cooperative learning
- Direct instruction
- Discovery learning
- Whole-group discussion
- Independent study
- Interdisciplinary instruction
- Concept mapping
- Inquiry method
- Questioning

Using textbooks and other sources as needed, make sure you can describe each of these strategies in your own words. Find materials that will help you identify examples of each and situations for which each is appropriate. On the test you may be asked direct questions on one or more of these topics, or you may be asked to evaluate the use or appropriateness of a strategy in a particular context.

Special questions marked with stars. Interspersed throughout the list of topics are questions that are preceded by stars (☆). These questions are intended to help you test your knowledge of fundamental concepts that apply to typical classroom situations. Most of the questions require you to combine several pieces of information in order to formulate an integrated understanding and response. Answering these questions will help you gain increased understanding of the subject matter covered on the test. You might want to discuss these questions and your answers with a teacher or mentor.

Note that the questions marked with stars are not short-answer or multiple-choice. These questions are intended as *study* questions, not practice questions. Thinking about the answers can improve your understanding of fundamental concepts and help you answer a broad range of questions on the test. For example, the following starred question appears in the list of study topics under "Planning Instruction."

If you think about the relationships among curriculum goals, scope, and sequence frameworks, and unit and lesson plans, you have probably prepared yourself to answer multiple-choice questions similar to the one below, which asks you to link a curricular goal with the most appropriate performance objective.

The goal of a particular mathematics curriculum is for students to use computational strategies fluently and estimate appropriately. Which of the following objectives for students best reflects that goal?

(A) Students in all grades will use calculators for all mathematical tasks.

(B) Students in all grades will be drilled daily on basic number facts.

(C) Students in all grades will know the connections between the basic arithmetic operations.

(D) Students in all grades will evaluate the reasonableness of their answers.

The correct answer is choice D. To "evaluate the reasonableness of their answers," students must understand the computational strategies involved in mathematical solutions before they are able to estimate or to evaluate estimated answers.

Teachers are responsible for connecting scope and sequence frameworks and curriculum goals into classroom lessons and groups of lessons. How does a teacher translate curriculum goals and disciplines-specific scope and sequence frameworks into units and lesson plans with objectives, activities, and assessments appropriate for the students being taught? Give an example of a curriculum goal and then write a lesson objective, one activity, and an idea for an assessment of student learning that would accomplish that goal.

Outline of Study Topics

I. Students as Learners

A. Student Development and the Learning Process

You will notice that in this section, the names of important theorists appear in more than one category. This is because the work of these theorists has implications for multiple domains that are important to effective teaching.

▸ Theoretical foundations about how learning occurs: how students construct knowledge, acquire skills, and develop habits of mind.

▸ Examples of important theorists
- Albert Bandura
- Jerome Bruner
- John Dewey
- Jean Piaget
- Lev Vygotsky
- Howard Gardner
- Abraham Maslow
- B. F. Skinner

☆ Knowing each theorist's major ideas and being able to compare and contrast one theory with another comprises basic professional knowledge for teachers. In addition, knowing how these ideas actually can be applied to teaching practice is important professional knowledge for teachers.

☆ What are the major differences between Jerome Bruner's and Jean Piaget's theories of cognitive development in young children?

☆ How might a teacher apply some of Lev Vygotsky's ideas about scaffolding and direct instruction in the classroom?

☆ What does Gardner's work on multiple intelligences suggest about planning instruction?

☆ What does Abraham Maslow's hierarchy of needs suggest about motivation for learning in the classroom?

▶ Important terms that relate to learning theory

- Constructivism
- Metacognition
- Readiness
- Schemata
- Transfer
- Scaffolding
- Loom's taxonomy
- Zone of proximal development
- Intrinsic and extrinsic motivation

▶ Human development in the physical, social, emotional, moral, and cognitive domains

- The theoretical contributions of important theorists such as Erik Erikson, Lawrence Kohlberg, Carol Gilligan, Jean Piaget, Abraham Maslow, Albert Bandura, and Lev Vygotsky.
- The major progressions in each developmental domain and the ranges of individual variation within each domain.
- The impact of students' physical, social, emotional, moral, and cognitive development on their learning and how to address these factors when making instructional decisions.
- How development in one domain, such as physical, may affect performance in another domain, such as social.

☆ Go beyond memorization of definitions: try to apply the terms to the theories behind them and think of applications in the classroom.

☆ What are some specific classroom-based examples of extrinsic and intrinsic motivators for students?

☆ Make sure you can recognize the differences between lower-order and higher-order thinking in classroom activities, using Bloom's taxonomy as a guide.

☆ What is an example of a schema, and what good is it?

☆ What is scaffolding, and why is it important for both teachers and students?

☆ When responding to case studies, you will be asked to perform the following kinds of tasks related to the area of human development and the learning process:

Identify and describe strengths and/or weaknesses in

- the instruction described in the case, in terms of its appropriateness for students at a particular age

Propose a strategy for

- instruction that would be appropriate for students at the age described in the case

☆ Give a specific example from your own classroom experience of the effects of differences in learning styles on how people understand and express what they know.

☆ What is an example of the way cultural expectations from a particular geographical region or ethnic group might affect how students learn or express what they know?

☆ What does the research reveal about gender differences and how they might affect learning?

☆ Know the major types of challenges in each category (e.g., dyslexia under "Learning Disabilities"), know the major symptoms and range of severity, and know the major classroom and instructional issues related to each area.

☆ Know the basic rights or responsibilities that the legislation established.

B. Students as Diverse Learners

▶ Differences in the ways students learn and perform
- Learning styles
- Multiple intelligences
- Performance modes
  ○ Concrete operational thinkers
  ○ Visual and aural learners
- Gender differences
- Cultural expectations and styles

▶ Areas of exceptionality in student learning
- Visual and perceptual differences
- Special physical or sensory challenges
- Learning disabilities
- Attention Deficit Disorder (ADD); Attention Deficit-Hyperactivity Disorder (ADHD)
- Functional mental retardation
- Behavioral disorders
- Developmental delays

▶ Legislation and institutional responsibilities relating to exceptional students
- Americans with Disabilities Act (ADA)
- Individuals with Disabilities Education Act (IDEA)
- Inclusion, mainstreaming, and "Least Restrictive Environment"
- IEP (Individual Education Program), including what, by law, must be included in each IEP
- Section 504 of the Rehabilitation Act
- Due process
- Family involvement

▶ Approaches for accommodating various learning styles, intelligences, or exceptionalities, including
- Differentiated instruction
- Alternative assessments
- Testing modifications

▶ The process of second-language acquisition, and strategies to support the learning of students for whom English is not a first language

▶ How students' learning is influenced by individual experiences, talents, and prior learning, as well as language, culture, family, and community values, including:

- Multicultural backgrounds
- Age-appropriate knowledge and behavior
- The student culture at the school
- Family backgrounds
- Linguistic patterns and differences
- Cognitive patterns and differences
- Social and emotional issues

When responding to case studies, you will be asked to perform the following kinds of tasks related to the area of students as diverse learners:

Identify and describe strengths and/or weaknesses in

- a lesson plan for meeting needs of individual students with identified special needs, as described in the case . . .
- the interaction described in the case between the teacher and students in terms of culturally responsive teaching . . .

Propose a strategy for

- helping the students with attention deficit problems described in the case stay on task (e.g., in listening to a lecture, following a demonstration, doing written work)
- improving performance of students in the case who do not perform well on homework, original compositions, or other assignments
- helping students in the case for whom English is not the first language to build literacy skills and/or improve in academic areas
- meeting the needs of a wide range of students (especially students with learning difficulties and students who are accelerated)
- building positive relationships with a student the case shows is very turned off to school
- adapting instruction and/or assessment for an individual student with identified needs described in the case
- helping the student described in the case see issues from different points of view

C. Student Motivation and the Learning Environment

▶ Theoretical foundations about human motivation and behavior

- Abraham Maslow
- Albert Bandura
- B. F. Skinner

▶ Important terms that relate to motivation and behavior

- Hierarchy of needs
- Correlational and casual relationships
- Intrinsic motivation
- Extrinsic motivation
- Learned helplessness
- Self-efficacy
- Operant conditioning
- Reinforcement
- Positive reinforcement
- Negative reinforcement
- Shaping successive approximations
- Prevention
- Extinction
- Punishment
- Continuous reinforcement
- Intermittent reinforcement

▶ How knowledge of human motivation and behavior should influence strategies for organizing and supporting individual and group work in the classroom

▶ Factors and situations that are likely to promote or diminish students' motivation to learn; how to help students become self-motivated

☆ Go beyond memorization of definitions; try to apply the terms to the theories behind them and think of applications in the teaching situations.

▶ Principles of effective classroom management and strategies to promote positive relationships, cooperation, and purposeful learning, including:

- Establishing daily procedures and routines
- Establishing classroom rules
- Using natural and logical consequences
- Providing positive guidance
- Modeling conflict resolution, problem solving, and anger management
- Giving timely feedback
- Maintaining accurate records
- Communicating with parents and caregivers
- Using objective behavior descriptions
- Responding to student misbehavior
- Arranging of classroom space
- Pacing and structuring the lesson

☆ Why is each of the principles on the left a good practice for teachers to cultivate and maintain in terms of its effect on student learning? How can each help you to be a more effective teacher? What are the characteristics of effective implementation of each of these practices? How can you structure your instructional planning to include these?

☆ What are the choices a teacher has in each of the last three bulleted items to the left? What are the most important considerations when you are making decisions about each one?

☆ Pacing and structuring of a lesson is a particularly challenging aspect of instruction. What factors can change the pace and structure of a lesson as it unfolds? How can you prepare *in advance* for adjusting the pace and the structure of a lesson for each of these factors?

☆ When responding to case studies, you will be asked to perform the following kinds of tasks related to the area of student motivation and the learning environment:

Identify and describe a strength and/or weakness in

- a lesson plan or instructional strategy described in the case with the intention of building a positive classroom environment

Propose a strategy for

- revising a lesson that is described in the case for improving student motivation and engagement
- improving motivation through means other than negative strategies described in the case
- addressing behavioral problems that are described in the case

What are some specific instructional goals in a particular content area that would be associated with each of these cognitive processes?

How are these cognitive processes connected with the developmental level of students?

How are these processes different from one another?

What are some ways that teachers can simulate each of these cognitive processes in a lesson?

What are the primary advantages of each of these strategies? In general terms, describe the kinds of situations or the kinds of goals and objectives for which each of these strategies is appropriate. What kinds of information about students' levels does each of these offer? When would you NOT use a particular instructional strategy?

II. Instruction and Assessment

A. Instructional Strategies

▶ The major cognitive processes associated with student learning, including:

- Critical thinking
- Creative thinking
- Higher-order thinking
- Inductive and deductive thinking
- Problem-structuring and problem-solving
- Invention
- Memorization and recall
- Social reasoning
- Representation of ideas

▶ Major categories of instructional strategies, including:

- Cooperative learning
- Direct instruction
- Discovery learning
- Whole-group discussion
- Independent study
- Interdisciplinary instruction
- Concept mapping
- Inquiry method
- Questioning
- Play
- Learning centers
- Small group work
- Revisiting
- Reflection
- Project approach

Principles, techniques, and methods associated with various instructional strategies, including:

- Direct instruction
  - Madeline Hunter's "Effective Teaching Model"
  - David Ausubel's "Advance Organizers"
  - Mastery learning
  - Demonstrations
  - Mnemonics
  - Note taking
  - Outlining
  - Use of visual aids
- Student-centered models
  - Inquiry model
  - Discovery learning
  - Cooperative learning (pair-share, jigsaw, STAD, teams, games, tournaments)
  - Collaborative learning
  - Concept models (concept development, concept attainment, concept mapping)
  - Discussion models
  - Laboratories
  - Project-based learning
  - Simulations

Give some examples of appropriate situations for grouping students heterogeneously.

Give some examples of grouping students homogeneously. Besides grouping by performance level, what other characteristics should a teacher sometimes consider when grouping students?

What is wait time? What does research suggest about wait time?

How might a teacher promote critical thinking among students in a discussion?

How can a teacher encourage student-to-student dialogue in a class discussion?

What kinds of classroom management procedures and rules would tend to make class discussion more productive?

How does the development level of students affect the way a teacher might handle classroom discussion?

In what kinds of discussions or situations should a teacher name a specific student before asking a question? When is it best *not* to name a specific student?

What should a teacher consider when planning to incorporate various resources into a lesson design?

 What are the advantages of these different resources?

 When responding to case studies, you will be asked to perform the following kinds of tasks related to the area of instructional planning:

Identify and describe a strength and/or weakness in

- specific activities that are described in the case

Propose a strategy for

- teaching critical thinking skills in a specific lesson described in the case
- achieving effectiveness with group work in a particular situation described in the case
- helping students stay on task in the situation described in the case
- helping students learn material presented through various media introduced in the case
- assigning students to group work appropriate to the case
- bringing closure to a lesson that stops abruptly as presented in the case
- improving student interaction during class discussion as described in the case
- addressing a "missed opportunity" during instruction that is described in the case

A. Instructional Strategies

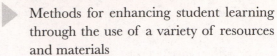 Methods for enhancing student learning through the use of a variety of resources and materials

- Computers, Internet resources, Web pages, e-mail
- Audiovisual technologies such as videotapes and compact discs
- Local experts
- Primary documents and artifacts
- Field trips
- Libraries
- Service learning

B. Planning Instruction

▶ Techniques for planning instruction to meet curriculum goals, including the incorporation of learning theory, subject matter, curriculum development, and student development

- National and state learning standards
- State and local curriculum frameworks
- State and local curriculum guides
- Scope and sequence in specific disciplines
- Units and lessons—rationale for selecting content topics
- Behavioral objectives: affective, cognitive, psychomotor
- Learner objectives and outcomes
- Emergent curriculum
- Antibias curriculum
- Themes/projects
- Curriculum webbing

▶ Techniques for creating effective bridges between curriculum goals and students' experiences

- Modeling
- Guided practice
- Independent practice, including homework
- Transitions

☆ Teachers are responsible for connecting scope and sequence frameworks and curriculum goals into classroom lessons and groups of lessons. How does a teacher translate curriculum goals and discipline-specific scope and sequence frameworks into units and lesson plans with objectives, activities, and assessments appropriate for the students being taught? Give an example of a curriculum goal, and then write a lesson objective, one activity, and an idea for an assessment of student learning that would accomplish that goal.

☆ How do behavioral objectives and learner objectives and outcomes fit into a teacher's planning for units and lessons?

☆ What criterion or criteria does a teacher use to decide when to use each of these techniques?

☆ Why is it so important for a teacher to plan carefully for transitions? What are the risks if transitions are not thought through and executed with care?

☆ Why is each of these actions a principle of effective instruction?

☆ What tools and techniques can a teacher plan to use to accomplish each one?

☆ What strategies can a teacher employ to monitor student understanding as a lesson unfolds?

☆ What evidence should the teacher observe in order to know whether to reteach a topic, move more quickly, or go back to material previously covered?

☆ When responding to case studies, you will be asked to perform the following kinds of tasks related to the area of instructional planning:

Identify and describe a strength and/or weakness in

- a unit plan that is described in the case
- specific strategies used in instruction (e.g., using lecture, using class discussion) in the case
- a sequence of lessons described in the case designed to achieve a goal or set of objectives
- one or more written assignments given to students in the case

Propose a strategy for

- meeting what may appear to be conflicting goals or objectives described in the case
- incorporating activities that will have students described in the case draw on their own experiences to understand the instruction
- stimulating prior knowledge in the situation described in the case

B. Planning Instruction (continued)

- Activating students' prior knowledge
- Anticipating preconceptions
- Encouraging exploration and problem-solving
- Building new skills on those previously acquired
- Predicting

C. Assessment Strategies

Measurement theory and assessment-related issues

- Types of assessments
  - Standardized tests, norm-referenced or criterion-referenced
  - Achievement tests
  - Aptitude tests
  - Structure observations
  - Anecdotal notes
  - Assessments of prior knowledge
  - Student response during a lesson
  - Portfolios
  - Essays written to prompts
  - Journals
  - Self-evaluations
  - Performance assessments
- Characteristics of assessments
  - Validity
  - Reliability
  - Norm-referenced
  - Criterion-referenced
  - Mean, median, mode
  - Sampling stratcgy
- Scoring assessments
  - Analytical scoring
  - Holistic scoring
  - Rubrics
  - Reporting assessment results
  - Percentile rank
  - Stanines
  - Mastery levels
  - Raw score
  - Scaled score
  - Grade equivalent score
  - Standard deviation
  - Standard error of measurement

What are the characteristics, uses, advantages, and limitations of each of the formal and informal types of assessments to the left?

When might you use "holistic scoring"?

Under what circumstances would "anecdotal notes" give a teacher important assessment information?

How might a teacher effectively use student self-evaluation?

What are some examples of informal assessments of prior knowledge that a teacher can easily use when a new topic is introduced?

What kind of assessment information can a teacher gather from student journals?

What is a structured observation in a classroom setting?

When responding to case studies, you will be asked to perform the following types of tasks related to the area of assessment:

Propose a strategy for

- assessing progress for students described in the case who are working toward specified goals or objectives
- assessing class progress toward achievement of specified goals or objectives
- gathering information to use to help understand classroom performance that is different from what was expected at the beginning of the year
- assessing language fluency of a student for whom English is not the first language

Propose a hypothesis or explanation for

- a student's strengths and/or weaknesses as a learner based on the evidence presented
- what might be important to explore in working with a student described in the case who is having difficulties academically, socially, or emotionally

C. Assessment Strategies (continued)

- Use of assessments
  - ○ Formative evaluation
  - ○ Summative evaluation
  - ○ Diagnostic evaluation
- Understanding measurement theory and assessment-related issues
- Interpreting and communicating results of assessments

III. Communication Techniques

A. Basic effective verbal and nonverbal communication techniques

B. Effect of cultural and gender differences on communications in the classroom

C. Types of questions that can stimulate discussion in different ways for particular purposes

- Probing for learner understanding
- Helping students articulate their ideas and thinking processes
- Promoting risk-taking and problem-solving
- Facilitating factual recall
- Encouraging convergent and divergent thinking
- Stimulating curiosity
- Helping students to question
- Promoting a caring community

What are some ways that a teacher's raising his or her voice might be interpreted differently by students with different cultural backgrounds?

What are specific examples of gestures and other body language that have different meanings in different cultures (e.g., looking someone directly in the eye, disagreeing openly during a discussion, pointing)?

What is an example of a question in a particular content area that probes for understanding?

What is an example of a question that would help a student articulate his or her ideas?

What is an example of a comment a teacher might make that would promote risk-taking? Problem-solving?

How would a teacher encourage divergent thinking on a particular topic?

How would a teacher encourage students to question one another and the teacher?

When responding to case studies, you will be asked to perform the following kinds of tasks related to the area of communication:

Identify and describe a strength and/or weakness in

- the teacher's oral or written communication with students in the case (e.g., feedback on assignments, interaction during class)

Propose a strategy for

- improving the self-image of a student described in the case or the student's sense of responsibility for his or her own learning

- involving all students in a class discussion described in the case in a positive way, showing respect for others

- helping a student described in the case to develop social skills in a specified situation

IV. Profession and Community

A. The Reflective Practitioner

▶ Types of resources available for professional development and learning

- Professional literature
- Colleagues
- Professional associations
- Professional development activities

▶ Ability to read, understand, and apply articles and books about current research, views, ideas, and debates regarding best teaching practices

▶ Why personal reflection on teaching practices is critical, and approaches that can be used to reflect and evaluate

- Code of ethics
- Advocacy for learners

▶ Major laws related to students' rights and teacher responsibilities

- Equal education
- Appropriate education for students with special needs
- Confidentiality and privacy
- Appropriate treatment of students
- Reporting in situations related to possible child abuse

☆ Be able to read and understand articles and books about current views, ideas, and debates regarding best teaching practices.

☆ What types of help or learning can each of these resources offer a new teacher?

☆ What are the titles of two professional journals of particular interest to you in your chosen field of teaching to which you might subscribe?

☆ What professional association(s) offer professional meetings, publications, and opportunities for collaborative conversation with other teachers?

☆ What might be a professional development plan for the first two years of a teacher's career that would support her or his learning and growth?

When responding to case studies, you will be asked to perform the following kinds of tasks related to the area of the larger community:

Identify and describe a strength and/or weakness in

- the communication with parents used by a teacher described in the case
- the approach taken by a teacher described in the case to involve parents

Propose a strategy for

- using parent volunteers during a lesson that is described in a case
- involving all parents or other caregivers
- helping students in areas specified in the case
- helping the family of a student described in the case work with the student's learning or other needs

B. The Larger Community

▶ The role of the school as a resource to the larger community

- Teachers as a resource

▶ Factors in the students' environment outside of school (family circumstances, community environments, health and economic conditions) that may influence students' life and learning

▶ Basic strategies for developing and utilizing active partnerships among teachers, parents/guardians, and leaders in the community to support the educational process

- Shared ownership
- Shared decision-making
- Respectful/reciprocal communication

HOW TO READ A CASE STUDY

ETS uses case studies as the basis for the assessment of a beginning teacher's professional and pedagogical knowledge for several important reasons.

- First, professional educators frequently use case studies of teaching situations as a method for representing the complex domain of professional practice. Carefully constructed, case studies can simulate actual teaching contexts, issues, and challenges. They also provide a platform for thinking about theoretical and practical pedagogical concerns, making them a professionally credible method for assessing an educator's knowledge.
- Second, case studies allow the presentation of sufficient detail about a particular teaching situation or series of classroom events. By identifying strengths and weaknesses in the teaching presented, case studies provide a medium in which hypotheses, conclusions, and suggestions for strategies that might accomplish particular pedagogical goals can be thoughtfully supported and explained.
- Third, case studies encourage questions that demand application of knowledge across a broad range of professional knowledge bases —developmental psychology, motivation, communication strategies, pedagogical methods and strategies, instructional design principles and strategies—rather than simple recognition and recall of facts without a meaningful context.

Simulations of teaching situations like those presented in the Principles of Learning and Teaching case studies offer the opportunity to ask questions that may have several acceptable answers. The open-ended questions that follow each case study encourage the beginning teacher to synthesize knowledge, much as he or she will have to in the day-to-day work of teaching. Because the open-ended questions can be satisfactorily answered from many different perspectives, they acknowledge that teachers have extremely varied backgrounds and experiences with students, and that there are often many possible effective responses in a given teaching situation.

Two Kinds of Cases: Teacher-Based and Student-Based

You may encounter either or both of two kinds of cases in the Principles of Learning and Teaching test. The first is a "teacher-based" case, and the second is a "student-based" case. A teacher-based case focuses on the teaching practice of one or more teachers. The case will present sufficient information about the teaching context, goals, objectives, lesson plans, assignments, teaching strategies, assessments, and interactions with students to enable you to identify the issues involved in the case and to respond fully to the questions about the teachers' practices. However, the information is carefully restricted to only what is required to understand the issues and respond to the questions. Additional information might be interesting to have but is not essential for understanding and responding. A response that says the question cannot be answered because more information is needed is not acceptable.

A student-based case focuses on one student, with information about the student's background, where appropriate, and the student's strengths and weaknesses. In addition, there may be examples of the student's work as well as excerpts of conversations between the student and a teacher, counselor, or interviewer.

Excerpts of a class discussion in which the student participated may also be provided. Again, the information provided is all you need to understand the issues involved and to respond to the questions. As with teacher-based cases, you might want to know more about the student, but all the information you need to respond fully to each question is presented.

Although cases are termed "student-based" and "teacher-based," both kinds of cases often have questions that deal with both teachers and students as learners. For example, one of the cases presented below is termed a student-based case because one student is the focus of the case. However, the teacher's practice is clearly an essential part of the case, and there are questions that focus both on the student as a learner and on the teacher's practice.

All case studies are approximately the same length, 800–850 words, and each is followed by three questions requiring a "constructed response." This means that for each question, you need to write one or two paragraphs to answer the question. In no case are there questions that require knowledge specific to academic disciplines such as language arts, history, science, or mathematics.

Expert Strategies for Reading Case Studies

There are two different strategies you can use for reading case studies. The key to both of them is a close and careful reading of the case, with attention focused on the important information in each paragraph or document. You will also want to consider how each paragraph or document relates to the central issues addressed in the case and in the questions.

Strategy 1. Read the case study with the major content categories clearly in mind. (You'll find those categories in the PLT Tests at a Glance chart on page 264.) Remember that each case and the questions are based directly on these categories. You will also want to keep in mind that each paragraph of the narrative or each document is included specifically to elicit understanding of an issue or to provide information for responding to the questions.

Therefore, for each section, narrative, or document, ask the following questions as you read:

- What issues about the teacher's planning, instruction, and assessment does this raise?
- What issues are raised about the student as a learner and the way teachers and others do and/or do not understand and address the student's strengths and needs?
- What specific information is presented here that addresses the way issues were faced and resolved? How else might they have been resolved?
- How, specifically, does this information address one or more of the questions?

Strategy 2. Before you read the case read the questions that follow the case first. Once you have carefully examined the questions and made mental notes about what kinds of issues to look for in the case, then you can read the case and take notes about how each paragraph, section, and/or document relates to particular questions.

Case Study 1: Content Category Approach

To help you understand more about what case studies look like and how the first expert approach might work for you, look at the sample case with annotations that follows. This narrative, about Sara, is a student-based case that involves issues about Sara as a learner and about Ms. Mercer, her first-grade teacher. Follow the case in the left column and note the questions raised in the marginal notes in the right column. These questions relate to the major content categories covered on the test.

CASE STUDY 1

SARA

Information Presented

Notes

Scenario

Six-year-old Sara lives with her mother, who has a relaxed schedule. Ms. Mercer, Sara's teacher, notes that Sara is often tired and inattentive after arriving late. Sara says she frequently stays up past midnight if others are up. Ms. Mercer, a second-year teacher, has asked her mentor to observe Sara and suggest ways to help Sara achieve Ms. Mercer's purposes.

What possible issues does this section suggest about Sara as a learner? How might this information be useful in thinking about these issues?

Observation: Ms. Mercer's Class, April 30

Pre-Observation Interview Notes

Ms. Mercer says, "The purposes of first grade are to teach children 'school survival skills' and reading, writing, and arithmetic." She adds, "Sara needs help with 'survival skills,' including following directions, concentrating on a task to its completion, and being attentive to the lessons I present."

What possible issues are raised about Ms. Mercer's approach to teaching first grade? How might these affect Sara?

Mentor Classroom Observation—Focus on Sara Porter

As Ms. Mercer's class begins, the children play with puzzles and other activities requiring construction or manipulation. Two children "write" on a flannel board, using letters kept in alphabetical stacks in a box. They return the letters so they fit exactly over their counterparts. Ms. Mercer praises them for neatness. She instructs them to return to their previously assigned groups as Sara enters the room.

What does this section tell us about Ms. Mercer's approach and how it might impact Sara?

What issues about Ms. Mercer's approach does this section raise? What strengths and/or areas for improvement in her use of group work might this suggest?

What information does this section present about Sara as a learner? How might this information be used?

What additional information about Sara as a learner is presented? What issues might this information raise? How does Ms. Mercer interact with Sara? How might this be important?

The students are seated at six tables, four students at each table. Ms. Mercer explains, "Tables one and two will work on reading first, while tables three and four will solve math problems, and tables five and six will draw page illustrations for your collaborative Big Book. After 25 minutes, the groups will stop the first activity and begin working on a second task without changing seats. Twenty-five minutes later, you will change again to work on the activity each group has not yet done. The math groups and those doing illustrations will hand in their work when time is called. I will work with the two groups who are reading aloud." She plans to monitor progress of students in the reading group.

Sara is at table one. Ms. Mercer begins with this table and table two, working on reading. Several children read aloud. Ms. Mercer praises them. When Ms. Mercer calls on Sara, she begins reading in the wrong place. Joyce, seated next to Sara, points to where they are. Ms. Mercer says, "Sara, you would know where we are if you were paying attention." She calls on another child. Sara looks hurt, but soon starts to follow along in the book. Subsequently, Ms. Mercer calls on Sara, who now has the right place. Ms. Mercer then calls on another child.

During the math activity, Sara, yawning frequently, is the last to open her workbook and write her name. When she completes the page, she waits. She seems puzzled, although Ms. Mercer has already given directions. Sara gets up, sharpens a pencil, and returns to the wrong seat. "That's MY seat," accuses an angry boy. Sara apologizes and returns to her seat. Later, she waits to have her workbook checked. She has not torn out pages as Ms. Mercer instructed. Sara is told to "do it right." Sara has not creased the paper as Ms. Mercer demonstrated, so the pages do not tear out easily. Sara sucks her thumb and holds her ear for a minute. Suddenly, she yanks the paper and the pages come out with jagged edges. She receives three dots for her work. Ms. Mercer says, "Sara, this is good. I wish you could earn four dots" (the maximum). Sara slaps herself on the forehead. During the illustration activity, Sara helps several others who have trouble thinking of ideas. Sara's illustration is among the best handed in.

After the group work, Ms. Mercer places a large pad on an easel and says, "Now we're going to write about our trip to the art museum yesterday. Raise your hand and tell me something you saw or did in the museum." No one responds. She says, "Tell me the first thing we did at the museum." Sara raises her hand, offering a first sentence. After each response, Ms. Mercer asks, "What happened next?" or "What did we see next?" She prints each child's contribution.

Our Trip to the Art Museum

We rode the elevator to the second floor. We looked at different shapes on the ceiling. We saw a statue with a white triangle. We went to another room where we saw some pictures. We rode back down to the first floor. On our way out, we saw a painting of a grandfather and a boy.

During the writing of the group story, Sara fidgets in her seat, stares out the window, and makes a face at her neighbor.

Post-Observation Interview Notes

Ms. Mercer says, "Sara is a top performer in academic achievement and on standardized tests, consistently scoring among the top five students in the class. She's so bright. It's a shame she's late and distracted so much." The mentor replies, "There may be something else bothering Sara. Although she is easily distracted, there may be other explanations for her behavior. Let's talk more."

What additional information about Sara is presented? How might this be important in addressing her strengths and needs? How might the information about Ms. Mercer's writing lesson be important? What strengths or areas for improvement might it suggest? How might it be built upon?

What are the implications of the mentor's comment?

Case Study 1: Question Approach

Now let's examine the same case using the second expert method. First, read through the questions below, then, read through the case again with question-related notes. Notice that this time the notes next to the case show how each paragraph or section relates to a particular question and propose some ideas that will eventually go into the actual response to the questions.

Questions Related to Case Study 1. Sara

1. Suppose that Ms. Mercer and her mentor discuss how to connect school and Sara's home environment for the benefit of Sara's learning.

   - Identify TWO specific actions Ms. Mercer might take to connect school and Sara's home environment for the benefit of Sara's learning.
   - Explain how each action you identified could benefit Sara's learning. Base your response on principles of fostering school-parent relationships to support student learning.

2. Review the pre-observation notes in which Ms. Mercer explains the purposes of first grade as she sees them. Suppose that her mentor suggests that Ms. Mercer consider other purposes of first grade and how she might modify her instruction to address those purposes and the related needs of Sara and her other students.

   - Identify TWO additional purposes of first grade that Ms. Mercer could consider when planning her instruction, in order to meet the needs of Sara and/or her other students.
   - For each purpose you identified, explain how Ms. Mercer might modify her instruction to address the purpose and meet the needs of Sara and/or her other students. Base your response on principles of planning instruction and learning theory.

3. Assume that the groups working on mathematics and illustrations for the Big Book become very noisy and unproductive over the course of the activity.

   - Suggest TWO changes Ms. Mercer could have made in the planning and/ or implementation of the group work that would have made the activity more successful.
   - Explain how each change you suggested could have made the group work activity more successful. Base your response on principles of planning instruction and human development.

4. In the activities described in the Mentor Classroom Observation, Ms. Mercer demonstrates understanding of developmentally appropriate instruction.

   - Identify TWO strengths in the instructional approaches Ms. Mercer uses in the activities that reflect understanding of the principles of developmentally appropriate instruction.
   - Explain how each of these strengths you identified provides evidence of an understanding of the principles of developmentally appropriate instruction. Base your response on principles of planning instruction and human development.

5. Assume that the day after the lesson was observed, Ms. Mercer's objective is to use the story about the museum visit to continue building students' literacy.

- Identify TWO strategies and/or activities involving the story about the museum visit that Ms. Mercer could use to continue building students' literacy.
- For each strategy and/or activity you identified, explain how it could help build literacy. Base your response on principles of language development and acquisition.

6. In the post-observation notes, Ms. Mercer's mentor suggests that they explore explanations for Sara's inattentive behavior.

- Suggest TWO hypotheses other than lack of sleep that Ms. Mercer and her mentor might explore to learn more about why Sara behaves as she does in class.
- For each hypothesis you suggested, describe at least one action that Ms. Mercer and her mentor might take to see if the hypothesis might be correct. Base your response on principles of human development, motivation, and diagnostic assessment.

CASE STUDY 1

SARA
Information Presented

Scenario

Six-year-old Sara lives with her mother, who has a relaxed schedule. Ms. Mercer, Sara's teacher, notes that Sara is often tired and inattentive after arriving late. Sara says she frequently stays up past midnight if others are up. Ms. Mercer, a second-year teacher, has asked her mentor to observe Sara and suggest ways to help Sara achieve Ms. Mercer's purposes.

Observation: Ms. Mercer's Class, April 30

Pre-Observation Interview Notes

Ms. Mercer says, "The purposes of first grade are to teach children 'school survival skills' and reading, writing, and arithmetic." She adds, "Sara needs help with 'survival skills,' including following directions, concentrating on a task to its completion, and being attentive to the lessons I present."

Mentor Classroom Observation—Focus on Sara Porter

As Ms. Mercer's class begins, the children play with puzzles and other activities requiring construction or manipulation. Two children "write" on a flannel board, using letters kept in alphabetical stacks in a box. They return the letters so they fit exactly over their counterparts. Ms. Mercer praises them for neatness. She instructs them to return to their previously assigned groups as Sara enters the room.

The students are seated at six tables, four students at each table. Ms. Mercer explains, "Tables one and two will work on reading first, while tables three and four will solve math problems, and tables five and six will draw page illustrations for your collaborative Big Book. After 25 minutes, the groups will stop the first activity and begin working on a second task without changing seats. Twenty-five minutes later you will change again to work on the activity each group has not yet done. The math groups and those doing illustrations will hand in their work when time is called. I will work with the two groups who are reading aloud." She plans to monitor progress of students in the reading group.

Notes

Question 1: Conference with mother about lateness and tiredness and their effects on learning. School nurse—advise mother about healthful sleep. Document Sara's behavior.

Question 2: First grade is also for building self-esteem, learning responsibility, beginning higher-order thinking skills, and dealing with the "whole child."

Question 2: Could praise students for something more demanding than neatness—beginning to "write."

Question 4: Puzzles and other manipulatives are good for this age, as is "writing" on flannel board.

Question 3:
- Could shorten the activity time
- Could have them move seats between activities
- Could make directions and expectations clearer

Sara is at table one. Ms. Mercer begins with this table and table two, working on reading. Several children read aloud. Ms. Mercer praises them. When Ms. Mercer calls on Sara, she begins reading in the wrong place. Joyce, seated next to Sara, points to where they are. Ms. Mercer says, "Sara, you would know where we are if you were paying attention." She calls on another child. Sara looks hurt, but soon starts to follow along in the book. Subsequently, Ms. Mercer calls on Sara, who now has the right place. Ms. Mercer then calls on another child.

During the math activity, Sara, yawning frequently, is the last to open her workbook and write her name. When she completes the page, she waits. She seems puzzled, although Ms. Mercer has already given directions. Sara gets up, sharpens a pencil, and returns to the wrong seat. "That's MY seat," accuses an angry boy. Sara apologizes and returns to her seat. Later, she waits to have her workbook checked. She has not torn out pages as Ms. Mercer instructed. Sara is told to "do it right." Sara has not creased the paper as Ms. Mercer demonstrated, so the pages do not tear out easily. Sara sucks her thumb and holds her ear for a minute. Suddenly, she yanks the paper and the pages come out with jagged edges. She receives three dots for her work. Ms. Mercer says, "Sara, this is good. I wish you could earn four dots" (the maximum). Sara slaps herself on the forehead.

During the illustration activity, Sara helps several others who have trouble thinking of ideas. Sara's illustration is among the best handed in.

Question 6: Hypothesis: ADHD?

Question 6:
- Physical/emotional problems?
- K–1 instruction so different she can't follow?
- Sara angry?—what about?
- Sara needs positive reinforcement?

After the group work, Ms. Mercer places a large pad on an easel and says, "Now we're going to write about our trip to the art museum yesterday. Raise your hand and tell me something you saw or did in the museum." No one responds. She says, "Tell me the first thing we did at the museum." Sara raises her hand, offering a first sentence. After each response, Ms. Mercer asks, "What happened next?" or "What did we see next?" She prints each child's contribution.

Our Trip to the Art Museum

We rode the elevator to the second floor. We looked at different shapes on the ceiling. We saw a statue with a white triangle. We went to another room where we saw some pictures. We rode back down to the first floor. On our way out, we saw a painting of a grandfather and a boy.

During the writing of the group story, Sara fidgets in her seat, stares out the window, and makes a face at her neighbor.

Post-Observation Interview Notes

Ms. Mercer says, "Sara is a top performer in academic achievement and on standardized tests, consistently scoring among the top five students in the class. She's so bright. It's a shame she's late and distracted so much." The mentor replies, "There may be something else bothering Sara. Although easily distracted, there may be other explanations for her behavior. Let's talk more."

These two versions of the same student-based case show that you should be well prepared to respond to each of the questions by following these steps:

- Read each case carefully, raising questions about each section as you read.
- After reading the questions, reread the section and make notes.

These questions call on your knowledge of effective teaching and learning as conceptualized in the content categories, and also on theories that support teaching and learning. With this foundation of knowledge, and careful reading and annotation of the case, you should find that you can respond to each of the questions fully.

Case Study 2: Content Category Approach

Below is a second case, this time a document-based, teacher-based case. It is presented first using strategy 1—reading and annotating with questions based on the major content categories covered in the test.

CASE STUDY 2

MS. RILEY
Information Presented

Scenario

Ms. Riley is a third-year teacher in an urban elementary school. She has a heterogeneously mixed class of twenty-six 9- and 10-year-olds. At the beginning of the second month of school, she introduces a long-term project called "Literature Log." She plans the project to support her long-term goals. The following documents relate to that project.

Document 1
Literature Log Project Plan

Long-term goals:

1. Improve reading, writing, speaking, and listening abilities.
2. Develop critical-thinking skills.
3. Address students' individual differences.
4. Build a positive classroom community.

Notes

> What information is given in this section that might be relevant to Ms. Riley's instruction?

> What details about the planning might be significant?

- Appropriateness of goals and objectives?
- Strengths and weaknesses of the assignment?
- Strengths and weaknesses of assessment?
- Match of goals and objectives, activities, and assessment?
- Ways to expand or build on goals and objectives beyond the assignment?

Objectives:

1. Students will use writing to link aspects of a text with experiences and people in their own lives.
2. Students will write accurate summaries of what they have read.

Project Assignment:

Independent Reading Assignment
Literature Logs

You are expected to read independently for about 2 hours each week (25 to 30 minutes every school night).

You may choose the book.

You are also expected to write four entries in your Literature Log every two weeks.

Each entry should be about one handwritten page in your log.

At the beginning of each entry you are to write the following:

- The title and author of the book you are reading
- The numbers of the pages you are writing about
- A summary of the part of the book you have just read

In addition to writing a summary, you are to include one or more of the following:

- Similar things that have happened in your life
- What you think might happen next in the story
- Dilemmas the characters are facing and how they solve them or how you would solve them

HAPPY READING!

Assessment:

Each week, each student's Literature Log will be assessed on the following criteria:

- Number of pages read during the week
- Number of entries in Literature Log during the week
- Ability to write effective summaries of what has been read

Document 2
Entries from Sharon's Literature Log and
Ms. Riley's comments

Sharon
October 13, 2002
pp. 240–267

Beth died. I almost didn't notice because the book didn't really say she died. The way I noticed was because they started talking about how everyone missed her humming when she did house-work and how she played the piano and all kinds of things. My mother explained to me about yufamisms, which are words people use for things they really don't like to talk about. Well, we don't like to talk about it either but we say died. My aunt came to live with us because she was very sick and last year she died. I wonder what it felt like. I wonder how she felt when she was dieing? I miss her lots of times too.

I think you are reading *Little Women* by Louisa May Alcott. Remember to state the book title, author, and pages read every time.

Euphemisms

I'm sorry.
dying

Sharon
October 27, 2002
Little Women
by Louisa May Alcott
pp. 268–296

Jo realy likd to write and she started selling her stories to the newspapper. But one of her frends didnt like that kind of story so she stoped signing her name.

Sharon—
I'm disappointed with your spelling in this entry in your log. You need to be more careful.

really liked

newspaper
friends didn't

stopped

Don't you have any thoughts about your own life to add?

- Why are there two different entries? Are there changes?
- Do the entries meet the assignment and/or the goals and objectives?
- Why are the teacher's comments given?

- What does the conversation show about Kenny as a learner?
- How does Ms. Riley interact with Kenny?
- How might Ms. Riley address Kenny as a learner based on what is learned?

Document 3
A Conversation with Kenny

Ms. Riley: Kenny, in my grade book I noticed I don't have a check for your Literature Logs. But I'm sure you've been reading, since I've seen you read at least two books a week since the beginning of the year.

Kenny: Yeah, I read three books last week.

Ms. Riley: I noticed how much you enjoyed one of them, at least you were laughing as you read during silent reading. Did you choose one you wanted to write about in your Literature Log?

Kenny: Well, right now I'm reading an interesting one that takes place in a museum.

Ms. Riley: Oh, what book is that?

Kenny: It's a long name, *From the Mixed-Up Files of Mrs. Basil E. Frankenweiler.* I just started it last night.

Ms. Riley: Oh, I know that book. It's very good.

Kenny: Great, because I have a question about it.

Ms. Riley: Is it a question that could help with your reading?

Kenny: Well, someone keeps explaining things to Saxonberg and I don't know who is explaining. I don't know who Saxonberg is either.

Ms. Riley: You know, Kenny, I think if you read a few more chapters you will probably find out, and then you can write about it in your Literature Log.

Kenny: Well, I can tell you about it tomorrow. It has a long name, but it's a small book. I'll finish it tonight.

Ms. Riley: Well, I'd really love to see it written in your Literature Log, or I won't be able to fill in that you've completed your homework.

Kenny: That's O.K.—I don't read to get credit. I just read for fun.

Case Study 2: Question Approach

Questions Related to Case Study 2. Ms. Riley

1. Review Document 1, the Literature Log Project Plan. The plan demonstrates both strengths and weaknesses.

   - Identify ONE strength and ONE weakness of the Literature Log Project Plan.
   - Describe how each strength or weakness you identified demonstrates a strength or weakness in planning instruction. Base your response on principles of effective instructional planning.

2. Review Sharon's first entry (dated October 13) in Document 2, her Literature Log. Suppose that Ms. Riley wants to evaluate how well the entry demonstrates achievement of her long-term goals and/or her objectives.

   - Identify TWO aspects of Sharon's October 13 entry in her Literature Log that an effective evaluation would identify as achieving one or more of Ms. Riley's goals and/or her objectives.
   - For each aspect you identified, explain how it demonstrates achievement of one or more of Ms. Riley's goals and/or her objectives. Base your response on principles of effective assessment and evaluation.

3. In Document 2, Sharon's Literature Log, there are significant differences between Sharon's entry dated October 13 and her entry dated October 27. It appears that Sharon is having less success meeting the objectives for the project in the October 27 entry than in the October 13 entry.

   - Identify TWO significant differences between the first and second entries that indicate that Sharon is having less success in meeting the objectives of the project in the second entry.
   - For each difference you identified, suggest how Ms. Riley might have responded differently to Sharon in order to help Sharon continue to meet the objectives of the project. Base your response on principles of communication, assessment, and/or effective instruction.

4. In Document 3, Kenny's conversation with Ms. Riley, Kenny reveals characteristics of himself as a learner that could be used to support his development of literacy skills.

   - Identify ONE characteristic of Kenny as a learner, and then, suggest ONE strategy Ms. Riley might use to address that characteristic in a way that will support his development of literacy skills.
   - Describe how the strategy you suggested addresses the characteristic of Kenny as a learner and how the strategy could support Kenny's development of literacy skills. Base your response on principles of varied instructional strategies for different learners and of human development.

5. Review Ms. Riley's long-term goals at the beginning of Document 1, the Literature Log Project Plan.

- Select TWO long-term goals and for each goal, and identify one strategy Ms. Riley might use to expand the Literature Log unit beyond the stated assignment and assessment plan to address the goal.
- Explain how the use of each strategy you identified could expand the Literature Log unit to address the selected goal. Base your response on principles of planning instruction and/or language development and acquisition.

6. Review the two objectives of the Literature Log Project Plan included in Document 1. Suppose that at the end of the project, as a culminating activity, Ms. Riley wants her students to use their Literature Logs to help them do a self-assessment of the two objectives.

- For each of the TWO project objectives described in Document 1, suggest one assignment Ms. Riley could give the students that would serve as a self-assessment.
- For each assignment you suggested, describe how Ms. Riley's students could use it as a self-assessment. Base your response on principles of effective assessment.

With these questions in mind, reread the text of the case and note marginal comments that would directly help in responding to the questions.

CASE STUDY 2

MS. RILEY

Scenario

Ms. Riley is a third-year teacher in an urban elementary school. She has a heterogeneously mixed class of twenty-six 9- and 10-year-olds. At the beginning of the second month of school, she introduces a long-term project called "Literature Logs." She plans the project to support her long-term goals. The following documents relate to that project.

Document 1
Literature Log Project Plan

Long-term goals:

1. Improve reading, writing, speaking, and listening abilities.
2. Develop critical-thinking skills.
3. Address students' individual differences.
4. Build a positive classroom community.

Objectives:

1. Students will use writing to link aspects of a text with experiences and people in their own lives.
2. Students will write accurate summaries of what they have read.

Questions 1 and 5: In evaluating project plan and ways to expand the unit, bear in mind the following:

- urban elementary
- heterogeneous
- 26 nine-/ten-year-olds
- second month of school

Question 1:

Strengths

- Independent reading two hours per week—strengthens reading skills, literacy
- Student choice of book—individual differences
- Four entries per week—writing practice, known topic
- Including summary—meets objective, builds specific writing/thinking skills
- Link to lives—student-based instruction
- Prediction—builds thinking skills
- Dilemmas of characters—thinking skills, individual differences

Weaknesses

- Assessing number of pages—unimportant, doesn't meet any objectives
- Assessing number of entries per week doesn't meet objectives, suggests low-level expectations

Question 5:

- Speaking/listening: report aloud, students listen and question
- Critical thinking: rubric for self- and teacher assessment
- Positive community: cooperative groups to share
- Individual differences: find ways students differ
- All skills: folders, students present two favorites, revise in response to input

Question 6:

- For Objective 1, could have class develop a rubric together for evaluating entries in terms of linking with personal experience—students use rubric to evaluate selected entries.
- For Objective 2, could have students write an essay about strengths and weaknesses they see in five or six of their own summaries.

Project Assignment:

Independent Reading Assignment

Literature Logs

You are expected to read independently for about 2 hours each week (25 to 30 minutes every school night).

You may choose the book.

You are also expected to write four entries in your Literature Log every two weeks.

Each entry should be about one handwritten page in your Literature Log.

At the beginning of each entry you are to write the following:

- The title and author of the book you are reading
- The numbers of the pages you are writing about
- A summary of the part of the book you have just read

In addition to writing a summary, you are to include one or more of the following:

- Similar things that have happened in your life
- What you think might happen next in the story
- Dilemmas the characters are facing and how they solve them or how you would solve them

HAPPY READING!

- Objective of building positive community never addressed
- Assessment doesn't match goals/objectives except for summaries—no critical thinking, individual differences, positive community, using writing to link reading and personal experience

Assessment:

Each week, each student's Literature Log will be assessed on the following criteria:

- Number of pages read during week
- Number of entries in Literature Log during week
- Ability to write effective summaries of what has been read

Document 2

Entries from Sharon's Literature Log and Ms. Riley's Comment.

Sharon
October 13, 2002
pp. 240–267

Beth died. I almost didn't notice because the book didn't really say she died. The way I noticed was because they started talking about how everyone missed her humming when she did housework and how she played the piano and all kinds of things. My mother explained to me about <u>yufamisms</u>, which are words people use for things they really don't like to talk about.

I think you are reading Little Women by Louisa May Alcott. Remember to state the book title, author, and pages read every time.

euphemisms

Well, we don't like to talk about it either but we say died. My aunt came to live with us because she was very sick and last year she died. I wonder what it felt like. I wonder how she felt when she was <u>dieing</u>? I miss her lots of times too.

I'm sorry.
dying

Sharon
October 27, 2002
Little Women
by Louisa May Alcott
pp. 268 – 296

Sharon—
I'm disappointed with your spelling in this entry in your log. You need to be more careful.

Jo <u>realy likd</u> to write and she started selling her stories to the <u>newspapper</u>.
But one of her <u>frends didnt</u> like that kind of story so she <u>stoped</u> signing her name.

really liked

newspaper
friends didn't
stopped

Don't you have any thoughts about your own life to add?

Question 2:
- Uses critical thinking to figure out Beth is dead.
- Uses mother's definition connecting to family.
- Writes accurate brief summary.
- Wrestles with dilemma: what is it like to die?
- Strong personal voice: individual differences

Question 3:
- Oct. 27 entry, no dilemmas of characters. Positive comment in Oct. 13 entry might have encouraged more.
- Oct. 27 entry, no reference to own life.
- Oct. 27 entry, no speculation; needed positive comment in Oct. 13 entry from teacher to encourage more.
- Oct. 27 entry is a short summary; no critical thinking. Positive reinforcement on Oct. 13 needed.
- Oct. 27 entry minimal; comments on Oct. 13 entry almost all on routine requirements and not on accurate summary or personal response.

Question 4:

- Loves to read; doesn't waste time writing about it—make writing more creative or provide alternate response mode like taping.
- Loves to read—ask to imitate book he likes to write own story.
- Loves to read—review favorites for other students.
- Insightful, curious reader—suggest reviews he might read to see how others respond.
- Enthusiastic about books—act out a scene from favorite for others.
- Curious mind—search Internet for Web sites with interesting facts about books he likes.

Document 3

A Conversation with Kenny

Ms. Riley:	Kenny, in my grade book I noticed I don't have a check for your Literature Logs. But I'm sure you've been reading, since I've seen you read at least two books a week since the beginning of the year.
Kenny:	Yeah, I read three books last week.
Ms. Riley:	I noticed how much you enjoyed one of them, at least—you were laughing as you read during silent reading. Did you choose one you wanted to write about in your Literature Log?
Kenny:	Well, right now I'm reading an interesting one that takes place in a museum.
Ms. Riley:	Oh, what book is that?
Kenny:	It's a long name, *From the Mixed-Up Files of Mrs. Basil E. Frankenweiler.* I just started it last night.
Ms. Riley:	Oh, I know that book. It's very good.
Kenny:	Great, because I have a question about it.
Ms. Riley:	Is it a question that could help with your reading?
Kenny:	Well, someone keeps explaining things to Saxonberg and I don't know who is explaining. I don't know who Saxonberg is either.
Ms. Riley:	You know, Kenny, I think if you read a few more chapters you will probably find out, and then you can write about it in your Literature Log.
Kenny:	Well, I can tell you about it tomorrow. It has a long name, but it's a small book. I'll finish it tonight.
Ms. Riley:	Well, I'd really love to see it written in your Literature Log. Or I won't be able to fill in that you've completed your homework.
Kenny:	That's O.K.—I don't read to get credit. I just read for fun.

With these strategies in mind, you may now want to go on to the next section, which takes a different focus: writing your answers to questions based on cases.

HOW TO ANSWER CONSTRUCTED-RESPONSE QUESTIONS

The previous section focused on strategies for reading, analyzing, and taking notes on case studies and how to relate each question to a particular section or concept in the case study. This section focuses on producing your response—making sure you understand what the question is asking and then using advice from experts to formulate a successful response.

Advice from the Experts

Scorers who have scored thousands of real tests were asked to give advice to students taking the Principles of Learning and Teaching test. Here is what they said:

1. **Answer all parts of the question.** This seems simple, but many test-takers fail to provide a complete response. If the question asks for two activities, don't forget the second one. If the question asks for a strength and a weakness, don't describe just a weakness. No matter how well you write about one activity or about a weakness, you will not get full credit for an answer that does not cover all aspects of the question.

2. **Show that you understand the pedagogical concepts related to the question.** This is a more subtle piece of advice. The scorers are looking to see not only that you can read the case study and make good observations, but also that you can relate those good observations to pedagogical concepts such as the principles of human development, the principles of motivation, the principles of effective instructional design, and the principles of diagnostic and evaluative assessment. To show that you understand these concepts, you have to do more than just mention that the concepts exist. You must also relate them to the specifics of your response. For example, in answering a question about identifying a weakness in a teacher's approach to assessment, instead of stating that "Mr. Taft didn't give the students very good tests," you could improve on this answer and state, "Given that assessment of student performance is most effective when evidence is gathered frequently and through a variety of exercises and assignments, Mr. Taft's reliance on end-of-chapter tests did not give students such as Paige adequate opportunities to demonstrate achievement."

3. **Show that you have a thorough understanding of the case.** Some answers receive partial credit because they are vague—they address the issues brought up in the case study at too general a level rather than at a level that takes into consideration the particulars given about a teacher, student, or assignment. If you are asked, for example, about the boy with learning disabilities whose patterns of behavior are described specifically in several sentences in the case study, don't answer the question in terms of children with disabilities in general. Instead, focus on the boy in the case study and all the particulars you know about him.

4. **Support your answers with details.** This advice overlaps, to some extent, with numbers 2 and 3 above. The scorers are looking for some justification of your answers. If you are asked to state a "strength" shown by the teacher in a case study, don't just state the strength in a few words. Write why this is a strength—perhaps because of a particular principle of effective instructional design, which you should briefly summarize, or perhaps because of a good outcome described in the case, to which you should refer.

5. **Do not change the question or challenge the basis of the question.** Stay focused on the question that is asked, and do your best to answer it. You will receive no credit or, at best, a low score if you choose to answer another question or you state that, for example, there really aren't any activities that could be proposed, or there aren't any strengths to mention, or in some other way deny the basis of the question.

How PLT Constructed-Response Questions Are Scored

The following guide provides the overarching framework that guides how constructed-response questions on the Principles of Learning and Teaching tests are scored and the method by which the question-specific scoring guide for each question is created and revised.

Principles of Learning and Teaching General Scoring Guide

All questions will be scored on a 0, 1, 2 scale.

A response that receives a score of 2

- demonstrates a thorough understanding of the aspects of the case that are relevant to the question
- responds appropriately (see next page) to all parts of the question
- if an explanation is required, provides a strong explanation that is well supported by relevant evidence
- demonstrates a strong knowledge of pedagogical concepts, theories, facts, procedures, or methodologies relevant to the question

A response that receives a score of 1

- demonstrates a basic understanding of the aspects of the case that are relevant to the question
- responds appropriately (see next page) to one portion of the question
- if an explanation is required, provides a weak explanation that is well supported by relevant evidence
- demonstrates some knowledge of pedagogical concepts, theories, facts, procedures, or methodologies relevant to the question

A response that received a score of 0

- demonstrates misunderstanding of the aspects of the case that are relevant to the question
- fails to respond appropriately (see next page) to the question
- is not supported by relevant evidence
- demonstrates little knowledge of pedagogical concepts, theories, facts, procedures, or methodologies relevant to the question

No credit is given for blank or off-topic response.

The criteria for evaluating whether a response is "appropriate" are established through a "model answers" methodology, which consists of the following steps:

- After a case and questions are written, three or four knowledgeable experts are asked to read the case and answer the questions, addressing each question exactly as it is worded. These experts are carefully chosen to represent the diverse perspectives and situations relevant to the testing population.
- The case writer uses these "model answers" to develop a question-specific scoring guide for each question, creating a list of specific examples that would receive full credit. This list is considered to contain examples of correct answers, not all the possible correct answers.

- These question-specific scoring guides based on model answers provide the basis for choosing the papers that serve as a benchmark and sample papers for the purpose of training the scorers at the scoring session.
- During the scoring sessions, while reading student papers, scorers can add new answers to the scoring guide as they see fit.
- Training at the scoring sessions is aimed to ensure that scorers do not score papers on the basis of their opinions or their own preferences, but rather make judgments based on the carefully established criteria in the scoring guide.

CHAPTER 13

Real PLT Questions for Practice

Now you can practice writing your own responses to the 12 questions based on the case studies you read in Chapter 12. When you read a question for the first time, it is helpful to think about what the question is really asking and then to think about which of the content categories the question assesses. Note in the samples below that the last sentence of each question contains a reference to the content category addressed. This is nearly always the case in the constructed-response questions on the Principles of Learning and Teaching test, although there may be instances when the category is not explicitly stated.

As you plan and evaluate your response to the question, think about the scoring criteria used by the scorers, and think about the advice given by the experts.

The two cases and 12 practice questions, with accompanying advice and commentary, begin on the next page.

CASE STUDY 1

SARA

Scenario

Six-year-old Sara lives with her mother, who has a relaxed schedule. Ms. Mercer, Sara's teacher, notes that Sara is often tired and inattentive after arriving late. Sara says she frequently stays up past midnight if others are up. Ms. Mercer, a second-year teacher, has asked her mentor to observe Sara and suggest ways to help Sara achieve Ms. Mercer's purposes.

Observation: Ms. Mercer's Class, April 30

Pre-Observation Interview Notes

Ms. Mercer says, "The purposes of first grade are to teach children 'school survival skills' and reading, writing, and arithmetic." She adds, "Sara needs help with 'survival skills,' including following directions, concentrating on a task to its completion, and being attentive to the lessons I present."

Mentor Classroom Observation—Focus on Sara Porter

As Ms. Mercer's class begins, the children play with puzzles and other activities requiring construction or manipulation. Two children "write" on a flannel board, using letters kept in alphabetical stacks in a box. They return the letters so they fit exactly over their counterparts. Ms. Mercer praises them for neatness. She instructs them to return to their previously assigned groups as Sara enters the room.

The students are seated at six tables, four students at each table. Ms. Mercer explains, "Tables one and two will work on reading first, while tables three and four will solve math problems, and tables five and six will draw page illustrations for your collaborative Big Book. After 25 minutes, the groups will stop the first activity and begin working on a second task without changing seats. Twenty-five minutes later, you will change again to work on the activity each group has not yet done. The math groups and those doing illustrations will hand in their work when time is called. I will work with the two groups who are reading aloud." She plans to monitor progress of students in the reading group.

Sara is at table one. Ms. Mercer begins with this table and table two, working on reading. Several children read aloud. Ms. Mercer praises them. When Ms. Mercer calls on Sara, she begins reading in the wrong place. Joyce, seated next to Sara, points to where they are. Ms. Mercer says, "Sara, you would know where we are if you were paying attention." She calls on another child. Sara looks hurt, but soon starts to follow along in the book. Subsequently, Ms. Mercer calls on Sara, who now has the right place. Ms. Mercer then calls on another child.

During the math activity, Sara, yawning frequently, is the last to open her workbook and write her name. When she completes the page, she waits. She seems puzzled, although Ms. Mercer has already given directions. Sara gets up, sharpens a pencil, and returns to the wrong seat. "That's MY seat," accuses an angry boy. Sara apologizes and returns to her seat. Later, she waits to have her workbook checked. She has not torn out pages as Ms. Mercer instructed. Sara is told to "do it right." Sara has not creased the paper as Ms. Mercer demonstrated, so the pages do not tear out easily. Sara sucks her thumb and holds her ear for a minute. Suddenly, she yanks the paper and the pages come out with jagged edges. She receives three dots for her work. Ms. Mercer says, "Sara, this is good. I wish you could earn four dots" (the maximum). Sara slaps herself on the forehead.

During the illustration activity, Sara helps several others who have trouble thinking of ideas. Sara's illustration is among the best handed in. After the group work, Ms. Mercer places a large pad on an easel and says, "Now we're going to write about our trip to the art museum yesterday. Raise your hand and tell me something you saw or did in the museum." No one responds. She says, "Tell me the first thing we did at the museum." Sara raises her hand, offering a first sentence.

After each response, Ms. Mercer asks, "What happened next?" or "What did we see next?" She prints each child's contribution.

Our Trip to the Art Museum

We rode the elevator to the second floor. We looked at different shapes on the ceiling. We saw a statue with a white triangle. We went to another room where we saw some pictures. We rode back down to the first floor. On our way out, we saw a painting of a grandfather and a boy. During the writing of the group story, Sara fidgets in her seat, stares out the window, and makes a face at her neighbor.

Post-Observation Interview Notes

Ms. Mercer says, "Sara is a top performer in academic achievement and on stand-ardized tests, consistently scoring among the top five students in the class. She's so bright. It's a shame she's late and distracted so much." The mentor replies, "There may be something else bothering Sara. Although she is easily distracted, there may be other explanations for her behavior. Let's talk more."

STRATEGIES FOR ANSWERING CONSTRUCTED-RESPONSE QUESTIONS FOR CASE STUDY 1

The questions that follow are the same questions you read in Chapter 12. Read each question again, then complete the exercises below it. These exercises are designed to help you think critically about what is being asked.

How to Answer Question 1

Question 1

Suppose that Ms. Mercer and her mentor discuss how to connect school and Sara's home environment for the benefit of Sara's learning.

- Identify TWO specific actions Ms. Mercer might take to connect school and Sara's home environment for the benefit of Sara's learning.

- Explain how each action you identified could benefit Sara's learning. Base your response on principles of fostering school–parent relationships to support student learning.

Step 1. Think About What Is Being Asked.

In the space below, state in your own words what you think the question is asking.

```



```

Compare your impression of what is being asked with the explanation below.
  The question asks for

- *two* things Ms. Mercer might do to help the school and parent work together to identify Sara's needs
- for *each* thing, an explanation of how it could help Sara's learning

Step 2. Think About the Category Being Assessed.

- The larger community

The important aspect of this content category is fostering relationships with . . . parents. Also, although they are not the focus of the question, you need to understand the underlying human development issues—the physical, social, emotional, moral, and cognitive development of children this age. Both aspects (fostering relationships . . . and human development) are critical in a teacher's responsibilities to meet the needs of all students, but especially students such as Sara.

Step 3. Write Your Response.

In the space below, write what you consider to be a response that directly addresses the question.

```



```

Step 4. Reflect on Your Response in Light of the Scoring Guide, Sample Responses, and Commentary.

Note that the scoring guide used to evaluate responses to this question specifies two actions and that they must be appropriate. Note the rubric contains bulleted possible answers, but that they are introduced by the statement ". . . such as the following." The list is neither prescriptive nor restrictive; all appropriate responses are given full credit. The experienced educators who score the test can evaluate the appropriateness of responses that are not contained in this list.

ETS Scoring Guide for Question 1

Score of 2

The response presents two appropriate actions Ms. Mercer might take to connect school and Sara's home environment and explanations of how each could benefit Sara's learning, such as the following:

- Ms. Mercer can seek a conference with Sara's mother to determine why Sara often arrives late and appears tired in class. Together they can discuss strategies to address Sara's problems.
- Ms. Mercer might ask the school nurse to schedule a conference with Sara, her mother, and Ms. Mercer to explore the reasons for Sara's tiredness in class. With the mediation of the school nurse, the adults and Sara can discuss ways to improve Sara's attentiveness and ability to follow directions.
- Ms. Mercer might telephone Sara's mother and explain that Sara is doing very well on tests, but that she is falling behind in class because she arrives late, appears very tired, reports she often stays up late, and finds it hard to follow directions or to contribute to discussions in class. Together they can explore ways to address Sara's problematic behavior.
- Ms. Mercer can document one or two weeks of Sara's inability to follow directions or to arrive on time and then call Sara's mother or schedule a conference to discuss what can be done at home and in school to improve Sara's ability to follow directions and to arrive on time.
- Ms. Mercer could gather a few articles about the necessity of at least 8 hours of sleep each night for 6-year-olds. She could ask for a conference with Sara's mother and discuss with her the harmful effects Sara's apparent lack of sleep is having on her school performance. Together they can seek solutions to Sara's tiredness.
- Ms. Mercer can discuss with second- and third-grade teachers the importance of a student's ability to follow directions and to contribute in class. She could then seek a conference with Sara's mother to show the negative effects of Sara's inability to follow

directions and contribute in class, indicating why that might be important for her present and future well-being.

Score of 1

The response presents two appropriate actions Ms. Mercer might take to connect school and Sara's home environment for the benefit of Sara's learning, without sufficient explanations, or presents one appropriate action with explanation, such as those described under 'Score of 2' above.

Score of 0

The response fails to address the question, presents inappropriate actions, or is vague.

Sample Responses and Commentary

Response That Would Receive a Score of 2

First, Ms. Mercer can collect as much information as possible to use in conferences with Sara's mother to help establish a positive relationship and to help identify Sara's strengths and needs. Ms. Mercer should do some systematic observation and objective description of Sara's performance and the effects of her late arrival and inattentiveness in class. Observation information should include Sara's good qualities. She might also gather information, with the help of the school nurse, about healthful habits for children Sara's age, including the amount of sleep needed. Second, Ms. Mercer then needs to seek a parent conference to discuss the areas in which Sara shows strengths as a student and to address her concerns about Sara's performance in class. By showing a sincere interest in Sara's positive growth and development as well as identifying the youngster's problems, Ms. Mercer can work to establish a positive working relationship with Sara's mother.

Commentary on the Above Response

The response presents two appropriate actions in considerable detail. The actions are related to each other, but are still clearly two separate steps in building a positive home–school relationship. The actions are clearly presented and directly applicable to the situation. The response receives full credit.

Response That Would Receive a Score of 1

Ms. Mercer needs to talk with Sara's mother in order to connect school and Sara's home environment for the benefit of Sara's learning. She should call her to make an appointment, and when Sara's mother comes to school for the meeting, they can begin to discuss Sara's behavior and the possible causes for it. In the same way, Ms. Mercer and perhaps the nurse or school psychologist know a lot about what Sara does at school and a lot of theory about child growth and development, and they can help Sara's mother understand what her problems are and how to approach them. In this way, Sara will benefit because both home and school will know more and be better able to help her.

Commentary on the Above Response

The response presents only one action. Calling the mother is not presented as a separate action that, in itself, would address the problem, but rather as a preliminary to the meeting. The response does present one action that is appropriate, clearly expressed, and applicable to the situation. The response receives partial credit.

Response That Would Receive a Score of 0

Although it sounds like a good idea, probably very little if anything will be gained by trying to establish contact with Sara's mother. From the way Sara behaves in school, it appears that a very likely cause of her problems lies at home, especially if her mother keeps her up very late at night and has little regard for her welfare. Therefore, in the best interests of Sara, Ms. Mercer should rely on the school to help her try to figure out what's going on with Sara and how best to help her and should not involve Sara's mother.

Commentary on the Above Response

The response presents an inappropriate action. The INTASC standard that reads "the teacher fosters relationships with school colleagues, parents, and agencies in the larger community to support students' learning and well being" clearly indicates that deliberately not involving Sara's mother is an inappropriate course of action. The response receives no credit.

How to Answer Question 2

Question 2

Review the pre-observation notes in which Ms. Mercer explains the purposes of first grade as she sees them. Suppose her mentor suggests that Ms. Mercer consider other purposes of first grade, and how she might modify her instruction to address those purposes and the related needs of Sara and her other students.

- Identify TWO additional purposes of first grade that Ms. Mercer could consider when planning her instruction, in order to meet the needs of Sara and/or her other students.
- For each purpose you identified, explain how Ms. Mercer might modify her instruction to address the purpose and meet the needs of Sara and/or her other students. Base your response on principles of planning instruction and learning theory.

Step 1. Think About What Is Being Asked.

In the space below, state in your own words what you think the question is asking.

Compare your impression of what is being asked with the explanation below.
The question asks for

- *two* additional purposes that might indicate needs of Sara and the other students
- for *each* purpose, an explanation of how Ms. Mercer might modify her instruction to meet these needs

Step 2. Think About the Categories Being Assessed.

- Planning instruction
- Learning theory

It is important to know how to establish appropriate purposes for specific groups of students, and how to plan instruction to meet those purposes in a way that will engage students fully in learning.

Step 3. Write Your Response.

In the space below, write what you consider to be a response that directly addresses the question.

Step 4. Reflect on Your Response in Light of the Scoring Guide, Sample Responses, and Commentary.

Remember, as you study the scoring guide below, that scorers use it as the primary means of evaluating responses, and use their professional knowledge to evaluate the appropriateness of responses. Remember, too, that the words "such as" introducing the bulleted examples of possible appropriate responses mean that these possible responses are neither prescriptive nor restrictive.

ETS Scoring Guide for Question 2

Score of 2

The response presents two additional appropriate purposes for first grade. For each, the response offers one modification for the teacher's instruction to better meet the needs of Sara or the other students, such as the following:

- The mentor can suggest that another purpose for first grade is to build self-esteem and confidence by providing success for all students in a variety of learning situations. Instead of pointing out Sara's weaknesses, she could praise her in class when she does well. By building in opportunities for success and building self-esteem and confidence, she can increase the engagement of Sara and other students.
- The mentor can suggest that another purpose of first grade is to offer students multiple opportunities to recognize and accept their responsibilities. For example, she could have a student repeat the directions she gives to each group and could have students identify what they are responsible for doing.
- The mentor can suggest that first grade should also be about developing more challenging skills than those for "survival," and could recommend that rather than just having the students learn survival routines. Ms. Mercer could introduce higher-order tasks, including evaluation, analysis, and/or synthesis, at an appropriate level for students to perform as part of each task.
- The mentor can suggest that another purpose for first grade is for students to learn to support one another in their learning. Instead of reprimanding Sara and other students for not hearing the directions the first time, she can appoint a buddy for each student so they can check with each other when they're unsure of what to do.
- The mentor can suggest that another purpose of first grade is to develop "the whole child," addressing physical, emotional, and intellectual growth and development. For example, Ms. Mercer might learn more about Sara's talents, interests, and problems so she can address Sara's strengths and needs in all three areas.

Score of 1

The response presents two additional purposes, but does not explain how Ms. Mercer might modify her instruction, or presents one additional purpose and explains how she might modify her instruction, in keeping with the purposes and modifications presented in score point 2.

Score of 0

The response fails to address the question, presents inappropriate additional purposes and modifications, or is vague.

Sample Responses and Commentary

Response That Would Receive a Score of 2

The mentor can point out to Ms. Mercer that an important additional purpose for first grade is to address the physical, emotional, and intellectual needs of all children. She could have modified her instruction by learning more about Sara and then addressing Sara's needs in a carefully planned way that supports Sara's growth and development. A second additional purpose for first grade is to build students' self-esteem and confidence. The mentor could point out that Ms. Mercer shows her concern about Sara to the mentor, but to Sara she generally shows her frustration and impatience with what Sara does wrong. If Ms. Mercer began by praising Sara for her ability and acknowledging her genuine contributions, she would take an important step toward building Sara's self-esteem and confidence.

Commentary on the Above Response

The response presents two appropriate additional purposes of first grade. For each, the response offers one modification for her instruction to better meet Sara's needs. The two purposes and the accompanying explanations of the modification are presented clearly and thoroughly. Therefore, the response receives full credit.

Response That Would Receive a Score of 1

One additional purpose of first grade is to begin introducing some of the higher-order thinking skills at a level appropriate for the age and grade level. Ms. Mercer is right that reading, writing, and arithmetic are important, but she could help the students grow much more effectively by helping them begin to use some synthesis, analysis, and evaluation skills in the tasks they are doing. For example, in her oral reading activity, she could ask some questions related to what the students are reading that would require them to use these higher-order thinking skills. She could ask how characters are alike, or ask them to name two things they really like about the story.

Commentary on the Above Response

The response presents one appropriate additional purpose for first grade and suggests an appropriate modification Ms. Mercer might make in her instruction. Both the purpose and the modification are explained with sufficient appropriate detail. However, the response does not present two additional purposes with modifications as the question requires, and so it receives partial credit.

Response That Would Receive a Score of 0

It seems to me that, with everything first-grade teachers are expected to do these days, Ms. Mercer has more than enough challenges with the purposes she has established. Yes, it might be nice if she could think of some "additional" purposes, but I think her students will be best served if she concentrates on the purposes she has established and works to give her students a solid foundation on which later grades can build.

Commentary on the Above Response

The response fails to address the question. Responses that argue with the premise of the question receive no credit.

How to Answer Question 3

Question 3

Assume that the groups working on mathematics and illustrations for the Big Book become very noisy and unproductive over the course of the activity.

- Suggest TWO changes Ms. Mercer could have made in the planning and/or implementation of the group work that would have made the activity more successful.
- Explain how each change you suggested could have made the group work activity more successful. Base your response on principles of planning instruction and human development.

Step 1. Think About What Is Being Asked.

In the space below, state in your own words what you think the question is asking.

Compare your impression of what is being asked with the explanation below.
   The question asks for

- *two* changes Ms. Mercer could have made to make the group work more successful
- for *each* change, an explanation of how the group work would have been more successful

Step 2. Think About the Categories Being Assessed.

- Planning instruction
- Human development

Again, note the importance of addressing each of these two categories. These two are especially important when a teacher is thinking about planning specific instructional strategies for specific groups of students. Note again that knowledge from learning theory and human behavior and motivation should be utilized to develop strategies for organizing and supporting individual and group work.

Step 3. Write Your Response.

In the space below, write what you consider to be a response that directly addresses the question.

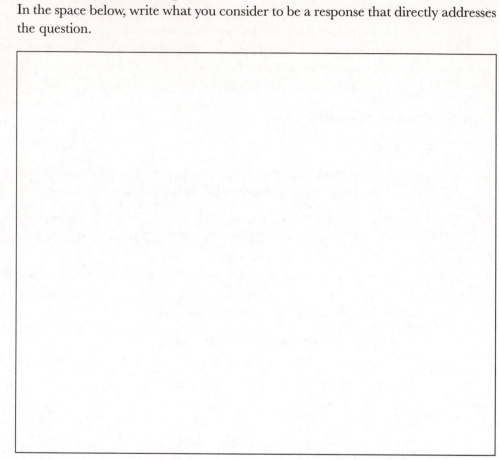

Step 4. Reflect on Your Response in Light of the Scoring Guide, Sample Responses, and Commentary.

Again, note that the scoring guide contains possible appropriate responses that are illustrative only and are neither prescriptive nor restrictive. Remember there are many appropriate ways in which the question could be answered, and these are illustrations only.

Score of 2

The response presents two appropriate changes Ms. Mercer could have made in planning and implementing the group work, and explanations of how they could make the activity more successful, such as the following:

- Ms. Mercer could shorten the amount of time for each activity, so that the students would be more likely to stay on task. Twenty-five minutes per activity is too much time for students this age to be expected to work independently or in small groups without direct supervision.
- Ms. Mercer should teach or review group work behavior and expectations before the work begins, so that her students would be more likely to participate appropriately in the activity.
- Ms. Mercer could have groups move seats between activities. Students this age need to move more frequently and have physical activity, rather than being expected to sit in the same seats for long periods.
- Ms. Mercer could use parent volunteers to help support and monitor the work of the two groups with whom she is not working directly.
- Ms. Mercer could give clear directions, with steps and models of what final products are to look like, before students begin to work, so that they would be more likely to understand and achieve the objectives of the activity.
- Ms. Mercer could display posters that illustrate what students are to do; posters can also indicate the location of each group activity. The posters would provide the students with clearer directions for completing the activity.

Score of 1

The response presents two appropriate changes Ms. Mercer could have made in planning and implementing the group work without explanations of how the changes make the activity more successful, or presents one change Ms. Mercer could have made with an explanation of how the activity could have been more successful, such as those described under "Score of 2" above.

Score of 0

The response fails to address the question, presents inappropriate ways to introduce and implement the group work, or is vague.

Sample Responses and Commentary

Response That Would Receive a Score of 2

First, Ms. Mercer should plan shorter times for the students to work on each activity, so that the students would be able to stay on task. Twenty-five minutes is too long to expect students this age to work alone or even in small groups on one activity. Next, she should plan to review much more carefully what she expects students in each group to do, showing them examples of what their finished work is supposed to look like. Providing clearer expectations would increase the likelihood that the students would complete the activity as desired.

Commentary on the Above Response

The response presents two appropriate changes Ms. Mercer could have made in the planning and implementation of the group work. They take into account the students' developmental levels and present approaches that would strengthen the group activities. The response receives full credit.

Response That Would Receive a Score of 1

Ms. Mercer should introduce the activity by teaching or reviewing rules for behavior and procedures for small group work. She can't expect students to know this, or even to remember it from day to day. She needs to explain rules for working independently, or rules for working cooperatively so students can help one another without disturbing other students. If she reviews these things, the groups will have a better chance of success.

Commentary on the Above Response

The response presents one appropriate change Ms. Mercer could have made in her planning. It is presented in detail, but constitutes only one change. The question requires two appropriate changes; the response receives partial credit.

Response That Would Receive a Score of 0

Ms. Mercer should not try to use small group work with students this age. They are too young to be expected to work independently or even in small groups. She should keep the class together so that she can have direct supervision over them at all times.

Commentary on the Above Response

The response argues with the question, rather than responding to it in an appropriate way. Responses that argue with the premise of the question receive no credit.

How to Answer Question 4

Question 4

In the activities described in the Mentor Classroom Observation, Ms. Mercer demonstrates understanding of developmentally appropriate instructions.

- Identify TWO strengths in the instructional approaches Ms. Mercer uses in the activities that reflect understanding of the principles of developmentally appropriate instructions.

- Explain how each of these strengths you identified provides evidence of an understanding of the principles of developmentally appropriate instruction. Base your response on principles of planning instruction and human development.

Step 1. Think About What Is Being Asked.

In the space below, state in your own words what you think the question is asking.

Compare your impression of what is being asked with the explanation below.
The question asks for

- *two* strengths in Ms. Mercer's instructional approaches
- for *each* strength, an explanation of how it demonstrates understanding of developmentally appropriate instruction

Step 2. Think About the Categories Being Assessed.

- Planning instruction
- Human development

Again, note the importance of addressing each of these two categories. These two are especially important in thinking about planning specific instructional strategies for specific groups of students. Note again that knowledge from learning theory and human behavior and motivation are utilized to develop strategies for organizing and supporting individual and group work.

Step 3. Write Your Response.

In the space below, write what you consider to be a response that directly addresses the question.

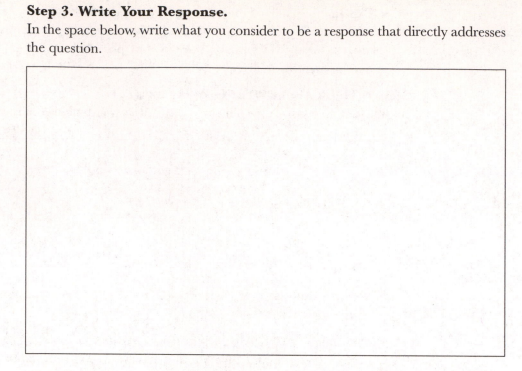

Step 4. Reflect on Your Response in Light of the Scoring Guide, Sample Responses, and Commentary.

ETS Scoring Guide for Question 4

Score of 2

The response presents two strengths in Ms. Mercer's instructional approaches, with evidence of understanding of developmentally appropriate instructions, such as the following:

- Having students engage in play with puzzles or other activities requiring construction and manipulation is very appropriate to the students' developmental levels.
- Having the students "write" on flannel boards is an appropriate language development activity for students this age.
- Having students work on a variety of tasks, rotating among three tasks, is an appropriate activity-centered approach for students this age.
- Connecting the writing activity to the students' previous experience on the field trip is an appropriate way to help students this age make connections and, therefore, perform well.
- Questioning and prompting students as they are developing the account of the trip is an appropriate way to help students this age develop writing fluency.

Score of 1

The response presents two strengths in Ms. Mercer's instructional approaches, without appropriate discussion of how they are developmentally appropriate, or presents one strength in Ms. Mercer's instructional approach with evidence of how it is developmentally appropriate, such as those described under 'Score of 2' above.

Score of 0

The response fails to address the question, presents inappropriate points as strengths, or is vague.

Sample Responses and Commentary

Response That Would Receive a Score of 2

Ms. Mercer's lesson does display strengths. She is developing students' writing skills in an appropriate way for students this age by having students "write" at the flannel board. They are developing an enthusiasm for writing and a sense of what it means to put letters together to form words. Another strength is the way she connects the writing of the story to their previous trip to the museum. When teachers connect one activity to previous knowledge or experience of students, the students this age have a better opportunity to learn and demonstrate their learning. It was also a strength to prompt and question students as they were developing ideas for the story. They were having trouble remembering, but without telling them what to say, she helped them develop ideas.

Commentary on the Above Response

The response presents more than two appropriate strengths. Each point presented is valid and explained in sufficient detail. No additional credit, however, is given for going beyond the requirement of the question. The response receives full credit.

Response That Would Receive a Score of 1

Ms. Mercer's use of rotating group activities for the students is a strength of the lesson. This activity-centered approach is very effective in helping students develop skills and remain engaged in the work. The activities are varied enough to keep the students interested and are all appropriate for students this age.

Commentary on the Above Response

The response presents one appropriate strength of her approach. It is explained in sufficient detail. However, the response presents only one strength, and the question calls for two. It receives partial credit.

Response That Would Receive a Score of 0

One appropriate strength in her approach is that she is very nice to the children. Boys and girls in first grade need lots of personal attention and a supportive classroom environment. Teachers who are enthusiastic and supportive of their students help students a lot more than teachers who are too stern and critical.

Commentary on the Above Response

The response refers to aspects for teaching first grade that are important. However, the discussion does not address the question of strengths of Ms. Mercer's instructional approaches. Discussing aspects of instruction stressed by the INTASC standards but not relevant to the question posed is not sufficient to receive credit.

How to Answer Question 5

Question 5

Assume that the day after the lesson was observed, Ms. Mercer's objective is to use the story about the museum visit to continue building students' literacy.

- Identify TWO strategies and/or activities involving the story about the museum visit that Ms. Mercer could use to continue building students' literacy.
- For each strategy and/or activity you identified, explain how it could help build literacy. Base your response on principles of language development and acquisition.

Step 1. Think About What Is Being Asked.

In the space below, state in your own words what you think the question is asking.

Compare your impression of what is being asked with the explanation below.
   The question asks for

- *two* strategies or activities the teacher could use to meet this objective
- an explanation of how *each* strategy or activity helps build literacy

Step 2. Think About the Category Being Assessed.

- Planning instruction

For students this age, building literacy skills is essential. The ability to address this need in practice is critical.

Step 3. Write Your Response.

In the space below, write what you consider to be a response that directly addresses the question.

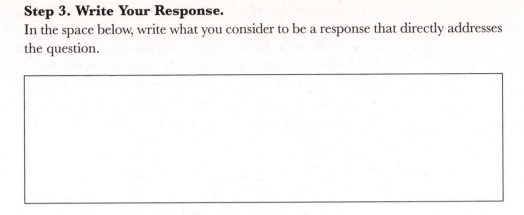

Step 4. Reflect on Your Response in Light of the Scoring Guide, Sample Responses, and Commentary.

ETS Scoring Guide for Question 5

Score of 2

The response offers two appropriate strategies Ms. Mercer could use and explains how each strategy meets her objective, such as the following:

- Ms. Mercer could tell the students their story is going to be shared with students in another class. Have them brainstorm ways to make the story more interesting for other children their age, including more information they remember that might be included. This activity would build their writing skills by adding information for a specific audience.
- Ms. Mercer could have copies of the story run off by the end of the day and give each student a copy of the story. She could ask them to have their parents read the story with them and ask questions about it. The next day they could use the questions they can remember to brainstorm more ideas. This activity would build their oral literacy through conversation with their parents and their writing skills through revision.
- Ms. Mercer can ask students to think about one thing they remember from the visit (the marble with the white triangle, the ceiling pictures, or the room full of statues) and draw a picture of it. She could post the pictures and use them as a basis for a word board of good descriptive language. This builds their writing skills by revising to add more specific, focused details about one aspect of the visit.
- Ms. Mercer might read the children a story about a visit. She could have children discuss what they liked about the story, and use this information to brainstorm ways to write about their own visit. This builds their writing skills by modeling an effective description,

and their speaking and listening skills as they share aloud ideas to revise their story.

- Ms. Mercer can show pictures of the various things the class saw at the museum. By asking the members of each group to identify an item that interests them and discuss what they could write to make another person their age interested in the item, Ms. Mercer could build on their discussion and listening skills and develop writing skills.

Score of 1

The response presents one appropriate strategy and explains how it meets the objective to develop students' literacy such as those presented in score point 2, or presents two appropriate strategies such as those presented in score point 2 but does not explain how the strategies meet the objective.

Score of 0

The response fails to address the question, presents inappropriate strategies and explanations of how the strategies meet the objective, or is vague.

Sample Responses and Commentary

Response That Would Receive a Score of 2

Ms. Mercer has many opportunities to develop the speaking, reading, writing, and listening skills of her students by using the description of the museum visit in creative ways. By having students revise the story for a specific audience, a group of children their age, and describe their visit in ways that would make the others want to go to the museum too, she can increase their ability to write for a specific audience. If she were to display pictures of things they saw, ask them to provide descriptive words, and then write the words beneath the pictures, she would help them develop vocabulary appropriate to their writing and to develop speaking and listening skills.

Commentary on the Above Response

The response identifies two specific ways in which Ms. Mercer could continue building students' literacy. The activities suggested are appropriate and described in detail. The response receives full credit.

Response That Would Receive a Score of 1

Ms. Mercer could use two additional activities to build students' literacy. The next day they could return to the story they have written, and could brainstorm some additional details that could be added to make the story more interesting. Ms. Mercer might have to prompt them a bit, but by giving them some hints, she could help them remember things that would make the story fuller and more detailed. She could also develop literacy by having "listening stations" where students can listen to tape-recorded stories and follow along in books. By connecting the story read aloud (on tape) and the story as it appears in print, she can help them understand that the words on the page have real meaning.

Commentary on the Above Response

The question specifically says her objective is "to use the story about the museum visit to continue building students' literacy" and asks for two strategies or activities to meet this objective. One of the activities presented does extend the lesson and receives credit. However, the second activity is unrelated to the story about the museum and therefore is considered unresponsive to the question. The response receives partial credit.

Response That Would Receive a Score of 0

I believe developing literacy is probably the most important academic objective first grade teachers can have. Literacy involves developing specifically the skills of reading, writing, speaking, and listening. There are many activities that first grade teachers can use to develop literacy. It is important to remember that for first graders, print is very confusing, and they often see little connection between ideas and print, so anything a teacher can do to help them make that connection will help.

Commentary on the Above Response

Merely selecting one word—even a critical word—from the question and writing about it does not constitute responding appropriately to the question. While the question does deal with developing literacy, the response does not address the specific requirements of the question and receives no credit.

How to Answer Question 6

Question 6

In the post-observation notes, Ms. Mercer's mentor suggests that they explore explanations for Sara's inattentive behavior.

- Suggest TWO hypotheses other than lack of sleep that Ms. Mercer and her mentor might explore to learn more about why Sara behaves as she does in class.
- For each hypothesis you suggested, describe at least one action that Ms. Mercer and her mentor might take to see if the hypothesis might be correct. Base your response on principles of human development, motivation, and diagnostic assessment.

Step 1. Think About What Is Being Asked.

In the space below, state in your own words what you think the question is asking.

Compare your impression of what is being asked with the explanation below. The question asks for

- *two* hypotheses that Ms. Mercer and the mentor might explore to learn more about Sara's behavior in class
- for *each* hypothesis, a description of one action Ms. Mercer and the mentor might take to learn more about why Sara behaves as she does

Step 2. Think About the Categories Being Assessed.

- Diagnostic and evaluative strategies in the areas of human development and learner motivation

The ability to make effective assessments, both of the needs of students and of the strengths and weaknesses in student performance, is essential. Here, the question asks for hypotheses to explore to learn more about Sara's behavior—in other words, for the beginning of a diagnostic assessment.

Step 3. Write Your Response.

In the space below, write what you consider to be a response that directly addresses the question.

Step 4. Reflect on Your Response in Light of the Scoring Guide, Sample Responses, and Commentary.

Score of 2

The response presents two appropriate hypotheses that the mentor and Ms. Mercer can explore to learn the causes for Sara's inattentiveness in class, and for each hypothesis, the response describes one action Ms. Mercer and her mentor could take to see if the hypothesis is correct, such as the following:

- One hypothesis is that Sara has ADHD or some other learning disability. They can have a member of the child study team or other trained staff member observe Sara and determine whether she needs further testing.
- One hypothesis is that there are physical or emotional factors in Sara's background that affect her behavior now. They could look for information in Sara's background data that suggests causes for her inattentiveness. They can examine Sara's folder and find out if any potential causes are listed in the data.
- One hypothesis is that Sara had a very different kind of teacher in kindergarten, and she may miss the kind of instruction with which she was familiar. Ms. Mercer and the mentor could talk with Sara's kindergarten teacher to find out what behavior patterns she exhibited and what kinds of approaches worked well with her.
- One hypothesis is that Sara is angry too about something, related either to school or to other areas of her life, as indicated by her angry gestures. They could explore a variety of sources including Sara's mother, Sara's records, or a discussion with Sara herself to determine if there is ongoing anger.
- One hypothesis is that Sara needs ongoing, frequent positive reinforcement in order to function well. They could try a program of greatly enhanced positive reinforcement and praise to see if Sara responds to this approach.
- One hypothesis is that Sara is bored. Ms. Mercer has noted her high test scores and identified her as very bright. She may be bored with activities that aren't challenging her. They could have a counselor or other trained staff member work with Sara to determine if she would respond to more intellectually challenging work.

Score of 1

The response presents two appropriate hypotheses that the mentor and Ms. Mercer can explore to learn the causes for Sara's inattentiveness in class, but no actions they could take to see if the hypotheses might be correct; or the response presents one appropriate hypothesis Ms. Mercer and the mentor could explore with one action they could take to see if the hypothesis might be correct, such as those presented in score point 2.

Score of 0

The response fails to address the question, presents inappropriate hypotheses, or is vague.

Sample Responses and Commentary

Response That Would Receive a Score of 2
The mentor may suspect that Sara has ADHD or some other learning disability that prevents her from maintaining concentration on her work. They can work with the member of the child study team or other trained staff member to explore this possibility. The mentor may also suggest that Sara needs consistent, ongoing positive reinforcement and performs poorly when exposed to criticism. She and Ms. Mercer could work together to provide consistent feedback to Sara that would build self-esteem and confidence, and see if this approach helps Sara be more fully engaged in the work.

Commentary on the Above Response
The response presents two appropriate hypotheses the mentor and Ms. Mercer could explore to learn more about Sara's behavior. They are presented briefly, but are specific and presented in sufficient detail. Responses need not be lengthy or elaborately written to receive full credit. This response does receive full credit.

Response That Would Receive a Score of 1
The mentor and Ms. Mercer could explore the possibility that Sara has some form of a learning disability that prevents her from paying attention. They could use a school psychologist to help them make this determination.

Commentary on the Above Response
The response presents only one hypothesis. It is appropriate and although very brief is sufficient for partial credit.

Response That Would Receive a Score of 0
The mentor and Ms. Mercer could look for the causes of Sara's behavior in class. The mentor seems to understand that there may be more involved than Sara's lack of sleep. She can clearly help Ms. Mercer and together, they can brainstorm possibilities about what may be causes of Sara's behavior. A second thing they could do would be to consult some of the professional staff of the school and ask them for help in figuring out what's going on with Sara so they can help her.

Commentary on the Above Response
The response fails to address the question. A response that paraphrases the question or offers related information that does not directly address the requirements of the question receives no credit.

Now let's look at how the questions for the teacher-based, document-based case "Ms. Riley" might be analyzed, responded to, and evaluated. Again, the materials below are intended as illustrative of how you might prepare for practice cases and respond to actual cases. As you prepare, remember that the critical factors to bear in mind as you read and respond to the questions are what is being asked and the categories being assessed.

MS. RILEY

Scenario

Ms. Riley is a third-year teacher in an urban elementary school. She has a heterogeneously mixed class of twenty-six 9- and 10-year-olds. At the beginning of the second month of school, she introduces a long-term project called "Literature Logs." She plans the project to support her long-term goals. The following documents relate to that project.

Document 1

Literature Log Project Plan

Long-Term Goals:

1. Improve reading, writing, speaking, and listening abilities.
2. Develop critical-thinking skills.
3. Address students' individual differences.
4. Build a positive classroom community.

Objectives:

1. Students will use writing to link aspects of a text with experiences and people in their own lives.
2. Students will write accurate summaries of what they have read.

Project Assignment:

Independent Reading Assignment

Literature Logs

You are expected to read independently for about 2 hours each week (25 to 30 minutes every school night).

You may choose the book.

You are also expected to write four entries in your literature logs every two weeks.

Each entry should be about one handwritten page in your log.

At the beginning of each entry you are to write the following:

- The title and author of the book you are reading
- The numbers of the pages you are writing about
- A summary of the part of the book you have just read

In addition to writing a summary, you are also to include one or more of the following:

- Similar things that have happened in your life
- What you think might happen next in the story
- Dilemmas the characters are facing and how they solve them or how you would solve them

HAPPY READING!

Assessment:

Each week, each student's Literature Log will be assessed on the following criteria:

- Number of pages read during the week
- Number of entries in Literature Log during the week
- Ability to write effective summaries of what has been read

Document 2

Entries from Sharon's Literature Log and Ms. Riley's comments

Sharon
October 13, 2002
pp. 240–267

Beth died. I almost didn't notice because the book didn't really say she died. The way I noticed was because they started talking about how everyone missed her humming when she did housework and how she played the piano and all kinds of things. My mother explained to me about yufamisms, which are words people use for things they really don't like to talk about. Well, we don't like to talk about it either but we say died. My aunt came to live with us because she was very sick and last year she died. I wonder what it felt like. I wonder how she felt when she was dieing? I miss her lots of times too.

I think you are reading *Little Women* by Louisa May Alcott. Remember to state the book title, author, and pages read every time.

euphemisms

I'm sorry.

dying

Sharon
October 27, 2002
Little Women
by Louisa May Alcott
pp. 268–296

Sharon—
I'm disappointed with your spelling in this entry in your log. You need to be more careful.

Jo <u>realy likd</u> to write and she started selling her stories to the <u>newspapper</u>. But one of her <u>frends didnt</u> like that kind of story so she <u>stoped</u> signing her name.

really liked
newspaper
friends didn't
stopped

Don't you have any thoughts about your own life to add?

Document 3

A Conversation with Kenny

Ms. Riley:	Kenny, in my grade book I noticed I don't have a check for your Literature Logs. But I'm sure you've been reading, since I've seen you read at least two books a week since the beginning of the year.
Kenny:	Yeah, I read three books last week.
Ms. Riley:	I noticed how much you enjoyed one of them, at least you were laughing as you read during silent reading. Did you choose one you wanted to write about in your Literature Log?
Kenny:	Well, right now I'm reading an interesting one that takes place in a museum.
Ms. Riley:	Oh, what book is that?
Kenny:	It's a long name, *From the Mixed-Up Files of Mrs. Basil E. Frankenweiler.* I just started it last night.
Ms. Riley:	Oh, I know that book. It's very good.
Kenny:	Great, because I have a question about it.
Ms. Riley:	Is it a question that could help with your reading?
Kenny:	Well someone keeps explaining things to Saxonberg and I don't know who is explaining. I don't know who Saxonberg is either.
Ms. Riley:	You know, Kenny, I think if you read a few more chapters you will probably find out, and then you can write about it in your Literature Log.
Kenny:	Well, I can tell you about it tomorrow. It has a long name, but it's a small book. I'll finish it tonight.
Ms. Riley:	Well, I'd really love to see it written in your Literature Log or I won't be able to fill in that you've completed your homework.
Kenny:	That's O.K.—I don't read to get credit. I just read for fun.

STRATEGIES FOR ANSWERING CONSTRUCTED-RESPONSE QUESTIONS FOR CASE STUDY 2

The questions that follow are the same questions you read in Chapter 12. Read each question again, then complete the exercises below it. These exercises are designed to help you think critically about what is being asked. Here is the first question related to the Ms. Riley case.

How to Answer Question 1

Question 1

Review Document 1, the Literature Log Project Plan. The plan demonstrates both strengths and weaknesses.

- Identify ONE strength and ONE weakness of the Literature Log Project Plan.
- Describe how each strength or weakness you identified demonstrates a strength or weakness in planning instruction. Base your response on principles of effective instructional planning.

Step 1. Think About What Is Being Asked.

In the space below, state in your own words what you think the question is asking.

Compare your impression of what is being asked with the explanation below.
   The question asks for

- *one* strength of the plan and one weakness of the plan
- explanations of why *each* is a strength or a weakness

Step 2. Think About the Categories Being Assessed.

- Planning instruction

As you saw in studying the questions and domains for the first case presented, planning instruction is a very important category and is addressed in many of the questions in the cases. Planning instruction draws on an understanding of learning theory, subject matter, curriculum development, and student development and a sense of how to use that knowledge in planning instruction. In the Principles of Learning and Teaching test, rather than being asked to plan a unit or lesson plan of your own, you are asked to analyze existing plans in terms of strengths and weaknesses or in terms of how to modify them for specific purposes.

Step 3. Write Your Response.

In the space below, write what you consider to be a response that directly addresses the question.

Step 4. Reflect on Your Response in Light of the Scoring Guide, Sample Responses, and Commentary.

Now consider your response in light of the following scoring guide used to evaluate test-takers' responses. Remember that the guide contains illustrative possible responses that are neither restrictive nor prescriptive.

Score of 2

The response presents one appropriate strength of the plan and one appropriate weakness of the plan and explains why each is a strength or a weakness. Here are some examples:

Strengths:

- Having students read independently for over two hours a week is likely to help them improve their reading skills.
- Letting each student choose the books to read reinforces the notion that individual differences are worth respecting.
- Writing four entries a week gives each student a significant amount of writing practice and can improve each student's writing fluency.
- The assignment to include a summary of the part of the book just read supports the objective of having students write accurate summaries.
- Having students link events in their lives to events in what they read directly supports the first objective.
- Having each student indicate what will happen next can build a student's critical thinking ability.
- Focusing on the dilemmas the characters face and how the reader would solve them promotes critical thinking and acknowledgment of individual differences.

Weaknesses:

- Assessing the number of pages read each week does not necessarily support any of the long-term goals or the objectives. It is, therefore, an inappropriate criterion for assessment.
- Keeping track of the number of entries in the log each week suggests that the teacher really wants more than the four entries she requires. Although having the students read more each week supports the goal of building reading skills, it does not necessarily promote the joy of reading suggested by the caps in the assignment: HAPPY READING!
- There is no aspect of the project assignment or the assessment that addresses the long-term goal of building a positive classroom community.
- The assessment does not match the goals and objectives, with the exception of the assessment of writing effective summaries. The assessment does not address critical thinking skills, individual differences, building a positive classroom community, or using writing to link reading and personal experience.

Score of 1

The response offers one appropriate strength or one appropriate weakness and appropriate reasons why it is a strength or weakness, such as those presented in score point 2, or one strength and one weakness without appropriate reasons why each is a strength or a weakness.

Score of 0

The response fails to address the question, presents inappropriate strengths and weaknesses, or is vague.

Sample Responses and Commentary

Response That Would Receive a Score of 2

Ms. Riley's goals and assignment are fairly well matched. She assigns a reasonable amount of reading for a week to address the goal of improving reading, attempts to help the students make personal connections to their lives, allows them to select their own books, and asks them to write regularly about what they read. Generally, her assignment develops her goals pretty well. However, her assessments are not well aligned with her goals. All her assessments focus on mechanical aspects of the tasks she assigns. By grading student summaries and the number of entries, and counting the number of pages, she is suggesting that she is not very interested in critical thinking or in helping students to acknowledge differences among people. She establishes these as her goals, but when it comes to assessing student performance in the project, most of the goals and objectives do not count toward a grade, and therefore they are undervalued.

Commentary on the Above Response

The response presents both: one appropriate strength and one appropriate weakness. The response is very fully developed; however, responses are evaluated on the appropriateness and/or accuracy of the information presented, not on the writing skill with which they are presented. The response receives full credit because it explains one appropriate strength and one appropriate weakness. Note that had the strength and weakness simply been named, without an explanation of why each was selected, the response would have received a score of 1.

Response That Would Receive a Score of 1

Having the students include a summary of the part of the book just read supports one of the objectives, the one that says students should write accurate summaries. In addition, having students link events in their lives to events in the books helps students see connections between their lives and what occurs in literature, and so matches another of the objectives.

Commentary on the Above Response

The response presents two appropriate strengths of the assignment. However, the question calls for one strength and one weakness. It therefore receives partial credit.

Response That Would Receive a Score of 0

I think having students keep Literature Logs is a very good idea. It helps them to think about what they have read, and gives them a chance to use their writing skills to write about something they know. A second good thing about these logs is that they give the teacher a way to assess what students have understood and are thinking.

Commentary on the Above Response

The response does not address the question. While a different question might have asked for advantages of this kind of assignment, the question as presented asks for one strength and one weakness of this specific plan. It therefore receives no credit.

How to Answer Question 2

Question 2

Review Sharon's first entry (dated October 13) in Document 2, her Literature Log. Suppose that Ms. Riley wants to evaluate how well the entry demonstrates achievement of her long-term goals and/or her objectives.

- Identify TWO aspects of Sharon's October 13 entry in her Literature Log that an effective evaluation would identify as achieving one or more of Ms. Riley's goals and/or her objectives.
- For each aspect you identified, explain how it demonstrates achievement of one or more of Ms. Riley's goals and/or objectives. Base your response on principles of effective assessment and evaluation.

Step 1. Think About What Is Being Asked.

In the space below, state in your own words what you think the question is asking.

Compare your impression of what is being asked with the explanation below.
The question asks for

- *two* aspects of the first entry that show achievement of one or more of Ms. Riley's long-term goals and/or objectives
- for *each* aspect, an explanation of how it meets one or more of the goals and/or objectives

Step 2. Think About the Categories Being Assessed.

- Assessment (diagnostic and evaluative)

An important aspect of this category is the ability to use formal and informal assessment strategies to evaluate the continuous intellectual development of the learner. This question asks for an assessment of Sharon's work and of Ms. Riley's ability to assess and respond to that work effectively.

Step 3. Write Your Response.

In the space below, write what you consider to be a response that directly addresses the question.

Step 4. Reflect on Your Response in Light of the Scoring Guide, Sample Responses, and Commentary.

Score of 2

The response identifies and explains two appropriate achievements of one or more instructional goals or objectives, such as the following:

- Sharon notes that characters miss hearing Beth humming. She figures out from this that Beth is dead. She is using her critical-thinking skills to figure out what is happening in the text.
- By including her mother's definition of "yufamisms" Sharon is connecting what happens in the book to her family, thereby making direct links between literature and her life.
- Sharon is writing an accurate summary of what happens in the book.
- By wondering what it is like to die, Sharon is indicating her own individuality and trying to wrestle with one of the dilemmas both she and the characters face.
- Sharon's entry is quite candid and unique, expressing her own point of view.
- Sharon trusts Ms. Riley to respect individual differences by "confessing" a great deal about her own private questions, family events, and dilemmas about the sensitive subject of death.

Score of 1

The response identifies and explains one appropriate achievement of one or more instructional goals or objectives, such as those presented in score point 2, or identifies but does not explain two aspects of the Literature Log entry that achieve one or more instructional goals or objectives.

Score of 0

The response fails to address the question, presents inappropriate achievements, or is vague.

Sample Responses and Commentary

Response That Would Receive a Score of 2

Sharon is a sensitive, thoughtful reader who in her first response offers Ms. Riley many of the things Ms. Riley wants to promote in readers. She talks about her own personal links to the characters when she discusses the death of Beth and her aunt, uses her analytic powers to figure out the meaning of dilemmas that characters face when she uses clues to figure out that Beth has died, and suggests how personally she responds to key events in the novel when she notes that she wonders what it felt like to die.

Commentary on the Above Response

The response presents and explains at least two appropriate ways in which Sharon's entry demonstrates achievement of the objectives. Adding a third appropriate way neither adds to nor subtracts from the effectiveness of the response. It receives full credit.

Response That Would Receive a Score of 1

In the first entry, Sharon does a wonderful job of connecting what she has read to her own life. When she talks about one of the characters dying and then connects that to her aunt's death, she has done a wonderful job of making a connection. She has really met her teacher's objective!

Commentary on the Above Response

The response presents and explains only one appropriate way in which Sharon's first entry demonstrates achievement of one or more of the objectives. It therefore receives partial credit.

Response That Would Receive a Score of 0

Sharon's first entry is wonderful! I wish I could get my students to write reading log entries like this one. She does everything her teacher wanted, and more! I just wish Ms. Riley had given her a lot more positive feedback.

Commentary on the Above Response

The response does talk about the first entry, but it does not address the question, which asks for specific ways in which the entry demonstrates achievement of one or more of the objectives. It receives no credit.

How to Answer Question 3

Question 3

In Document 2, Sharon's Literature Log, there are significant differences between Sharon's entry dated October 13 and her entry dated October 27. It appears that Sharon is having less success meeting the objectives for the project in the October 27 entry than in the October 13 entry.

- Identify TWO significant differences between the first and second entries that indicate that Sharon is having less success in meeting the objectives of the project in the second entry.
- For each difference you identified, suggest how Ms. Riley might have responded differently to Sharon in order to help Sharon continue to meet the objectives of the project. Base your response on principles of communication, assessment, and/or effective instruction.

Step 1. Think About What Is Being Asked.

In the space below, state in your own words what you think the question is asking.

```

```

Compare your impression of what is being asked with the explanation below.

The question asks for

- *two* specific differences between the first entry and the second
- for *each* difference, how Ms. Riley might have helped Sharon continue to meet her goals

Step 2. Think About the Categories Being Assessed.

- Planning instruction
- Communication, social organization, classroom management
- Assessment

The question addresses all three of these important domains in one way or another. Part of planning instruction is using an understanding of student development. Communication addresses using knowledge of effective verbal communication techniques to foster active inquiry, while assessment involves formal and informal assessment strategies to evaluate the continuous intellectual development of the learner. The ways in which Ms. Riley thinks about her responses as she plans, the way in which she assesses the achievement of her objectives, and the way in which she communicates with Sharon all directly address these domains.

Step 3. Write Your Response.
In the space below, write what you consider to be a response that directly addresses the question.

Step 4. Reflect on Your Response in Light of the Scoring Guide, Sample Responses, and Commentary.

Score of 2

The response presents two significant differences between Sharon's October 13 and October 27 entries and offers appropriate suggestions about how Ms. Riley could have helped Sharon to meet the teacher's goals, such as the following:

- As Ms. Riley requested, Sharon's second entry summarizes what happened in the book, but doesn't discuss any of the dilemmas the characters face. Because Ms. Riley doesn't comment on the dilemma Sharon included in the first entry, Sharon probably believes that it is not important. Had Ms. Riley praised Sharon for including her remarks on the dilemmas faced in the first entry, Sharon might have included dilemmas in the second entry.

- Sharon's first entry draws connections to the student's life with her reference to her mother's definition and to her aunt's death. Had Ms. Riley noted how interesting those comments were, Sharon might have included similar comments in the second entry.

- Sharon's first entry engages in introspective speculation when she comments, "I wonder what it felt like." This is a kind of thinking skill Ms. Riley suggests she wants to develop. Had she commented positively about it, Sharon would have been more likely to continue doing this kind of thinking.

- The second entry is a minimal summary and does not give any evidence of Sharon's using critical-thinking skills, such as her ability to figure out Beth's death in the first entry. Had Ms. Riley praised Sharon's ability to think critically to figure out that Beth had died, Sharon would have been more likely to continue using this critical-thinking skill.

- By focusing her comments in response to the October 13 entry largely on matters of routine requirements (title, author, pages read) and on spelling, with only a two-word comment on a personal response, Ms. Riley implies that the routine requirements are much more important than the ability to write an accurate summary or to link aspects of the text with experiences and people in their own lives. Had she focused on the summary and the connections, Sharon would have been more likely to continue developing the skills to address these aspects of the assignment.

Score of 1

The response presents one significant difference between the October 13 and the October 27 entries and offers one appropriate way in which Ms. Riley could help Sharon to meet the teacher's goals, such as those presented in score point 2; or the response presents two significant differences between the October 13 and the October 27 entries with no ways in which Ms. Riley could have responded differently to Sharon.

Score of 0

The response fails to address the question, presents inappropriate differences, or is vague.

Sample Responses and Commentary

Response That Would Receive a Score of 2

In Sharon's second entry, the student includes the kinds of things Ms. Riley says she wants to see when she comments on Sharon's first entry. She gives title and author and pages read, and does include a very short summary. However, she omits any personal connections to the literature or focusing on any dilemmas the characters face because Ms. Riley makes no comment on those aspects of Sharon's first entry. If Ms. Riley had sympathized with Sharon when she gave Ms. Riley what she asked for or praised her for including some of the aspects the teacher requested, Sharon might have included them in the second entry.

Commentary on the Above Response

The response presents two appropriate and significant differences (the second entry does include all the specific information the teacher says she wants about title, author, and pages read but omits any personal connections to literature or discussion of dilemmas the characters face). It also presents appropriate suggestions for how Ms. Riley might have responded in a way that would have helped Sharon meet the goals. The response receives full credit.

Response That Would Receive a Score of 1

One significant difference is that Sharon stopped sharing ways that the book reminded her of her own life. If Ms. Riley had commented favorably and constructively on the connections Sharon made in the first entry, Sharon might have continued working in this way to achieve the objective. The second difference is that the first entry is a lot longer. If Ms. Riley had praised her for writing a lot, she might have continued developing her fluency in this way.

Commentary on the Above Response

The response presents one appropriate difference, but then discusses a difference that does not indicate that Sharon is having less success meeting the objectives for the project. The response therefore receives partial credit.

Response That Would Receive a Score of 0

Ms. Riley is really missing an opportunity to help Sharon. Students this age are very sensitive and I suspect Sharon had a pretty negative reaction when she got her Literature Log back after the first entry. Ms. Riley could profit from a professional development workshop that helps teachers develop effective ways to respond to student logs.

Commentary on the Above Response

The response, while it makes some valid points, does not address the question, which requires an identification of significant differences between the two entries and ways Ms. Riley might help Sharon continue to meet her goals. It therefore receives no credit.

How to Answer Question 4

Question 4

In Document 3, Kenny's conversation with Ms. Riley, Kenny reveals characteristics of himself as a learner that could be used to support his development of literacy skills.

- Identify ONE characteristic of Kenny as a learner, and then suggest ONE strategy Ms. Riley might use to address that characteristic in a way that will support his development of literacy skills.
- Describe how the strategy you suggested addresses the characteristic of Kenny as a learner and how the strategy could support Kenny's development of literacy skills. Base your response on principles of varied instructional strategies for different learners and of human development.

Step 1. Think About What Is Being Asked.

In the space below, state in your own words what you think the question is asking.

Compare your impression of what is being asked with the explanation below.
   The question asks for

- *one* characteristic of Kenny as a learner and *one* strategy Ms. Riley might use to address that characteristic to support his development of literacy skills
- descriptions of how the strategy addresses the characteristics of Kenny as a learner and supports development of his literacy skills

Step 2. Think About What Is Being Assessed.

- Human development
- Varied instructional strategies for different kinds of learners

These two domains are both very important in understanding students and their needs and in planning instruction to meet those needs. Both are directly involved in understanding Kenny and his needs as a learner and in planning strategies to meet his specific needs.

Step 3. Write Your Response.

In the space below, write what you consider to be a response that directly addresses the question.

Step 4. Reflect on Your Response in Light of the Scoring Guide, Sample Responses, and Commentary.

Score of 2

The response identifies and describes one appropriate characteristic of Kenny as a learner, and one appropriate strategy Ms. Riley can use to address that characteristic and support the development of Kenny's literacy skills.

- Kenny loves to read, but doesn't want to take the time to write about what he's read. Ms. Riley might make the writing more creative to match Kenny's interest in books. She could ask Kenny to think about what makes a book interesting to him, thereby supporting his critical thinking, or might provide an alternate mode, such as a tape-recording, for Kenny to record his thoughts.
- Ms. Riley might ask Kenny to imitate the plot of a book he likes in order to create his own story. That would link Kenny's love of reading with writing that would indicate what Kenny takes from the books he reads.
- Ms. Riley might ask Kenny to write a review of one of the books he likes so that others in the class will want to read it. That links Kenny's writing to a purpose supported by his inherent interest in books.
- Ms. Riley might give Kenny some reviews or analysis of the books he's read and ask him to analyze whether the reviews or analysis are accurate from his perspective. That will give Kenny insights into the act of reviewing as well as reading books.
- Because Kenny is intrigued by books, Ms. Riley might ask Kenny to select a small group and act out a scene from one of his favorite books. That will allow Kenny to develop a more critical perspective on a book he's reading.
- Ms. Riley might ask Kenny to search the Internet for Web sites about an author Kenny admires. She might then have him analyze the book from the perspective of the author. This activity might spark Kenny's interest in the connections between an author's life and some of the characters in his or her books.

Score of 1

The response identifies and describes one appropriate characteristic of Kenny as a learner such as those presented in score point 2, but does not present a strategy Ms. Riley can use to address that characteristic and support the development of Kenny's literacy skills, or identifies an appropriate characteristic of Kenny as a learner and a strategy Ms. Riley could use to address that characteristic, but does not sufficiently describe either the characteristic or the strategy.

Score of 0

The response fails to address the question, presents inappropriate identification of characteristics of Kenny as a learner and strategies to address those characteristics, or is vague.

Sample Responses and Commentary

Response That Would Receive a Score of 2

Because Kenny is an avid reader, Ms. Riley needs to think of a strategy that might engage Kenny in critical thinking that can enhance his literacy. Since one of her long-term goals includes developing speaking abilities, she might offer him the opportunity to tape-record his comments about the book, moving the apparent focus from writing to talking about the book—something it appears he likes to do. To address her goal of developing critical-thinking skills, she might give him a few analyses of books by reviewers and ask Kenny to support or refute the reviews from his reading of the book.

Commentary on the Above Response

The response begins by identifying an appropriate characteristic of Kenny as a learner, and then presents and describes an appropriate strategy Ms. Riley might use to address that characteristic in a way that would address her first long-term goal. The response receives full credit, score point 2.

Response That Would Receive a Score of 1

Kenny is a very interesting learner. He obviously loves to read; Ms. Riley comments she's seen him read at least two books a week, and he himself says he just reads "for fun." But he candidly admits he doesn't "read to get credit," and so he isn't concerned about the assignment Ms. Riley has given or about meeting her objectives. Students such as Kenny are a challenge: he loves reading (good for him!) but doesn't want to jump through Ms. Riley's hoops. She has to be creative to figure out how to challenge him!

Commentary on the Above Response

The response analyzes Kenny as a learner with appropriate commentary. However, simply saying that Ms. Riley "has to be creative to figure out how to challenge him" is not sufficient to meet the second requirement of the question. The response therefore receives partial credit.

Response That Would Receive a Score of 0

There isn't really enough information given here to do an analysis of Kenny as a learner, or to suggest how his teacher could work to support his development of literacy skills. A much fuller presentation of his work, his thoughts, and his interactions with his teacher and the other students would be needed.

Commentary on the Above Response

As was pointed out earlier, saying that "more information is needed" is not an acceptable response or a viable excuse for not responding to the question. While it is true that more information could and would be sought to do a full analysis of Kenny or a complete plan for addressing his needs, there is sufficient information in the short conversation presented to warrant "one characteristic of Kenny as a learner" and one strategy to address that characteristic.

How to Answer Question 5

Question 5

Review Ms. Riley's long-term goals at the beginning of Document 1, the Literature Log Project Plan.

- Select TWO long-term goals, and for each goal, identify one strategy Ms. Riley might use to expand the Literature Log unit beyond the stated assignment and assessment plan to address the goal.
- Explain how the use of each strategy you identified could expand the Literature Log unit to address the selected goal. Base your response on principles of planning instruction and/or language development and acquisition.

Step 1. Think About What Is Being Asked.

In the space below, state in your own words what you think the question is asking.

Compare your impression of what is being asked with the explanation below. The question asks for

- *two* goals
- for *each* goal, explanation of one strategy to expand the Literature Log

Step 2. Think About the Categories Being Assessed.

- Planning instruction
- Language development and acquisition

Both planning instruction and planning strategies to support the language learning of all students are important skills. The Literature Log is a part of Ms. Riley's literacy program; by asking you to plan strategies she might use to expand the Literature Log assignment, the question directly assesses both categories.

Step 3. Write Your Response.

In the space below, write what you consider to be a response that directly addresses the question.

Step 4. Reflect on Your Response in Light of the Scoring Guide, Sample Responses, and Commentary.

Score of 2

The response selects two long-term goals and identifies an appropriate strategy to address each goal with explanations of how the use of each strategy could address the selected goal, such as the following:

- One goal is to develop speaking and listening abilities. To develop these skills, Ms. Riley can include activities such as having students report aloud about the books read while other students note what is important about each and ask questions about the books.

- One goal is to develop critical-thinking skills. Ms. Riley could have included in her assessment plan a rubric that would provide a means for student self-assessment and for her own assessment of the kinds of critical-thinking skills she has included in the assignment.

- One goal is to build a positive classroom community, but this goal is never addressed. Ms. Riley might form cooperative groups based on principles of teaching social skills and have the groups read members' Literature Logs, identifying positive ways to see the differences in how members of the group responded to what they read.

- One goal is to address students' individual differences. Ms. Riley could read all the Logs and find significant differences among the ways students responded. She could then present those examples to the class and conduct a class discussion about how interesting and valuable those differences are.

- To address the goal of linking aspects of a text with experiences and people in their own lives, Ms. Riley could use an overhead projector to display features of the logs that presented intriguing ways in which individuals made connections between what they read and their own lives. In this case, she should check first with students to be sure she has not invaded their privacy. The class could discuss those connections and offer further suggestions about how individual class members might respond.

- To address the goal of improving reading, writing, speaking, and listening, Ms. Riley can have each student maintain a folder of Literature Log entries for several weeks and select two for public presentation. The student could then rewrite each entry to present to the class in published form. This adds audience and purpose to the assignment.

- To address the goal of improving speaking and listening skills, Ms. Riley can form groups and have students present an oral summary of their book and why it was important to them. They can also explain to their group why others might want to read the book as well. Each group could then select one or two books for presentation to the whole class. The activity could develop speaking and listening skills and generate greater interest in books that students might want to read.

- To address the goal of building a positive classroom community, Ms. Riley can form groups of those who have read the same or similar books. She could then have the members of the group explain some of the individual connections they made to what happened in the book, or comment about one or two things each finds interesting about each student's response to the characters. By sharing responses to books, students build a sense of a community.

- To address the goal of building critical-thinking skills, Ms. Riley can ask students who identified interesting dilemmas in books to explain what was problematic for the characters and why. Ms. Riley could use these dilemmas to begin a class discussion about human dilemmas all people face.

- To address her long-term goal of building a positive classroom community and her objectives of both linking reading to experience and developing summary writing skills, Ms. Riley can form response groups in which students share their logs. She could establish the principle that there are to be no "put downs," and that students must find one or two positive things to say about the connections others draw to the texts or about the summaries.

Score of 1

The response selects two long-term goals and, for each, identifies but does not explain an appropriate strategy to address the goal, such as those presented in score point 2, or selects one long-term goal and identifies and explains an appropriate strategy to address the goal.

Score of 0

The response fails to address the question, presents inappropriate goals and strategies, or is vague.

Sample Responses and Commentary

Response That Would Receive a Score of 2

Ms. Riley has many valuable long-term goals that could be developed through additional activities or assessments. For example, one of her goals is to build a positive classroom community. To address this goal, she could create cooperative groups and have students respond in positive ways to the connections other students have made between their books and their own lives or to the summaries that are written. If several students have read the same book, she could have them share their summaries and personal responses, developing a sense of the commonality of their reading and personal experiences. Another of her goals is to address students' individual differences. After checking with students to be sure they are comfortable with sharing, she might discuss or present on an overhead projector a variety of kinds of connections students make between books and their own lives, to show how each reader responds in ways that are unique.

Commentary on the Above Response

The response presents two goals and fully discusses an appropriate strategy Ms. Riley might use to expand the Literature Log to implement the goal. The response fully and appropriately addresses the question and receives full credit.

Response That Would Receive a Score of 1

One of her goals is to build critical-thinking skills. To address this goal, Ms. Riley can ask students who came up with some interesting dilemmas in books to explain what was difficult for the characters and to tell why they thought the situation was difficult. Ms. Riley could use these dilemmas to start a class discussion about problems all people face. In this way, she would be addressing one of her important goals and at the same time extending the lesson.

Commentary on the Above Response

The response only partially addresses the requirements of the question. The question calls for an identification of "two goals" and one strategy for each that can be used to expand the Literature Log unit. The response identifies only one goal and does present a strategy to address it in a way that would expand the unit. The response receives partial credit.

Response That Would Receive a Score of 0

I don't think it would really be a good idea to try to expand the Literature Log unit at this time. Third-grade teachers have an enormous amount of material to cover. For each subject, there are state, district, and school standards of objectives to meet. If she adds to this unit, she is going to be taking away time and emphasis from other subjects like social studies, mathematics, or science. All of these need a lot of instructional time. I think she should leave well enough alone.

Commentary on the Above Response

Arguing with the question is not an acceptable way to respond. While the points made in the response may be seen as having some validity, it must be assumed that Ms. Riley could expand the unit within the time she has for her language arts program. Because the response does not address the question, it receives no credit.

How to Answer Question 6

Question 6

Review the two objectives of the Literature Log Project Plan included in Document 1. Suppose that at the end of the project, as a culminating activity, Ms. Riley wants her students to use their Literature Logs to help them do a self-assessment of the two objectives.

- For each of the TWO project objectives described in Document 1, suggest one assignment Ms. Riley could give the students that would serve as a self-assessment.
- For each assignment you suggested, describe how Ms. Riley's students could use it as a self-assessment. Base your response on principles of effective assessment.

Step 1. Think About What Is Being Asked.

In the space below, state in your own words what you think the question is asking.

Compare your impression of what is being asked with the explanation below.

The question asks for two proposed assignments

- *one* to serve as a self-assessment for students based on the *first* objective mentioned in Document 1
- *one* to serve as a self-assessment for students based on the *second* objective mentioned in Document 1

Step 2. Think About the Categories Being Evaluated.

- Assessment

Part of the assessment domain involves teaching students how to assess their own work. Self-assessment can help students make connections between learning objectives and their own performance.

Step 3. Write Your Response.

In the space below, write what you consider to be a response that directly addresses the question.

Step 4. Reflect on Your Response in Light of the Scoring Guide, Sample Responses, and Commentary.

ETS Scoring Guide for Question 6

Score of 2

The response presents an explanation of two appropriate culminating activities: one that will help students do a self-assessment of the first objective and one that will help students do a self-assessment of the second objective, such as the following:

Objective 1

- She could have them select three entries that they believe meet the objective of linking aspects of their reading with experiences and people in their own lives. For each entry, explain why it meets the objective.
- She could have them write a new paragraph about a character or event they felt strongly connected to, and explain why.
- She could have them select one entry they feel they could improve in terms of making connections to their own lives, and could have them write a revision and one entry they feel meets the objective and tell why.
- She could have the class develop a rubric for evaluating entries in terms of making connections between reading and personal experience, and use the rubric to evaluate selected entries.

Objective 2

- She could have the class develop a rubric for an effective summary and have individuals use it to evaluate three of their own entries.
- She could have each student read five or six of their summaries and write a reflective assessment about the strengths or weaknesses she or he sees in the summaries.
- She could have the class write a summary of a short selection they all read and use a class-developed rubric to have them evaluate their own summaries.

Score of 1

The response presents an explanation of one appropriate culminating activity that will help students do a self-assessment of either the first objective or the second objective, such as those presented in score point 2; or the response suggests two culminating activities related to the objectives but does not describe how the students could use them as self-assessments.

Score of 0

The response fails to address the question, presents inappropriate culminating activities, or is vague.

Response That Would Receive a Score of 2

For both objectives, her activity for the students to do self-assessment could begin with the development of a rubric for evaluating success in meeting the objective. Students could work together to develop both rubrics. Then, for the first objective, she could have students select three of their own entries and use the rubric to evaluate how well each student met the objective. For the second objective, Ms. Riley could have the students write a summary of a new selection, and then use the rubric to evaluate how well they have learned to write an effective summary.

Commentary on the Above Response

The response presents one appropriate assignment for each objective. Although the response begins by explaining something that both activities could have in common, it includes separate appropriate activities for each of the two objectives. It receives full credit.

Response That Would Receive a Score of 1

Following up with a culminating self-assessment is a very good way to end the project. It will help students internalize what they have learned. There are many different activities she could use. One is that she could have them select one entry they feel could be improved in terms of making connections to their own lives. They could then write a revision and one entry they feel meets the objective and tell why. Doing these two things would really help them take a fresh look at what it means to connect literature to their own lives.

Commentary on the Above Response

The response suggests that there are two activities, but they address only one of the objectives. The question specifically calls for one activity for each of the two objectives. It therefore receives only partial credit.

Response That Would Receive a Score of 0

In a sense, it's a very good idea for her to do a culminating activity. But, on the other hand, it's very possible that by now the students have learned everything there is to learn about writing Literature Logs. They have been doing it for several months, and I have found that students of this age get tired of activities after a while. I would therefore suggest that she just wrap up the Literature Logs with a celebration in which she praises them for what they have done well, and then move on to some other aspect of literature study.

Commentary on the Above Response

The response begins with what appears to be a direct response to the question, but moves off the point and fails to address the question, instead arguing with its premise. Responses that argue with the question are deemed nonresponsive and receive no credit.

Praxis™ II Elementary Education

CHAPTER 14

Elementary Education: Curriculum, Instruction, and Assessment

The Elementary Education: Curriculum, Instruction, and Assessment Test, (Test Code 0011), is designed for prospective teachers of students in the elementary grades. Most people who take the test have completed a bachelor's degree program in elementary or middle school education or have prepared themselves through some alternative certification program.

PREPARING FOR THE CURRICULUM, INSTRUCTION, AND ASSESSMENT TEST

The 110 questions on the Curriculum, Instruction, and Assessment test covers the breadth of material a new teacher needs to know and assesses knowledge of both principles and processes. Some questions assess basic understanding of curriculum planning, instructional design, and assessment of student learning. Many questions pose particular problems that teachers routinely face in the classroom, and many are based on authentic examples of student work. Although some questions concern general issues, most questions are set in the context of the subject matter most commonly taught in elementary school: reading/language arts, mathematics, social studies, science, fine arts, and physical education.

In developing assessment material for this test, ETS has worked in collaboration with educators, higher education content specialists, and accomplished practicing teachers to keep the test updated and representative of current standards.

Elementary Education: Curriculum, Instructions, and Assessment (0011)

Test at a Glance

Time	2 hours	
Format	110 multiple-choice questions	
Content Categories	**Approximate Number of Questions**	**Approximate Percentage of Examination**
I. Reading and Language Arts Curriculum, Instruction, and Assessment	38	35%
II. Mathematics Curriculum, Instruction, and Assessment	22	20%

III. Social Studies Curriculum, Instruction, and Assessment	11	10%
IV. Science Curriculum, Instruction, and Assessment	11	10%
V. Arts and Physical Education Curriculum, Instruction, and Assessment	11	10%
VI. General Information about Curriculum, Instruction, and Assessment	17	15%

The test is structured in the following way:

- The questions are grouped into the six content areas listed above (e.g., with all mathematics questions together), and in each content area you will answer questions that measure your understanding of curriculum, instruction, and assessment.

You are not allowed to use a calculator during the test. One or more of the questions on the test may not count toward your score.

Preparing on Your Own

As you use this chapter, set the following tasks for yourself:

- **Become familiar with the test content.** Learn what will be tested. You will find a list of topics covered in the Test at a Glance bulletins available on the *Praxis* Web site (www.ets.org/praxis).
- **Assess how well you know the content in each area.** After you learn what topics the test contains, you should assess your knowledge in each area. How well do you know the material? In which areas do you need to learn more before you take the test? It is quite likely that you will need to brush up on most of or all the areas. If you encounter material that feels unfamiliar or difficult, mark the pages with sticky notes to remind yourself to spend extra time reviewing these topics.
- **Read the section in this chapter on multiple-choice questions to sharpen your skills in reading and answering multiple-choice questions.** To succeed on questions of this kind, you must focus carefully on the question, avoid reading things into the question, pay attention to details, and sift patiently through the answer choices.
- **Develop a study plan.** Assess what you need to study and create a realistic plan for studying. You can develop your study plan in any way that works best for you. A Study Plan Sheet is included in this chapter as a possible way to structure your planning. Remember that you will need to allow time to find books and other materials, time to read the materials and take notes, and time to apply your learning to the practice questions.

- **Identify study materials.** Most of the material covered by the test is contained in standard textbooks in the field. If you no longer own the texts you used in your undergraduate course work, borrow texts from friends or from a library. Use standard textbooks and other reliable, professionally prepared materials. Information provided by friends or obtained from searching the Web is not as uniformly reliable as information found in your textbooks and other relevant course materials.

- **Work through your study plan.** Whether you choose to work alone or with a study group, don't just memorize definitions from books. Instead, prepare to define and discuss the topics in your own words, and make sure you understand the relationships between diverse topics and concepts. If you are working with a group or mentor, you can also try informal quizzes and questioning techniques.

- **Proceed to the practice questions.** Once you have completed your review, you are ready to benefit from the practice questions on page 370. Use the Answers and Explanations to mark the questions you answered correctly and the ones you missed. Read the explanations of the questions you missed and see whether you understand them.

- **Decide whether you need more review.** After you have looked at your results, decide whether there are areas that you need to brush up on before taking the actual test. Go back to your textbooks and reference materials to see if the topics are covered there. You might also go over your questions with a friend or teacher who is familiar with the subjects.

- **Assess your readiness.** Do you feel confident about your level of understanding in each of the subject areas? If not, where do you need more work? If you feel ready, complete the Readiness Checklist to double-check that you've thought through the details.

Readiness Checklist

- Do you know the testing requirements for your teaching field in the state(s) where you plan to teach?
- Have you followed all the test registration procedures?
- Do you know how long the test will take and the number of questions it contains? Have you considered how you will pace your work?
- Are you familiar with the test directions and the types of questions for the test?
- Are you familiar with the recommended test-taking strategies and tips?
- Have you practiced by working through the practice questions at a pace similar to that of an actual test?
- If you are repeating a *Praxis* Series Assessment, have you analyzed your previous score report to determine areas in which additional study and test preparation could be useful?

Preparing with a Study Group

There are several advantages to forming a study group with others preparing for the same test.

- Study groups give members opportunities to ask questions and get detailed answers.
- In a group, some members usually have a better understanding of certain topics, while others may be better at other topics. As members take turns explaining concepts to one another, everyone builds self-confidence.
- Because study groups schedule regular meetings, group members study in a more disciplined fashion.

The group should be large enough so that various people can contribute different kinds of knowledge, but small enough so that it stays focused. Often, three to six people makes a good-sized group.

Here are some ways to use this chapter as part of a study group:

- **Plan the group's study program.** Parts of the Study Plan Sheet on page 369 can help to structure your group's study program. By filling out the first five columns and sharing the work sheets, everyone will learn more about your group's mix of abilities and about the resources (such as textbooks) that members can share with the group. In the sixth column ("Dates planned for study of content"), you can create an overall schedule for your group's study program.
- **Plan individual group sessions.** At the end of each session, the group should decide what specific topics will be covered at the next meeting and who will present each topic.
- **Prepare your presentation for the group.** When it's your turn to present, prepare something that's more than a lecture. Write five to ten original questions to pose to the group. Writing test questions can help you better understand the topics covered as well as the types of questions you will encounter on the test. It will also give other members of the group extra practice at answering questions.
- **Take the practice test together.** The idea of the practice test is to simulate an actual administration of the test, so scheduling a test session with the group will add to the realism and will also help boost everyone's confidence.

Whether you decide to study alone or with a group, remember that the best way to prepare is to have an organized plan. The plan should set goals based on specific topics and skills that you need to learn, and it should commit you to a realistic set of deadlines for meeting these goals. Stick with your plan, and you will accomplish your goals on schedule.

Study Plan Sheet

Content covered on test	How well do I know the content?	What materials do I have for study-ing this content?	What materials do I need for study-ing this content?	Where could I find the materials I need?	Dates planned for study of content	Dates completed

The questions that follow illustrate the kinds of questions on the test. They are not, however, representative of the entire scope of the test in either content or difficulty. Answers and Explanations follow the question section.

Directions: Each of the questions or statements below is followed by four suggested answers or completions. Select the one that is best in each case.

1. During a unit on folktales, a second-grade teacher wants to help students engage in higher-order thinking skills. After the students read *The Little Red Hen,* the teacher asks the students to justify the Little Red Hen's decision to eat the bread herself. Which of the levels of Bloom's taxonomy does this activity address?
   (A) Application
   (B) Analysis
   (C) Synthesis
   (D) Evaluation

2. During which of the following stages in the writing process are students most likely to share their writing with the entire class?
   (A) Drafting
   (B) Revising
   (C) Editing
   (D) Publishing

3. A first-grade student wrote, "R dg is bg n blk" and read aloud: "Our dog is big and black." Which of the following instructional activities is most likely to help the student become a more competent speller?
   (A) Discussion of the difference between "our" and "are"
   (B) Demonstration of left-to-right movement
   (C) Explicit instructions in phonics and phonemic awareness
   (D) Review the rules of capitalization and punctuation

4. The goal of a particular mathematics curriculum is that students in all grades will use computational strategies fluently and estimate appropriately. Which of the following objectives for student's best reflects that goal?
   (A) Students will use calculators for all mathematical tasks.
   (B) Students will be drilled daily on basic number facts.
   (C) Students will know the connections between the basic arithmetic operations.
   (D) Students will evaluate the reasonableness of their answers.

$$\begin{array}{r} 29 \\ \times 57 \\ \hline \end{array}$$

5. Before the students in a fifth-grade class solve the problem above, the teacher has them use mental mathematics to compute 9×7, 20×7, 9×50, and 20×50. For which of the following reasons would it be appropriate to have the students use mental mathematics in this way?
   (A) To show the connection between multiplication and addition
   (B) To prepare for an activity involving rounding to the nearest ten
   (C) To introduce the associative property of multiplication
   (D) To reinforce understanding of a multiplication algorithm

6. A fifth-grade teacher is reviewing percentages with a class. Which of the following strategies would provide effective practice while also motivating students?
   (A) Instructing the students to review the basic concepts of percentages in small heterogeneous groups
   (B) Assigning a homework sheet that includes various types of problems about percentages
   (C) Pretending to be a salesperson in a music store and having the students determining percentage discounts off their favorite CDs
   (D) Rereading out loud the pages in the textbook that cover percentages and working sample problems on the board

7. The table and graph below were produced by a group of students during an activity designed to help them collect and graph data and organize information.

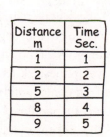

Distance m	Time Sec.
1	1
2	2
5	3
8	4
9	5

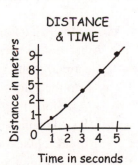

Which feedback from the teacher would best facilitate student understanding?
(A) "You should always use units when measuring variables."
(B) "You should produce a data table to organize your information."
(C) "You should keep the intervals of each axis consistent."
(D) "You should use an appropriate title when producing your graph."

8. The following is an excerpt from a whole scope and sequence for a second-grade science class.

> The teacher will open various sealed containers one at a time. Each container will hold one of the following: chocolate, bananas, perfume, soup, oranges, soap, vinegar, and strawberries. The teacher will ask students to raise their hands as soon as they are able to smell the substance. The class will discuss the reason why students closest to the open container usually notice the odor first.

The activity above can best be integrated into which of the following modules from a science textbook?

(A) Life science: Classifying living things

(B) Physical science: Properties of matter

(C) Earth science: Weather and climate

(D) Environmental science: Endangered plant species

9. Students in a science class have been learning how to separate various mixtures into individual components. Which of the following is the best instructional method to identify a student's acquired skills in this area?

(A) Have the student separate a few mixtures and solutions while the teacher observes.

(B) Have the student write an essay about the proper method to separate a few mixtures and solutions.

(C) Have the student work with a small group whose objective is to separate a few mixtures and solutions.

(D) Have the student describe for the teacher how to separate a few mixtures and solutions.

10. At the beginning of the school year, a first-grade teacher observes that a student is unable to use beginning and final consonants correctly while reading. Which of the following is most likely to help the student develop these skills?

(A) Modeling words in context and teaching decoding skills

(B) Showing a video of a popular children's story and stopping to discuss words that appear in the story

(C) Pairing the student with another student who is able to use consonants correctly

(D) Displaying pictures and corresponding printed words around the room

11. As part of a social studies unit on Aztec culture, a lower elementary teacher has students make papier-mâché masks that resemble those used by the Aztec peoples in ritual dances. This activity is an example of which of the following?

(A) Content integration

(B) Assessing prior knowledge

(C) Brainstorming

(D) Using metacognitive skills

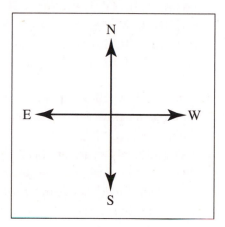

12. After a geography lesson on cardinal points, nearly one-half of the students in a first-grade class label a compass as shown above. Which of the following is the LEAST developmentally appropriate strategy to help these students?

(A) Place an "E" sticker on the students' right hand and a "W" sticker on their left hand

(B) Have students use hand-held compasses to find their way around the school

(C) Teach students a song that names each direction as they move clockwise around a compass on the floor

(D) Assign students to locate and list ten cities in the Eastern Hemisphere and ten in the Western Hemisphere

13. A physical education teacher is planning a unit on basketball. Which of the following is this teacher most likely to teach last?

(A) Some simple offensive plays

(B) Dribbling the ball

(C) Passing the ball

(D) How to shoot a layup

14. The following steps should be used to teach a music concept in a general music class:

I. Preparation
II. Extension
III. Practice
IV. Presentation

Which of the following is the most appropriate sequence for these steps?

(A) I, II, III, IV
(B) III, I, IV, II
(C) I, IV, III, II
(D) IV, II, I, III

15. Which of the following is the most appropriate statement to make to students who will be engaging in a brainstorming activity in their art class?

(A) "Say only your very best idea."
(B) "We want original ideas from your own mind."
(C) "Don't judge ideas now; we can do that later."
(D) "Make sure your ideas make sense before saying them."

16. "Wait time" is most useful as a strategy when a student is

(A) not focused
(B) thinking
(C) embarrassed
(D) speaking

17. According to Howard Gardner's theory of multiple intelligences, a student with high kinesthetic intelligence and low interpersonal and linguistic intelligence would be most likely to learn science concepts in which of the following ways?

(A) Discussing them with other students
(B) Finding ways to act them out
(C) Writing about them
(D) Reading about them

18. Which one of the following types of portfolios is generally considered to present the most accurate picture of a student's progress and development over time?

(A) Working portfolio
(B) Showcase portfolio
(C) Record-keeping portfolio
(D) Teacher portfolio

EXPLANATIONS OF RIGHT ANSWERS

1. In asking the students to "justify the Little Red Hen's decision," the teacher is helping the students to reason and make judgments and is encouraging them to develop and defend their decisions based on criteria they establish. "Evaluation" is the level of this task. Therefore, (D) is the correct answer.

2. During the publishing phase of the writing process, students make their writing public by reading, putting the writings in a booklet, and so on. The correct answer, therefore, is (D).

3. Analyzing student work can provide valuable insights into what a student can do and what additional work and activities are needed. A teacher needs to select developmentally appropriate strategies and adjust instructions accordingly to meet the needs of individual students. In this question, a first-grade student writes the words phonetically, as they are heard and not as they are spelled. Of all the options presented, "Explicit instruction in phonics and phonemic awareness" is most likely to assist the student in becoming a better speller. Therefore, (C) is the correct answer.

4. Teachers must be able to develop objectives that help their students meet overall curriculum goals. Here the goal is to use computational strategies accurately and to estimate appropriately. (D) is the correct answer because it covers both parts of the curricular goal. Students must understand the computational strategies involved in mathematics solutions before they are able to estimate or to evaluate estimated answers. None of the objectives reflected in the other options is as likely to meet the goal.

5. Here a teacher is "preteaching" students by having them use "mental mathematics" to compute simple multiplication problems before they tackle the actual problem that they will be asked to solve. Understanding the algorithm involved in multiplication is essential to success in solving multiplication problems. Using mental mathematics is a useful way to comprehend the algorithm. Therefore, (D) is the correct answer.

6. Teachers play a vital role in providing motivation for students. Practice is an important part of learning. Each of the four possible actions offered in the question deals with percentages, but the students are most likely to be motivated and achieve practice by the action described in (C). It involves them actively in applying what they know about percentages to a task that is likely to interest them: buying CDs at discount prices.

7. Presenting information graphically is a common goal of most science curriculums, and a useful teaching technique is to have students create their own graphs. In this question, students have produced both a table and a graph, but the results are in error because the students did not keep the intervals consistent on their vertical axis ("distance in meters"). Therefore, (C) is the correct answer. To facilitate their understanding, the teacher should explain (and demonstrate) how to use units of measure consistently on a graph.

8. Effective teachers are able to guide students from the specific findings of a "hands-on" experiment to the broader principles and theories behind the experimental results. The experiment described in the question exposes students to the odors of various familiar substances. The students observe the connection between the odor and the substance, plus the way odor is dispersed over distance. Since odor is a property of matter, this activity would fit into a science textbook under the heading "Physical Science: Properties of Matter." Therefore, (B) is the correct answer.

9. Teachers often need to identify and assess their students' acquisition of skills in a content area. In this example, having the individual student perform the required task is often the best way to identify and assess skills. It can be time-consuming, but it can also be the best method of assessment. (A), therefore, is the correct answer.

10. Choices (B) and (D) may be appropriate for building interest in reading and enhancing reading readiness. (C) might be appropriate for practicing new skills. Only (A) combines teaching of the needed skills with meaningful contexts in which to use them. Therefore, (A) is the correct answer.

11. (A) is the correct answer. "Content integration" is the appropriate term for the activity presented in this scenario, where students use art to explore another culture as part of a social studies unit.

12. (D) is the correct answer. The assignment is too abstract for students of this age, who would not have a good concept of hemispheres. All the other activities are more appropriate for these students, since each one has a concrete task to encourage learning.

13. When planning units of instruction, a teacher needs to be aware of the sequence as well as the content of the material. At times, lessons build on previous information or skills. At other times, lessons are developmentally appropriate for students only at a specific age. In this example, the teacher will most probably give instruction on team plays last, after basic individual skills have been developed. All the other answers represent individual skills and need to be developed before team play. Therefore, (A) is the correct answer.

14. Music concepts should be prepared through various musical experiences prior to the formal presentation of the concept. Then the students should be given opportunities to use and practice this new knowledge. As students gain confidence and competence, opportunities to extend learning should be provided. The correct answer, therefore, is (C).

15. Brainstorming is most useful for teachers when it is most spontaneous. Students should be encouraged to contribute their ideas on a topic or answers to a question without "prescreening" their responses. This allows the teacher to see more accurately what the students know or believe. Statements (A), (B), and (D) all ask students to screen what they say before they say it. Only statement (C) accurately reflects the goal of brainstorming, and therefore it is the correct answer.

16. "Wait time" is often "thinking time." It allows students to comprehend a teacher's question and come up with an answer. Therefore, (B) is the correct answer. Other strategies are more effective when students are not focused, are embarrassed, or are already speaking.

17. Kinesthetic learners are most likely to learn from acting out the concepts being taught. Discussing, writing, and reading are approaches that are not likely to be as successful with kinesthetic learners. Therefore, (B) is the correct answer.

18. A "working" portfolio is generally considered to be the most accurate because it contains all of the student's work to date in a specific subject. It allows both the teacher and the student to see the progress that has been made and to identify areas in which the student still needs to develop. Therefore, (A) is the correct answer. A "showcase" portfolio usually contains a student's best work in a subject. A "record-keeping" portfolio usually refers to a portfolio kept by the teacher for each student, with contents such as notes from the student's parents and anecdotal records taken by the teacher based on observing the student. A "teacher" portfolio usually describes a portfolio kept by the teacher that includes assignments given to the class, along with data on student performance and notes about the success of each assignment.

CHAPTER 15

Elementary Education: Content Knowledge

The Elementary Education: Content Knowledge test is designed for prospective teachers of children in primary through upper elementary school grades. The 120 multiple-choice questions focus on four major subject areas: reading/language arts, mathematics, history/social studies, and science. Test questions are arranged by subject area.

PREPARING FOR THE CONTENT KNOWLEDGE TEST (0014)

The Content Knowledge test is not intended to be a test of your teaching skills. Rather, it is intended to demonstrate that you possess fundamental knowledge in the subject areas you will be required to teach.

Elementary Education: Content Knowledge

Test at a Glance

Time	2 hours	
Format	120 multiple-choice questions, scientific or four-function calculator use permitted	
Content Categories	**Approximate Number of Questions**	**Approximate Percentage of Examination**
I. Reading/Language Arts	30	25%
II. Mathematics	30	25%
III. History/Social Studies	30	25%
IV. Science	30	25%

Advice from the Experts

The test makers recommend the following approach to prepare for the test:

- **Become familiar with the test content.** Learn what will be tested in the four sections of the test. Consult the Study Topics section of the Test at a Glance bulletin available at the *Praxis* Web site (www.ets.org/praxis/testprep).
- **Assess how well you know the content in each area.** It is likely that you will need to study in most of or all the four content areas. After you learn what the test contains, assess your knowledge in each area. How well do you know the material? In which areas do you need to learn more before you take the test?

- **Develop a study plan.** Assess what you need to study and create a realistic plan for studying. You can develop your study plan in any way that works best for you. The Study Plan Sheet on page 369 is one possible way to structure your planning. Remember that this is a licensure test and covers a great deal of material. Plan to review carefully. You will need to allow time to find the books and other materials, time to read the material and take notes, and time to go over your notes.

- **Identify study materials.** Most of the material covered by the test is contained in standard introductory textbooks in each of the four fields. If you do not own an introductory text in each area, borrow one or more from friends or from a library. You should also obtain a copy of your state's standards for the subject areas for elementary-grade students. (One way to find these standards quickly is to go to the Web site for your state's Department of Education.) The textbooks used in elementary classrooms may also prove useful to you, since they also present the material you need to know. Rely on standard school and college introductory textbooks and other professionally prepared materials, rather than on information provided by friends or from searching the Web. Neither of these sources is as uniformly reliable as textbooks.

- **Work through your study plan.** You may want to work alone, or you may find it more helpful to work with a group or with a mentor. Be able to define and discuss the topics in your own words rather than memorizing definitions from books. If you are working with a group or mentor, you can also try informal quizzes and questioning techniques.

- **Proceed to the practice questions.** Once you have completed your review, you are ready to benefit from the Real Questions for Practice starting on page 381.

- **Answer the Real Questions for Practice at the end of this chapter.** Make your own test-taking conditions as similar to actual testing conditions as you can. Work on the practice questions in a quiet place without distractions. Remember that the practice questions are only examples of the way the topics are covered in the test. The test you take will have different questions.

- **Score the practice questions.** Go through the detailed answers in Answers and Explanations, and mark the questions you answered correctly and the ones you missed. Look over the explanations of the questions you missed and see if you understand them.

- **Decide whether you need more review.** After you have looked at your results, decide if there are areas that you need to brush up on before taking the actual test. (The practice questions are grouped by topic, which may help you spot areas of particular strength or weakness.) Go back to your textbooks and reference materials to see if the topics are covered there. You might also want to go over your questions with a friend or teacher who is familiar with the subject.

- **Assess your readiness.** Do you feel confident about your level of understanding in each of the subject areas? If you feel ready, complete the Readiness Checklist on page 367 to double-check that you've thought through the details.

REAL QUESTIONS FOR PRACTICE

The questions that follow indicate the kinds of questions in the test. They are not, however, representative of the entire scope of the test in either content or difficulty. Answers with explanations follow the questions.

Directions: Each of the questions or statements below is followed by four suggested answers or completions. Select the one that is best.

I. Reading/Language Arts

1. Which of the following is an example of internal conflict?

(A) "All the way home, Emilio felt angry with himself. Why couldn't he have spoken up at the meeting? Why was he always so shy?"

(B) "Juanita and Marco disagreed about where they should take the money they had found."

(C) "In the high winds, the crew was barely able to keep the sails from dipping sideways. Each time the wind accelerated, the crew almost lost the boat."

(D) "Celine struggled to walk through the cold, blowing wind."

Question 2 is based on the following poem:

The fallen leaves are cornflakes
That fill the lawn's wide dish,
And night and noon
The wind's a spoon
That stirs them with a swish.

Excerpted from "December Leaves" in Don't
Ever Cross a Crocodile by *Kaye Starbird.*
Copyright © 1963, 1991 Kaye Starbird.

2. Which of the following devices or figures of speech appears most frequently in the poem?

(A) Foreshadowing
(B) Personification
(C) Metaphor
(D) Hyperbole

We came back to the city Labor Day Monday—us
and a couple million others—traffic crawling, a
hot day, the windows practically closed up tight to
keep Cat in. I sweated, and then cat hairs
stuck to me and got up my nose. Considering
everything, Pop acted quite mild.

I met a kid up at the lake in Connecticut who had skin-diving equipment. He let me use it one day when Mom and Pop were off sight-seeing. Boy, this has fishing beat hollow! I found out there's a skin-diving course at the Y, and I'm going to begin saving up for the fins and mask and stuff. Pop won't mind forking out for the Y membership, because he'll figure it's character building.

Meanwhile, I'm wondering if I can get back up to Connecticut again one weekend while the weather's still warm, and I see that Rosh Hashanah falls on a Monday and Tuesday this year, the week after school opens. Great. So I ask this kid— Kenny Wright—if I can maybe come visit him that weekend so I can do some more skin diving.

   I. First-person narrative
  II. Use of slang
 III. Use of dialect
 IV. Anthropomorphism

3. The selection contains which of the above?

    (A) I and II only
    (B) II and IV only
    (C) I, III, and IV only
    (D) I, II, III, and IV

II. Mathematics

4. Which of the following numbers is least?

    (A) 0.103
    (B) 0.1041
    (C) 0.1005
    (D) 0.11

5. The Statue of Liberty casts a shadow 37 meters long at the same time that a vertical 5-meter pole nearby casts a shadow that is 2 meters long. The height, in meters, of the Statue of Liberty is within which of the following ranges?

    (A) 115 m to 120 m
    (B) 105 m to 110 m
    (C) 90 m to 95 m
    (D) 60 m to 65 m

III. History/Social Studies

6. What major geographic feature in North America separates the rivers and streams that flow toward the Pacific Ocean from those that flow toward the Atlantic Ocean?

(A) Appalachian Mountains
(B) Continental Divide
(C) Great Plains
(D) San Andreas Fault

IV. Science

Use the map below to answer question 7.

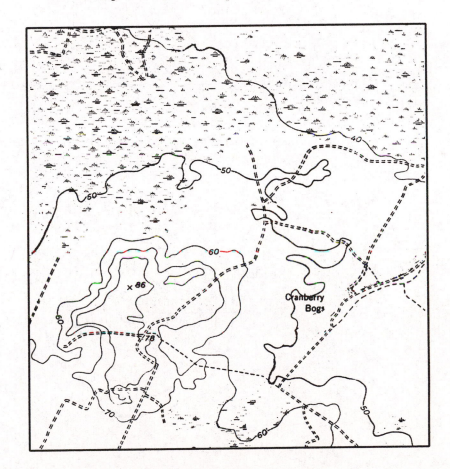

7. What do the solid lines on the map above represent?

(A) Levels of snow accumulation
(B) Lines above which certain trees do not grow
(C) Elevation of land above sea level
(D) The advance of glaciers in the region

8. As altitude increases, atmospheric pressure decreases, but not at a constant rate. Which of the following graphs best represents this relationship?

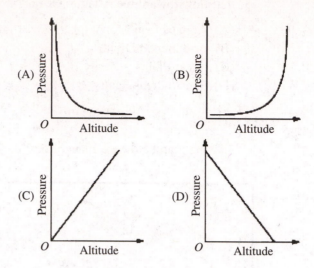

Question 9 refers to the following model:

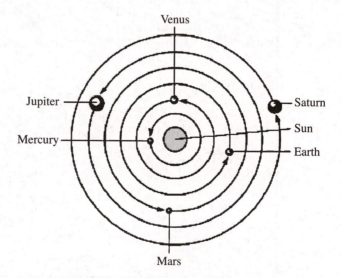

9. A model of the solar system is shown above. Which of the following is LEAST accurately shown in the model?

(A) The relative distance of each planet from the Sun

(B) The order of the planets from nearest to the Sun to farthest from the Sun

(C) The direction of the planetary orbits

(D) The shapes of the planetary orbits

10. A rock picked up on a hillside was found to contain tiny pieces of seashells. Which of the following is the best explanation of how this rock was formed?

(A) It was formed when sediments sank to the bottom of an ancient sea and were subjected to great pressure for long periods of time.

(B) It was formed on or near Earth's surface from magma or lava that flowed during a volcanic eruption.

(C) It was formed when minerals deep inside Earth were subjected to great heat and pressure.

(D) It was formed by seafloor spreading and erosion of the mid-ocean ridge deep in the ocean.

Answers and Explanations

1. This question asks you to recognize an example of a particular literary element. Internal conflict is a struggle between opposing forces in the mind of a single character. Choice A is the only choice where conflict is taking place in the mind of a character; accordingly, choice A is the correct answer.

2. This question asks you to apply your knowledge of figures of speech. A metaphor is a figure of speech that vividly describes a thing by identifying it directly with something else (for example, in line 4, "The wind's a spoon"). In line 1, the poet identifies fallen leaves with cornflakes. In line 2, the poet identifies the lawn with a wide dish. In line 4, the poet identifies the wind with a spoon. Therefore choice C is the correct answer.

3. This question asks you to apply your knowledge of narrative, structural, and stylistic elements to the selection. The narrator constantly says "I," and so the selection is written in first-person narrative. The narrator also uses slang (for example, "this has fishing *beat hollow!*" and "forking out for the Y membership"). There is no particular dialect represented, nor is the cat in the passage portrayed anthropomorphically—that is, as having human qualities. The correct answer, therefore, is choice A.

4. This question tests your knowledge of decimal values. Without the decimal, 1041 would be the greatest number and 11 would be the least, but because these are decimals, the position in relation to the decimal point is crucial in determining the value. It is helpful to work from left to right to determine which number is least. In this case, 0.1005 is the least number, and choice C is the correct answer. Another way to approach this kind of problem is to add a zero to the end of 0.103 in choice A, and two zeros to the end of 0.11 in choice D so that all four choices represent so many ten-thousandths. This does not change the numbers' values, but makes it easier to determine that choice D is the greatest, being equal to 1,100 ten-thousandths, and choice C is the least, being equal to 1,005 ten-thousandths. Again, choice C is the correct answer.

5. This question can be solved by setting up a proportion. The ratio between the height of the Statue of Liberty and the length of its shadow is equal to the ratio between the height of the pole and the length of its shadow. The proportion will look like this (where L represents the height of the Statue of Liberty):

$$\frac{L}{37} = \frac{5}{2}$$

Multiplying both sides by 37 and then simplifying both sides of the equation give you $L = 92.5$ m. Note that other proportions can be set up, such as: Statue height (L) divided by pole height (5 meters) equals statue shadow length (37 meters) divided by pole shadow length (2 meters). This will also give the correct result. Therefore, choice C is the correct answer.

6. This question tests your knowledge of important geographic features of North America. The Continental Divide is the series of mountain ridges extending from Alaska to Mexico that forms the watershed of North America. Most of the Divide runs along peaks of the Rocky Mountains. In the United States, it is often called the Great Divide. The correct answer, therefore, is choice B.

7. This question asks you to identify the purpose of a feature in a common topological map. This kind of map has contour lines, one line for each major level of elevation. All the land at the same elevation is connected by a line. These lines often form circles or ovals—one inside the other. If contour lines are very close together, the surface is steep. If the lines are spread apart, the land is flat or rises very gradually. The correct answer is choice C.

8. In this question, you are asked to interpret graphs and match the correct graph with a relationship expressed in words. Choices B and C are wrong, because they show that as altitude increases (i.e., left to right), pressure *increases* rather than decreases. Choice D is wrong because, although pressure does decrease (i.e., high to low), the relationship is linear and therefore *constant* rather than not constant. Choice A shows that as altitude increases pressure decreases, but not at a constant rate: the degree of decrease gets smaller as altitude increases. The correct answer, therefore, is choice A.

9. This question asks you to put together your knowledge of the solar system with a simple model representing part of the solar system. Models such as this are often found in textbooks, and it is important to distinguish what each model represents well and what each one represents poorly. In this model, the order of the planets going outward from the Sun is correct, as is the direction of the planetary orbits. The shapes of the planetary orbits are represented by circles. While the orbits are actually elliptical, the eccentricities of most of the orbits are so small that they are nearly circular. Even in a correctly scaled diagram, the small elongations of the orbits may not be discernable, thus, the circular representation is close to being accurate. The relative distance of each planet from the Sun is inaccurate, since the inner four planets are significantly more closely spaced than the two outer planets shown. The correct answer, therefore, is choice A.

10. This question asks you to apply your knowledge of rock formation and the processes of Earth's history to a single sample, a rock containing tiny pieces of seashells. The presence of seashells in a rock on a hillside indicates that the hillside was under water many years ago. During the time that the ancient sea existed, shells, which are the "houses" of sea creatures, would have fallen to the seabed when the animals died. The pressure of the water over very long periods of time would have compacted and cemented the shells and sediment into rocks that were later exposed when the sea dried up. The correct answer, therefore, is choice A.

CHAPTER 16

Elementary Education: Content Area Exercises

The Praxis Elementary Education: Content Area Exercises test is designed to measure how well prospective teachers of students in the elementary grades can respond to extended exercises that require thoughtful, written responses. The exercises pose challenging, complex problems to assess examinees' in-depth understanding of elementary education.

The test is designed to reflect current standards for knowledge, skills, and abilities in teaching elementary education. ETS works in collaboration with teacher educators, higher education content specialists, and accomplished practicing teachers in the field of education to keep the tests updated and representative of current standards.

PREPARING FOR THE CONTENT AREA EXERCISES TEST

The Elementary Education: Content Area Exercises test consists of four essay exercises set in the context of a subject area (or integrated subject areas) and in the context of a classroom situation. The essays are graded on how well they answer all parts of the exercise and demonstrate understanding of the subject matter and pedagogy required by the exercise.

Elementary Education: Content Area Exercises (0012)

Test at a Glance

Time	2 hours
Format	Four 30-minute exercises pose problems requiring extended responses

Content Categories	Approximate Number of Questions	Approximate Percentage of Examination
I. Reading/Language Arts	1	25%
II. Mathematics	1	25%
III. Science or Social Studies	1	25%
IV. Interdisciplinary Instruction	1	25%

The main purpose of the Elementary Education: Content Area Exercises test is to ensure that candidates who pass the test possess fundamental pedagogical content knowledge of the subject areas that they may be required to teach in elementary school.

Preparing on Your Own

If you are working by yourself to prepare for the Elementary Education: Content Area Exercises test, you may find it helpful to copy and fill out the Study Plan Sheet on page 369. This work sheet will help you to focus on what topics you need to study most, identify materials that will help you study, and set a schedule for doing the studying.

Preparing with a Study Group

Here are some ways to use this book as part of a study group:

- **Plan the group's study program.** Parts of the Study Plan Sheet can help structure your group's study program. By filling out the first five columns and sharing the work sheets, everyone will learn more about your group's mix of abilities and about the resources (such as textbooks) that members can share with the group. In the sixth column ("Dates planned for study of content"), you can create an overall schedule for your group's study program.

- **Plan individual group sessions.** At the end of each session, the group should decide what specific topics will be covered at the next meeting and who will present each topic.

- **Prepare your presentation for the group.** When it's your turn to present, prepare two or three original questions to pose to the group. Writing sample test questions can help you better understand the topics covered as well as the types of questions you will encounter on the test. It will also give other members of the group extra practice at answering questions.

- **Take the practice questions together.** The idea of the practice questions are to simulate an actual administration of the test, so scheduling a test session with the group will add to the realism and will also help boost everyone's confidence.

- **Learn from the results of the practice questions.** Score each other's responses. Then, try to follow the same guidelines that the test scorers use to score each other's responses.

  Be as critical as you can. You're not doing your study partner a favor by letting him or her get away with an answer that does not cover all parts of the question adequately.

  Be specific. Write comments that are as detailed as the comments made in the section 'Sample Responses and Commentary.' Indicate *where and how* your study partner is doing a poor job of answering the question. Writing notes in the margins of the response may also help.

Be supportive. Include comments that point out what your study partner got right and, therefore, earned points.

Then, plan one or more study sessions based on aspects of the questions on which group members performed poorly. For example, each group member might be responsible for rewriting one paragraph of a response in which someone else did an inadequate job of answering the question.

Whether you decide to study alone or with a group, remember that the best way to prepare is to have an organized plan. The plan should set goals based on specific topics and skills that you need to learn, and it should commit you to a realistic set of deadlines for meeting these goals.

REAL QUESTIONS FOR PRACTICE

Question 1

Directions: Read the following scenario and then answer parts (A), (B), and (C) of this question on the lined pages in the space provided.

Scenario: A third-grade class is exploring the theme of friendship in language arts.

One of the stories the class will be reading is *Angelina and Alice* by Katharine Holabird. The book is about friends who help each other learn gymnastic tricks to perform at the town fair. The friends learn that by working together and helping each other, they not only improve their performance but also become closer friends.

Use the story *Angelina and Alice* as the core of a lesson on friendship. Be sure to explain why each activity or technique you suggest is appropriate.

Here is a summary of the story:

> Two young mice meet at school and become friends because they enjoy doing gymnastics. They are both good at most gymnastic tricks, but Alice can do a perfect handstand, while Angelina always falls over when she tries. The other mice in their class laugh at Angelina and call her names, and Alice joins the other mice and doesn't play with Angelina anymore. One day their gymnastics teacher announces that the class will put on a gymnastics show at the town fair and asks the students to practice for the show with a partner. Alice comes up to Angelina and asks her to be her partner. The two mice begin practicing, and Alice teaches Angelina how to do handstands. Angelina and Alice become very good friends again, and all their practicing makes their act the best at the show.

(A) Describe a prereading activity for this third-grade class. The activity should be age-appropriate and should reflect the friendship theme of the book that the students will be reading. The activity you describe should be focused and detailed, and should demonstrate an understanding of the principles of reading instruction, as well as an understanding of how children learn.

(B) Describe an instructional technique or strategy that you would use during the reading of the story to enhance the children's comprehension. Explain how you would determine whether the strategy did enhance comprehension.

(C) Describe an after-reading activity that would be an extension of the theme of friendship. The activity you describe should be focused and detailed. Carefully explain why you would develop the activity; your explanation should demonstrate an understanding of principles of literacy instruction, as well as an understanding of how children learn.

Begin your response to Question 1 here.

(Question 1—*continued*)

(Question 1—*continued*)

(Question 1—*continued*)

Question 2

Directions: Read the following scenario and then answer parts (A), (B), and (C) of this question on the lined pages in the space provided.

Scenario: Suppose that you have a second-grade class with 25 students in a small elementary school. It is the first month of a new school year. Your objective is to teach addition of two- and three-digit numbers without regrouping, but you find that 10 of your students do not know basic addition facts (0 to 18) and do not understand place value. The remaining 15 students know the basic addition facts well and understand place value, and would very likely be bored by a lesson in which you reteach these concepts.

(A) Describe three different activities that would help the 10 children who need help with addition facts. The activities should help the children develop conceptual understanding and familiarity with the basic facts, as well as the ability to recall the facts with speed and accuracy. Provide examples of what the children would be doing during the activities and, to justify your choices, explain what is known about how children learn mathematics.

(B) Describe three different activities that would help the 10 children who do not understand place value. Provide examples of what the children would be doing during the activities, and explain how you would assess their understanding of place value after they have completed the activities.

(C) Describe two activities that would reinforce and extend the skills of the 15 children who do not need reteaching. Provide examples of what the children would be doing during the activities and, to justify your choices, explain what is known about how children learn mathematics.

Begin your response to Question 2 here.

(Question 2—continued)

(Question 2—*continued*)

(Question 2—*continued*)

(Question 2—*continued*)

Sample Responses and Commentary

Question 1

Response That Would Receive a Score of 6

Learning the importance of friendship is vital to any child. I would begin my lesson with the following prereading activity. Together as a class, we would complete a K-W-L chart on the chalkboard. I would write the word "friendship" at the top to designate our area of interest for the length of this unit.

I would allow the children to raise their hands and name one aspect of "friendship" that we know. I would list these under the "K" column. Then we would collectively list the aspects about friendship that we want to know under the column marked "W." Finally, I would explain to the children that the column marked "L" stands for what we have learned through this unit. The children would be asked throughout the length of this unit to keep a personal list of what he/she has learned. At the end of the unit, we would list these on the board together and note how much we had learned. An example of a K-W-L of friendship might be:

Friendship

K	W	L
1. We all have friends	1. Why do we have to be nice to everyone?	1. Kindness is part of kind makes us better friendship and being citizens
2. Friends are kind		

Using a K-W-L chart as a prereading activity would be effective because it gets the children to thinking. Each child has to critically decide what he/she knows about friendship, wants to know, and evaluate what he/she has learned when the entire reading activity is completed. This activity is appropriate because it carries the children through; it foreshadows some of the learning that will take place throughout the unit. It also aids the teacher in knowing exactly where the children's interests lie. Their interests may or may not correlate with the teacher's objectives; however, by knowing their interests, the teacher is given an advantage. She can better keep their attention and promote further comprehension when she incorporates the children's interests into her important objectives.

During the reading of the story, the children need to be reading for comprehension. It is the obligation of the teacher to encourage that this is a main goal for each child. In order to do this, I would have the children read it separately then I would assign the children into groups of four and ask them to complete a list of vital notes from the story. Each child must contribute at least one fact. One child will naturally assume the role of the leader. When the children are finished I would allow them to stay in their groups and orally share with the rest of the class the points they listed. As each group shares, I would point out similarities and differences to the class as they are noticed. We would discuss the completed list as a class.

This during reading activity is appropriate because it is not fully teacher directed. They read the book separately, quietly at first. This enables each to read unintimidated at his/her own pace. In their groups, one child will naturally become the leader. They are not asked to reread the material, implying that they had read the book the first time they were asked. They must each contribute one fact from the book which causes each child to summarize and think critically to decide on what the important aspects of the book were as I list the aspects on the board. By having the compiled list on the board, the visual learners have the material reinforced. As we orally discuss similar and different facts each group gave, the audial learners have the material reinforced. Therefore, the teacher would know that comprehension was enhanced.

After this activity, we would summarize the lesson by allowing each child to write his/her own story about friendship. It could be factual or fiction. By allowing the children to complete their own story, they are reinforcing their reading skills. Reading and writing go hand in hand. They complement each other. The children would be using very high levels of thinking. They have now moved from listing facts to summarizing to applying their knowledge from comprehending the book. We would share these as a class and possibly hang them on the walls or in the hall to show pride in each child's work.

Commentary on the Above Response

This well-organized and coherent response addresses all three parts of the question and reflects a thorough understanding of the principles of reading instruction. All the activities are developmentally appropriate for third-grade students. The response describes the reading activities in detail and explains how and why each activity enhances students' reading comprehension. The first part of the response (the K-W-L chart) offers a focused activity that presents students with a clear purpose for reading, involves all children, and reflects the friendship theme. The response directly explains how the individual and group strategies used during reading provide for enhanced comprehension. The response also demonstrates how the after-reading summary activity would extend student knowledge and allow the teacher to assess comprehension and reinforce the theme.

Response That Would Receive a Score of 5

Before reading ANGELINA AND ALICE I would ask my students to think of some characteristics that a friend should have. In small groups I would have them share their characteristics with group members and agree on the top five characteristics. I then would ask each group to tell me their five most important characteristics and list them on the board. A discussion of why the listed characteristics are so important in a friend would conclude the prereading activity. I believe this activity is appropriate because it stimulates the children's thoughts on friendship and may introduce a concept.

During the reading of ANGELINA AND ALICE I would pose questions to the students at key times to enhance comprehension. One example may be, "why do you suppose Alice joined in with the others and decided not to be Angelina's friend anymore?" Another may be "what kind of characteristic is Alice showing when she asks Angelina to be her partner for the show?" Yet another may be "Why do you suppose that the two mice had the best act?" Each of these questions should stimulate good conversation about what is happening in the story and therefore should enhance comprehension.

As an extension to the reading I would have the students write about a friend that they might have. Their writing should include some characteristics that they like about the friend and why the characteristics are something the student values in a friend. If they choose I would allow them to write in the form of a letter to that specific friend so that the friend may know as well. Later, in a whole group session, I would ask if anyone would like to share their paper and I would read my own paper about a friend I had. I believe this extension activity is appropriate for the theme of friendship because it asks students to write about their own friend and to reflect on why that friend is special.

Commentary on the Above Response

All three activities are developmentally appropriate, and the descriptions show a good understanding of the principles of reading instruction. The choice of activities, however, is less directly focused on the specific goals of the unit. The prereading activity—listing the characteristics of a friend—introduces the concept of friendship, but does not explain how the introduction of that concept will assist the students' reading development. Also, the discussion of how the chosen activities reflect the principles of literacy instruction and pedagogy is less well developed than in the response rated a 6. The postreading activity accomplishes the goal of extending the theme through a creative activity that requires higher-order thinking skills. The response, however, does not directly explain why the letter-writing activity contributes to the children's growth or extends their academic and social knowledge. If the activities had been more diverse and the explanations had been better developed, this response would have received a higher score.

Response That Would Receive a Score of 4

Before I read the book to the children I would have them think about what being a friend means and what they think the qualities of a friend are. I would have them write them down and then discuss and share their thoughts as a class. As I read the story I would stop periodically and ask them questions about what was going on in the story, such as "Do you think that those who were laughing at Angelina were her friends? Why or why not?" I would also have them predict what is going to happen at the end of the story. After reading the story we would then discuss what happened in the story. So I could see if they understand it and if they understood the sequence of story beginning, middle and end etc. After we talk about the story and have discussed friendship then they will write their own story about their friend(s) and an experience of how they became friends or something that a friend did for them.

I would develop this activity to enhance the students' writing and have them use their own experiences to relate to the story and what happened in it. This helps them open up about their background/prior knowledge of friendship, the sequence of story and shows them that they can relate stories to their own lives.

Commentary on the Above Response

This response adequately describes three activities that are developmentally appropriate and enhance students' development, but offers only a partial explanation of why the activities are effective. While an explanation of part (C), the extension of the theme, is provided, similar explanations for parts (A) and (B) would have raised the score. The response also lacks clear paragraph organization to show the distinction between the three separate activities. The response demonstrates an accurate, if limited, understanding of the principles of reading instruction.

Response That Would Receive a Score of 3

I believe that it is very important for children to learn about the interactions between friends and the qualities that promote friendship. As a teacher doing a unit on friendship, I would focus on forming a community of learners that would appreciate and understand the overall theme of friendship.

During the reading of the story Angelina and Alice, I would set up cooperative learning groups. Through these groups children can take control of their own learning and enhance their comprehension of the story. I would choose heterogeneous groups to form small literature circles. In these groups, I would have the children discuss their observations and reflections. The children would be free to discuss the book and form their own understanding. In order to assess this strategy I would observe the groups and make anecdotal notes on their progress. Through this authentic assessment I could gain an understanding as to the level of comprehension that the children had developed from the book.

(C) After reading the book, I would have the children take part in an interesting, interactive learning activity. The children would be instructed to interview people in their families, communities, etc. to find out what qualities people look for in a friend. This is important for children to see the many commonalities that form the basis of a friendship. After the children have interviewed several people, I would call the class together and discuss their findings. As a group we would list and discuss the qualities of friendship found. The class would then be broken into several groups to develop an advertisement for a friend. This advertisement should include the specific details that one would look for in a friend. After the students have developed ideas, they will be able to complete their projects with any necessary materials. The groups will then be able to share with the class their advertisements. Through this activity, children will see the basic fundamental qualities that form a friendship.

Commentary on the Above Response

This response does not provide a prereading activity or explanation for part (A). The omission of this part automatically limits the score to 3 or a below. The reading activity for part (B) is adequate, although more explanation of the activity would help clarify its instructional purpose. The activity described for part (C), extension of the theme, reflects a good understanding of principles of learning and human growth and development. Unfortunately, the overall score can be no more than 3 because part (A) is missing.

Response That Would Receive a Score of 2

The prereading activity would be for the students to go to the library and check out a book relating to a friendship. When the students return to class, they will have 20–25 minutes to read their book silently. After the students have read their books, they will tell the class the title of their book, what the book is about, and why they chose that book. Then the class as a group will discuss the meaning of the word "friendship". Students will tell who their best friends are and how long they have been friends. This activity will develop listening skills and cooperating learning.

The teacher will have 2 students in the class to play the role of best friends. One friend will say something to hurt the other one's feelings. Then that student will tell how she is feeling and why did it hurt her feelings. Then the class will have the other student say something nice to her to make her feel better. This demonstrates just because they are your best friend they still have feelings too.

Commentary on the Above Response

The response omits both parts (B) and (C), and part (A) is answered only partially. The prereading activity described reflects a limited understanding of reading instruction at the third-grade level. Because of these omissions and lack of demonstrated knowledge of reading pedagogy, no score above 2 can be awarded.

Response That Would Receive a Score of 1

(A) The prereading activity would be to ask students their knowledge on gymnastics. This would be appropriate because third graders love to move around.

(B) The instructional technique would be to "act out." I would have a number of selected students to act like gymnasts. This would give the students a visual idea of the story.

(C) The technique would be a discussion with the students. This is the only idea I can come to you with as far as postreading.

Commentary on the Above Response

The response does not adequately answer any part of the question, and demonstrates a serious lack of understanding about reading instruction at the third-grade level. The activity for part (A) focuses on neither reading nor friendship, and the explanation provided does not demonstrate knowledge of reading pedagogy. The activity for part (B) would lead to serious classroom management difficulties and raises possible safety issues. The activity for part (C) is not clearly defined or explained. Because of the inappropriateness of the activities and lack of supporting details, no score above a 1 can be awarded.

Question 2

Response That Would Receive a Score of 6

We will now look at scored responses to Question 2 and see comments from the scoring leader about why each response received the score it did.

(A) The children need to understand what the abstract numbers represent before they can begin performing mathematical operations. In this case, they need to understand numbers as individual entities before they can begin to add two- and three-digit numbers without regrouping (and eventually, with regrouping). Before advancing to addition, I would first call together the group of 10 students who do not know basic addition facts and discuss numbers with them. I would ask the children, "What does 12 mean? Could you show me 12 with the counting chips?" We could discuss how to arrange the chips to make it easier to count, such as, placing them in groups of 2s to show 12 or groups of 5s to show 10. Each child would be given a container of counting chips and would practice showing abstract numbers in the concrete forms. Once the children understand the concept of numbers, it is appropriate to advance to basic addition facts. Write a problem on the board and ask the children to show the fact with counting chips (e.g., $5 + 7 =$). Discuss strategies used to determine the answer to the number model. Repeat this process with several more problems. Then give the students a number fact that they know automatically (e.g., $2 + 2 =$). Allow them to use the number chips to solve the problem. Discuss which method is quicker, using the number chips or knowing the answer automatically. Tell them that a goal for second grade is to be able to answer facts quickly and correctly.

Before beginning the games, remind the children of all the facts that they probably know. Begin with the facts for 10 and ask the children to tell you facts they know where the answer is 10 (e.g., $5 + 5$ or $9 + 1$). As the children give you the facts, add them to a list on the board. Discuss facts that are doubles ($5 + 5$) or turn around facts (if you know $8 + 2$, then you also know $2 + 8$). Extend the list to include all the doubles facts ($2 + 2$, $3 + 3$, etc.) and then discuss near doubles facts (if you know that $7 + 7 = 14$, then what would $7 + 6$ equal?).

It is important to provide the children with models of all the information that they know. This provides the children with the proper mindset for retrieving the information independently when they are playing the games with their peers. It is important in second grade that the children know the facts fluently as well as accurately. The following three activities will help children gain fluency.

1. Addition Top It (this game is played in pairs)—the children are given a pile of cards with numbers (initially, the children can use cards with the numbers 0 to 9). Each child takes 2 cards from the pile and says the complete number model (e.g., child one gets cards with a 5 and 6 and says "5 plus 6 equals 11"; child two gets 8 and 7 and says "8 plus 7 equals 15; 15 is higher than 11 so I win this round of Top It"). The children continue until the pile is gone. Children may use counting chips or number grids to solve difficult problems or to verify an answer.

2. Domino Addition (this game is played in pairs)—the children are given a pile of dominoes with the dots facing down. One child takes a domino and gives two number models for the fact (e.g., if the domino has 3 dots on one half and 5 dots on the other half, the child says "$3 + 5 = 8$ and $5 + 3 = 8$"). The other child takes a domino and gives two number models (e.g., if the domino has 3 dots on one half and 3 dots on the other half, the child says "$3 + 3 = 6$ and the turn around fact is the same, $3 + 3 = 6$ and that is less than 8 so you get my domino"). The children continue until the pile is gone.

3. Computer Programs—this may be done individually or in pairs. Children solve math problems on the computer at adaptive sites such as www.funbrain.com or Accelerated Math.

(B) It is also important that the children understand the concrete representation of abstract numbers for place value. The Base-10 Blocks are valuable in visually representing numbers. First we would discuss as a group what the different blocks represent (the cubes represent ones, the longs represent tens). Then we would discuss how the blocks would represent numbers (e.g., 27 would be 2 longs and 7 cubes). It is also important to discuss how to exchange blocks (e.g., 10 cubes would be exchanged for one long). The following three different activities will help the children to understand place value:

1. Reach 1,000 (played in pairs)—The children are given a pile of Base-10 Blocks, a Place Value Mat and a die. As each child takes turns rolling the die, the child takes that number of cubes, making exchanges when possible (e.g., a child has 1 flat, 4 longs and 8 cubes on the Place Value Mat and rolls a 6 on the die; the child takes 6 cubes and adds those to the 8 already on the mat; then the child exchanges 10 of those cubes for a long, resulting in 1 flat, 5 longs and 4 cubes on the Place Value Mat; the child then has to identify how many blocks are on the mat by saying "I have 154 blocks"). The game continues until one of the children reaches 1,000.

2. Base-10 Blocks (this is played in pairs)—The child places any combination of flats, longs and ones on the Place Value Mat and then the child turns over a card that says "hundreds place", "tens place" or "ones place". The child must identify how many blocks are in that place. For example, if the child has placed 6 flats, 5 longs and 9 cubes on the Place Value Mat and then turns over a card that says "tens place" the child would say "I have 659 blocks and there are 5 tens."

3. Show the Number (this is played in pairs)—the child turns over cards with riddles and must show the number with Base-10 Blocks. For example, the riddle says, 1 ten and 3 ones. The child shows that with Base-10 Blocks and says "1 ten and 3 ones is 13". Call the children together as a group and give a large number such as 173. Ask which number is in the ten's place. Advance to basic addition without regrouping, asking the children to solve problems, such as 23 + 31 using the Base-10 Blocks. Observe how the children arrange the blocks to determine understanding of place value.

(C) As the 10 children above are strengthening their understanding of basic addition facts and place value, the 15 remaining students will reinforce and extend their skills through the following activities:

1. The children will be invited to create number problems involving two- and three-digit numbers. The students will create number problems by reviewing the aspects of number stories (unit, story, question, solution, number model, and illustration). The stories will be shared with the class, placed in a class number story book and used as models for other students. These students will then write a number story that their classmates will answer. This time the number story should have three components (unit, story and question) and the classmates will provide the other three components (solution, number model and illustration). Children learn from peer interaction

and by encouraging students to solve number stories that were developed by classmates. Two important functions are being accomplished: the child writing the story must present information clearly and the child solving the story must use that information, along with problem solving strategies, to determine a solution.

2. Have students create their own fact triangles with higher facts. Fact triangles are triangles in which the answer is placed at the highest point and the two numbers that are added together to get that number are placed in the two lower corners. Once the children have made 20 fact triangles with more complex facts, they can join a partner and play the fact triangle game. It is important to challenge students who have acquired basic facts and build on the basic foundation in order to advance learning to higher levels. Children learn best when they are actively involved and are completing new and exciting activities that require problem solving but are within their understanding.

Commentary on the Above Response

This response shows that the test taker has a superior understanding of the subject matter and pedagogy required by the question. The response provides good strategies for helping students develop mathematical understanding (Base-10 Blocks, Show the Number) and then offers explanations for why these strategies work for different populations of children. These activities extend and generalize learning in a social context.

Response That Would Receive a Score of 5

The first activity I would do with my students would be to play math bingo addition. The students' card has addition facts only. The teacher calls out the number. For Ex: The number is "14." The students that have addition facts that equal that number place a token on their card. The students who cover the board get bingo.

The second activity that I would have my students play would be "Do or Die." For example, I give the students a math addition fact sheet. The students are timed. The table that has the most answers correct is the winner. The third activity I would have my students play is a card game, and they have a magic number. For example, 4 students per deck of cards. The magic number is "13." Each person would take a card and they would go counterclockwise. When one student who had two cards that equaled "13" they lay those cards down. The students keep going until the deck is gone. The student who has laid down the most cards win. These three different activities build accuracy and speed. This allows the student to become familiar with addition fact families. It also speeds up their process of learning: when you give them a timed test. I also encourage my students to try, because it gets easier everyday. To help my students learn place value, the first activity we do is a calendar activity. How many days we have been in school? 72 days. I have straws and containers. The student would come up and be the teacher and ask, "What place is the "two" in?" The student would reply, " The one's column." The teacher-student would then ask, "What place is the seven in?" The students would reply, " The ten's column." Then the students would place the straws in the correct column.

The second activity would be to give the students a sheet that has place value. The students must write the number in the correct place value that the teacher calls out. The third activity would be to write a number on the board. For example, 1,753. Call students up to the board and ask them to write the number that is in the hundred column. If they did it correctly they would write "7." I would be able to assess these types of activities very quickly. The student would also get immediate feedback. If the student still didn't understand, then I would do different activities using Cuisinart rods to show place value. One activity I would do for the 15 students who didn't need reteaching is peer tutoring. I find that my students enjoy working together to help their classmates. So the student who needs help would get w/ a student who doesn't and drill that student.

The second activity would be for the students who didn't need any help. I would give them enrichment problems that would expand their level of thinking. Students who do very well in math are sometimes analytical thinkers. Therefore, I always like to have a challenging math and problem solving center they can go to.

Commentary on the Above Response

This response answers all parts of the question clearly, but some of the explanations lack depth and detail. Part (A) represents the strongest part of the response; each of the three basic addition activities listed is supported with clear examples. While part (B) clearly describes three place value activities, the explanation of assessment as done "very quickly" is vague; it does not offer a description of how assessment would be accomplished. Part (C) describes the two enrichment and reinforcement activities only in very general terms; no specific details are offered, and there is no evidence for how problems would "expand their level of thinking." Although the response often lacks such reflection and analysis, the activities described do demonstrate a strong understanding of the subject matter and pedagogy required by the situation.

Response That Would Receive a Score of 4

The first thing I would do with children who are having trouble with Basic math facts is pull out the unifix cubes. I need to be sure they know what it is they are doing in a concrete manner. We would complete simple addition problems using the blocks to demonstrate that 1 block and 2 blocks is 3 blocks etc. I would also use everyday items such as pencils or books. Once the students seem comfortable with the concept of adding I would teach them about fact families in order to help them see the relationship as well as aid in recall of the basic facts. When students understand that and are the same their speed and accuracy will increase. Finally, a fun way to help increase speed and accuracy is to play addition bingo. The student must recognize the facts quickly but because it is presented as a game it is an enjoyable activity that helps with memorization of facts.

These activities will be effective because children must start with concrete, manipulative activities moving on to more abstract activities. As knowledge builds their speed and accuracy follow. This holds true for all areas of math education so for students needing help with place value, I would again turn to manipulatives. I would have them begin with unit blocks to complete simple addition problems. Next I would discover how the units must stay in the tens. They would work problems until they were clearly comfortable left moving onto flats of 100. This process of manipulating concrete objects would be repeated until students demonstrate the ability to transfer the information to the abstract. Another activity I would do with these blocks is play a game called "First to Fifty". Children work as teams or as individuals by rolling dice and taking a block for every roll.

When necessary they trade in units for rods and try to be the first to reach 50. Finally I would ask them to make up problems of their own to use with each other in order to assess their understanding of what they are doing. At any time during these activities I can do individual spot assessments and correct any misconceptions I see.

The students who have a solid understanding of these concepts can center to increase speed and accuracy of the facts by playing the same game as the others but at a higher level. For example they can increase place value concepts by playing 'First to One Hundred' or 'First to One Thousand' etc. the same method of assessment and evaluation can be used. Also they can play math Bingo like the others but use higher level of facts for the game. This will allow the more advanced students to be challenged while their peers receive needed help.

Commentary on the Above Response

While this response answers all parts of the question, the activities, examples, explanations, and assessment are not fully developed. The three activities provided for part (A) need more detailed description and explanation of how and why the activities would achieve the instructional goal. The first activity described in part (B) is more appropriate for simple addition than for place value. Also, there is no explanation of how the rods, blocks, and flats will be used in the place value activities. The third activity described in part (B) is appropriate, but the description of its assessment lacks depth. Part (C) only briefly describes two enrichment and reinforcement activities; neither is explained in detail, and more analysis of why these activities are effective is needed. The lack of detail and analysis shows an accurate but limited understanding of the subject matter and pedagogy required by the question.

Response That Would Receive a Score of 3

(A) One activity that the 10 children who need help with basic addition facts could participate in would be a flash card game. (The students would be in a circle). I would choose one student to hold up the flash card to the first person, if that person gets the answer right, he/she gets another problem to figure out—if he/she misses the problem, the card is shown to the next person. The most cards one individual student can answer correctly is 3 in one turn, then the next person automatically gets a turn. The "card holder" would switch after each round. Everyone would get practice during this activity, even if it wasn't their turn, because they would realize that if someone missed the problem they would be next. The cardholder gets practice just by looking at the flash cards. I would also pass out an "addition fact" worksheet time test to these students. Just by seeing the problem over and over, they will learn them, and learn to do the problem with speed and accuracy. I would also have those 10 students answer addition problems with manipulatives. (for ex: counting bears, cubes, etc.). I feel that it is very important for children to understand what they are actually doing. Children learn math many different ways. Some have to actually visualize what is happening in the problem, until you show them with counting bears. On the other hand, some students memorize the problems right away and don't care to see visuals. Everyone learns differently and teachers need to be able to accommodate every type of learner.

(B) One activity that would help the 10 children with place value would be to give them a piece of paper with a line down the middle and labeled 10's on the left side and ones on the right side. Each student would have several individual straws and some grouped in tens with rubber bands. I would tell them that the group is 10 straws. Then I'd show an example: "If I called out the number 22, I would put 2 groups of 10's on the 10's side and 2 ones (individual straws) on the right side. Following that activity I would give them a worksheet with place value problems on it. (For example, the problem may say "if a number has two 10's and three 1's, what is it?") Another activity that you could use would be to group the students into partners and have one student say a number, (e.g., 15), and the other partner would say one 10's and five 1's. They would switch off turns. I would be constantly monitoring.

(C) While the 10 students were working on worksheets, I would hand out a tougher worksheet on addition and place value for them to be working on. If the 10 students still don't seem to be catching on after a few days, I would go ahead and start the 15 students on the new harder material. They could also be assisting me in helping out the other students (flash cards, straw games). This would help the 10 students out greatly plus enrich their understanding of the material better (as a review.)

Commentary on the Above Response

The test-taker answers some parts of the question adequately and shows some understanding of the subject matter and pedagogy required by the exercise. However, the activities, examples, explanations, and assessment are not fully developed. While the first activity in part (A) is explained in detail, the second and third activities are not fully developed, and the explanation as to why these activities were chosen is only adequate. For part (B), once again the first activity is explained in detail, but the second and third activities are weakly explained, and no mention of assessment is provided. The explanations for the two activities listed in part (C) are very weakly developed. More supporting details are needed throughout the response to receive a higher score.

Response That Would Receive a Score of 2

(A) <u>Activity 1</u>
Working in pairs, and with unifix cubes, or any other manipulatives, students will practice their addition facts with each other. The manipulatives provide the students with concrete examples.

<u>Activity 2</u>
Pairing students with the 15 other children and having them practice basic facts together with manipulatives. This allows the students to learn from each other, and also helps with reinforcing skills in 15 other children.

Activity 3

Testing students everyday basic facts, with worksheets, and verbally. Develop a game where the teacher passes around a beach ball that has basic facts written on them, and the students catches it and gives the answer to one of the basic facts that are on the ball. This allows students to have fun and math don't be so stressful and helps with speed.

(B) <u>Activity 1</u>

Having each student use a roll of toilet paper, I would have write their numbers 0 to 18 on the paper as it unrolls. This would give them a visual picture of place value: Ex.

Activity 2

Have students make place cards showing place value. This provides another concrete example.

Activity 3

With worksheets, students will do math problems, using manipulatives to represent problems.

(C) <u>Activity 1</u>

Students will work in pairs with students who need additional help. This would reinforce these students math skills and provide them an opportunity to help other students.

Activity 2

Students will work by themselves on higher order math skills.

Commentary on the Above Response

The response demonstrates a weak understanding of the subject matter and pedagogy required by the question. In part (A), the response does not provide examples for each of the activities, and the descriptions lack supporting details and depth of analysis. Part (B) is particularly weak; the few examples provided lack clarity, are not fully developed, and do not mention assessment practices. Part (C) provides only very brief descriptions of the activities, and does not offer any explanation of how the activities extend and reinforce math skills. No part of the question is answered adequately because supporting details are underdeveloped or omitted.

Response That Would Receive a Score of 1

Children who don't understand math need lots of hands on exposure.

First thing is using manipulatives having children group different things. If children can touch it and move it they have a better understanding.

2nd is board games. Playing in sm groups with each other. I would also have the ones that did understand help the students who didn't.

3rd I would have a sm group w/ dry erase boards. And we would go over math. I would be there to help them one-to-one.

Commentary on the Above Response

Many parts of the question are not answered in this response. Only three activities are described, and it is unclear to which parts of the question they apply. No examples of how the activities would be used are given. Explanations of assessment are also missing. This response does not reflect an understanding of the subject matter and pedagogy.

PART VI

Praxis™ *II* Subject Assessments

Your Goals for This Part:

- Identify the format and content of 34 popular Subject Assessments.
- Learn what kinds of questions are asked on Subject Assessment tests and how to answer them correctly.

417

CHAPTER 17

All About the Subject Assessments

Praxis Subject Assessments are designed to assess your knowledge of specific subject areas. They test your grasp of the actual content you will be expected to teach once you are licensed. This chapter and the three following chapters describe 34 assessment tests. They provide sample questions to help you become familiar with the question formats that will actually appear on the test and answer explanations to help you understand the kinds of knowledge and reasoning you will need to apply to choose correct answers.

To determine which test or tests you need to take, consult Appendix A: The Praxis Series™ Passing Scores by Test and State or contact your state's teacher licensing commission, usually located in the state department of education.

Praxis II Subject Assessments include two types of tests: multiple-choice tests, for which you select your answer from a list of choices, and constructed-response tests, for which you write a response of your own. Multiple-choice tests measure a broad range of knowledge across your content area. Constructed-response tests measure your ability to provide in-depth explanations of a few essential topics in a particular subject area.

This chapter covers the following Subject Assessments:

- Fundamental Subjects: Content Knowledge
- Education of Young Children
- Special Education: Application of Core Principles Across Categories of Disability
- Educational Leadership: Administration and Supervision
- School Psychologist
- School Guidance and Counseling
- Library Media Specialist

FUNDAMENTAL SUBJECTS: CONTENT KNOWLEDGE (0511)

2 hours   100 multiple-choice questions

The Fundamental Subjects: Content Knowledge examination assesses candidates' skills and understanding broadly across four subjects:

- English Language Arts
- Mathematics
- Citizenship and Social Science
- Science

Questions are arranged by subject, with approximately 25 questions in each topic area. An index on the back page of the test book identifies the page locations where each subject can be found. Candidates may answer the questions in any order they choose.

The content of the examination is *not* predicated on the assumption that the candidates should be experts in all the subjects. Since the purpose of this examination is to assess knowledge and skills in subject matter that may lie outside an individual candidate's teaching specialization, the questions in each subject focus on key indicators of general knowledge and understanding. The questions require examinees to use fundamental skills that are founded upon broad concepts in each of the subjects.

EDUCATION OF YOUNG CHILDREN (0021)

2 hours   Part A—60 multiple-choice questions
                    Part B—6 short constructed-response questions

The Education of Young Children test is intended primarily for prospective teachers of preschool through primary grade students. It is based on a teaching approach that emphasizes the active involvement of young children in a variety of play and child-centered activities that provide opportunities for choices, decision-making, and discovery. The test is designed to assess the examinee's knowledge about pedagogy and content, the relationship of theory to practice, and how theory can be applied in the educational setting. Also included are multicultural influences, diversity, variations in development, including atypical development, and how they affect children's development and learning. Each of the six constructed-response questions will focus on one of the following areas: the learning environment, working with families, instruction, assessment, professionalism, and diversity.

The test was designed to align with the National Association for the Education of Young Children's *NAEYC Standards for Early Childhood Professional Preparation* (2001).

SPECIAL EDUCATION: APPLICATION OF CORE PRINCIPLES ACROSS CATEGORIES OF DISABILITY (0352)

1 hour   50 multiple-choice questions

The Special Education: Application of Core Principles Across Categories of Disability test is designed for examinees who plan to teach in a special education program at any grade level from preschool through grade 12. The 50 multiple-choice questions assess the knowledge and understanding of applying the basic principles of special education in a wide variety of settings for students with disabilities. Some of these questions are based on a case study related to the teaching of students with disabilities. Extensive knowledge of individual specialty areas, such as education of students with visual impairments or hearing impairments, is not required.

EDUCATIONAL LEADERSHIP: ADMINISTRATION AND SUPERVISION (0410)

2 hours   120 multiple-choice questions

The Educational Leadership: Administration and Supervision test is intended to assess a candidate's knowledge of the functions of an administrator or supervisor, including the background information needed to implement these functions. The examination is intended primarily for those who are candidates for master's degrees or who already possess a master's degree and are seeking first appointments as administrators or supervisors. This assessment instrument reflects the most current research and professional judgment and experience of educators across the country. The test is designed to capture what is essential about the role of a school leader; what makes the difference in whether a school community can provide experiences that ensure all students succeed.

The 120 multiple-choice questions cover five content areas: determining educational needs, curriculum design and instructional improvement, staff development and program evaluation, school management, and individual and group leadership skills. The test questions are structured to measure knowledge and cognitive skills in application, analysis, synthesis, and evaluation as described in *Bloom's Taxonomy of Educational Objectives*. For example, some questions emphasize knowledge of trends, principles, and theories; others require interpretation of data and identification of implications or consequences. Still others emphasize ability to generalize, determine priorities and relationships, integrate knowledge of theory to produce new information or patterns, and judge the value of a process or product on the basis of logical consistency

SCHOOL PSYCHOLOGIST (0401)

2 hours   120 multiple-choice questions

The School Psychologist test is designed for 60-hour master's- and specialist's-degree-level candidates wishing to serve as school psychologists in educational settings. The test assumes that candidates have had some form of supervised practicum or internship experience.

The 120 multiple-choice test questions focus on both content and process issues that are relevant to the school setting. Note that certain areas relevant to the practice of a school psychologist are not assessed in this examination because they do not lend themselves readily to multiple-choice assessment. It is assumed that candidates' competence in these other areas will have been evaluated using other methodologies during the course of academic training. The main content areas of the test include diagnosis and fact finding, prevention and intervention, psychological foundations, educational foundations, and ethical and legal issues. In measuring the six content areas, a variety of contexts are used as settings: consultation, assessment, intervention, research, professional standards, and in-service.

SCHOOL GUIDANCE AND COUNSELING (0420)

2 hours   120 multiple-choice questions, 40 based on the listening section

The School Guidance and Counseling test is intended primarily for persons who are completing master's-level programs for counselors and intend to become counselors in the public schools. It measures knowledge and skills required of the professional school counselor in relation to those developmental areas that constitute most of the work of the counselor. The test is designed to measure counselor functions and skills related to the primary and secondary school levels. A number of questions are applicable across school levels; other questions are especially applicable to the elementary school level, the middle or junior high school level, or the high school level. The content of the test is focused on questions that relate to the following four major categories: counseling and guidance, consulting, coordinating, and professional issues.

The 120 multiple-choice questions generally are intended to measure how the counselor skills and functions are applied to the following areas of student development:

- Identity and self-concept, covering student intrapsychic factors such as identity development, self-appraisal, and internal conflicts regarding the individual's actions, decisions, and values.
- Interpersonal, including the full range of interpersonal relationships, with emphasis on the student's relationships with peers, adults within the family, and adults outside the family, such as teachers.
- Career and leisure, covering the exploration and broadening of the student's options in planning such career and leisure activities as locating occupational information, interviewing for a job, and finding recreational facilities.
- Academic and cognitive, focusing on learning in the classroom and other educational contexts, with particular attention to the individual student's needs, abilities, and approach to the learning situation.
- Health and physical well-being, including student concerns about such matters as physical maturation, sexuality, fitness, injury and disease, handicapping conditions, chemical dependency, eating disorders, stress, abuse, and neglect.

The test is divided into two sections, one of which is based on a CD. Approximately 40 questions require listening to this CD and then, responding to written questions. The CD includes brief client responses, client statements followed by counselor responses, and extended client–counselor interactions. The questions based on the CD cover such counseling processes as identifying client feelings, identifying client problems or critical issues, and identifying the appropriateness of various counselor responses. Consisting of interactions between clients and counselors, the questions emphasize the knowledge and skills included in counseling and guidance content but may also include material related to consulting, coordinating, and professional issues content.

During the test, examinees will have 40 minutes to work on the taped questions and will see only the questions and/or possible choices. The script of the CD does not appear in the test book.

LIBRARY MEDIA SPECIALIST (0311)

2 hours   120 multiple-choice questions

The Library Media Specialist test is designed to measure the knowledge and abilities of examinees who have had preparation in a program for school library media specialists, grades K–12. Because programs in school librarianship are offered at both the undergraduate and graduate levels, the test is appropriate for examinees at either level. The test content is aimed at the level of knowledge appropriate for the person who is responsible for administering the library media program at the individual school level. The material in the test, therefore, would not be suitable for those in systems with differentiated staffing or for those at the district level. The 120 multiple-choice questions cover program administration; collection development; information access and delivery; learning and teaching; and professional development, leadership, and advocacy.

REAL QUESTIONS FOR PRACTICE

The following real test questions illustrate the types of items on the actual exams. Answers and explanations follow the last question.

Directions: Each of the questions or statements below is followed by four (or five) suggested answers or completions. Select the one that is best.

Fundamental Subjects: Content Knowledge

1. The following excerpt is from a speech by William Safire.

Is the decline of the written word inevitable? Will the historians of the future deal merely in oral history? I hope not. I hope that oral history will limit itself to the discovery of toothpaste and the invention of mouthwash. I don't want to witness the decomposing of the art of composition, or be present when we get in touch with our feelings and lose contact with our minds.

It can be inferred from the passage that the author believes that, in contrast to oral history, the written word is

(A) able to convey emotions more accurately
(B) a more intellectual exercise
(C) doomed to describe mundane historical events
(D) already obsolete

2. To make 36 5-inch pancakes, mix 4½ cups of water with 2 pounds of pancake mix.

When Mark goes shopping at Food Warehouse, he often buys food in large quantities in order to save money. A problem that sometimes arises is that large packages give directions for making food for large groups. Last week he brought home pancake mix with the directions shown above. If Mark wants to make 10 5-inch pancakes, how many cups of water should he use?

(A) $4\frac{1}{20}$ cups
(B) 1¾ cups
(C) 1½ cups
(D) 1¼ cups

3. Which of the following is true for both Martin Luther King, Jr. and Mahatma Gandhi, shown above?

(A) They based their movements for social change on Christian faith.
(B) They led mass movements based on nonviolent civil disobedience.
(C) They believed in achieving their goals by any means necessary.
(D) They urged their followers to cooperate with the rules laid down by established authorities.

4. During the nineteenth century, some bird species, such as starlings, were introduced into the United States from Europe. Since then they have spread throughout the country and become a nuisance, or pest species, especially in urban areas. They often drive native birds out of their habitats. Factors that have contributed to the starling's success in the United States most likely include all of the following EXCEPT

(A) appropriate locations for nesting
(B) suitable range of temperatures
(C) an abundance of natural predators
(D) availability of a variety of food sources

Education of Young Children

5. The portfolio a teacher keeps on each child in a class for assessment purposes needs to include all of the following EXCEPT

(A) dated work samples accompanied by teacher commentary
(B) anecdotal records and records of systematic observations
(C) checklists, rating scales, and screening inventories
(D) weekly classroom lesson plans and curriculum goals

6. Kate and Marc are working in the art center making a bird using paper-towel rolls, Styrofoam, feathers, sequins, scissors, scraps of material, and glue. The children are engaged in which type of play?

(A) Dramatic
(B) Constructive
(C) Exploratory
(D) Parallel

Special Education

7. For a special education teacher, which of the following is the best example of collaborative goal setting?

(A) Developing IEP goals with the regular classroom teacher and then presenting the completed goals to the student's parents
(B) Reaching a consensus on goals by consulting with parents and the multidisciplinary team
(C) Allowing parents to choose from goals designed by the multi-disciplinary team
(D) Encouraging students to select goals for IEP inclusion from teacher-approved lists

Educational Leadership: Administration and Supervision

8. The primary role of the supervising or cooperating teacher in the education of the student teacher is most appropriately described as

(A) setting a good example for the student teacher to follow
(B) helping the student teacher develop effective ways of teaching
(C) determining the educational philosophy to be implemented by the student teacher
(D) providing the student teacher with information on classroom management techniques
(E) facilitating the proper placement of the student teacher in his or her initial position

School Psychologist

9. The decisions in *Tarasoff v. Board of Regents of California* (1974, 1976) establish which of the following principles regarding confidentiality in counseling relationships?

(A) Duty to warn and protect
(B) Responsibility to maintain privacy
(C) Need to obtain informed consent
(D) Need to maintain accurate records
(E) Duty to limit access to student records

School Guidance and Counseling

10. When should the counselor inform a student about conditions that may require the provision of more than routine counseling?

(A) At a time halfway through the counseling relationship
(B) Only when an ethical issue arises during the counseling relationship
(C) Only while giving the student advice on which the counselor expects the student to act
(D) Near the close of the counseling relationship
(E) At or before the time the student enters the counseling relationship

Library Media Specialist

11. All of the following awards recognize excellence in children's literature EXCEPT

(A) Michael Printz Award
(B) John Newbery Medal
(C) Randolph Caldecott Medal
(D) Mildred Batchelder Award
(E) Coretta Scott King Award

Answers and Explanations

Fundamental Subjects: Content Knowledge

1. The correct answer is choice B. In the final sentence of the passage, Safire suggests that if we stop engaging with the written word ("the art of composition"), we may also "lose contact with our minds," or miss out on the intellectual rewards of the written word.

2. The correct answer is choice D. According to the recipe, 36 5-inch pancakes require 4½ cups of water. The proportion of the number of pancakes to the number of cups of water is

$$\frac{\text{Number of 5-inch pancakes}}{\text{Number of cups of water}} = \frac{36}{4\frac{1}{2}} = \frac{36}{\frac{9}{2}} = \frac{72}{9} = \frac{8}{1}$$

Since Mark is using the same recipe to make 10 5-inch pancakes, the proportion of the number of pancakes to the number of cups of water is still

$$\frac{\text{Number of 5-inch pancakes}}{\text{Number of cups of water}} = \frac{8}{1}$$

The number of cups of water needed to make 10 5-inch pancakes is

$$\frac{\text{Number of 5-inch pancakes}}{\text{Number of cups of water}} = \frac{8}{1} = \frac{10}{\text{Number of cups of water}}$$

$$\text{By cross-multiplying,} = \frac{8}{1} = \frac{10}{\text{Number of cups of water}}$$

can be written as: Number of cups of water = 10/8, which is equal to 1¼ cups of water.

3. The correct answer is choice B. Both King and Gandhi led movements for social change based on principles of nonviolence. King was a Christian minister, but Gandhi did not base his movement on Christian faith (choice A). "By any means necessary" (choice C) is a phrase often associated with Malcolm X, another civil rights leader in the United States in the 1960s. Choice D is incorrect: both King and Gandhi urged their followers to conduct nonviolent acts of civil disobedience when faced with unjust laws or policies.

4. The correct answer is choice C. The European starling was introduced into the United States in 1890. Environmental conditions in the United States were appropriate for the reproduction and survival of this species. However, as happens with many exotic species, there are few if any natural predators or competitors in their new habitats. This allowed starlings to thrive in their new ecosystems and reduce populations of native species. An abundance of predators would have kept the number of starlings from increasing greatly and, therefore, choice C would *not* be a factor that contributed to their success.

Education of Young Children

5. The correct answer is choice D. Choices A, B, and C are types of items that may be found in a portfolio kept to assess student progress. Weekly lesson plans and curriculum goals are items that do not need to be in such a portfolio.

6. The correct answer is choice B, the students are constructing a bird sculpture. Because Kate and Marc have a goal in mind and are using the materials to create a specific structure, it would be incorrect to characterize their behavior as simply exploratory play (choice C). Additionally, as the two are working together with a shared focus, this would not be considered parallel play (choice D). Dramatic play (choice A) may occur after the students have completed their project but is not described in the given scenario.

Special Education

7. The correct answer is choice B, since collaborative goal setting requires the sharing of ideas among all those involved with the student—educators, parents, related services providers, etc. It is not appropriate in collaborative goal setting for one person or group to present previously prepared goals to the student and his or her family. There must be collaboration among all concerned to develop appropriate goals for the student.

Educational Leadership: Administration and Supervision

8. The correct answer is choice B. The primary role of a supervising teacher regarding the education of a student teacher is to help develop effective ways of teaching. Among the choices provided, choice B is the only answer that addresses this point and is also the only choice that focuses on the development of the student teacher, not on the control exercised by the cooperating teacher.

School Psychologist

9. The correct answer is choice A. Choices B through E are good ethical practices but were not decided in the Tarasoff case.

School Guidance and Counseling

10. The correct answer is choice E. According to the American School Counselors Association, the counselor must inform the client of the purposes, goals, techniques, rules of procedure, and limitations that may affect the relationship at or before the time the counseling relationship is entered. Issues of violating the rights of clients are raised when counselors fail to provide adequate information that may affect the clients' welfare.

Library Media Specialist

11. The correct answer is choice C. The Randolph Caldecott Medal is awarded in recognition of outstanding illustration in a children's book.

Reading, English, Language Arts

This chapter covers the following Subject Assessments:

- Middle School: English Language Arts
- English Language, Literature, and Composition: Content Knowledge
- English Language, Literature, and Composition: Essays
- English Language, Literature, and Composition: Pedagogy
- English to Speakers of Other Languages
- Reading Across the Curriculum: Elementary
- Reading Across the Curriculum: Secondary

MIDDLE SCHOOL: ENGLISH LANGUAGE ARTS (0049)

2 hours   90 multiple-choice questions (Part A)
                   2 constructed-response questions (Part B)

The Middle School: English Language Arts test is designed to assess whether an examinee has the knowledge and competencies necessary for a beginning teacher of English Language Arts at the middle school level. The 90 multiple-choice questions constitute approximately 75 percent of the examinee's score and fall into three categories: knowledge of concepts relevant to reading and literature study, knowledge of the development and use of the English language, and knowledge of concepts relevant to the study of composition and rhetoric. The two equally weighted constructed-response questions constitute approximately 25 percent of the examinee's score and emphasize the use of critical-thinking skills. One question will ask examinees to interpret a piece of literary or nonfiction text and/or to discuss an approach to interpreting text; the other question will ask examinees to discuss the rhetorical elements of a piece of writing. The sections are not separately timed. However, examinees should allow about 90 minutes for the multiple-choice section and about 15 minutes for each essay question (for an approximate total of 30 minutes on the constructed-response portion).

ENGLISH LANGUAGE, LITERATURE, AND COMPOSITION: CONTENT KNOWLEDGE (0041)

2 hours   120 multiple-choice questions

The English Language, Literature, and Composition: Content Knowledge test is designed to assess whether an examinee has the broad base of knowledge and competencies necessary to be licensed as a beginning teacher of English in a secondary school. The 120 multiple-choice questions are based on the material typically covered in a bachelor's degree program in English and English education. The test covers literature and reading (55 percent), the English language (15 percent), and composition and rhetoric (30 percent).

ENGLISH LANGUAGE, LITERATURE, AND COMPOSITION: ESSAYS (0042)

2 hours   4 essay questions

The English Language, Literature, and Composition: Essays test is designed for those who plan to teach English at the secondary level. The test addresses two key elements in the study of literature: the ability to analyze literary texts and the ability to understand and articulate arguments about key issues in the study of English. The test consists of four essay questions, which are weighted equally. Two questions ask examinees to interpret literary selections from English, American, or world literature of any period. The first question always focuses on a work of poetry, while the second always features a work of prose. The third question asks examinees to evaluate the argument and rhetorical features of a passage that addresses an issue in the study of English. The fourth question asks examinees to take and defend a position on an issue in the study of English, using references to works of literature to support that position. The issue questions may deal with such matters as the nature of literary interpretation, the value of studying literature, the qualities that define the discipline of literary study, the kinds of literary works we choose to read and teach and why we make those choices, and so on.

ENGLISH LANGUAGE, LITERATURE, AND COMPOSITION: PEDAGOGY (0043)

1 hour   2 constructed-response questions

The English Language, Literature, and Composition: Pedagogy test is designed for those who plan to teach English at the secondary school level. The test assesses how well examinees can perform two tasks that are required of a teacher of English: teaching literature and responding to student writing.

The first question presents a list of literary works commonly taught at the secondary level and asks examinees to choose one work from the list as the basis for their response to the three-part question. The parts of this question are as follows:

1. Identify two literary features of the particular work that are central to teaching the work.
2. Identify two obstacles to understanding that students might experience when encountering the work.
3. Describe two instructional activities that could be used to help students understand the literary features and/or overcome obstacles to understanding.

Examinees should be sure to include specific examples from the work in their discussion. A general discussion of problems students tend to have when encountering any work of literature would be inappropriate; similarly, a discussion that does not demonstrate familiarity with the work and its literary features would be unacceptable. In responding to this question about teaching literature, examinees should show that they understand the various kinds of knowledge, abilities, and skills that students bring to the English classroom; that they can identify important literary features central to teaching a particular work of literature; that they can anticipate likely obstacles for students encountering a work of literature; and that they can plan and describe relevant instructional activities.

The second question requires examinees to read an authentic piece of student writing and then assess the strengths and weaknesses of the writing, identify errors in the conventions of standard written English, and create a follow-up assignment that addresses the strengths or weaknesses of the student's writing. Responses that focus on too general a strategy (e.g., "revise the essay"), identify only minor problems, or merely rewrite portions of the essay for the student, would not meet the demands of the task. In responding to this question about student writing, examinees should demonstrate how well they can assess student writing and design instructional activities that take into account student abilities. Examinees should also show that they can determine appropriate objectives for teaching composition, while at the same time demonstrating their understanding of the knowledge, skills, and abilities that different students bring to the English classroom.

The suggested time for each question is 30 minutes. Each question represents one-half of the total test score.

ENGLISH TO SPEAKERS OF OTHER LANGUAGES (0360)

2 hours, with a 30-minute listening section

120 multiple-choice questions, with 20 based on the listening section

The English to Speakers of Other Languages (ESOL) test is designed to measure basic pedagogical knowledge within the context of teaching ESOL in elementary or secondary schools. The test consists of two timed 15-minute listening sections and a 90-minute writing section.

Taped Portion: Section I, Parts A and B

- The 20 questions in Section I, Parts A (Oral Grammar and Vocabulary) and B (Pronunciation), are on an audio recording.
- The recorded questions in Section I are based on speech samples recorded by ESOL students who are not native speakers; examinees will be asked to identify errors in the students' speech. Therefore, before taking the test, they should be familiar with the speech of nonnative speakers who are learning English.

- Each of the recorded speech samples is printed in the test book. Examinees should mark the students' errors directly on the printed version of the speech samples to help focus their listening.
- After each speech sample, there will be a pause to allow examinees to choose and mark their answer. Examinees must answer within the time provided. The speech samples in Part A will be played one time only. The speech samples in Part B will be played twice.

Section I, Part C, and Section II

- After the recorded portion, examinees have 90 minutes to answer the remaining 100 questions in the test: Section I, Part C (Writing Analysis), and Section II (Language Theory and Teaching). Although there is a suggested time for each section, examinees will be able to work at their own pace. Those who finish the test before time is called can use any extra time to check their answers in either Section I, Part C, or Section II.
- The questions in Section I, Part C (Writing Analysis), are based on writing samples produced by ESOL students who are not native speakers; examinees will be asked to identify errors in the students' writing. Therefore, before taking the test, examinees should be familiar with the writing of nonnative speakers who are learning English.

READING ACROSS THE CURRICULUM: ELEMENTARY (0201)

2 hours   60 multiple-choice questions (Part A)
                 3 constructed-response questions (Part B)

The Reading Across the Curriculum: Elementary test is designed for persons completing teacher training programs with at least two or three courses in reading who are planning to teach at the elementary level or persons who are currently teaching and have the option of taking this test in lieu of state-mandated course work. The 60 multiple-choice questions and the 3 constructed-response questions assess knowledge of the content and skills necessary to be an effective teacher of reading, as well as the ability to apply knowledge of content and skills in the teaching of reading to all students. The multiple-choice questions and the constructed-response questions each constitute about one-half of the total test. The test questions involve the selection and application of ideas and practices to reading instruction from the earliest stages of language acquisition through the development of literacy skills across the curriculum. The content is based on categories and competencies developed by the Professional Standards and Ethics Committee of the International Reading Association.

READING ACROSS THE CURRICULUM: SECONDARY (0202)

2 hours   60 multiple-choice questions (Part A)
                3 constructed-response questions (Part B)

The Reading Across the Curriculum: Secondary test is designed for persons completing teacher training programs with at least two or three courses in reading who are planning to teach at the secondary level, or persons who are currently teaching and have the option of taking this test in lieu of state-mandated course work. The 60 multiple-choice questions and the 3 constructed-response questions assess knowledge of the content and skills necessary to be an effective teacher of reading, as well as the ability to apply knowledge of content and skills in the teaching of reading to all students. The multiple-choice questions and the constructed-response questions each constitute about one-half of the total test. The test questions involve the selection and application of ideas and practices to reading instruction from the different stages of language acquisition through the development of literacy skills across the curriculum. The content is based on categories and competencies developed by the Professional Standards and Ethics Committee of the International Reading Association.

REAL QUESTIONS FOR PRACTICE

The following real test questions illustrate the types of items on the actual exams. Answers and Explanations follow the last question.

> **Directions:** Each multiple-choice question below is followed by four suggested answers or completions. Select the one that is best. For questions that are not multiple-choice, follow the directions given.

Middle School: English Language Arts

1. Freewriting, brainstorming, clustering, and idea mapping are most important during which stage of the writing process?

(A) Prewriting
(B) Drafting
(C) Revising
(D) Proofreading

English Language, Literature, and Composition: Content Knowledge

Questions 2 and 3 refer to the following paragraphs.

I. On a dark, secluded street stood three abandoned houses. The first had broken shutters and shattered windows. Next to it stood a dilapidated structure badly in need of paint. Adjacent, amid debris, stood a shack with graffiti scrawled across the door.

II. Weeks before they decided on their destination, the seniors had already begun a massive fundraising project to help finance their class trip. When they were offered the choice between Rome and London, an overwhelming majority chose Rome. Then preparations began in earnest. In the months that followed, the students' enthusiasm escalated until the day the plane finally took off, carrying them toward an experience they would remember forever.

III. Selecting a new car requires each buyer to weigh a number of factors. First to be considered is the car's appearance. Next, and even more critical, are the car's performance and safety ratings. Most significant to any prospective buyer, however, is the car's price.

2. Which of the following best describes the organization of paragraph II?

(A) Chronological order
(B) Spatial order
(C) Cause and effect
(D) Order of importance

3. Which of the following best describes the organization of paragraph III?

(A) Chronological order
(B) Spatial order
(C) Cause and effect
(D) Order of importance

English Language, Literature, and Composition: Essays

Below is a sample of the first question in this test, which presents a poem and asks examinees to analyze some of the literary elements in the poem. The second question in the test is similar in format, except that it will ask examinees to analyze literary elements in a prose selection instead.

4. Read carefully the following poem by Louis MacNeice. Then discuss how MacNeice uses imagery and diction to convey the qualities of what the narrator calls "world." Be sure to use at least THREE specific examples from the poem to support your points about MacNeice's use of imagery and diction.

Snow

The room was suddenly rich and the great
bay-window was
Spawning snow and pink roses against it
Soundlessly collateral and incompatible:
World is suddener than we fancy it.

World is crazier and more of it than we think,
Incorrigibly plural. I peel and portion
A tangerine and spit the pips and feel
The drunkenness of things being various.

And the fire flames with a bubbling sound for world
Is more spiteful and gay than one supposes—
On the tongue on the eyes on the ears
in the palms of one's hands—
There is more than glass between the snow
and the huge roses.

English Language, Literature and Composition: Pedagogy

5. Assume you are teaching a literature unit to a ninth-grade class. Your overall goal is to help your students recognize and understand important literary features of the works they read. Your choices of literary works to use as part of this unit are:

William Golding, *Lord of the Flies*
Lorraine Hansberry, *A Raisin in the Sun*
S. E. Hinton, *The Outsiders* **or** *That Was Then, This Is Now*
William Shakespeare, *Romeo and Juliet* **or** *Macbeth*
John Steinbeck, *The Grapes of Wrath* **or** *The Pearl*
Amy Tan, *The Joy Luck Club*
Mark Twain, *The Adventures of Huckleberry Finn*

Choose ONE of the works listed above. Choose a work that you know well enough to identify and cite examples of its central literary features. Such features include, but are not limited to, specific methods of characterization and narration; characteristics of specific genres and subgenres; specific literary devices; and specific poetic techniques. Once you have chosen the literary work, answer the following three-part question.

A. Identify and describe TWO literary features central to the work that you would want ninth-grade students to be able to recognize and understand. In your discussion
- be specific about what students should know about each literary feature
- include specific examples from the work that are relevant to each literary feature
- be sure the literary features are appropriate for teaching to ninth-grade students

B. Identify and describe TWO obstacles to understanding this work that you anticipate these students might have. In your discussion
- explain **why** each obstacle is likely for ninth-grade students encountering the particular work; include specific examples from the work that are relevant to each obstacle

C. Describe TWO instructional activities you would use while teaching this particular work that would help students understand the literary features you described in Part A and/or overcome the obstacles to understanding you described in Part B. In your discussion
- present clear, well-formulated activities in which students are actively involved
- explain **how** each activity would help students understand the literary features and/or overcome the obstacles of the particular work
- describe activities that are appropriate for ninth-grade students

English to Speakers of Other Languages

Questions 6 and 7 are based on the following section of a table of contents in an ESOL textbook.

CONTENTS

Lesson 1 Try Our Special Offer . . . . Page 1
WHAT: to describe specific people and things; to give reasons; to emphasize; to show uncertainty
HOW: relative clauses

Lesson 2 An "Excellent Opportunity". . . . . Page 8
WHAT: to read an ad; to write a letter of application
HOW: paragraph construction

Lesson 3 Buying a Computer . . . . Page 35
WHAT: to discuss the future; to read ads; to describe features of a computer; to use some language of contemporary technology
HOW: collective nouns; "the" with plural and mass nouns; "the" with the names of places

---

6. For which of the following students is this text most appropriate?

    I. Preschool
   II. Elementary
  III. Secondary
  IV. Postsecondary

(A) I and II only
(B) III and IV only
(C) I, II, and III only
(D) II, III, and IV only

7. For which of the following programs would this text be most appropriate?

(A) English for Academic Purposes
(B) Coping Skills in ESOL
(C) English for Science and Technology
(D) ESL Current Events

Reading Across the Curriculum: Elementary

8. According to research, effective vocabulary instruction integrates new information with the familiar. Students are most likely to achieve that integration by

(A) using a dictionary
(B) developing a semantic map
(C) analyzing word structure
(D) memorizing words

9. A teacher is leading a Directed Reading–Thinking Activity while using a piece of informational text with the class. The teacher is most likely to ask the students which of the following questions initially?

(A) What part of the text gave you a clue about the writer's purpose?
(B) What do you think the writer intended to say?
(C) How do you know what references the writer used?
(D) How might the information in the text be used?

Reading Across the Curriculum: Secondary

10. According to research, effective vocabulary instruction integrates new information with the familiar. Students are most likely to achieve that integration by

(A) using a dictionary
(B) developing a semantic map
(C) analyzing word structure
(D) memorizing words

11. A teacher is leading a Directed Reading-Thinking Activity while using a piece of informational text with the class. The teacher is most likely to ask the students which of the following questions initially?

(A) What part of the text gave you a clue about the writer's purpose?
(B) What do you think the writer intended to say?
(C) How do you know what references the writer used?
(D) How might the information in the text be used?

Answers and Explanations

Middle School: English Language Arts

1. The correct answer is choice A. The terms mentioned are processes and devices associated with generating new ideas and organizing them. These processes and devices would not be associated with proofreading (choice D). While they might be part of drafting (choice B) or revising (choice C), they are most important during the prewriting stage of the writing process.

English Language, Literature, and Composition: Content Knowledge

2. The correct answer is choice A. Paragraph II describes a series of events that take place over the course of several months. Words and phrases such as "weeks before," "when," "then," and "in the months that followed" relate events sequentially.

3. The correct answer is choice D. The organization of paragraph III reflects an order of increasing importance. The features of the car are arranged from the one that should least affect the prospective buyer's decision (appearance) to the one that should most influence the buyer's decision (price). Words such as "more" and "most" help establish the comparative importance of each feature.

English Language, Literature, and Composition: Essays

4. Sample Response That Received a Score of 3

In the poem "Snow," by Louis MacNeice, the narrator uses conflicting imagery and unusual diction to draw a picture of a strange and contradictory world. Throughout the poem, the narrator uses conflicting images to create his "world." The first is the description of snow and roses at a single bay-window. This image confuses the sense of season. Snow normally falls in the winter, while roses bloom in the summer months. Then the narrator remarks that the two are "collateral and incompatible," again employing conflicting imagery. Another example of the narrator's use of conflicting imagery is his description of the fire bubbling. Usually, fire is expected to crackle and water is expected to bubble; people usually talk about "fire and water" as if they are two conflicting things. The narrator's use of imagery and description in the poem gives the reader a greater concept of the contradictory world he is describing. This world is full of contradictions and incompatible things. While the images illustrate the poem, it is the narrator's use of language that brings it to life. In this poem, the narrator uses vivid but odd diction in order to add life to his idea of "world." For example, he never refers to "a world" or "the world," but only "world," like it is something strange and new. The elaborate language creates an illustration of what the narrator is describing. For example, he refers to feeling the "drunkenness of things being various." Not only do things change in "world," but the changes are sharp and quick, enough so that one can feel intoxicated by the experience. The language even sounds intoxicated when it says, "On the tongue on the eyes on the ears . . . ." The narrator also uses a variety of vivid and surprising verbs throughout the poem. This tactic avoids stale, repetitive language that can often bore readers. In one case, the window in the first stanza was said to be "spawning snow and pink roses." While the idea is physically impossible, the word choice creates an unmistakable picture for the reader. It also emphasizes the idea that "world" is contradictory and strange. The overall effect of the narrator's use of imagery and diction was brilliant. The elaborate descriptions, verb variance, and conflicting images created a beautifully "crazy" world for the reader.

English Language, Literature, and Composition: Pedagogy

5. Sample Response That Received a Score of 6

Work Chosen: John Steinbeck's *The Pearl*

A. One literary feature of *The Pearl* is its form as a modern-day parable of Everyman and ultimately Everyman's quest for the "American dream." The protagonist Kino is an Everyman who must deal with his new-found promise of wealth and the false hope it instills in him. In an allegory/parable such as this one, a simple style is used to represent characters who often have very little individual personality but who embody moral qualities and other abstractions. In this way, the novel's significance as a universal fable can be appreciated. Symbolism is another important feature of *The Pearl*. Symbols are used in literature to reveal abstract ideas or truths. Steinbeck's hero, Kino, finds The Pearl of the World, an object that promises hope and prosperity. Kino believes that with the money the pearl will earn him, he will be able to legitimize his family (with a real wedding) and provide better for them (his son will attend school, he will purchase a new rifle). But as the piece unfolds, the pearl ironically becomes a symbol of greed and evil that steals the prosperity and joy that Kino actually did enjoy as peasant husband, father, and provider. He loses his ability to provide for his family, and his first son is killed. Kino's real hope for the family's future is destroyed. The pearl as a symbol of false hope and greed is at the center of the novel.

B. Students might find the simple style of this novel to be an obstacle. Steinbeck strips down the narrative by using short, repetitive sentences and plain language. For example, he often begins sentences with "And" several times in a row. Students might miss the point that simple language is used to make the parable clearer. Another obstacle for students might be the archetypal characters. Not only are the main family members described as predictable types but also the doctor, the priest, and the pearl buyers are all developed as stick figures. Again, students might miss the depth of the text because they do not get to know well-rounded, fully developed characters.

C. One instructional activity that I might use to help students understand the story as a fable would be to read a fable before reading *The Pearl*. This could help them anticipate the style. They would also be prepared for understanding the theme better. I would read the fable and ask them to write a short reflection in their journals or notebooks. We would then engage in a small-group discussion about this question: Why is the fable told so simply? I would then bring them into a large-group discussion and lead them to an understanding of the concept of allegory and universal application. The concept of simplicity of style would help them to understand allegory. An instructional activity I might use to help students become interested in the seemingly "flat" characters in the novel would be to show the purpose of archetypal characters in a narrative. I'd ask the students to discuss common TV/movie characters: policeman, hero, queen, newspaper reporter under deadline, president. Then I'd have them determine the values, beliefs, or actions of their characters. Then I might pose the question: when is an archetypal character a useful character in a movie? Can you think of any examples? Then I'd pull the discussion into the concept of universal application again.

Rationale for the Score

This response earned a 6 on a scale of 0–6. Points were awarded as follows:

- **Part A:** 2 points awarded. The examinee identifies two central literary features (the form of the allegory/parable and symbolism) and clearly connects those objectives to specific examples from the novel.
- **Part B:** 2 points awarded. The examinee identifies two obstacles to understanding (the simple style and flat characterization), explains why they would likely pose problems for student understanding, and cites specific examples from the novel.
- **Part C:** 2 points awarded. The examinee describes two instructional activities that are appropriate for the grade level and that address the literary features and obstacles to understanding. The instructional activities are designed to help students understand specific elements of the novel.

English to Speakers of Other Languages

6. The correct answer is choice B. The text would necessarily use and require language of both lexical and syntactic complexity greater than that which is likely to be possible or appropriate for levels I and II. The contexts or situations are more appropriate for teenagers and adults.

7. The correct answer is choice B. The lessons described in the table of contents would be most appropriate for a life skills or coping skills program (applying for a job, making purchases, etc.).

Reading Across the Curriculum: Elementary

8. The correct answer is choice B. A semantic map is a visual representation of ideas and the relationships among them. It usually has a key word or concept at the center, with other information radiating outward. It may be used before, during, and after reading to represent what students already know about a topic, to keep ongoing notes, to reorganize information, and to review and enhance information because of new information gained.

9. The correct answer is choice B. A Directed Reading–Thinking Activity is a guided reading method in which the teacher divides the text into shorter segments and then leads the students in predicting; reading silently to confirm predictions; discussing to refine and clarify predictions; and then formulates the new predictions about the remainder of the text. The process is repeated until the reading of the text is completed.

Reading Across the Curriculum: Secondary

10. The correct answer is choice B. A semantic map is a visual representation of ideas and the relationships among them. It usually has a key word or concept at the center, with other information radiating outward. It may be used before, during, and after reading to represent what students already know about a topic, to keep ongoing notes, to reorganize information, and to review and enhance information because of new information gained.

11. The correct answer is choice B. A Directed Reading-Thinking Activity is a guided reading method in which the teacher divides the text into shorter segments and then leads the students in predicting; reading silently to confirm predictions; discussing to refine and clarify predictions; and then formulates the new predictions about the remainder of the text. The process is repeated until the reading of the text is completed.

CHAPTER 19

Social Studies, Math, Science

This chapter covers the following Subject Assessments:

- Social Studies: Content Knowledge
- Citizenship Education: Content Knowledge
- Mathematics: Content Knowledge
- Middle School: Science
- Middle School: Social Studies
- Middle School: Mathematics
- Biology: Content Knowledge
- Chemistry: Content Knowledge
- Earth and Space Sciences: Content Knowledge
- Physics: Content Knowledge

SOCIAL STUDIES: CONTENT KNOWLEDGE (0081)

2 hours   130 multiple-choice questions

The Social Studies: Content Knowledge test is designed to determine whether an examinee has the knowledge and skills necessary for a beginning teacher of social studies in a secondary school. The test requires the examinee to understand and apply social studies knowledge, concepts, methodologies, and skills across the fields of United States history (22 percent); world history (22 percent); government/civics/political science (16 percent); geography (15 percent); economics (15 percent); and the behavioral science (10 percent).

A number of the questions are interdisciplinary, reflecting the complex relationships among the social studies fields. Answering the questions correctly requires knowing, interpreting, and integrating history and social science facts and concepts.

The 130 equally weighted multiple-choice questions consist of no more than 60 percent knowledge, recall, and/or recognition questions and no less than 40 percent higher-order thinking questions. Some questions are based on interpreting material such as written passages, maps, charts, graphs, tables, cartoons, diagrams, and photographs. Between 10 and 15 percent of the questions contain content reflecting the diverse experiences of people in the United States as related to gender, culture, and/or race, and/or content relating to Latin America, Africa, Asia, or Oceania.

Note: This examination uses the chronological designations B.C.E. (before the common era) and C.E. (common era). These labels correspond to B.C. (before Christ) and A.D. (anno Domini), which are used in some world history textbooks.

CITIZENSHIP EDUCATION: CONTENT KNOWLEDGE (0087)

2 hours   115 multiple-choice questions

The Citizenship Education: Content Knowledge test is designed to determine whether an examinee has the knowledge and skills necessary for a beginning teacher of citizenship education in a secondary school. The test requires the examinee to understand and apply knowledge, concepts, methodologies, and skills across the fields of United States history (25 percent); world history (25 percent); government/civics/political science (18 percent); geography (16 percent); and economics (16 percent). A number of the questions are interdisciplinary, reflecting the complex relationships among the social studies fields. Answering the questions correctly requires knowing, interpreting, and integrating history and social science facts and concepts.

The 115 equally weighted multiple-choice questions consist of no more than 60 percent knowledge, recall, and/or recognition questions and no less than 40 percent higher-order thinking questions. Some questions are based on interpreting material such as written passages, maps, charts, graphs, tables, cartoons, diagrams, and photographs. Between 10 and 15 percent of the questions contain content reflecting the diverse experiences of people in the United States as related to gender, culture, and/or race, and/or content relating to Latin America, Africa, Asia, or Oceania.

MATHEMATICS: CONTENT KNOWLEDGE (0061)

2 hours   50 multiple-choice questions, graphing calculator required

The Mathematics: Content Knowledge test is designed to assess the mathematical knowledge and competencies necessary for a beginning teacher of secondary school mathematics. Examinees have typically completed a bachelor's program with an emphasis in mathematics or mathematics education. The examinee will be required to understand and work with mathematical concepts, to reason mathematically, to make conjectures, to see patterns, to justify statements by using informal logical arguments, and to construct simple proofs. Additionally, the examinee will be expected to solve problems by integrating knowledge from different areas of mathematics, to use various representations of concepts, to solve problems that have several solution paths, and to develop mathematical models and use them to solve real-world problems.

The test is not designed to be aligned with any particular school mathematics curriculum, but it is intended to be consistent with the recommendations of national studies on mathematics education, such as the National Council of Teachers of Mathematics (NCTM) *Principles and Standards for School Mathematics* (2000) and the National Council for Accreditation of Teacher Education (NCATE) *Program Standards for Initial Preparation of Mathematics Teachers* (2003). Graphing calculators without QWERTY (typewriter) keyboards are required for this test. Some questions will require the use of a calculator. Because many test questions may be solved in more than one way, examinees should first decide how to solve each problem and then, decide whether to use a calculator. On the test day, examinees should bring a calculator they are comfortable using. Selected notations, formulas, and definitions are printed in the test book.

MIDDLE SCHOOL: SCIENCE (0439)

2 hours   90 multiple-choice questions (Part A)
                 3 constructed-response questions (Part B)

The Middle School: Science test is designed to measure the knowledge and competencies necessary for a beginning teacher of middle school science, such as knowledge of scientific principles, facts, methodology, philosophy, scientific concepts, and an ability to integrate basic knowledge from all the sciences. Teachers need to understand the subject matter from a more advanced viewpoint than is actually presented to the students. Accordingly, some questions of a more advanced nature are included. These questions deal with topics typically introduced in freshman college-level courses in chemistry, physics, life sciences, and Earth/space sciences. The questions require a variety of abilities, including definition of terms, comprehension of critical concepts, application, and analysis, to address and solve problems. Some questions may require the examinee to integrate concepts from more than one content area.

The constructed-response questions assess the examinee's ability to use and analyze critical concepts in science and to integrate knowledge from science, technology, and society. One question deals with a topic in the physical sciences (chemistry/physics), the second with a topic in the life sciences, and the third with a topic in the Earth/space sciences. One question will assess an examinee's understanding of concepts and models; the second will assess skills in data analysis, experimental design, and investigations; and the third will assess understanding of the patterns and processes that occur in natural systems. In addition, one of the questions will contain a component that assesses the ability to deal with issues concerning science, technology, and society.

The 90 multiple-choice questions make up 75 percent of the total score. The 3 equally weighted constructed-response questions make up 25 percent of the total score. Examinees should plan to allow about 90 minutes for the multiple-choice section and about 30 minutes for the constructed-response section.

MIDDLE SCHOOL: SOCIAL STUDIES (0089)

2 hours   90 multiple-choice questions (Part A)

                      3 constructed-response questions (Part B)

The Middle School: Social Studies test assesses the knowledge and skills necessary for a beginning middle school social studies teacher. The test is based on the understanding and application of social studies knowledge, concepts, methodologies, and skills across the fields of U.S. History, world history, government/civics, geography, economics, sociology, and anthropology. Some of the multiple-choice and all the short essay questions are interdisciplinary, reflecting the complex relationship among the social studies fields. Some questions are based on interpreting stimulus material such as written passages, maps, charts, graphs, tables, cartoons, diagrams, and photographs.

The three equally weighted short-answer/essay questions will focus on important historical events and issues as well as on fundamental social studies concepts. These questions, which should take about 10 minutes each to complete and will together comprise 25 percent of the examinee's score, will emphasize the exercise of critical-thinking skills, requiring the reading and interpreting of social studies materials (such as maps, charts, quotations), drawing inferences from such materials, and placing these materials in their historical, geographical, political, and economic contexts. The 90 equally weighted multiple-choice questions will constitute 75 percent of the examinee's score. Examinees should plan to spend about 90 minutes on the multiple-choice section and about 30 minutes on the constructed response section.

MIDDLE SCHOOL: MATHEMATICS (0069)

2 hours   40 multiple-choice questions (Part A)

                      3 short constructed-response questions (Part B)

The Middle School: Mathematics test is designed to certify examinees as teachers of middle school mathematics. Examinees have typically completed a bachelor's program with an emphasis in mathematics education, mathematics, or education. Course work will have included many of the following topics: theory of arithmetic, foundations of mathematics, geometry for elementary and middle school teachers, algebra for elementary and middle school teachers, the big ideas of calculus, data and their uses, elementary discrete mathematics, elementary probability and statistics, history of mathematics, mathematics appreciation, and the use of technology in mathematics education. The examinee will be required to understand and work with mathematical concepts, to reason mathematically, to make conjectures, to see patterns, to justify statements using informal logical arguments, and to construct simple proofs.

Additionally, the examinee will be expected to solve problems by integrating knowledge from different areas of mathematics, to use various representations of concepts, to solve problems that have several solution paths, and to develop mathematical models and use them to solve real-world problems.

The 40 multiple-choice questions make up 67 percent of the total score. The 3 constructed-response questions make up 33 percent of the total score. Examinees should plan to spend 80 minutes on the multiple-choice section and 40 minutes on the constructed-response questions.

Examinees are allowed to use a four-function, a scientific, or a graphing calculator during the examination; however, calculators with QWERTY keyboards will not be allowed. More information on the calculator use policy for *Praxis* tests can be found at www.ets.org/praxis/prxcalc.html. The test is not designed to be aligned with any particular school mathematics curriculum, but it is intended to be consistent with the recommendations of national studies on mathematics education such as the National Council of Teachers of Mathematics (NCTM) *Principles and Standards for School Mathematics* (2000) and the National Council for Accreditation of Teacher Education (NCATE) *Program Standards for Initial Preparation of Mathematics Teachers* (2003).

BIOLOGY: CONTENT KNOWLEDGE (0235)

2 hours   150 multiple-choice questions

The Biology: Content Knowledge test is designed to assess whether an examinee has the knowledge and competencies necessary for a beginning teacher of biology in a secondary school. The development of the test questions and the construction of the test reflect the National Science Education Standards and recognize that there are conceptual and procedural schemes that unify the various scientific disciplines. The 150 multiple-choice questions are derived from topics typically covered in an introductory college-level biology course. They cover the following content categories: basic principles of science (8 percent); molecular and cellular biology (25 percent); classical genetics and evolution (15 percent); diversity of life, plants, and animals (30 percent); ecology (15 percent); and science, technology, and society (7 percent). Within these content areas, the test questions require a variety of abilities and knowledge, including definition of terms, comprehension of critical concepts, and application and analysis, to address and solve problems.

CHEMISTRY: CONTENT KNOWLEDGE (0245)

2 hours   100 multiple-choice questions

The Chemistry: Content Knowledge test measures the knowledge and competencies necessary for a beginning teacher of chemistry in a secondary school. Examinees have typically completed or nearly completed a bachelor's degree program in chemistry, with appropriate course work in education. The 100 multiple-choice questions address examinees' breadth of knowledge of the physical and philosophical bases of chemistry, and issues related to laboratory practice (including data manipulation and analysis) and the importance of science in the community.

The test covers the following seven broad content areas: matter and energy; heat, thermodynamics and thermochemistry (16 percent), atomic and nuclear structure (10 percent), nomenclature; the mole, chemical bonding, and geometry (14 percent), periodicity and reactivity; chemical reactions; biochemistry and organic chemistry (23 percent), solutions and solubility; acid/base chemistry (12 percent), history and nature of science; science, technology, and social perspectives (11 percent), and mathematics, measurement, and data management; and laboratory procedures and safety (14 percent).

Topics are typically covered in introductory college-level chemistry and physical science courses, although some questions of a more advanced nature are included because secondary school instructors must understand the subject matter from a more advanced viewpoint than that presented to their students.

Examinees are not permitted to use calculators in taking this test. Test books contain a periodic table and a table of information that presents various physical constants and a few conversion factors among SI units. Whenever necessary, additional values of physical constants are printed with the text of the question.

EARTH AND SPACE SCIENCES: CONTENT KNOWLEDGE (0571)

2 hours   100 multiple-choice questions

The Earth and Space Sciences: Content Knowledge test is designed to assess whether an examinee has the knowledge and competencies necessary for a beginning teacher of Earth and space sciences in a secondary school. The 100 multiple-choice questions address the examinee's knowledge of fundamental scientific concepts, methods, principles, phenomena, and interrelationships.

Questions are derived from topics typically covered in introductory college-level courses in Earth and space sciences, including geology, meteorology, oceanography, astronomy, and environmental science. The questions require a variety of abilities, including an emphasis on the comprehension of critical concepts, analysis to address and solve problems, and an understanding of important terms. Some questions may require the examinee to integrate concepts from more than one content area.

The test covers the following six broad content areas: basic scientific principles of Earth and space sciences (8–12 percent); tectonics and internal Earth processes (18–22 percent); Earth materials and surface processes (23–27 percent); history of Earth and its life-forms (13–17 percent); Earth's atmosphere and hydrosphere (18–22 percent); and astronomy (8–12 percent). In addition, a substantial number of the questions require knowledge and/or abilities listed under the content area of history and nature of science.

PHYSICS: CONTENT KNOWLEDGE (0265)

2 hours   100 multiple-choice questions

The Physics: Content Knowledge test measures the knowledge and competencies necessary for a beginning teacher of physics in a secondary school. Examinees have typically completed or nearly completed a bachelor's degree program in physics, with appropriate course work in education. The 100 multiple-choice questions address examinees' breadth of knowledge in physics, embracing scientific principles, facts, methodology, and philosophy in the following content areas: mechanics (32 percent); electricity and magnetism (23 percent); optics and waves (17 percent); heat and thermodynamics (8 percent); modern physics, atomic, and nuclear structure (8 percent); and history and nature of science; and science, technology and social perspectives (STS) (12 percent). Topics are typically covered in an introductory college-level physics course, although some questions of a more advanced nature are included since secondary school instructors must understand the subject matter from a more advanced viewpoint than that presented to their students.

Examinees are not permitted to use calculators in taking this test. The test books contain a periodic table and a table of information that presents various physical constants and a few conversion factors among SI units. Whenever necessary, additional values of physical constants are printed with the text of the question. Also, since a major goal of science education is to have students develop an understanding of science and the impact of science and technology on the environment and human affairs, these areas are included in the assessment. The questions include definition of terms, comprehension of critical concepts, application, analysis, and problem solving.

REAL QUESTIONS FOR PRACTICE

The questions that follow illustrate the types of questions in the test. Answers and Explanations follow the questions.

> **Directions:** Each of the questions or statements below is followed by four suggested answers or completions. Select the one that is best in each case.

Social Studies: Content Knowledge

1. Demographic transition

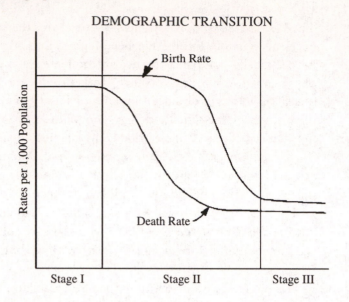

DEMOGRAPHIC TRANSITION

The graph above indicates that rapid population growth is most likely to occur in

(A) stage I only
(B) stage II only
(C) stages I and III only
(D) stages II and III only

Citizenship Education: Content Knowledge

2. Which of the following people would benefit most if the value of the U.S. dollar increased relative to the Japanese yen?

(A) A United States car dealer importing Japanese cars
(B) A Japanese tourist vacationing in the U.S.
(C) A worker in the United States beer industry
(D) A Japanese baker buying U.S. wheat

Mathematics: Content Knowledge

3. Given the recursive function defined by

$f(1) = -3,$
$f(n) = f(n-1) - 6$ $for\ n \geq 2$

what is the value of $f(4)$?

(A) -2
(B) -9
(C) -10
(D) -21

4. For lines in the plane, the relation "is perpendicular to" is

(A) reflexive but not transitive
(B) symmetric but not transitive
(C) transitive but not symmetric
(D) both symmetric and transitive

Middle School: Science

5. Which of the following is most directly involved with controlling levels of sugar in blood?

(A) Hemoglobin
(B) Calcitonin
(C) Thyroid-stimulating hormone
(D) Insulin

Middle School: Social Studies

6. "I was adamant about getting fathers into the labor room and into the delivery room. I was insistent about fathers attending parenting classes. The only way I would take parents was as couples. I wrote an article for a family magazine and encouraged them to put a father holding a baby on the cover. Today we see fathers pushing baby strollers, carrying babies on slings. We see men doing commercials for diapers and showing tender loving care. There have been tremendous changes. It is no longer considered 'unmasculine' to be affectionate."

The quote above is from a 1987 interview with an obstetrician who has been practicing medicine for decades. The changes mentioned by the obstetrician refer to changes in social

(A) regulations
(B) norms
(C) policies
(D) instincts

ROBIN'S TEST SCORES

| 88, 86, 98, 92, 90, 86 |

7. In an ordered set of numbers, the median is the middle number if there is a middle number; otherwise, the median is the average of the two middle numbers. If Robin had the test scores given in the table above, what was her median score?

(A) 89
(B) 90
(C) 92
(D) 95

Biology: Content Knowledge

8. A visual representation of an individual's chromosomes that have been stained, photographed, enlarged, and arranged in order of size from largest to smallest is known as a

(A) karyotype
(B) linkage map
(C) pedigree chart
(D) DNA fingerprint

Chemistry: Content Knowledge

9. The solubility product, K_{sp}, for $Mg(OH)_2$ is 1.0×10^{11}. What is the concentration of Mg^{2+} in a saturated solution of this base?

(A) $\sqrt[2]{5.0 \times 10^{-12}}$ M
(B) $\sqrt{1.0 \times 10^{-11}}$ M
(C) $\sqrt[3]{2.5 \times 10^{-12}}$ M
(D) $\sqrt[3]{1.0 \times 10^{-11}}$ M

10. When 0.50 mol of octane, C_8H_{18}, is burned completely and the reaction products are brought to 10°C and 1 atm, the products include approximately

(A) 18 mol of water
(B) 100 L of carbon dioxide
(C) 200 L of carbon dioxide
(D) 220 L of water vapor

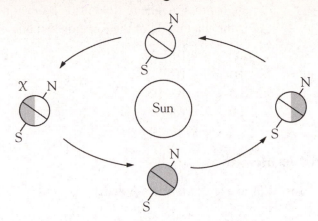

11. In the illustration above of the Earth's orbit about the Sun, which of the following is true of the Earth at location *X*?

(A) The spring equinox occurs.
(B) The fall equinox occurs.
(C) It is winter in the northern hemisphere.
(D) It is summer in the northern hemisphere.

12. Which of the following has provided evidence that the Sun's atmosphere contains sodium atoms?

(A) Stars with the same spectral class as the Sun are made mostly of sodium.
(B) The Sun gives off energy produced by the nuclear fusion of sodium in its core.
(C) Light from the Sun has absorption lines that are consistent with the presence of sodium.
(D) Solar samples returned to Earth by the Voyager spacecraft contained sodium.

Physics: Content Knowledge

13. In a test of an automobile air bag, a mannequin with a mass of 70 kilograms hits a stationary air bag. The velocity of the mannequin at the instant of impact is 25 meters per second. After 0.25 second the mannequin has come to a complete stop and the air bag has deflated. The average force on the mannequin during this interval is most nearly

(A) 70 N
(B) 700 N
(C) 7,000 N
(D) 70,000 N

14. If electrons have a velocity of 4.0×10^6 meters per second at right angles to a magnetic field of 0.20 newton per ampere-meter, what is the magnitude of the force on a single electron?

(A) 1.3×10^{-13} N
(B) 1.6×10^{-14} N
(C) 6.4×10^{-19} N
(D) 3.2×10^{-26} N

Answers and Explanations

Social Studies: Content Knowledge

1. The correct answer is choice B. In stages I and III, birth and death rates are approximately equal. Therefore, the rate of natural increase (population growth) would be quite low, even in the first stage in which the birth rate is high. In stage II, a decline in the death rate precedes a decline in the birth rate. It is in this middle stage that rapid and dramatic population growth would occur.

Citizenship Education: Content Knowledge

2. The correct answer is choice A. Appreciation in the value of the dollar results in a decline in the relative cost of importing foreign goods. An importer of foreign goods would thus benefit. U.S. goods would be relatively more expensive, so choices B and D are incorrect. Choice C is also incorrect; a change in the value of the dollar would have no beneficial effect on a worker in the U.S. beer industry.

Mathematics: Content Knowledge

3. The correct answer is choice D. Given the recursive function defined in the question, in order to find $f(4)$, you need first to find $f(2)$ and $f(3)$. [$f(1)$ is given.]

$$\text{Since } f(1) = -3 \text{ and } f(n) = f(n-1) - 6$$
$$f(2) = -3 - 6 = -9$$
$$\text{for } n \geq 2, \text{ then } f(3) = -9 - 6 = -15$$
$$f(4) = -15 - 6 = -21$$

4. The correct answer is choice B. To answer this question, you must read each answer choice and find the statement that correctly describes the properties of the relation defined as "is perpendicular to." You can see that each answer choice includes two of three properties: reflexivity, symmetry, or transitivity. It may be most efficient to first consider each of these properties and then, find the statement that describes these properties correctly for the given relation. The definition of these properties can be found in the Notation,

Definitions, and Formulas pages that are included in this document and at the beginning of each of the Mathematics: Content Knowledge tests.

A relation $\Re$ is reflexive if $x \Re x$ for all x. In this case, a line cannot be perpendicular to itself, so the relation given in the question is *not* reflexive. A relation $\Re$ is symmetric if $x \Re y \rightarrow y \Re x$ for all x and y. In this case, if line j is perpendicular to line k, it follows that line k is perpendicular to line j. So this relation is symmetric. A relation $\Re$ is transitive if $(x \Re y$ and $y \Re z) \rightarrow x \Re z$ for all x, y, and z. In this case, if line j is perpendicular to line k and line k is perpendicular to line l, then lines j and l either are the same line or are parallel to each other. Thus, line j is not perpendicular to line l. So this relation is not transitive. The answer choice that correctly describes the relation "is perpendicular to" is choice B, "symmetric but not transitive."

Middle School: Science

5. The correct answer is choice D. In response to rising levels of glucose in the blood, cells in the pancreas secrete the hormone insulin. Circulating insulin lowers blood sugar levels by enhancing the transport of glucose and other simple sugars into body cells, especially muscle cells.

Middle School: Social Studies

6. The correct answer is choice B. The obstetrician is discussing changes in people's learned behavior made through education, encouragement, and example. No actions by government or another official body are mentioned, therefore, eliminating regulations (choice A) and policies (choice C). Instincts (choice D) are not learned behavior, but rather are innate and would not be affected by the obstetrician's actions. "Norms," society's often unwritten and unspoken rules, serve to guide and control proper and acceptable behavior and can be affected by the type of actions that the obstetrician describes taking.

Middle School: Mathematics

7. The correct answer is choice A. The problem gives a set of test scores and the definition of median. The first part of the definition tells you to order the scores, that is, to arrange them in order from smallest to largest. Here are the numbers ordered from smallest to largest:

$$86, 86, 88, 90, 92, 98$$

Because there are an even number of scores (6), there are two middle numbers in the set, 88 and 90, and the average of the two middle numbers is

$$\frac{88+90}{2} = \frac{178}{2} = 89$$

Thus the median of Robin's scores is 89 and the answer is choice A. (Notice that the median of a set of numbers need not be one of the numbers in the set.)

Biology: Content Knowledge

8. The correct answer is choice A. A karyotype is basically a pictorial representation of the chromosomes contained in a cell.

Chemistry: Content Knowledge

9. The correct answer is choice C.
The K_{sp} of a salt is the product of the ion concentrations in a saturated solution. In the present case, $K_{sp} = [Mg^{2+}] [OH^-]^2$.
Since $[OH^-] = 2[Mg^{2+}]$, $K_{sp} = [Mg^{2+}] (2[Mg^{2+}])^2 = 4[Mg^{2+}]3 = 1.0 \times 10^{-11}$.
Solving for $[Mg^{2+}]$, one obtains $[Mg^{2+}] = [1 \times 10^{-11}/4]^{1/3}$.

10. The correct answer is choice B.
The balanced equation for the reaction is
$2C_8H_{18} + 25O_2 \rightarrow 16CO_2 + 18H_2O$.
0.5 mol octane produces 4 mol of CO_2, which at 10°C STP, occupies

$$\frac{(4\,mol \times 22.4\,L/mol)\,293\,K}{273\,K} = 96\,L \cong 100\,L$$

Earth and Space Sciences: Content Knowledge

11. The correct answer is choice D. When Earth is at location X, the northern hemisphere receives the most direct rays of the Sun and experiences the greatest number of daylight hours. Under these conditions, it is summer in the northern hemisphere.

12. The correct answer is choice C. The chemical composition of the Sun's atmosphere has been inferred primarily from absorption lines observed in the solar spectrum.

Physics: Content Knowledge

13. The correct answer is choice C.
The average force $\bar{F}$ is equal in magnitude to the change in the momentum of the mannequin divided by the elapsed time, or

$$\bar{F} = \frac{m\,\Delta V}{\Delta t} = \frac{(70\,kg)(25\,m/s)}{0.25s} = 7,000\,N$$

14. The correct answer is choice A.
According to the Lorentz force law, $F = qvB = (1.6 \times 10^{-19}\,C) (4.0 \times 10^6\,m/s) (0.20\,N/Am) = 1.3 \times 10^{-13}\,N$.

CHAPTER 20

Other Subjects

This chapter covers the following Subject Assessments:

- Spanish: Content Knowledge
- French: Content Knowledge
- German: Content Knowledge
- Business Education
- Art: Content Knowledge
- Physical Education: Content Knowledge
- Health Education
- Audiology
- Speech-Language Pathology
- ParaPro Assessment

SPANISH: CONTENT KNOWLEDGE (0191)

2 hours   120 multiple-choice questions based on recorded and printed materials in Spanish

The Spanish: Content Knowledge test is designed to assess the knowledge and competencies necessary for a beginning or entry-year teacher of Spanish. The 120 multiple-choice questions measure the test-takers' competence in various language skills and their knowledge of the cultures of Spanish-speaking regions. The test contains the following four sections: I. Interpretive Listening (27 percent); II. Structure of the Language (28 percent); III. Interpretive Reading (26 percent); and IV. Cultural Perspectives (19 percent). In the first, third, and fourth sections, all questions and answer choices are in Spanish. All the questions in the Interpretive Listening section, as well as the first part of the Structure of the Language section, are based on recorded materials.

FRENCH: CONTENT KNOWLEDGE (0173)

2 hours   120 multiple-choice questions based on recorded and printed materials in French

The French: Content Knowledge test is designed to assess the knowledge and competencies necessary for a beginning or entry-year teacher of French. The 120 multiple-choice questions measure the test-takers' competence in various language skills and their knowledge of the cultures of France and French-speaking regions.

The test contains the following four sections: I. Interpretive Listening (27 percent); II. Structure of the Language (28 percent); III. Interpretive Reading (26 percent); and IV. Cultural Perspectives (19 percent). In the first, third, and fourth sections, all questions and answer choices are in French. All the questions in the Interpretive Listening section, as well as the first part of the Structure of the Language section, are based on recorded materials.

GERMAN: CONTENT KNOWLEDGE (0181)

2 hours   120 multiple-choice questions based on recorded and printed materials in German

The German: Content Knowledge test is designed to assess the knowledge and competencies necessary for a beginning or entry-year teacher of German. The 120 multiple-choice questions measure the test-takers' competence in various language skills and their knowledge of the cultures of Germany and German-speaking regions. The test contains the following four sections: I. Interpretive Listening (27 percent); II. Structure of the Language (28 percent); III. Interpretive Reading (26 percent); and IV. Cultural Perspectives (19 percent). In the first, third, and fourth sections, all questions and answer choices are in German. All the questions in the Interpretive Listening section, as well as the first part of the Structure of the Language section, are based on recorded materials.

BUSINESS EDUCATION (0100)

2 hours   120 multiple-choice questions

The Business Education test is intended primarily for persons planning to teach in business education programs at the high school level. The test concentrates on the core of knowledge and cognitive skills common to all business teachers, including content that contributes to business and economic literacy. Also included are questions about professional information related to business education in general and questions about areas of specialization within business education. Because of the variations among business education programs, some questions may refer to areas that may not have been studied. Therefore, no one is expected to answer all the questions on the test correctly. In general, the topics concern areas broadly defined as business and economic literacy; professional business education, including knowledge, comprehension, and application of pedagogical techniques; and business specialization, including specific background and application knowledge considered essential for a business education teacher.

The examination is typically taken by examinees who have completed a bachelor's degree program in education with appropriate course work in business education. Examinees are allowed to use a calculator during the examination. Calculators with QWERTY keyboards will not be allowed.

ART: CONTENT KNOWLEDGE (0133)

2 hours   120 multiple-choice questions

The Art: Content Knowledge test is intended primarily for individuals completing teacher training programs who plan to become art teachers. The multiple-choice test questions focus on those concepts that are considered central to the subject matter of art. The test measures knowledge of the traditions in art, architecture, design, and the making of artifacts (36 percent); art criticism and aesthetics (25 percent); and the making of art (39 percent). Illustrations may be included with some of the questions. The majority of these illustrations are printed in color. Test-takers have typically completed a bachelor's degree program in art or art education.

PHYSICAL EDUCATION: CONTENT KNOWLEDGE (0091)

2 hours   120 multiple-choice questions

The Physical Education: Content Knowledge test is designed to measure the professional knowledge of prospective teachers of physical education in elementary through senior high schools. The test assesses whether an examinee has the knowledge and competencies necessary for a beginning teacher of physical education.

The 120 multiple-choice questions cover knowledge of fitness, fundamental movements, and sports that comprise the content of physical education classes; knowledge of areas in the natural and social sciences that provide the foundation for teaching these activities; and knowledge of crucial topics in health and safety. Knowledge of these subject areas enables teachers to understand the nature and purpose of the activities in the physical education curriculum; to evaluate and interpret the physical characteristics and performances of students in physical education classes; and to make decisions about the ongoing conduct of physical education classes and the needs of students in those classes. Questions will test knowledge of essential facts, including the meaning of terms and placement of content elements in proper categories; understanding of relationships between and among areas of content; and the ability to apply concepts appropriately.

HEALTH EDUCATION (0550)

2 hours   120 multiple-choice questions

The Health Education test is designed to measure the professional knowledge of prospective teachers of health education in elementary schools, junior high schools, and senior high schools. The questions invite examinees to recall basic knowledge and to apply education and health principles to real-life situations. The content is appropriate for examinees who have completed a bachelor's degree program in health education. The 120 multiple-choice questions cover health education as a discipline (15 percent); promoting healthy lifestyles (30 percent); community health advocacy (10 percent); healthy relationships (20 percent); disease prevention (15 percent); and health education pedagogy (10 percent).

AUDIOLOGY (0340)

2 hours   120 multiple-choice questions

The Audiology test measures knowledge important for independent practice as an audiologist in all primary employment settings including schools, hospitals, clinics, private practice, etc. The examination assesses knowledge important for the beginning practitioner in all primary employment settings. The examination is typically taken by examinees who are in or who have completed a master's or doctoral degree program that prepares individuals to enter professional practice. Recognized as the national examination in audiology, the test is one of several requirements for the Certificate of Clinical Competence issued by the American Speech-Language-Hearing Association (ASHA). Some states use the examination as part of the licensure procedure. Examinees may obtain complete information about certification or licensure from the authority (ASHA, 2200 Research Boulevard, Rockville, MD 20850) or state or local agency from which certification or licensure is sought.

The 120 multiple-choice test questions focus on content related to the major practice areas of basic human communication processes, prevention, identification, behavioral assessment and interpretation, electrophysiological measurement and interpretation, rehabilitative assessment, rehabilitative technology, rehabilitative management, and professional issues/psychometrics/research. Case studies assess the candidate's knowledge of possible applications to clinical situations and issues. Research articles are included to assess the examinee's ability to synthesize information and to apply it to specific examples. The distribution of the test questions across the areas of practice was based on a national survey, commissioned by ASHA, of audiologists in a variety of employment settings. The Audiology test is regularly updated to take into account new developments in the field.

SPEECH-LANGUAGE PATHOLOGY (0330)

2 hours   120 multiple-choice questions

The Speech-Language Pathology test measures knowledge important for independent practice as a speech-language pathologist in all primary employment settings, including schools, hospitals, clinics, private practice, etc. The examination assesses knowledge important for the beginning practitioner in all primary employment settings. The examination is typically taken by examinees who are in or who have completed a master's degree program. Recognized as the national examination in speech-language pathology, the test is one of several requirements for the Certificate of Clinical Competence issued by the American Speech-Language-Hearing Association (ASHA, 2200 Research Boulevard, Rockville, MD 20850). Some states use the examination as part of the licensure procedure. Examinees may obtain complete information about certification or licensure from the authority or state or local agency from which certification or licensure is sought.

The 120 multiple-choice test questions focus on content related to the major practice areas of basic human communication processes, phonological and language disorders, speech disorders, neurogenic disorders, audiology/hearing, clinical management, and professional issues/psychometrics/research. Case studies assess the examinee's knowledge of possible applications to clinical situations and issues. Research articles are included to assess the examinee's ability to synthesize information and to apply it to specific examples.

The distribution of the test questions across the areas of practice was based on a national survey, commissioned by ASHA, of speech-language pathologists in a variety of employment settings. The Speech-Language Pathology test is regularly updated to take into account new developments in the field.

PARAPRO ASSESSMENT (0755)

2½ hours   90 multiple-choice questions

The ParaPro Assessment for prospective and practicing paraprofessionals measures skills and knowledge in reading, mathematics, and writing, as well as the ability to apply those skills and knowledge to assist in classroom instruction. The test consists of 90 multiple-choice questions across the three subject areas of reading, mathematics, and writing. Approximately two-thirds of the questions in each subject area focus on basic skills and knowledge, and approximately one-third of the questions in each subject area focus on the application of those skills and knowledge in a classroom context. This test may contain some questions that do not count toward your score. The test questions are arranged by subject area, with reading first, then mathematics, and finally writing.

REAL QUESTIONS FOR PRACTICE

The following real test questions illustrate the types of items on the actual exams. Answers and explanations follow the last question.

> **Directions:** Each of the questions or statements below is followed by four or five suggested answers or completions. Select the one that is best in each case.

Spanish: Content Knowledge

1. Un magnífico ejemplo de la arquitectura Inca es:

(A) Chichén Itzá
(B) Machu Picchu
(C) Tikal
(D) Teotihuacán

French: Content Knowledge

2. À quelle heure les gens ont-ils le plus de chance de dîner en France?

(A) 15h30
(B) 16h30
(C) 20h00
(D) 23h00

German: Content Knowledge

3. Welches der folgenden Länder grenzt an Österreich?

(A) Polen
(B) Rumänien
(C) Ungarn
(D) Frankreich

4. Das Ruhrgebiet ist allgemein bekannt

(A) für seinen Weinanbau
(B) als populäres Ferienziel
(C) für seine Milchwirtschaft
(D) als Industrieregion

Business Education

5. In connection with the purchase of a house, the term "abstract" refers to a document that

(A) transfers the title of the property from one party to another
(B) provides a history of the ownership of the property
(C) quits a claim against a property that one may have held at any time
(D) guarantees that there is no encumbrance against the property
(E) certifies that the records of the property have been examined

6. The flowchart symbol ∇ means that data are

(A) collated
(B) displayed
(C) sorted
(D) stored off-line
(E) handled manually

Art: Content Knowledge

7. In painting, which of the following techniques generally makes the objects in a composition appear closer to the viewer?

(A) Drawing the objects as relatively large compared with other objects in the composition
(B) Drawing the objects in three-point rather than two-point perspective
(C) Using analogous colors for all the objects that are in the fore-ground
(D) Outlining the objects in black or dark colors

8. In storing printmaking supplies, it is most important to store which of the following separately from the other materials?

(A) Acetic acid
(B) Rosin powder
(C) Nitric acid
(D) Solvents

Physical Education: Content Knowledge

9. Which of the following practice alternatives would best promote motor learning and safety for potentially injurious sports such as pole vaulting and downhill skiing?

(A) Whole
(B) Part
(C) Progressive-part
(D) Distributed

10. All of the following are direct physiological consequences of warm-down (cool-down) activities following vigorous physical activity EXCEPT

(A) preventing blood from pooling in the legs
(B) increasing the rate of lactic acid removal from the blood and skeletal muscle
(C) promoting the reduction of cholesterol in the blood
(D) reducing the risk of cardiac irregularities

Health Education

11. Amniocentesis is most often used to

(A) facilitate artificial insemination
(B) measure immune response capability in transplant recipients
(C) determine the presence of certain disorders in the fetus
(D) estimate the mother's potential for maintaining a pregnancy to term

12. Compared to younger women, women over age 35 have an increased risk of giving birth to children with which of the following genetic disorders?

(A) Cystic fibrosis
(B) Down syndrome
(C) Hemophilia
(D) Sickle cell anemia

Audiology

13. In the measurement of real-ear sound-pressure levels with a probe-tube microphone system, insufficient probe-tube depth will tend to

(A) increase the high-frequency response
(B) decrease the high-frequency response
(C) decrease the response at all frequencies
(D) decrease the low-frequency response
(E) increase the low-frequency response

14. Click-evoked otoacoustic emissions are most likely to be recorded from the ears of which of the following individuals?

(A) A person with a profound hearing loss
(B) A person with severe presbycusis
(C) A person with an upper brain stem lesion
(D) A person with otitis media
(E) A person who has ingested large quantities of aminoglycosides

Speech-Language Pathology

15. A speech-language pathologist is behaving ethically if he or she does which of the following?

(A) Refuses to deliver professional services on the basis of a client's sexual orientation

(B) Offers to provide speech or language services solely by correspondence for an individual whose handicapping condition prevents easy access to the professional's office

(C) Diagnoses a speech disorder solely through correspondence as long as the correspondence is thorough and careful

(D) Offers general information of an educational nature by correspondence

(E) Indicates the specific duration of the therapeutic program

16. Which of the following statements best characterizes the ethics of formulating prognoses for clients with speech and language disorders?

(A) No assessment is complete until a precise statement can be formulated regarding the prognosis.

(B) Since offering a favorable prognosis is essentially equivalent to guaranteeing the results of a therapy program, it is unethical to make specific statements regarding prognosis.

(C) The extreme complexity of speech and language processes and behaviors makes it impossible to formulate prognoses.

(D) After an assessment has been completed, it is usually appropriate to make some general statements about prognosis.

(E) A clinician's ability to make prognostic statements depends on the availability of standardized tests to quantify the severity of a speech and language disorder.

ParaPro Assessment

Questions 17 and 18 are based on the following rough draft written by a student.

How to Teach Your Dog to Sit by Kiara

(1) First hold a dog biscuit so the dog pays attention. (2) Say "Sit!" (3) When you say it, use a loud and firm voice. (4) Move the hand holding the biscuit over the dog's nose, don't let him grab it. (5) You may have to give a light backwards tug on the dog's leash. (6) When the dog sits down, give him the treat and lots of praise. (7) Repeat this a few times, and he'll probably understand the command.

17. Kiara is writing an introductory sentence that summarizes the main points of the paragraph. What sentence would be the strongest introductory sentence for the paragraph?

(A) Dogs are naturally very intelligent and obedient.
(B) Your dog probably likes some dog biscuits better than others.
(C) It is easy to teach your dog the command "Sit!"
(D) Nobody likes a dog that can't play catch.

18. Kiara is learning how to use transition words (words that clarify the relationships between ideas). What transition word or words should Kiara use before the word "don't" in sentence 4 in order to clarify the meaning of the sentence?

(A) "but"
(B) "because"
(C) "for example"
(D) "so"

Answers and Explanations

Spanish: Content Knowledge

1. The correct answer is choice B. Machu Picchu was built by the Incas.

French: Content Knowledge

2. The correct answer is choice C. "Le dîner" (dinner) generally takes place around *"20 heures"* (8 o'clock in the evening). The other choices (3:30 p.m., 4:30 p.m., 11:00 p.m.) are not likely times for French people to have dinner.

German: Content Knowledge

3. The correct answer is choice C because Hungary borders Austria.
4. The correct answer is choice D because das Ruhrgebiet is the largest industrial area in Germany.

Business Education

5. The correct answer is choice B. An abstract of title provides a listing of the transfers of title to land. It is often obtained by a buyer as a means of protection, but it is not a guarantee.
6. The correct answer is choice D. The shape pictured is the standard symbol for off-line storage.

Art: Content Knowledge

7. The correct answer is choice A. Relative size is a powerful tool for making objects appear closer or farther away in pictorial space. The other techniques listed do not affect the viewer's impression of the nearness of the objects.

8. The correct answer is choice C. Nitric acid is an oxidizing agent that can react with any of the other supplies to cause an explosion or fire.

Physical Education: Content Knowledge

9. The correct answer is choice C. It describes a method of practice that involves working on specific elements of a skill in isolation. This method allows those elements of a skill that present the greatest risk of injury to be mastered under controlled conditions, before the skill is attempted "whole" and under real conditions.

10. The correct answer is choice C. This question is based on a standard textbook discussion of the rationale for warm-down following vigorous physical activity, which clearly establishes choices A, B, and D as real effects of proper warm-down procedures.

Health Education

11. The correct answer is choice C. Amniocentesis involves the removal and examination of a small sample of cells from the amniotic cavity, enabling doctors to detect genetic disorders.

12. The correct answer is choice B. The incidence of Down syndrome increases with the age of the mother. In the United States, for example, among mothers in the age range 20 to 30, about 1 in 800 newborns has Down syndrome, whereas the incidence of Down syndrome in newborns of mothers over age 40 is 1 in 100.

Audiology

13. The correct answer is choice B. Probe tubes for measuring real-ear sound-pressure levels (SPLs) should be inserted as close to the tympanic membrane as possible, since it is the SPL at the tympanic membrane that is being measured. If the probe tube is too far from the tympanic membrane, high-frequency sound waves bounced off the eardrum will dissipate before reaching the probe, but low-frequency sound waves, which do not dissipate as easily, will be essentially unaffected. The overall effect will thus be a decrease only in the high-frequency response.

14. The correct answer is choice C. Upper brainstem lesions do not always interfere with otoacoustic emissions, so otoacoustic emissions can be recorded from the ears of persons with upper brain stem lesions. Choices A, B, and E are incorrect because severe or profound hearing loss and ototoxic medications such as aminoglycosides cause a loss of spontaneous emissions. Choice D is incorrect because transmission of emissions is poor when the impedance of the middle ear is abnormal, as in cases of otitis media.

Speech-Language Pathology

15. The correct answer is choice D. According to the 1995 Code of Ethics of the American Speech-Language-Hearing Association (ASHA), the best answer, choice D, is allowed. The other choices are not approved and are discussed in Principle of Ethics I, Rule C, Rule F, and Rule G, among others.

16. The correct answer is choice D. According to the 1995 ASHA Code of Ethics, Principle of Ethics I, Rule F, a speech-language pathologist can make general statements about a client's prognosis. The other choices are contrary to the spirit of this ethical position.

ParaPro Assessment

17. The correct answer is choice C. Kiara's paragraph is concerned with discussing what steps to take when teaching a dog to sit. Choice A is too general, choice B concerns a minor element of the paragraph, not its primary focus, and choice D concerns playing catch, which is not discussed in the paragraph at all.

18. The correct answer is choice A. The word "but" is used to emphasize the contrast expressed in the sentence: "Move the hand holding the biscuit over the dog's nose, **but** don't let him grab it."

Passing Scores by Test and State

This chapter lists the passing scores for Praxis tests by test and state. Because guidelines vary widely between states, **before you register for a test, we strongly urge you to review your state requirements in more depth by contacting the appropriate agency for your state**. A list of contact information for each state appears in Appendix B. States that are not listed do not support the *Praxis* series of tests.

THE **PRAXIS**™
S E R I E S

The Praxis Series™ Passing Scores by Test and State

This list shows the minimum/passing scores of user states/agencies for **The Praxis Series** tests. To determine if you passed a test in a particular state, compare your test score with the score listed for the state in which you are interested and read all related footnotes. If your scaled score equals or exceeds the printed score for that state, you have passed. (**Note:** Number in parentheses following the test name is the test code.) **These scores are current as of May 1, 2009.** Passing score information is subject to change. To verify the latest score information for your state, go to www.ets.org/praxis.

PRAXIS I®: ACADEMIC SKILLS ASSESSMENTS				
PRE-PROFESSIONAL SKILLS TEST: MATHEMATICS (0730)				
COMPUTERIZED PPST®: MATHEMATICS (5730)				
AK - 173	AR - 171	CT - 171	DC - 174	DE - 174
HI - 173[a]	IN - 175	KY - +	LA - 172	MD - 177[d]
ME - [c]	MN - 171	MS - 169	NC - 173[f]	ND - 170[g]
NE - 171	NH - 172[e]	NJ - 174	NV - 172	OH - 172
OK - 171	OR - 175	PA - 173[i]	SC - 172	TN - 173
VA - 178[k]	VT - 175[j]	WI - 173	WV - 172	DODEA - 175
GUAM - 170	VI - 171			

* = Test required – passing score not set – verify with state.
** = Target score for ETS Recognition of Excellence.
+ = Each preparation program may have different requirements. Before registering for Praxis I, please contact your advisor/program coordinator to determine your requirements.

‡ = Multiple scores required – verify with state.
a–k = See state notes at end of this section.

KEY TO AGENCIES:	ASHA = American Speech-Language-Hearing Association	NASP = National Association of School Psychologists
	BCASP = British Columbia Association of School Psychologists	DODEA = Department of Defense Education Activity

PRE-PROFESSIONAL SKILLS TEST: READING (0710)
COMPUTERIZED PPST: READING (5710)

AK - 175	AR - 172	CT - 172	DC - 172	DE - 175
HI - 172[a]	IN - 176	KY - +	LA - 174	MD - 177[d]
ME - [c]	MN - 173	MS - 170	NC - 176[f]	ND - 173[g]
NE - 170	NH - 174[e]	NJ - 175	NV - 174	OH - 173
OK - 173	OR - 174	PA - 172[i]	SC - 175	TN - 174
VA - 178[k]	VT - 177[j]	WI - 175	WV - 174	DODEA - 177
GUAM - 173	VI - 173			

PRE-PROFESSIONAL SKILLS TEST: WRITING (0720)
COMPUTERIZED PPST: WRITING (5720)

AK - 174	AR - 173	CT - 171	DC - 171	DE - 173
HI - 171[a]	IN - 172	KY - +	LA - 173	MD - 173[d]
ME - [c]	MN - 172	MS - 172	NC - 173[f]	ND - 173[g]
NE - 172	NH - 172[e]	NJ - 173	NV - 172	OH - 172
OK - 172	OR - 171	PA - 173[i]	SC - 173	TN - 173
VA - 176[k]	VT - 174[j]	WI - 174	WV - 172	DODEA - 174
GUAM - 170	VI - 172			

PRAXIS II: PRINCIPLES OF LEARNING AND TEACHING (PLT)
PLT: EARLY CHILDHOOD (0521)

AR - 159	HI - 158	KS - 161	LA - 172	MD - 169
ME - 172	MN - 164	OH - 166	SD - 160	TN - 155
UT - 160				

PLT: GRADES K–6 (0522) ** ROE: 185

HI - 163	ID - 161	KS - 161	KY - 161	LA - 161
ME - 166	MN - 159	MS - 152	ND - 162	NV - 169
OH - 168	RI - 167	SC - 165	SD - 153	TN - 155
UT - 160	VI - 162	WV - 165	DODEA - 156	

* = Test required – passing score not set – verify with state.

** = Target score for ETS Recognition of Excellence.

+ = Each preparation program may have different requirements. Before registering for Praxis I, please contact your advisor/program coordinator to determine your requirements.

‡ = Multiple scores required – verify with state.

a–k = See state notes at end of this section.

KEY TO AGENCIES:	ASHA = American Speech-Language-Hearing Association	NASP = National Association of School Psychologists
	BCASP = British Columbia Association of School Psychologists	DODEA = Department of Defense Education Activity

PLT: GRADES 5–9 (0523) ** ROE: 184

AR - 164	HI - 157	ID - 162	KS - 161	KY - 161
LA - 154	MN - 155	MO - 160	MS - 152	OH - 168
SC - 165	SD - 153	TN - 154	UT - 160	WV - 159
WY - 157	DODEA - 153			

PLT: GRADES 7–12 (0524) ** ROE: 184

AR - 164	HI - 157	KS - 161	KY - 161	LA - 161
MD - 162	ME - 162	MN - 157	MO - 160	MS - 152
NV - 161	OH - 165	RI - 167	SC - 165	SD - 153
TN - 159	UT - 160	WV - 156	WY - 161	DODEA - 158

PRAXIS II®: SUBJECT ASSESSMENTS/SPECIALTY AREA TESTS
AGRICULTURE (0700)

AL - 460	AR - 510	DE - 530	ID - 510	KS - 470
KY - 520	LA - 510	MN - 490	MO - 520	SD - 480
TN - 530	UT - *	WA - 520	WI - 510	WV - 430
WY - 540				

AGRICULTURE (CA) (0900)

OR - 590

AGRICULTURE (PA) (0780)

PA - 520

ART MAKING (0131)

AR - 146	CT - 148	KY - 154	NC - [f]	NV - 154
SC - 155	TN - 155	VT - 148		

ART: CONTENT KNOWLEDGE (0133)

AK - 155	AL - 150	AR - 157	CT - 157	DE - 161
HI - 166	ID - 155	IN - 149	KS - 156	KY - 158
LA - 155	MD - 159[d]	ME - 151	MN - 164	MO - 153
MS - 139	NC - [f]	ND - 146	NJ - 150	NV - 156
OH - 157	OR - 156	PA - 161	SC - 149	SD - 143
TN - 150	UT - *	VA - 159	WA - 155	WI - 155
WV - 160	WY - *			

* = Test required – passing score not set – verify with state.

** = Target score for ETS Recognition of Excellence.

+ = Each preparation program may have different requirements. Before registering for Praxis I, please contact your advisor/program coordinator to determine your requirements.

‡ = Multiple scores required – verify with state.

a–k = See state notes at end of this section.

KEY TO AGENCIES:	ASHA = American Speech-Language-Hearing Association	NASP = National Association of School Psychologists
	BCASP = British Columbia Association of School Psychologists	DODEA = Department of Defense Education Activity

ART: CONTENT, TRADITIONS, CRITICISM, & AESTHETICS (0132)

AR - 140	CT - 130	HI - 135	MD - 145[d]	OR - 145
TN - 140				

AUDIOLOGY (0340)

State Departments of Education:　　CO - 600　　MS - 610　　NC - 590

OH - 600　　VT - 600

ASHA and All State Boards of Examiners - 600

BIOLOGY & GENERAL SCIENCE (0030)

OH - 560　　SC - 570

BIOLOGY: CONTENT ESSAYS (0233)

NH - 143　　TN - 146　　VT - 150

BIOLOGY: CONTENT KNOWLEDGE, PART 1 (0231)

HI - 161　　NV - 154　　WV - 148

BIOLOGY: CONTENT KNOWLEDGE (0235) ** ROE: 179

AK - 139	AL - 143	AR - 142	CT - 152	DC - 150
DE - 157	ID - 139	IN - 154	KS - 150	KY - 146
LA - 150	MD - 150	ME - 150	MN - 152	MO - 150
MS - 150	MT - *	NC - [f]	ND - 153	NH - 153
NJ - 152	OH - 148	OR - 153	PA - 147	SD - 147
TN - 148	UT - 149	VA - 155	VT - 151	WA - 152
WV - 152	WY - 148			

BUSINESS EDUCATION (0100)

AL - 570	AR - 550	CT - 620	DE - 600	HI - 570
ID - 580	IN - 480	KS - 590	KY - 590	LA - 570
MD - 590	ME - 560	MN - 610	MO - 590	MS - 560
NC - 580	NJ - 580	NV - 560	OH - 610	OR - 600
PA - 560	SC - 540	SD - 560	TN - 570	UT - 590
VA - 590	WA - 560	WI - 580	WV - 570	WY - *

* = Test required – passing score not set – verify with state.

** = Target score for ETS Recognition of Excellence.

+ = Each preparation program may have different requirements. Before registering for Praxis I, please contact your advisor/program coordinator to determine your requirements.

‡ = Multiple scores required – verify with state.

a–k = See state notes at end of this section.

KEY TO AGENCIES:	ASHA = American Speech-Language-Hearing Association	NASP = National Association of School Psychologists
	BCASP = British Columbia Association of School Psychologists	DODEA = Department of Defense Education Activity

CHEMISTRY: CONTENT ESSAYS (0242)

CT - 140	NH - 140	NV - 145	VT - 150

CHEMISTRY: CONTENT KNOWLEDGE (0241)

HI - 144

CHEMISTRY: CONTENT KNOWLEDGE (0245) ** ROE: 184

AK - 139	AL - 150	CT - 151	DC - 152	DE - 158
ID - 139	IN - 151	KS - 152	KY - 147	LA - 151
MD - 153	MN - 152	MO - 152	MS - 151	MT - *
NC - f	ND - 147	NH - 153	NJ - 152	NV - 151
OH - 152	OR - 146	PA - 154	SD - 135	TN - 152
UT - 151	VA - 153	VT - 160	WA - 152	WV - 157
WY - 151				

CHEMISTRY, PHYSICS, & GENERAL SCIENCE (0070)

AL - 560	MD - 520	OH - 520	OR - 540	SC - 540
UT - 570				

CITIZENSHIP EDUCATION : CK (0087)

PA - 148	RI - 160

COMMUNICATION (0800)

PA - 530

COOPERATIVE EDUCATION (0810)

PA - 770

DRIVER EDUCATION (WV) (0867)

AL - 149	WA - 150	WV - 141	WY - *

EARLY CHILDHOOD EDUCATION (0020)

IN - 510	PA - 530	WV - 530

EARLY CHILDHOOD: CONTENT KNOWLEDGE (0022)

AR - 157	CT - 156	KY - 165	MD - 160	MN - 155
NC - 155	ND - 158	NH - 161	NJ - 159	NV - 158
RI - 169	WY - 143			

* = Test required – passing score not set – verify with state.

** = Target score for ETS Recognition of Excellence.

+ = Each preparation program may have different requirements. Before registering for Praxis I, please contact your advisor/program coordinator to determine your requirements.

‡ = Multiple scores required – verify with state.

a–k = See state notes at end of this section.

KEY TO AGENCIES:	ASHA = American Speech-Language-Hearing Association	NASP = National Association of School Psychologists
	BCASP = British Columbia Association of School Psychologists	DODEA = Department of Defense Education Activity

EARTH AND SPACE SCIENCES: CONTENT KNOWLEDGE (0571)

AK - 144	AL - 150	AR - 145	CT - 157	DE - 150
ID - 144	IN - 150	KS - 150	KY - 145	MD - 152
MN - 149	MO - 147	MT - *	NC - 136	ND - 149
NH - 148	NJ - 153	OH - 151	PA - 157	SD - 150
TN - 146	UT - 153	VA - 156	VT - 158	WA - 150
WY - 150				

ECONOMICS (0910)

AK - 460	AL - 520	ID - 460	MT - *	ND - 510
SD - 500	TN - 530	UT - 560	WY - 510	

ED. LEADERSHIP: ADMINISTRATION & SUPERVISION (0410)

AL - 610	KS - 590	NC - 590	NV - 590	OH - 610
OR - 600	PA - 580	SC - 590	SD - 590	UT - 620
WV - 570				

EDUCATION OF DEAF & HARD OF HEARING STUDENTS (0271)

AR - 160	ID - 162	KS - 163	KY - 167	LA - 160
ME - *	MO - 161	MS - 151	OH - 158	OR - 144
PA - 164	SC - 161	TN - 163	UT - *	WA - 167

EDUCATION OF EXCEPTIONAL STUDENTS: CORE CONTENT KNOWLEDGE (0353)

CT - 158	DC - 146	HI - 152	ID - 156	IN - 150
KS - 160	KY - 157	LA - 143	MD - 148[d]	ME - 157
MN - 158	MO - 160	MS - 136	OH - 160	OR - 162
PA - 136	SC - 150	SD - 150	TN - 144	UT - 155
VI - 148	WA - 152	WV - 146	WY - *	

EDUCATION OF EXCEPTIONAL STUDENTS: LEARNING DISABILITIES (0382)

SC - 158	WV - 133

EDUCATION OF EXCEPTIONAL STUDENTS: MILD TO MODERATE DISABILITIES (0542)

ID - 168	IN - 156	KS - 169	KY - 172	LA - 141
MO - 172	NC - 159	SC - 165	TN - 164	UT - 155
WV - 153				

* = Test required – passing score not set – verify with state.

** = Target score for ETS Recognition of Excellence.

+ = Each preparation program may have different requirements. Before registering for Praxis I, please contact your advisor/program coordinator to determine your requirements.

‡ = Multiple scores required – verify with state.

a–k = See state notes at end of this section.

EDUCATION OF EXCEPTIONAL STUDENTS: SEVERE TO PROFOUND DISABILITIES (0544)

KS - 159	KY - 156[b]	LA - 147	MO - 153	NC - 144
SC - 148	TN - 155	UT - 159	WV - *	

EDUCATION OF YOUNG CHILDREN (0021)

CT - 158	DC - 174	DE - 167	HI - 160	ID - 169
KS - 172	ME - 166	MO - 166	MS - 165	NV - 160
OH - 166	OR - *	RI - 171	SC - 158	SD - 166
TN - 155	UT - 168	WA - 170	WY - *	

ELEM ED.: CONTENT AREA EXERCISES (0012)

CT - 148	DC - 148	HI - 135	MD - 150	NC - [f]
NV - 135	RI - 148	SC - 145	UT - 150	

ELEM ED.: CONTENT KNOWLEDGE (0014) ** ROE: 181

AK - 143	AL - 137	CO - 147	DC - 145	DE - 151
IA - 142	ID - 143	KY - 148	LA - 150	MD - 142
ME - 145	MN - 145	MS - 153	MT - *	NH - 148
NJ - 141	OH - 143	RI - 145	SD - 140	TN - 140
UT - 150	VA - 143	VI - 140	VT - 148	WA - 141
WI - 147				

ELEM ED.: CURRICULUM, INSTRUCTION, & ASSESSMENT (0011)

AK - 156	CT - 163	HI - 164	IA - 151	IN - 165
KS - 163	MO - 164	MS - 158	NC - [f]	ND - 158
NE - 159	NV - 158	PA - 168	SC - 164	TN - 159
WV - 155	WY - 160			

* = Test required – passing score not set – verify with state.

** = Target score for ETS Recognition of Excellence.

+ = Each preparation program may have different requirements. Before registering for Praxis I, please contact your advisor/program coordinator to determine your requirements.

‡ = Multiple scores required – verify with state.

a–k = See state notes at end of this section.

KEY TO AGENCIES:	ASHA = American Speech-Language-Hearing Association	NASP = National Association of School Psychologists
	BCASP = British Columbia Association of School Psychologists	DODEA = Department of Defense Education Activity

ENGLISH LANG., LIT., & COMP.: CONTENT KNOWLEDGE (0041) **ROE: 192

AK - 158	AL - 151	AR - 159	CO - 162	CT - 172
DC - 142	DE - 163	HI - 164	ID - 158	IN - 153
KS - 165	KY - 160	LA - 160	MD - 164	ME - 160
MN - 157	MO - 158	MS - 157	MT - *	NC - f
ND - 151	NH - 164	NJ - 162	NV - 150	OH - 167
OR - 159	PA - 160	SC - 162	SD - 154	TN - 157
UT - 168	VA - 172	VI - 161	VT - 172	WA - 158
WI - 160	WV - 155	WY - 163		

ENGLISH LANG., LIT., & COMP.: ESSAYS (0042)

AK - 160	AR - 150	CT - 160	KY - 155	NH - 155
OR - 145	SC - 150	UT - 160	VT - 160	

ENGLISH LANG., LIT., & COMP.: PEDAGOGY (0043)

AR - 145	DC - 150	HI - 150	LA - 130	MD - 155
NC - f	NV - 140	TN - 145	UT - *	

ENGLISH TO SPEAKERS OF OTHER LANGUAGES (0360)

AL - 540	DC - 520	HI - 510	ID - 580	KS - 500
KY - 620	MD - 570	ME - 540	MN - 600	NC - 520
OH - 420	OR - 520	SC - 540	TN - 530	VI - 570
WA - 580	WI - 530	WY - 560		

ENVIRONMENTAL EDUCATION (0830)

PA - 600

FAMILY AND CONSUMER SCIENCES (0121)

AL - 146	AR - 153	CT - 168	HI - 153	ID - 157
IN - 148	KS - 162	KY - 162	LA - 141	MD - 159
ME - 155	MN - 162	MO - 162	MS - 153	NC - 148
NJ - 150	NV - 164	OH - 148	OR - 168	PA - 162
SC - 148	SD - 150	TN - 157	UT - 159	VA - 150
WA - 139	WI - 159	WV - 146	WY - *	

* = Test required – passing score not set – verify with state.

** = Target score for ETS Recognition of Excellence.

+ = Each preparation program may have different requirements. Before registering for Praxis I, please contact your advisor/program coordinator to determine your requirements.

‡ = Multiple scores required – verify with state.

a–k = See state notes at end of this section.

KEY TO AGENCIES:	ASHA = American Speech-Language-Hearing Association	NASP = National Association of School Psychologists
	BCASP = British Columbia Association of School Psychologists	DODEA = Department of Defense Education Activity

FOREIGN LANGUAGE PEDAGOGY (0840)

ID - 158

FRENCH: CONTENT KNOWLEDGE (0173)

AK - 162	AL - 148	AR - 158	DC - 155	DE - 157
HI - 158	ID - 157	IN - 160	KS - 166	KY - 159
LA - 156	MD - 161[d]	ME - 157	MO - 161	NC - [f]
ND - 156	NJ - 156	NV - 152	OH - 160	OR - 146
PA - 170	SC - 160	SD - 150	TN - 160	UT - 161
VA - 169	VT - 157	WA - 158	WI - 156	WV - 131

FRENCH: PRODUCTIVE LANGUAGE SKILLS (0171)

AK - 171	AR - 167	DC - 173	DE - 168	HI - 164
MD - 170[d]	MN - 158	MS - 161	NC - [f]	NV - 162
OR - 160	SC - 166	TN - 165	VT - 163	

FUNDAMENTAL SUBJECTS: CONTENT KNOWLEDGE (0511)

MS - 142	NC - 148	PA - 150	RI - 160	UT - 161

GENERAL SCIENCE: CONTENT ESSAYS (0433)

AK - 145	CT - 145	NH - 135	NV - 135	TN - 130
VT - 145				

GENERAL SCIENCE: CONTENT KNOWLEDGE, PART 1 (0431)

AK - 155	HI - 150	NV - 150	TN - 145

GENERAL SCIENCE: CONTENT KNOWLEDGE, PART 2 (0432)

AK - 149	WV - 149

GENERAL SCIENCE: CONTENT KNOWLEDGE (0435) ** ROE: 185

AK - 149	AL - 147	CO - 152	CT - 157	DC - 157
DE - 160	ID - 149	LA - 156	MO - 154	NC - [f]
ND - 150	NH - 147	NJ - 152	OR - 146	PA - 146
SD - 143	UT - 166	VI - 154	VT - 157	WA - 153
WI - 154				

---

* = Test required – passing score not set – verify with state.

** = Target score for ETS Recognition of Excellence.

+ = Each preparation program may have different requirements. Before registering for Praxis I, please contact your advisor/program coordinator to determine your requirements.

‡ = Multiple scores required – verify with state.

a–k = See state notes at end of this section.

KEY TO AGENCIES:	ASHA = American Speech-Language-Hearing Association	NASP = National Association of School Psychologists
	BCASP = British Columbia Association of School Psychologists	DODEA = Department of Defense Education Activity

GEOGRAPHY (0920)

AK - 590	AL - 560	ID - 600	MT - *	ND - 530
SD - 520	TN - 580	UT - 630	WY - 620	

GERMAN: CONTENT KNOWLEDGE (0181)

AK - 153	AL - 142	HI - 148	ID - 159	IN - 147
KS - 158	KY - 157	LA - 151	MD - 153[d]	ME - 156
MO - 161	NC - 153	ND - 150	NJ - 157	OH - 165
OR - 156	PA - 165	SC - 151	SD - 143	TN - 149
UT - 153	VA - 162	VT - 148	WA - 160	WI - 153
WV - 132				

GERMAN: PRODUCTIVE LANGUAGE SKILLS (0182)

AK - 178	HI - 169	MD - 164[d]	MN - 179	MS - 160
OR - 160	SC - 181	VT - 169		

GIFTED EDUCATION (0357)

AR - 156	KY - *

GOVERNMENT/POLITICAL SCIENCE (0930)

AK - 610	AL - 570	ID - 610	MT - *	ND - 490
SD - 540	TN - 600	UT - *	WY - 640	

HEALTH EDUCATION (0550)

AL - 580	CT - 680	HI - 560	ID - 630	IN - 420
KS - 620	KY - 630	MD - 630	ME - 640	MN - 580
MO - 620	NC - 640	NV - 600	OH - 480	OR - 690
PA - 650	SC - 680	SD - 580	TN - 570	UT - 670
WI - 610	WV - 640	WY - *		

HEALTH & PHYSICAL EDUCATION: CONTENT KNOWLEDGE (0856)

AR - 144	NJ - 151	NV - 159	PA - 146	VA - 151
WA - 149				

INTERDISCIPLINARY EARLY CHILDHOOD EDUCATION (IECE) (0023)

KY - *

* = Test required – passing score not set – verify with state.

** = Target score for ETS Recognition of Excellence.

+ = Each preparation program may have different requirements. Before registering
   for Praxis I, please contact your advisor/program coordinator to determine
   your requirements.

‡ = Multiple scores required – verify with state.

a–k = See state notes at end of this section.

INTRODUCTION TO THE TEACHING OF READING (0200)

IN - 510	NC - 540	NJ - 560	NV - 560	OH - 540
SC - 560				

LATIN (0600)

AL - 590	KY - 700	MD - 610	ME - 610	NC - 570
ND - 500	PA - 610	TN - 540	UT - 610	VT - 580
WV - 480				

LIBRARY MEDIA SPECIALIST (0310)

AL - 600	AR - 610	HI - 610	ID - 620	IN - 530
KS - 630	KY - 640	LA - 560	ME - 590	MN - 630
MO - 630	MS - 590	NC - 610	OH - 610	OR - 610
PA - 620	SC - 620	TN - 600	UT - *	WA - 600
WV - 570	WY - *			

LIFE SCIENCE: PEDAGOGY (0234)

AR - 146	DC - 147	HI - 139	MD - 144	NC - [f]
NV - 150	UT - *			

MARKETING EDUCATION (0560)

AL - 500	AR - 620	ID - 630	MO - 660	MS - 590
NC - 690	NJ - 630	OH - 440	OR - 660	PA - 550
TN - 640	UT - *	VA - 570	WA - 640	WI - 600
WV - 600	WY - *			

MARKETING EDUCATION (0561)

AL - 135	AR - 156	ID - 158	MO - 163	MS - 151
NC - 169	NJ - 158	OH - 124	OR - 163	PA - 144
TN - 160	UT - *	VA - 147	WA - 160	WI - 153
WV - 153	WY - *			

* = Test required – passing score not set – verify with state.

** = Target score for ETS Recognition of Excellence.

+ = Each preparation program may have different requirements. Before registering for Praxis I, please contact your advisor/program coordinator to determine your requirements.

‡ = Multiple scores required – verify with state.

a–k = See state notes at end of this section.

MATHEMATICS: CONTENT KNOWLEDGE (0061) ** ROE: 165

AK - 146	AL - 126	AR - 125	CO - 156	CT - 137
DC - 141	DE - 141	HI - 136	ID - 129	IN - 136
KS - 137	KY - 125	LA - 130	MD - 141	ME - 126
MN - 125	MO - 137	MS - 123	MT - *	NC - [f]
ND - 139	NH - 127	NJ - 137	NV - 133	OH - 139
OR - 139	PA - 136	SC - 131	SD - 124	TN - 136
UT - 138	VA - 147	VI - 125	VT - 141	WA - 134
WI - 135	WV - 133	WY - 136		

MATHEMATICS: PEDAGOGY (0065)

AR - 135	DC - 135	HI - 135	MD - 145	NC - [f]
NV - 135	TN - 125			

MATHEMATICS: PROOFS, MODELS, & PROBLEMS, PART 1 (0063)

AK - 171	AR - 144	DC - 154	KY - 141	NH - 140
OR - 144	SC - 137	UT - *	VT - 154	

MIDDLE SCHOOL: CONTENT KNOWLEDGE (0146)

AK - 140	AL - 141	AR - 144	SD - 141	TN - 150
WI - 146	WY - 150			

MIDDLE SCHOOL ENGLISH LANGUAGE ARTS (0049)

AK - 154	AL - 148	CT - 164	DE - 161	HI - 160
IN - 152	KS - 165	KY - 157	LA - 160	MD - 160
ME - 155	MN - 161	MO - 163	MS - 145	NC - 145
ND - 157	NH - 155	NJ - 156	NV - 158	OH - 156
OR - 152	PA - 163	RI - 162	SC - 155	SD - 150
TN - 145	UT - 155	VA - 164	VT - 154	WA - 158
WV - 147	WY - 160			

* = Test required – passing score not set – verify with state.
** = Target score for ETS Recognition of Excellence.
+ = Each preparation program may have different requirements. Before registering for Praxis I, please contact your advisor/program coordinator to determine your requirements.

‡ = Multiple scores required – verify with state.
a–k = See state notes at end of this section.

KEY TO AGENCIES:	ASHA = American Speech-Language-Hearing Association	NASP = National Association of School Psychologists
	BCASP = British Columbia Association of School Psychologists	DODEA = Department of Defense Education Activity

MIDDLE SCHOOL MATHEMATICS (0069)

AK - 145	AL - 149	AR - 161	CT - 158	DE - 148
HI - 143	ID - 150	IN - 156	KS - 158	KY - 148
LA - 148	MD - 152	ME - 148	MN - 152	MO - 158
MS - 140	NC - 141	ND - 148	NH - 151	NJ - 152
NV - 139	OH - 143	OR - 156	PA - 151	RI - 158
SC - 149	SD - 140	TN - 143	UT - 145	VA - 163
VT - 161	WA - 152	WV - 148	WY - 152	

MIDDLE SCHOOL SCIENCE (0439)

AK - 136	AL - 142	CT - 162	DE - 146	HI - 148
IN - 137	KS - 149	KY - 139	LA - 145	MD - 145
ME - 142	MN - 150	MO - 149	MS - 135	NC - 134
ND - 145	NJ - 145	NV - 143	OH - 144	OR - 142
PA - 144	RI - 154	SC - 145	SD - 138	TN - 135
VA - 162	VT - 157	WA - 145	WV - 151	WY - 147

MIDDLE SCHOOL SOCIAL STUDIES: (0089)

AK - 147	AL - 149	CT - 160	DE - 164	HI - 152
IN - 153	KS - 155	KY - 149	LA - 149	MD - 154
ME - 153	MN - 151	MO - 154	MS - 140	NC - 149
ND - 152	NH - 153	NJ - 158	NV - 148	OH - 151
OR - 140	PA - 152	SC - 150	SD - 145	TN - 140
VA - 160	VT - 165	WA - 157	WV - 151	WY - 153

MUSIC: ANALYSIS (0112)

AR - 150	MD - 147[d]	OR - 167

MUSIC: CONCEPTS & PROCESSES (0111)

AR - 145	CT - 150	HI - 145	KY - 145	NC - [f]
NV - 150	SC - 145	TN - 145	VT - 150	

MUSIC: CONTENT KNOWLEDGE (0113)

AK - 148	AL - 150	AR - 150	CT - 153	DE - 155
HI - 139	ID - 148	IN - 140	KS - 152	KY - 154
LA - 151	MD - 154[d]	ME - 151	MN - 149	MO - 151
MS - 139	NC - [f]	ND - 149	NJ - 153	NV - 149
OH - 154	OR - 162	PA - 158	SC - 151	SD - 150
TN - 150	UT - *	VA - 160	VT - 153	WA - 150
WI - 150	WV - 155	WY - *		

PARAPRO ASSESSMENT (PAPER & PENCIL) (0755); (WEB-BASED) (1755)

AR - 457	CO - 460	CT - 457	DC - 461	DE - 459
HI - 459	ID - 460	IL - 460	IN - 460	KS - 455
LA - 450	MA - 464	MD - 455	ME - 459	MI - 460
MN - 460	MO - 458	ND - 464	NE - 456	NJ - 456
NM - 457	NV - 460	OH - 456	OR - 455	RI - 461
SC - 456	SD - 461	TN - 456	UT - 460	VA - 455
VI - 466	VT - 458	WA - 461	WY - 462	

PHYSICAL ED.: CONTENT KNOWLEDGE (0091)

AL - 141	AR - 149	CT - 154	DE - 152	HI - 155
ID - 143	IN - 150	KS - 148	KY - 147	LA - 146
MD - 153	ME - 149	MN - 143	MO - 153	MS - 138
NC - 158	NJ - 148	NV - 154	OH - 153	OR - 156[h]
SC - 146	SD - 140	TN - 152	UT - 152	VT - 147
WI - 150	WV - 150	WY - *		

PHYSICAL ED.: MOVEMENT FORMS-ANALYSIS & DESIGN (0092)

AR - 150	CT - 154	HI - 145	KY - 151	NV - 149
OR - 141[h]	TN - 148	UT - *	VT - 154	

PHYSICAL ED.: MOVEMENT FORMS-VIDEO EVALUATION (0093)

MD - 155	OR - 145[h]	SC - 160

KEY TO AGENCIES:	ASHA = American Speech-Language-Hearing Association	NASP = National Association of School Psychologists
	BCASP = British Columbia Association of School Psychologists	DODEA = Department of Defense Education Activity

PHYSICAL SCIENCE: CONTENT KNOWLEDGE (0481)

AK - 145	AR - 145	DE - 154	HI - 149	ID - 145
ME - 147	MT - *	NH - 148	SD - 143	UT - *
WV - 142	WY - 153			

PHYSICAL SCIENCE: PEDAGOGY (0483)

AR - 145	DC - 145	HI - 151	MD - 151	NC - [f]
NV - 147				

PHYSICS: CONTENT ESSAYS (0262)

CT - 135	NH - 140	TN - 135	VT - 150

PHYSICS: CONTENT KNOWLEDGE (0261)

DE - 136	HI - 144

PHYSICS: CONTENT KNOWLEDGE (0265) ** ROE: 177

AK - 129	AL - 138	CT - 141	ID - 129	IN - 149
KS - 141	KY - 133	LA - 141	MD - 143	MN - 137
MO - 141	MS - 139	MT - *	ND - 132	NH - 146
NJ - 141	OH - 132	OR - 147	PA - 140	SD - 130
TN - 144	UT - 136	VA - 147	VT - 140	WA - 140
WV - 126	WY - 137			

PRE-KINDERGARTEN EDUCATION (0530)

IN - 390	WV - 590

PSYCHOLOGY (0390)

AL - 550	ID - 600	KS - 550	NV - 550	SC - 720
SD - 520	TN - 560	UT - *	WY - 580	

READING ACROSS THE CURRICULUM: ELEMENTARY (0201)

MD - 173	TN - 151	VI - 149	WY - *

READING ACROSS THE CURRICULUM: SECONDARY (0202)

WY - *

READING SPECIALIST (0300)

AL - 530	AR - 560	DE - 560	HI - 540	ID - 480
KS - 560	ME - 530	MN - 590	NC - 570	OR - 610
PA - 570	TN - 510	WA - 540	WV - 520	

SAFETY/DRIVER EDUCATION (0860)

PA - 520

SCHOOL GUIDANCE & COUNSELING (0420)

AL - 520	AR - 600	HI - 580	KS - 600	ME - 570
MO - 590	MS - 580	NC - 570	NV - 610	OH - 510
OR - 600	PA - 590	SC - 550	TN - 580	UT - *
WI - *	WV - 580			

SCHOOL PSYCHOLOGIST (0401)

State Boards of Education:

AL - 143	AR - 159	CO - 165	KS - 157	KY - 161
MD - 161	MO - 157	MS - 154	NC - 159	NM - 156
OH - 161	OR - 154	PA - 150	SC - 165	TN - 154
UT - *	VT - 165	WI - 165	WV - 148	

Boards of Psychology:

BCASP - 165	FL - 165	MA - 165	NASP - 165	OH - 164
TX - 165	WI - 159			

SCHOOL SOCIAL WORKER: CONTENT KNOWLEDGE (0211)

WI - 161

SOCIAL SCIENCES: CONTENT KNOWLEDGE (0951)

PA - *

SOCIAL STUDIES: ANALYTICAL ESSAYS (0082)

AR - 140	NH - 145

SOCIAL STUDIES: CONTENT KNOWLEDGE (0081) ** ROE: 184

AK - 150	AL - 153	AR - 155	CO - 150	CT - 162
DC - 145	DE - 157	HI - 154	ID - 150	IN - 147
KS - 158	KY - 151	LA - 149	MD - 154	ME - 157
MN - 146	MO - 152	MS - 143	NC - [f]	ND - 153
NH - 155	NJ - 157	NV - 152	OH - 157	OR - 153
PA - 157	SC - 158	SD - 146	UT - 159	VA - 161
VT - 162	WA - 157	WI - 153	WV - 148	WY - 158

SOCIAL STUDIES: INTERPRETATION AND ANALYSIS (0085)

OR - 156

SOCIAL STUDIES: INTERPRETATION OF MATERIALS (0083)

KY - 159	LA - 152	SC - 160	VT - 165

SOCIAL STUDIES: PEDAGOGY (0084)

DC - 169	HI - 144	MD - 164	NC - [f]	UT - 180

SOCIOLOGY (0950)

AL - 550	ID - 570	SD - 540	TN - 540	UT - *
WY - 620				

SPANISH: CONTENT KNOWLEDGE (0191)

AK - 152	AL - 147	AR - 155	DC - 153	DE - 157
HI - 171	ID - 152	IN - 159	KS - 167	KY - 160
LA - 160	MD - 162[d]	ME - 158	MO - 158	NC - [f]
ND - 155	NJ - 159	NV - 160	OH - 160	OR - 161
PA - 166	RI - 156	SC - 148	SD - 135	TN - 152
UT - 161	VA - 161	VT - 163	WA - 160	WI - 158
WV - 143				

SPANISH: PEDAGOGY (0194)

AR - 160	DC - 170	HI - 150	UT - 175

---

* = Test required – passing score not set – verify with state.

** = Target score for ETS Recognition of Excellence.

+ = Each preparation program may have different requirements. Before registering for Praxis I, please contact your advisor/program coordinator to determine your requirements.

‡ = Multiple scores required – verify with state.

a–k = See state notes at end of this section.

KEY TO AGENCIES: ASHA = American Speech-Language-Hearing Association   NASP = National Association of School Psychologists
                  BCASP = British Columbia Association of School Psychologists   DODEA = Department of Defense Education Activity

SPANISH: PRODUCTIVE LANGUAGE SKILLS (0192)

AR - 141	DC - 166	DE - 156	MD - 168[d]	MN - 162
MS - 155	NC - [f]	NV - 156	OR - 160	RI - 174
SC - 161	TN - 154	UT - *	VT - 165	

SPECIAL EDUCATION: APPLICATION OF CORE PRINCIPLES ACROSS CATEGORIES OF DISABILITY (0352)

AR - 141	DE - 139	HI - 141	MD - 147[d]	MS - 139
NC - 136				

SPECIAL EDUCATION: KNOWLEDGE-BASED CORE PRINCIPLES (0351)

AR - 150	NV - 150

SPECIAL EDUCATION: PRESCHOOL/EARLY CHILDHOOD (0690)

AR - 610	ID - 550	ME - 550	MO - 620	ND - *
OR - 530	SD - 550	TN - 560	WA - 550	WV - 550

SPECIAL EDUCATION: TEACHING STUDENTS WITH BEHAVIORAL DISORDERS/EMOTIONAL DISTURBANCES (0371)

MS - 150	NC - 147	SC - 153	WV - 156

SPECIAL EDUCATION: TEACHING STUDENTS WITH LEARNING DISABILITIES (0381)

NC - 139

SPECIAL EDUCATION: TEACHING STUDENTS WITH MENTAL RETARDATION (0321)

ME - 140	NC - 144	SC - 143

SPEECH COMMUNICATION (0220)

AK - 560	AL - 580	AR - 550	ID - 560	KS - 590
KY - 580	LA - 580	MO - 530	MS - 510	NC - 560
NJ - 560	NV - 580	OR - 610	SD - 560	TN - 570
UT - *	WV - 600	WY - *		

KEY TO AGENCIES:	ASHA = American Speech-Language-Hearing Association	NASP = National Association of School Psychologists
	BCASP = British Columbia Association of School Psychologists	DODEA = Department of Defense Education Activity

SPEECH-LANGUAGE PATHOLOGY (0330)

State Boards of Education:

AR - 600	CA - 600	CO - 600	GA - 600	KY - 600
MO - 600	MS - 600	NC - 550	NJ - 550	NY - 600
OH - 600	OR - 600	PA - 600	SC - 530	TN - 600
VT - 600	WI - 600	WV - 600		

ASHA and All State Boards of Examiners: 600

TEACHING FOUNDATIONS: ENGLISH (0048)

CA - 173

TEACHING FOUNDATIONS: MATHEMATICS (0068)

CA - 153

TEACHING FOUNDATIONS: MULTI SUBJECTS (0528)

CA - 155

TEACHING FOUNDATIONS: SCIENCE (0438)

CA - 171

TEACHING SPEECH TO STUDENTS WITH LANGUAGE IMPAIRMENTS (0880)

ME - 540	NV - 500	PA - 590

TEACHING STUDENTS WITH VISUAL IMPAIRMENTS (0280)

AR - 690	ID - 660	KS - 710	KY - 700	ME - 660
MO - 660	MS - 660	NC - 550	OH - 580	OR - 730
PA - 620	SC - 690	TN - 700	WV - 660	

TECHNOLOGY EDUCATION (0050)

AL - 540	AR - 550	CT - 640	HI - 560	ID - 590
IN - 590	KS - 570	KY - 600	LA - 600	MD - 580
ME - 570	MN - 600	MO - 570	MS - 560	NC - 580
NJ - 570	NV - 580	OR - 620	PA - 620	SC - 570
SD - 560	TN - 580	UT - 600	VA - 610	WA - 590
WI - 590	WV - 570	WY - *		

---

* = Test required – passing score not set – verify with state.

** = Target score for ETS Recognition of Excellence.

+ = Each preparation program may have different requirements. Before registering for Praxis I, please contact your advisor/program coordinator to determine your requirements.

‡ = Multiple scores required – verify with state.

a–k = See state notes at end of this section.

KEY TO AGENCIES:	ASHA = American Speech-Language-Hearing Association	NASP = National Association of School Psychologists
	BCASP = British Columbia Association of School Psychologists	DODEA = Department of Defense Education Activity

THEATRE (0640)

AK - 560	AL - 510	AR - 580	ID - 540	KY - 630
MD - 560	ME - 530	MN - 560	NJ - 570	SC - 590
SD - 540	TN - 610	UT - *	WA - 560	WI - 600
WY - 630				

VOCATIONAL GENERAL KNOWLEDGE (0890)

ME - 540

WORLD & US HISTORY (0940)

NV - 470

WORLD & US HISTORY (0941)

AK - *	AL - 143	ID - 141	MT - *	ND - 151
SD - 135	TN - 136	UT - 156	WY - 146	

KEY TO AGENCIES:	ASHA = American Speech-Language-Hearing Association	NASP = National Association of School Psychologists
	BCASP = British Columbia Association of School Psychologists	DODEA = Department of Defense Education Activity

a = HAWAII Notes

HI Licensure for all areas requires (1) achieving a combined total score of 516 and meeting the minimum score of 170 on each of the three tests or (2) meeting the passing score of 173 for PPST or CPPST Mathematics (0730, 5730), meeting the passing score of 172 for PPST or CPPST Reading (0710, 5710), and meeting the passing score of 171 for PPST or CPPST Writing (0720, 5720).

ETS no longer offers the CBT tests; however, the scores for the CBT tests are reportable for ten years. Hawaii allows combining the PPST/CPPST scores with CBT scores to meet passing score requirements. The options are as follows:

(a) Combining two PPST/CPPST tests with one CBT test: Meeting a composite score of 647 and meeting the minimum score of 170 on the PPST/CPPST tests and a minimum score of 300 on the CBT test.

(b) Combining one PPST/CPPST test with two CBT tests: Meeting a composite score of 778 and meeting the minimum score of 170 on the PPST/CPPST test and a minimum score of 300 on the CBT tests.

(c) Combining three CBT tests: Meeting a composite score of 910 and meeting the minimum score of 300 on each of the three CBT tests.

(d) Meeting the passing score of 318 on CBT Mathematics (0731), meeting the passing score of 319 on CBT Reading (0711), and meeting the passing score of 316 on CBT Writing (0721).

b = KENTUCKY Notes

KY license for Moderate and Severe Disabilities – Please
visit www.kyepsb.net/for current requirements.

c = MAINE Notes

All Areas, K–12 (except Career and Technical Education)
require (1) achieving a combined total score of 526 and meeting the minimum score of 172 on PPST or CPPST Mathematics (0730, 5730), meeting the minimum score of 173 on PPST or CPPST Reading (0710, 5710), and meeting the minimum score of 172 on PPST or CPPST Writing (0720, 5720) or (2) meeting the passing score of 175 for PPST or CPPST Mathematics (0730, 5730), meeting the passing score of 176 for PPST or CPPST Reading (0710, 5710), and meeting the passing score of 175 for PPST or CPPST Writing (0720, 5720).

Career and Technical Education requires
(1) achieving a combined total score of 513 and meeting the minimum score of 169 on PPST or CPPST Mathematics (0730, 5730), meeting the minimum score of 170 on PPST or CPPST Reading (0710, 5710), and meeting the minimum score of 165 on PPST or CPPST Writing (0720, 5720) or (2) meeting the passing score of 172 for PPST or CPPST Mathematics (0730, 5730), meeting the passing score of 173 for PPST or CPPST Reading (0710, 5710), and meeting the passing score of 168 for PPST or CPPST Writing (0720, 5720).

d = MARYLAND Notes

MD Initial Licensure (all areas) requires (1) achieving a combined total score of 527 for all three PPST or CPPST tests (there are no minimum scores) or (2) meeting the passing score of 177 on PPST or CPPST Mathematics (0730, 5730), meeting the passing score of 177 on PPST or CPPST Reading (0710, 5710), and meeting the passing score of 173 on PPST or CPPST Writing (0720, 5720). ETS no longer offers the CBT tests; however, the scores for the CBT tests are reportable for ten years. Therefore, the CBT test requirements were (1) achieving a combined score of 966 for all CBT tests, (2) meeting the passing score of 322 on CBT: Mathematics (0731), meeting a passing score of 325 on CBT: Reading (0711), and meeting the passing score of 319 on CBT: Writing (0721).

MD license for Art requires (1) a combined score of 304 from Art: Content, Traditions, Criticism and Aesthetics (0132) and Art: Content Knowledge (0133) or (2) meeting the passing score of 145 on Art: Content, Traditions, Criticism and Aesthetics (0132) and meeting the passing score of 159 on Art: Content Knowledge (0133).

MD license for French requires (1) a combined score of 331 from French: Productive Language Skills (0171) and French: Content Knowledge (0173) or (2) meeting the passing score of 170 on French: Productive Language Skills (0171) and meeting the passing score of 161 on French: Content Knowledge (0173).

MD license for German requires (1) a combined score of 317 from German: Content Knowledge (0181) and German: Productive Language Skills (0182) or (2) meeting the passing score of 153 on German: Content Knowledge (0181) and meeting the passing score of 164 on German: Productive Language Skills (0182).

MD license for Music requires (1) a combined score of 301 from Music: Analysis (0112) and Music: Content Knowledge (0113) or (2) meeting the passing score of 147 on Music: Analysis (0112) and meeting the passing score of 154 on Music: Content Knowledge (0113).

MD license for Spanish requires (1) a combined score of 330 from Spanish: Content Knowledge (0191) and Spanish: Productive Language Skills (0192) or (2) meeting the passing score of 162 on Spanish: Content Knowledge (0191) and meeting the passing score of 168 on Spanish: Productive Language Skills (0192).

MD license for Special Education requires (1) a combined score of 295 from Education of Exceptional Students: Core Content Knowledge (0353) and Special Education: Application of Core Principles Across

---

KEY TO AGENCIES: ASHA = American Speech-Language-Hearing Association   NASP = National Association of School Psychologists
BCASP = British Columbia Association of School Psychologists   DODEA = Department of Defense Education Activity

Categories of Disability (0352) or (2) meeting the passing score of 147 on Special Education: Application of Core Principles Across Categories of Disability (0352) and meeting the passing score of 148 on Education of Exceptional Students: Core Content Knowledge (0353).

e = NEW HAMPSHIRE Notes

NH initial licensure (all areas) requires (1) achieving a combined total score of 518 for all three PPST or CPPST tests and meeting the minimum score of 170 on PPST or CPPST Mathematics (0730, 5730), meeting the minimum score of 172 on PPST or CPPST Reading (0710, 5710), and meeting the minimum score of 170 on PPST or CPPST Writing (0720, 5720) or (2) meeting the passing score of 172 on PPST or CPPST Mathematics (0730, 5730), meeting the passing score of 174 on PPST or CPPST Reading (0710, 5710), and meeting the passing score of 172 on PPST or CPPST Writing (0720, 5720).

f = NORTH CAROLINA Notes

Entry into a teacher training program requires (1) achieving a combined total score of 522 for all three PPST or CPPST tests (there are no minimum scores) or (2) meeting the passing score of 173 on PPST or CPPST Mathematics (0730, 5730), meeting the passing score of 176 on PPST or CPPST Reading (0710, 5710), and meeting the passing score of 173 on PPST or CPPST Writing (0720, 5720).

ETS no longer offers the CBT tests; however, the scores for the CBT tests are reportable for ten years. Therefore, the CBT test requirements for entry into teacher training programs are (1) achieving a combined score of 960 for all CBT tests, or (2) meeting the passing score of 318 on CBT: Mathematics (0731), meeting a passing score of 323 on CBT: Reading (0711), and meeting the passing score of 319 on CBT: Writing (0721).

NC license for Art requires a combined score of 322 from Art Making (0131) and Art: Content Knowledge (0133). There are no minimum scores.

NC license for Biology requires a combined score of 302 from Biology: Content Knowledge (0235); and Life Science: Pedagogy (0234). There are no minimum scores.

NC license for Chemistry requires a combined score of 307 from Chemistry: Content Knowledge (0245), and Physical Science: Pedagogy (0483). There are no minimum scores.

NC license for Elementary K–6 requires a combined score of 313 from Elementary Education: Curriculum, Instruction, and Assessment (0011) and Elementary Education: Content Area Exercises (0012). There are no minimum scores.

NC license for English requires a combined score of 321 from English Language, Literature and Composition: Content Knowledge (0041) and English Language, Literature and Composition: Pedagogy (0043). There are no minimum scores.

NC license for French requires a combined score of 335 from French: Content Knowledge (0173) and French: Productive Language Skills (0171). There are no minimum scores.

NC license for Mathematics requires a combined score of 281 from Mathematics: Content Knowledge (0061) and Mathematics: Pedagogy (0065). There are no minimum scores.

NC license for Music requires a combined score of 299 from Music: Concepts and Processes (0111), and Music: Content Knowledge (0113). There are no minimum scores.

NC license for Science Comprehensive requires a combined score of 303 from General Science: Content Knowledge (0435) and Life Science: Pedagogy (0234), OR, a combined score of 305 from General Science: Content Knowledge (0435) and Physical Science: Pedagogy (0483). There are no minimum scores.

NC Social Studies Licenses (Anthropology, Economics, Geography, History, Political Science, Social Studies Comprehensive, and Sociology) require a combined score of 320 from Social Studies: Content Knowledge (0081), and Social Studies: Pedagogy (0084). There are no minimum scores.

NC license for Spanish requires a combined score of 327 from Spanish: Content Knowledge (0191) and Spanish: Productive Language Skills (0192). There are no minimum scores.

g = NORTH DAKOTA Notes

ND Licensure for all areas requires (1) achieving a combined total score of 516 and meeting the passing scores on any two of the three tests or (2) meeting the passing score of 170 for PPST or CPPST Mathematics (0730, 5730), meeting the passing score of 173 for PPST or CPPST Reading (0710, 5710), and meeting the passing score of 173 for PPST or CPPST Writing (0720, 5720).

h = OREGON Notes

OR license for Elementary Education requires achieving either (1) meeting the passing score of 155 on MSAT: Content Knowledge (0140) and meeting the passing score of 155 on MSAT: Content Area Exercises (0151) OR (2) achieving a combined score of 310 and meeting/exceeding the minimum score of 147 on Content Knowledge and meeting/exceeding the minimum score of 147 on Content Area Exercises.

KEY TO AGENCIES: ASHA = American Speech-Language-Hearing Association   NASP = National Association of School Psychologists
BCASP = British Columbia Association of School Psychologists   DODEA = Department of Defense Education Activity

OR Certification in Physical Education requires (1) achieving a combined total score of 446 for three tests and (2) meeting/exceeding the passing score of 156 on Physical Education: Content Knowledge (0091), meeting/exceeding the passing score of 141 on Physical Education: Movement Forms - Analysis and Design (0092), and meeting/exceeding the passing score of 145 on Physical Education: Movement Forms - Video Evaluation (0093).

i = PENNSYLVANIA Notes

PA Initial Licensure (all areas, Instructional I, Educational Specialist I) requires (1) achieving a combined total score of 521 for all three PPST or CPPST tests and meeting or exceeding the minimum score of 170 on PPST or CPPST Mathematics (0730, 5730), and meeting or exceeding the minimum score of 169 on PPST or CPPST Reading (0710, 5710), and meeting or exceeding the minimum score of 170 on PPST or CPPST Writing (0720, 5720), or (2) meeting or exceeding the passing score of 173 on PPST or CPPST Mathematics (0730, 5730) and meeting or exceeding the passing score of 172 on PPST or CPPST Reading (0710, 5710) and meeting or exceeding the passing score of 173 on PPST or CPPST Writing (0720, 5720).

PA Vocational Instructional I requires meeting the passing score of 172 on PPST or CPPST Reading (0710, 5710) and meeting the passing score of 173 on PPST or CPPST Writing (0720, 5720).

PA Vocational Instructional II requires meeting the passing score of 173 on PPST or CPPST Mathematics (0730, 5730).

j = VERMONT Notes

VT Initial Licensure (all areas) requires either (1) achieving a combined total score of 526 for all three PPST or CPPST tests (there are no minimum scores) or (2) meeting the passing score of 175 on PPST or CPPST: Mathematics (0730, 5730), meeting the passing score of 177 on PPST or CPPST: Reading (0710, 5710), and meeting the passing score of 174 on PPST or CPPST: Writing (0720, 5720).

k = VIRGINIA Notes

Entry into teacher training programs requires (1) achieving a combined total score of 532 for all three PPST or CPPST tests (there are no minimum scores) or (2) meeting the passing score of 178 on PPST or CPPST Mathematics (0730, 5730), meeting the passing score of 178 on PPST or CPPST Reading (0710, 5710), and meeting the passing score of 176 on PPST or CPPST Writing (0720, 5720).

ETS no longer offers the CBT tests; however, the scores for the CBT tests are reportable for ten years. Therefore, the CBT test requirements for initial licensure were (1) achieving a combined score of 973 for all CBT tests, or (2) meeting the passing score of 323 on CBT: Mathematics (0731), meeting a passing score of 326 on CBT: Reading (0711), and meeting the passing score of 324 on CBT: Writing (0721).

KEY TO AGENCIES: ASHA = American Speech-Language-Hearing Association   NASP = National Association of School Psychologists
BCASP = British Columbia Association of School Psychologists   DODEA = Department of Defense Education Activity

For More Information

For more information about state teacher certification testing requirements, contact the agencies listed below:

Alabama
Teacher Education and Certification Office
State Department of Education
50 North Ripley St.
P.O. Box 302101
Montgomery, AL 36130-2101
Web site: www.alsde.edu

Alaska
Alaska Teacher Certification
Web site: www.eed.state.ak.us/teachercertification

Arkansas
Office of Professional Licensure
Arkansas Department of Education
#4 State Capitol Mall, Rooms 106B/107B
Little Rock, AR 72201

California
California Commission on Teacher Credentialing (CTC)
Information Services Unit
P.O. Box 944270
1900 Capitol Avenue
Sacramento, CA 94233-2700
Telephone: 916-445-7254 or 888-921-2682, 12:00 p.m. to 4:45 p.m. (PST)
E-mail: credentials@ctc.ca.gov

Colorado
Educator Licensing
Colorado Department of Education
201 E. Colfax Avenue, Room 105
Denver, CO 80203-1799
Telephone: 1-303-866-6628
Web site: www.cde.state.co.us/index_license.htm

Connecticut

Connecticut State Department of Education

Bureau of Educator Standards and Certification

PO Box 150471, Room 243

Hartford, CT 06115-0471

Telephone: 860-713-6969

Fax: 860-713-7017

Delaware

Delaware Educator Data System

Web site: https://deeds.doe.k12.de.us/default.aspx

District of Columbia

Office of the State Superintendent of Education

Educator Licensing and Quality

51 N St., NE

Third Floor

Washington, DC 20002

Telephone: 202-741-5881

Web site: www.osse.dc.gov

Georgia

The Georgia Professional Standards Commission

Two Peachtree Street, Suite 6000

Atlanta, GA 30303

Telephone: 1-404-232-2500 in Georgia, 1-800-869-7775 (outside metro Atlanta)

Web site: www.gapsc.com

Hawaii

Hawaii Teacher Standards Board

ATTN: Licensing Section

650 Iwilei Road, Suite 201

Honolulu, HI 96817

Telephone: 1-808-586-2600

Fax: 1-808-586-2606

Iowa

Web site: www.iowacte.org

Idaho

http://www.sde.idaho.gov/site/teacher_certification/

Indiana

Indiana Division of Professional Standards
Indiana Department of Education
Room 229, State House
Indianapolis, IN 46204-2798
Telephone: 1-317-232-9010

Kansas

Kansas Certification and Teacher Education
Web site: http://www.ksde.org/Default.aspx?tabid=1648

Kentucky

Kentucky Education Professional Standards Board
Web site: http://www.kyepsb.net/

Louisiana

Louisiana Department of Education
Division of Certification and Preparation
P.O. Box 94064
Baton Rouge, LA 70804-9064
Telephone: 1-877-453-2721
Web site: www.teachlouisiana.net

Maine

For further information about education and initial certification, visit the Maine Certification Office, at www.maine.gov/education/cert/index.html

Maryland

For further information, visit Maryland State Department of Education or call the Maryland Certification Information Line at 1-410-767-0412 or 1-866-772-8922. Web site: www.marylandpublicschools.org/msde/divisions/certification/certification_branch/

Minnesota

Minnesota Department of Education
Personnel Licensing Team
1500 Highway 36 West
Roseville, MN 55113-4266
Telephone: 1-651-582-8691
Web site: http://education.state.mn.us/html/mde_home.htm

Mississippi

For further information about education and teacher licensure in Mississippi, visit the Mississippi Department of Education at http://www.mde.k12.ms.us/ed_licensure/index.html

Missouri

Visit the Missouri Department of Elementary and Secondary Education, at http://www.dese.mo.gov/

Nebraska

Teacher Education and Certification
Nebraska Department of Education
301 Centennial Mall South
P.O. Box 94987
Lincoln, NE 68509
Telephone: 1-402-471-2496
Fax: 1-402-471-9735 or 8127
Web site: http://www.nde.state.ne.us/TCERT/

Nevada

Nevada Department of Education
9890 S. Maryland Parkway
Las Vegas, NV 89183
Telephone: 1-702-486-6458
Web site: http://nvteachers.doe.nv.gov

New Hampshire

For more information, visit the New Hampshire Department of Education, at http://www.ed.state.nh.us/

New Jersey

New Jersey Department of Education
Office of Licensing and Credentials
CN 500
Trenton, NJ 08625-0500
Telephone: 1-609-292-2070
Web site: http://www.state.nj.us/njded/educators/license

New Mexico

For further information, visit the New Mexico Department of Education, at http://sde.state.nm.us/index.html.

New York

For further information, visit the New York Office of Teaching, at http://www.highered.nysed.gov/tcert/certificate/.

North Carolina
Department of Public Instruction
Licensure Section
301 North Wilmington Street
Raleigh, NC 27601-2825
Telephone: 1-919-807-3310
Web site: http://www.ncpublicschools.org/

North Dakota
Web site: http://www.nd.gov/espb/

Ohio
For additional information, visit the Ohio Department of Education, Center for the Teaching Profession, at http://www.ode.state.oh.us/.

Oklahoma
Oklahoma Department of Education
Professional Standards Section
Hodge Education Building, Room 211
2500 North Lincoln Boulevard
Oklahoma City, OK 73105
Telephone: 1-405-521-3337
Web site: http://sde.state.ok.us/

Oregon
Visit Oregon's Teacher Standards and Practices Commission, at http://www.tspc.state.or.us/.

Pennsylvania
Bureau of School Leadership and Teacher Quality
Pennsylvania Department of Education
333 Market Street
Harrisburg, PA 17126-0333
Telephone: 1-717-787-3356
Web site: http://www.teaching.state.pa.us

Rhode Island
Please refer to the Rhode Island Web site (http://www.ride.ri.gov/EducatorQuality/Certification/default.aspx) for the most current information.

South Carolina

Division of Educator Quality and Leadership
South Carolina Department of Education
3700 Forest Drive, Suite 500
Columbia, SC 29204
Telephone: 1-803-734-8446 or 1-877-885-5280 (toll free in-state only), between
1:00 p.m. and 4:30 p.m. each business day
Fax: 1-803-734-2873
Web site: http://www.scteachers.org/Cert/index.cfm

South Dakota

South Dakota Department of Education
Office of Accreditation and Teacher Quality
700 Governors Drive
Pierre, SD 57501
Telephone: 1-605-773-3553
Web site: http://doe.sd.gov/oatq/praxis/index.asp

Tennessee

Office of Teacher Licensing
State Department of Education
4th Floor, Andrew Johnson Tower
710 James Robertson Parkway
Nashville, TN 37243-0377
Telephone: 1-615-532-4885
Web site: http://www.tennessee.gov/education/lic/

Texas

Texas State Board for Educator Certification.
Web site: http://www.sbec.state.tx.us/SBECOnline/default.asp

Utah

Certification and Personnel Development
Utah State Office of Education
250 East 500 South
P.O. Box 144200
Salt Lake City, UT 84111
Telephone: 1-801-538-7500
Web site: http://www.usoe.k12.ut.us/

Vermont

For questions concerning teacher licensure, call 1-802-828-2445 or visit Vermont
Department of Education, at http://www.state.vt.us/educ.

Virginia

Virginia Department of Education

Web site: http://www.pen.k12.va.us/VDOE/newvdoe/teached.html

Washington

Professional Educator Standards Board

Old Capitol Building

P.O. Box 47236

Olympia, WA 98504-7236

E-mail: pesbassessment@k12.wa.us

Telephone: 1-360-725-6275

Fax: 1-360-586-4548

TTY: 1-360-664-3631

Web site: http://www.k12.wa.us/certification/TeacherMain.aspx

To obtain additional information about teacher certification, please contact:

OSPI Office of Professional Education and Certification

Telephone: 1-360-725-6400

E-mail: cert@k12.wa.us

Web site: http://www.k12.wa.us/certification/TeacherMain.aspx

West Virginia

Office of Professional Preparation

West Virginia Department of Education

1900 Kanawha Blvd. East

Building 6, Room 252

Charleston, WV 25305-0330

Telephone: 1-304-558-7826

Web site: http://wvde.state.wv.us/

Wisconsin

Teacher Education, Professional Development and Licensing Team

Wisconsin Department of Public Instruction

125 South Webster Street

P.O. Box 7841

Madison, WI 53707-7841

Telephone: 1-800-266-1027

E-mail: licensing@dpi.state.wi.us

Web site: http://www.dpi.state.wi.us/dpi/dlsis/tel/licguide.html

Wyoming

Wyoming Professional Teaching Standards Board

Web site: http://ptsb.state.wy.us/

American Speech-Language Hearing Association (ASHA)
Web site: http://www.asha.org/students/praxis

Department of Defense Education Activity (DODEA)
Web site: http://www.dodea.edu

National Association of School Psychologists (NASP)
Web site: http://www.nasponline.org